Rethinking Psychiatric Drugs
A GUIDE FOR INFORMED CONSENT

by
Grace E. Jackson, MD

authorHOUSE™

1663 LIBERTY DRIVE, SUITE 200
BLOOMINGTON, INDIANA 47403
(800) 839-8640
WWW.AUTHORHOUSE.COM

First published by AuthorHouse 07/26/05

ISBN: 1-4208-6742-3 (sc)
ISBN: 1-4208-6741-5 (dj)

Library of Congress Control Number: 2005905714

Printed in the United States of America
Bloomington, Indiana

Dedication

To my family...

> for their unwavering support, integrity, and love... particularly, throughout the transformative journey which has culminated in the writing of this book

To my teachers...

> for inspiring me to think critically, act morally, and listen gently...

Contents

List of Illustrations

Prologue

In 2004, an on-line medical newsletter posted an article with a captivating title: "All the Things They Taught Us That Were Wrong."[1] Penned by an academic psychiatrist who completed his post-graduate training nearly two decades before my own, the essay resonated with my own discoveries during residency and beyond. Probably like him, my patient care and research experiences transformed me until I, too, developed the painful awareness of "all the things my teachers taught me" which proved to be untrue.

This book is the culmination of many of those discoveries. It is the result of a five-year (and continuing) process of corrective self-education. It is the philosophically, epidemiologically, and scientifically supported revelation of how and why clinicians have often failed their mental health patients, partly because the information upon which they have relied (Evidence Based Medicine) has become increasingly *unreliable*. This development, along with many more, has compromised the ability of physicians and patients to participate in the construction of viable, informed consents to care:

> **"Informed consent ...is about the right to make choices and the right to refuse consent; it is about the right of individuals to preserve their integrity and dignity whatever physical and mental deterioration they may suffer through ill health; it is about our duty always and in all circumstances to respect each other as fellow human beings and as persons."[2]**

The chapters which follow are intended to facilitate the shared decision making of consumers and health care providers. First, the public's opinion about psychiatric drugs is explored through research conducted in several countries. Next, the sources of professional opinion are reviewed, beginning with the drug development process and the philosophy of Evidence Based Medicine. Chapter four explains the gold standard of medical research – the Randomized Controlled Trial – along with an emphasis upon the methodological deficiencies which commonly distort the value of drug treatments. Chapter five is an overview of the human brain. This is offered for the reader who desires a more detailed understanding of the targets of psychiatric drugs in terms of their chemical and structural effects. Chapter six introduces the concept of allostatic load – a phenomenon of *maladaptive changes made by the body* in response to stimuli, such as medication. The chapter includes discussions of tolerance (an important mechanism of decreasing responsivity to treatment over time) and drug discontinuation syndromes (withdrawal and rebound). It presents the concept of sensitization as a possible explanation for the phenomenon through which pharmacological therapies may effect a progressive worsening or prolongation of initial symptoms.

At the heart of the book is a detailed examination of three major classes of psychiatric drugs: antidepressants, antipsychotics, and stimulants (the latter, given for Attention Deficit Hyperactivity Disorder). The history of each drug class is reviewed. A neuroscience section explains contemporary hypotheses about presumed mechanisms of action. A special emphasis is placed upon the topics of drug effectiveness and safety, including *long term effects*, uncommonly acknowledged dangers, and alternatives to medication. The book closes with a discussion of the current crises in psychiatric research and practice, particularly as these problems continue to undermine the capacity of physicians and patients to collaborate in authentically informed decisions about health care.

Chapter One
PUBLIC OPINION ABOUT PSYCHIATRIC DRUGS

How likely would you be to take a prescribed psychiatric medication...

> ➤ if you were having trouble in your personal life?

> ➤ if you needed help in coping with life's stresses?

> ➤ if you experienced poor sleep, tiredness, depressed mood, or feelings of worthlessness?

> ➤ if you felt like you were "going crazy" while experiencing periods of intense fear, trembling, sweating, and dizziness?

Do you believe that psychiatric drugs are effective...

> ➤ in helping with day-to-day stress?

> ➤ in improving relationships with family and friends?

> ➤ in controlling symptoms?

> ➤ in assisting people in feeling better about themselves?

Do you agree that psychiatric drugs...

> ➤ are harmful the body?

> ➤ interfere with daily activities?

Public Opinion in the U.S.

In the winter of 1998, these were precisely the questions which University of Chicago researchers posed to 1387 members of the general public.[1] Investigating the willingness of Americans to use a psychiatric drug, the Chicago investigators were surprised by the results of their study (76% response rate). Except for situations involving intense physical and emotional symptoms ("going crazy"), *most respondents stated that they would be unwilling to take a medication.* While 41% stated that they would take a drug for depression, 45% stated that they would not (the rest were unsure). Over one-third of the respondents (37%) said they would refuse psychiatric medication for any of the conditions specifically identified.

Opinions about medication effectiveness were more favorable: 73% of the respondents believed psychiatric drugs successful for coping with stress; 62% for relationship difficulties; 77% for the control of symptoms; 55% for improving self-image. Approximately 25% of the participants viewed drugs as harmful to the body; 36% believed they would interfere with daily functioning.

Through a variety of statistical analyses, the research team calculated the strength of association between several variables and consumer opinion about drug use. Although respondents voiced concern about *potential problems* related to medication, their views about *effectiveness* accounted for most of the variance in willingness to use. Even so, the majority of subjects seemed reticent to take medication for their own problems. The Chicago researchers found this perplexing, concluding that the "gap between attitudes and willingness to use psychiatric medications remains to be fully explained."[2]

Public Opinion in the UK

In 1991, the Royal College of Psychiatrists and Royal College of General Practitioners launched a five-year educational effort named the Defeat Depression Campaign.[3] Motivated by the concerns that "50% of depressed people do not consult their physician," and that "general practitioners do not always recognize depression," the Royal Colleges prepared and delivered (1992-1996) an informational blitz involving media releases, professional conferences, training tapes, treatment guidelines, and publications. A major source of funding for the project was the drug industry.[4]

The starting point was a pre-campaign survey involving 2003 members of the general public throughout the UK. Information was gathered using a combination of direct questions and show cards with graduated answers (strongly agree, tend to agree, neither agree nor disagree, tend to disagree, strongly disagree, don't know).

When asked about the cause of depression, life events assumed a dominant role. For example, 77% of the respondents identified unemployment; 77% identified death in the family; 67% mentioned the break-up of a relationship. Three-quarters (73%) of the respondents believed that depression was a medical condition like physical illness,[5] but only 33% believed that biological changes in the brain were the *cause*.[6]

The UK survey asked the public if they would consult their own general practitioner if they experienced depression: 60% of the respondents volunteered that they would start by seeing a physician (79% said "yes" when specifically prompted); 60% thought that most people would be too embarrassed to see a physician, feeling that the doctor would view them as "unbalanced" or would be "irritated or annoyed" by such a consultation.

With regards to drug treatment, fewer than half (46%) believed that antidepressants were effective for depression; 30% thought that antidepressants were of minimal or no effectiveness at all; and 78% of the respondents considered antidepressants to be addictive. By comparison, 85% believed that counseling was effective. Only 16% of those surveyed thought that people with depression should even be offered antidepressants.

Faced with a majority who seemed skeptical about the latest pharmacological therapies, the Royal Colleges worried that perceptions about drug effectiveness might have been caused by inadequate prescribing habits (pills not taken at doses high enough, nor for periods long enough, to make an impact). Moreover, they believed that the public had falsely attributed to antidepressants the addictive qualities associated with the minor tranquilizers (the benzodiazepines, whose potential to induce physiological and psychological dependence was only belatedly recognized by the medical profession some twenty years ago). Thus, the Defeat Depression Campaign was pursued as a corrective action to re-educate physicians about the proper use of antidepressant medications, and to reassure the public about the appropriateness of consuming them.

At the end of the campaign, surveys were conducted to assess its impact. Among 2046 general practitioners responding to a structured questionnaire,[7] two-thirds expressed an awareness of the campaign; 25% had read associated consensus statements and guidelines; 40% had made changes in their practice because of them. The collective impact of the campaign was highest among younger physicians, females, those in larger practices, and those with less experience in psychiatry. Preliminary data obtained in 1994 showed that antidepressant prescriptions had increased significantly.[8]

The impact upon the general public was less striking but still important. Changes were seen in perceptions of drug effectiveness and the appropriateness of that treatment:

	Respondents Agreeing	
	Before Campaign (1991)	After Campaign (1997)
Drugs Effective	46%	60%
Drugs should be given	16%	24%

Nevertheless, the majority of the public continued to regard antidepressants as addictive (74%) and less effective than psychotherapy.[9]

Public Opinion in Germany

A 1990 survey conducted in the Federal Republic of Germany[10] revealed an attitude of suspicion towards psychotropic drugs, not unlike the situation in the UK. Among 2184 Germans responding, the use of drugs for the treatment of three different mental disorders (schizophrenia, major depression, and panic disorder with *agoraphobia) was rejected twice as often as it was embraced. In the western part of the country, 52% of the respondents recommended psychotherapy as the method of choice for all three conditions; only 19% favored drug treatment. In the eastern part

---

* agoraphobia – fear of open spaces; more commonly used to refer to the fear of situations or contexts from which escape is perceived to be difficult

4

of the country, 51% recommended psychotherapy for all three conditions; only 16% supported drug treatment. Respondents familiar with psychiatric medications were most likely to hold a negative attitude about their use, and more likely to hold a positive view towards psychotherapy.

The argument most frequently cited in favor of psychotherapy was the hope that it would identify and treat the causes of the particular mental disorder. It was also seen as an effective means of restoring mental balance, promoting self-awareness, and allowing for the unburdening of one's thoughts and feelings. Perhaps for cultural and historical reasons, Germans chose psychoanalysis more frequently than behavioral therapy as the treatment of choice for depression, panic disorder, and schizophrenia, leading the researchers to comment:

> **"respondents preferred not the method recommended by the majority of experts, but precisely the method which, according to experts, is completely inappropriate for the treatment of schizophrenia, and only of limited use for treatment of the other two disorders."[11]**

Arguments against the use of pharmacotherapy (drug treatment) included perceptions of doubtful or only temporary effectiveness; risks of unwanted side effects, including physiological dependency (66%); and limited scope of action (50% believing that drugs lead to treatment of symptoms without the elimination of their underlying cause). Interestingly, more respondents advocated the use of alternative methods (yoga, meditation, natural remedies) than psychotropic drugs. A follow-up study performed in 2001 revealed continuing skepticism about the value of drug treatment, leading the researchers to conclude that "further efforts to improve public knowledge about pharmacotherapy of mental disorders are needed."[12]

Clinical Utility: The Foundation of Informed Consent

Multiple, contemporary surveys around the world reflect a public preference for the non-drug treatment of psychiatric conditions. Consumers convey significant doubt about the effectiveness of psychotropic medications, and substantial concern about their potential to harm the body or cause maladaptive changes (addiction). Translating these findings into the language of medicine, one can calculate the relative perceptions of drug utility in each country:

Psychotropic Drugs

	Perception of Effectiveness (Benefits)	-	Perception of Harm (Risks)	=	Clinical Utility	Prefer to Use Drug ?
United States	high		moderate / low	=	moderate	no
United Kingdom	low		high (addiction)	=	low	no
Germany	low		high	=	low	no

In the case of the Chicago survey, the research team speculated that the *expressed unwillingness* of the American public to use psychiatric drugs, despite a favorable assessment of utility, may have reflected a number of uninvestigated factors:

- a preference for psychosocial treatments (while the survey asked respondents about the effectiveness of drugs, it did not inquire about the effectiveness of alternatives)

- a fear of stigmatization associated with seeking treatment for oneself (i.e., the survey may have captured opinions about treatments appropriate for "others" but not personally desirable because of concerns about labeling)

- a belief system prioritizing personal autonomy and self-control, which some individuals might perceive as incompatible either with psychiatric treatment, in general; or with pharmacological treatments, in particular.

Clearly, clinical utility is not the only variable which shapes a patient's desires for treatment (other factors being economic, philosophical, and sociopolitical). Nevertheless, it is the cornerstone of the physician-patient relationship, where a dialogue about risks versus benefits is the foundation of each patient's *informed consent to care*.

How is it that clinicians and consumers hold such different opinions about the utility of drug treatments? One answer lies in the fact that physicians have come to rely increasingly upon information from published sources (e.g., clinical drug trials), rather than direct observation. Because of the medical profession's dependence upon data from clinical trials, it is important to understand the process through which new products reach the market and undergo further testing and monitoring.

Chapter Two
How A Psychiatric Drug Comes to Market[1-3]

It is important to understand the steps involved in drug development, in order to comprehend the sources of data which medical professionals rely upon for their treatment decisions. The process of developing a new psychiatric drug currently spans ten to twenty years, reflecting the efforts of drug companies, research facilities, and the Food and Drug Administration (FDA). Established in 1938, and empowered by Congress in 1962 to establish *not only the safety but also the therapeutic efficacy* of new chemical entities,[4-5] the FDA is the governmental authority entrusted with the approval and regulation of medications and medical devices in the United States.

Pre-Clinical Investigations

The production of a new medication begins with "pre-clinical investigations" involving the study of a drug's effects upon cell cultures, tissue samples, and laboratory animals. These early inquiries are undertaken with the goal of determining toxicity, metabolic pathways, and possible mechanisms of action. If a company then decides to study the compound in humans, it must submit an Investigational New Drug Application to the FDA. Once this is approved, the drug company is permitted to begin clinical trials in human subjects.

Pre-Marketing Clinical Investigations: Phase I, II, III

Phase I studies are the first level of human investigations with a new drug. Typically, the trials include one hundred healthy volunteers who provide information about the approximate dose range which will be safe when the drug is consumed by patients via the intended route of administration (oral, intravenous, subcutaneous, etc.). These subjects also provide further data about drug metabolism and potential adverse effects which might not have emerged in other species. If the preliminary results and safety profiles are favorable, the drug company may advance to Phase II.

8

Phase II studies involve 100-300 volunteers who are suffering from the condition which the new product is intended to treat. The goal of these trials is to establish an optimal dose range and a tentative idea about predicted efficacy (benefit) in real patients. If the data from these studies are favorable, the drug company can proceed to Phase III.

Phase III studies are the last group of trials required by the FDA before approval. Research is conducted in randomized, controlled, double-blinded trials (see chapter four) involving approximately 1000 subjects. These are short-term trials (usually 4-8 weeks in length) in which the drug is tested against other treatments and *placebo to establish efficacy and potential risks. Following the completion of this phase, the drug company files a New Drug Application (NDA) with the Food and Drug Administration, outlining the product's developmental history from initial synthesis through the completion of Phase III.

The FDA Approval Process

In evaluating experimental compounds for approval, the FDA looks for proof of efficacy in at least "two similar and well monitored Phase III trials."[6] Efficacy means that a new drug produces "a statistically significant, therapeutic effect in the absence of unacceptable toxicities,"[7] where effect is defined by comparing untreated with drug-treated outcomes. There is no limit on the number of studies which a drug company may submit in pursuit of this goal. Furthermore, there is no requirement that a new drug demonstrate superiority to competitors which are already on the market.

Following a comprehensive review of the New Drug Application, the FDA "will approve a drug if [it] determines that it is safe and effective in its proposed use(s), and if the benefits outweigh the risks."[8] Due to the lack of objective measures for psychiatric conditions, however, the FDA's standard for psychotropic drugs is far more ambiguous than may be commonly assumed. According

---

*placebo – any treatment which improves a patient's condition due to the expectation of beneficial effects. In drug trials, placebos commonly consist of sugar pills. Placebos are described in greater detail in future chapters (see chapters 3, 4, 7).

to internal memoranda prepared during the recent approval of a top-selling neuroleptic, the FDA acknowledges approving products based on *"efficacy in principle"* rather than *efficacy in fact*:

> **"...The evidence adduced in the sponsor's short term studies, although it unquestionably provides compelling** *proof in principle* **[emphasis added] of (the drug's) acute action, does not provide a useful quantitative estimate of how effective (the drug) actually will be in the population for whom it is likely to be prescribed upon marketing."[9]**

This uncertainty is also reflected in the FDA's internal debates about the clinical relevance of rating tools commonly used in psychopharmacology research:

> **"The size of a drug's effect is... an abstraction, a notion that is not yet fully reified. Importantly, the agency, wisely, given the potential difficulties involved in reifying the concept, has steered clear of the issue."[10]**

Post-Marketing Investigations: Phase IV Trials and Safety Surveillance

The process of drug development does not end with the FDA approval of each new product. The agency may require further investigations to clarify issues pertaining to safety. Alternatively, the FDA may request new trials if a company seeks approval for additional indications or populations (such as children). This latter aspect of drug design has become increasingly complicated, due to a series of legislative, administrative, and judicial acts which have alternately expanded or restricted the requirements for separate testing in children. A drug company may also conduct further studies comparing its product to other treatments, in order to gain leverage against its competitors. All of these post-marketing trials are subsumed under the category of Phase IV.[11-12] Critics express concern that much of the post-marketing research has been hijacked by contract research organizations (CROs) – the private businesses which conduct trials on behalf of the drug companies in order to enhance marketing and sales. Their apprehension pertains to the poor quality of these studies, many of which are never submitted to the FDA for regulatory review.[13]

Evaluations of product safety continue indefinitely. The pharmaceutical industry is required to perform observational studies related to risk assessment, issuing periodic post-marketing and adverse reaction reports to the FDA. The medical community at large is another source of long-term product surveillance, via publications in peer-reviewed journals and adverse drug reaction reports which are filed directly (MedWatch) or indirectly (via the drug manufacturer) with the FDA.[14] Unfortunately, it is estimated that only 1% of all adverse drug reactions are ever reported to the regulatory agency,[15-16] presumably for a variety of reasons:

> ➤ no mandatory reporting requirement for clinicians

> ➤ overflow of paperwork competing for physicians' time and attention

> ➤ inefficient system for communications between health care providers and the FDA

Implications for Informed Consent

What are the implications of the drug development process for informed consent?

First, the FDA acknowledges that it approves psychotropic drugs based solely upon efficacy *in principle*. Presumably, this difficulty reflects the lack of objective criteria within psychiatry for determining a treatment's clinical significance. It also reflects the fact that alternatives to drug therapy are typically so beneficial that the effect size of medications is comparatively quite small. Second, the existing mechanisms for safety oversight are failing. As both problems contribute prominently to the present culture of psychiatry, it is to that subject which the next chapter turns.

Chapter Three
EVIDENCE BASED MEDICINE AND THE
RANDOMIZED CONTROLLED TRIAL:
THE SOURCES OF PROFESSIONAL CONSENSUS

The Empirical Tradition

The Greek physician, Galen (129-200 AD) is credited with the identification of two distinct cultures among physicians: the Empiricists (evidence based) and the Rationalists (reason based).[1] While both cultures were dedicated observers of patients, the Empiricists (named in the 3rd century BC for a discrete school of Greek medical practitioners) attached a priority to the *effects of treatment* and *experimentation*.[2] The Rationalists (referring to the amorphous collection of healers who adhered to the Platonic principles of deductive reasoning) emphasized the importance of understanding the *theoretical mechanisms* responsible for disease.

Although modern medicine evolved from the gradual integration of these perspectives, the fundamental tensions (Empiricism vs. Rationalism, Materialism vs. Idealism) remained. Today, these clashing epistemologies are reflected in the fields of neuroscience and philosophy. On the one hand, the descendants of Empiricists (e.g., "emergent materialists" and many neuropsychiatrists) contend that all aspects of human experience can be explained in terms of brain cell activity.[3-4] On the other hand, the descendants of Rationalists (e.g., dualists and metaphysicists) suggest that key aspects of the human condition (creating, intending, intuiting) cannot be adequately explained by the methods or discourse of science alone.[5]

While the tradition of Empiricism played a vital role in the evolution of Western medicine, it achieved hegemony in 1992 with the *JAMA publication of an article announcing the arrival of Evidence Based Medicine:[6]

---

* JAMA – the *Journal of the American Medical Association*

"A new paradigm for medical practice is emerging. Evidence-based medicine de-emphasizes intuition, unsystematic clinical experience, and pathophysiologic rationales as sufficient grounds for clinical decision making and stresses the examination of evidence from clinical research."[7]

Evidence Based Medicine (EBM), as it entered the medical lexicon in the 1990s, referred specifically to:

"the conscientious, explicit, and judicious use of current best evidence in making decisions about the care of individual patients. The practice of EBM means integrating individual clinical expertise with the best available external clinical evidence from systematic research."[8]

To fully appreciate the impact of these developments,[9] it is useful to compare the differences between EBM and the model of healing which it has attempted to displace.

I will refer to the latter model as Reality Based Medicine:[10-12]

Evidence Based Medicine	Reality Based Medicine
emphasizes perspective of the scientific investigator	emphasizes the perspective of the clinical provider
seeks to *establish* general truths and probabilities from randomized placebo controlled trials, meta-analyses, and systematic reviews	seeks to *use* established truths from pathophysiology & experience; may include conscious dismissal of probabilities in the context of each unique patient
focuses on *populations*	focuses on the *individual patient*
wants to *minimize* the placebo response to demonstrate beyond any doubt the "true" effect of the active medication	wants to *maximize* the placebo response to any active medication in order to reduce the need for that treatment over the long term
eliminates sources of individual variability by using broad exclusion criteria	*incorporates* sources of individual variability by using broad inclusion criteria
relies upon statistical manipulation of quantitative measures to establish *general efficacy* of treatments	relies upon directly experienced qualitative and quantitative changes to establish *specific effectiveness* of treatments

Implications of Evidence Based Medicine for Psychiatry

Under the construct of Evidence Based Medicine, knowledge within the specialty of psychiatry has become increasingly defined by the results of published research, focusing particularly upon the *Randomized Controlled Trial* or *RCT*. Resting upon the assumption that biases can and should be eliminated from the research process, the RCT emerged in England in 1948 as a specific research design, intended to "represent the way things really are."[13] *Randomization* refers to the process by which subjects in a study are distributed, by chance, to any one of the treatment conditions. The term *controlled* refers to the use of a reference group whose members receive either a standard therapy different from the investigational drug (in other words, a substance or procedure known to exert specific physiological effects) or an inactive substance called a *placebo* (a substance or procedure thought to produce non-specific effects, due to patient or clinician beliefs and expectations). Although it took centuries to develop, the integration of the placebo with the randomized controlled trial (only possible after the creation of statistics, and its application to medical research by R.A. Fisher following the 1935 publication of *The Design of Experiments*) provided the medical community and the post-World War II pharmaceutical industry with the tools they both desired for establishing the efficacy of new drug treatments.[14-15]

Despite Fisher's enthusiasm for medical statistics, there are three major problems with the RCT in relation to the field of psychiatry. From a *philosophical perspective*, it is doubtful that the use of large, population-based and statistically driven studies form an appropriate standard for a healing specialty[16] dedicated to matters of the Psyche or soul:

> "....If illness can be viewed only in the context of the individual who is ill, not as a distinct and disembodied concept of a disease, then population based studies are methodologically inappropriate..."[17]

> "...When the individuality of the patient and the individuality of the practitioner are seen as vital to healing, the tools of EBM which are designed to obscure these effects (blinding, randomization, placebos) cannot be used...EBM is an incomplete guide to optimal clinical practice for disciplines that assert that non-measurable but detectable differences between individuals are important to the diagnosis and treatment of illness."[18]

From a *practical perspective*, there are many situations in medicine *and* psychiatry in which published empirical research fails to provide the most effective guidance for clinicians and patients. Other kinds of evidence[19] – *qualitatively different from the Randomized Controlled Trial* – are frequently more important in

15

shaping treatment decisions, but these are precisely the forms of knowledge which Evidence Based Medicine degrades:

Non-Empirical Guides to Clinical Decision Making

Patient Values	Physician Values	Theory	Direct Observation
quality of life	Primum non nocere	biological	case series
cost	"first, do no harm"	sociological	individual narratives
sociocultural	fear of litigation	anthropological	"n of 1" designs
context	influence of expert opinion	psychodynamic	naturalistic studies
fear of death	patient autonomy	transpersonal	direct clinical experience
or injury	spirituality	behavioral	
spirituality	distributive justice		

From a *logical perspective*, the methodologies used in psychopharmacology RCTs are characterized by such critical deficiencies that their findings are commonly incoherent, unreliable, or moot. It would be difficult to overstate the ethical crisis which has emerged in the field of psychiatry, due to conflicts of interest[20-22] and the intentional manipulation of trial designs.[23-24] The next chapter explores many of the key deficiencies in psychotropic drug research, in order to demonstrate how the "best available evidence" has produced a standard of care which inappropriately inflates the efficacy and minimizes the risks of many medications.

Chapter Four
THE RANDOMIZED CONTROLLED TRIAL:
ORIGINS, ASSUMPTIONS, AND DEFICIENCIES

How is it possible for patients and physicians to hold widely divergent views of treatments? One answer lies in the fact that physicians have been encouraged to base their opinions upon the evidence which appears in medical references. That evidence, as the previous chapter has reviewed, focuses almost exclusively on the results of the Randomized Controlled Trial (RCT):

"a prospective scientific experiment comparing the value of a treatment strategy in an experimental group with an alternative strategy in a control group, in which allocation to experimental or control group is determined by chance."[1]

Although medical journals routinely discuss the RCT as if it were a modern invention, the practice of identifying the value of specific treatments by comparing them against alternative therapies dates back to the 18th century. One prominent authority on the subject[2] has described five discrete phases in the development of the current gold standard: *the randomized, placebo controlled trial*.

Origins of the RCT

Phase I: Placebos and Blind Assessments to Reveal Charlatans

In the late 1700s, *blind assessment* (where the patient was prevented from seeing the treatment) was a preferred method for revealing charlatanism. Three discrete forms of medicine were subjected to the principles of blinded research: Mesmerism (a form of healing based upon the belief that a fluid in nature, called animal magnetism, was responsible for health or illness); Perkinism (a form of healing which used metal rods, called Perkins tractors, to conduct fluid away from the body); and homeopathy (a form of healing based upon the use of dilute substances to produce symptoms similar to the underlying condition). In each case, inert substances (such as bread pills or sugar pills), blindfolds, or curtains were used in order to prevent the patient from knowing the identity of the treatment which was being administered.

Phase II: Placebos to Reinforce Existing Healing Philosophies

In the middle of the 1800s, two medical communities incorporated blind assessments as a tool for strengthening their own agendas. Homeopaths in Vienna used blinding to investigate the effects of their remedies in healthy volunteers. Concerned about "imagined symptoms" in patients receiving their homeopathic remedies, they believed that testing in normal controls would enable them to discern the "true" or objective effects of their healing compounds. Sham treatments were also used by the Therapeutic Nihilists as a means of testing the strength of their own healing philosophy, which maintained that "no treatment at all" was as good or better than the routine practices of the day.[3]

Phase III: Blind Assessments to Validate Psychic Phenomena and Hypnotism

By the late 1800s, blind assessments (in the form of curtains or black boxes) came to be used as a method of testing the validity of psychic phenomena and hypnotism. In France, Charles Richet (1850-1953) experimented with telepathy using playing cards. The experiment involved a telepathic communicator who would attempt to transmit the identity of a certain card to another person who was concealed (blinded) behind a screen. Around this same time in history, controversy emerged around the practice of hypnotism.

Jean-Martin Charcot and his followers believed that hypnotic induction involved an objective process with concrete, material stages. The capacity to be "hypnotized" was interpreted as proof of a neurological disorder (hysteria). Critics of Charcot, such as Hippolyte Bernheim (1840-1919), believed that hypnotism involved nothing more than the "power of suggestion," where specific ideas of the hypnotist achieved influence because of the receiver's mind. (None of these parties considered the possibility that hypnosis might involve innate physiological capacities, as neurotechnologies have subsequently affirmed.)

Phase IV: Placebos to Demonstrate Drug Efficacy

Around the turn of the century, blind assessments came to be used in pharmaceutical research. In 1889, Charles Edouard Brown-

Sequard (1810-1894) claimed that injections of animal testicles could rejuvenate physical and mental health. This touched off a series of trials in France, Austria, and Germany, where researchers compared the effects of injected testicular extract against injections of water. In 1895, German investigators used placebos (bread pills, saline injections) to control for the influence of suggestion in the study of stimulants (caffeine, cocaine, alcohol, tea, cola). In English speaking countries, the work of W.H.R. Rivers (British experimental psychologist and anthropologist) incorporated blinding procedures to test the possibility that patients' responses to drugs were caused or enhanced by the excitement of participating in the research project. Rivers' work was widely known, and the use of placebo controls entered the methodology of investigators at Columbia and Johns Hopkins Universities in the United States shortly before World War I (1914-1918).

Phase V: Placebos and the Randomized Controlled Trial

The first large scale clinical research involving placebo controls occurred in Germany in the early 1900s. Adolf Bingel (1879-1950) studied 937 patients between 1911 and 1914, exposing subjects in a double-blind fashion to a diphtheria antitoxin or to normal horse serum (the placebo control). In 1932, a Berlin medical researcher named Paul Martini published the first monograph to outline a precise methodology for clinical drug trials. Experiments in Germany became more frequent thereafter, with placebos administered in order to control for the "expectations of the patient" and the "physician's personality."

In the United States, the initial use of placebo controls was motivated by very different reasons. Recognizing the impossibility of recruiting subjects to participate in research designs where some subjects would receive "no treatment" at all (in an attempt to study the natural progression of the underlying illness), it was decided that placebos should be used to disguise the "no treatment arm" of each study. In 1937, a research group at Cornell University (led by Harry Gold) recommended the use of placebos for purposes other than disguising the "no treatment group." Gold speculated that inert substances could be effective for a variety of reasons: a patient's confidence in receiving any treatment (even if inert); the encouragement afforded by receiving a *novel* procedure; or the beneficial effects of receiving treatment from a new clinician.

19

Despite these realizations, however, Gold clung to the limited belief system of his peers, all of whom devalued improvements in placebo subjects as nothing more than "spontaneous variations" in the underlying disease.

It was not until well after World War II that the *randomized, placebo controlled trial* became the *gold standard* for medical research. The contributions of two Englishmen were central. First, it was necessary for Sir Ronald Fisher (the father of modern statistics) to introduce randomization (a method of assigning study participants randomly, or by chance, to different treatment groups) and probability statistics to medical research. It was Fisher's belief that both features were necessary if medical experiments were to achieve the precision of the hard sciences. Second, it was necessary for a medical investigator to execute the first successful RCT. This second task was accomplished in 1948 under the leadership of Austin Bradford Hill (1897-1991), the British epidemiologist who coordinated a large trial with the antibiotic streptomycin.

Assumptions of the RCT

With the rise of the pharmaceutical industry in the latter half of the 20th century, the Randomized Controlled Trial became the major methodology for the testing of new drug products in allopathic medicine. While it is not entirely clear why or how medical practitioners came to embrace the new statistical approach to research, one might speculate that the appeal of the RCT was predicated upon three crucial assumptions: 1) that objective research designs were possible and desirable; 2) that the RCT would be a reliable means of producing unbiased results; and 3) that a standard of medical care based upon RCTs would lead to superior outcomes. Each of these assumptions demands critical review.

Assumption #1: Objectivity Is Possible and Desirable

Advocates of the RCT believe that randomization eliminates conscious (deliberate) and unconscious (subtle) influences upon the assignment of research subjects to different groups in a study. The use of a *double blind* (where neither the investigator, nor the patient knows the identity of the treatments being given) is supposed to remove the effect of expectations upon outcomes.

Together, these strategies are seen as ways of accomplishing objective results. The problem, however, is that the RCT *itself* may be a source of systematic error.[4]

The fundamental claim to the RCT's objectivity lies in its capacity to identify differences between the efficacy or effectiveness of competing therapies. The assumption is that the more stringent (the more unbiased) the research methodology becomes, the more likely it is to produce statistically significant differences between an active drug and a placebo. Equal outcomes are assumed to be the byproduct of *faulty trial design*. However, there is no *logical* reason why a placebo must perform less effectively than an active drug. The historical belief that placebos are essentially "non-treatments" has been disproven by neuroscience, and more than a few observers have commented that the placebo may very well *be* the treatment of choice for many conditions,[5-6] particularly in the field of psychiatry. These ideas have been corroborated by the latest medical technologies which have demonstrated the very tangible effects of placebos both within and beyond the human brain.[7-8] To the extent that the placebo effect is dismissed by RCT enthusiasts as a non-objective phenomenon (equivalent to "no treatment" at worst; or psychosomatic delusion at best), one must question the desirability of the kind of objectivity which the RCT is alleged to obtain.

The RCT presents another problem in relation to objectivity. Critics wonder how possible it is for a methodology which seeks to eliminate all bias, to produce unbiased results. What this means is that *elements of the RCT introduce their own biases*, because the conditions of participation are so dissimilar from treatment conditions in the real world. First, there is nothing *unbiased* about a process which requires subjects to volunteer for potential assignment to placebo. Second, there is nothing *unbiased* about study conditions in which participants are carefully screened, vigilantly monitored, and routinely measured with tools that are rarely seen outside of the medical research setting.

In other words, the very process of participation in a research trial sets up its own expectations (biases for positive and/or negative effects) in patients and investigators alike. Even the best clinical design can influence findings in an unpredictable way. This is because human research participants, as conscious beings, are always reflecting about their experiences, and these experiences are unavoidably subjective. In the words of Kaptchuk: "...it may be that a residue of irreducible uncertainty can cloud even an ideal scientific methodology."[9] Despite its claims to objectivity, the RCT cannot eliminate the influence of human consciousness or interrelatedness in the therapeutic process.

Assumption #2: The RCT is a Reliable Source of Unbiased Medical Information

Even if one agreed that unbiased research designs were *theoretically* possible *and* desirable, it would not necessarily follow that human subjects could achieve them. In theory, there are several elements to a well-designed RCT:[10]

➤ Clear statement of the hypothesis being tested

➤ Identification of the population for whom results will be relevant

➤ Precisely defined, clinically relevant outcomes

➤ Blinded randomization with patients distributed to treatment groups equally with respect to important characteristics (age, gender, diagnoses, medication)

➤ Explicit revelation of minimum clinically worthwhile difference in main outcome measure

➤ Limited exclusion criteria (the fewer the exclusion criteria, the more generalizable the results)

➤ Adequate sample size (based upon minimum expected difference between treatment groups) to achieve sufficient power (confidence level that difference between groups will be found) and statistical significance (probability that findings are not due to chance)

➤ Intention to Treat analysis of outcomes (results for all participants are recorded by intervention group to which each patient was randomly assigned; no patient outcomes unacknowledged or untracked)

> ➢ Treatment effects reported in absolute and proportional terms, with confidence levels to describe a range of plausible values on either side of the mean observed outcome

In practice, these elements are rarely obtained. Partly because of the medical community's growing concern about the poor quality of much published research, a group of epidemiologists, statisticians, journal editors, and clinical trialists convened in the mid-1990s to produce a guideline for the reporting of RCTs.[11-14] Their efforts resulted in the production of the CONSORT (Consolidated Standards of Reporting Trials) statement – a specific checklist and flow chart to be used by clinical investigators, in the hopes that the quality of RCT summaries would be considerably improved:

> **"Inadequate reporting makes the interpretation of RCT results difficult if not impossible. Moreover, inadequate reporting borders on unethical practice when biased results receive false credibility."[15]**

Adopted by a growing number of medical and health care journals, and revised since 1996 to incorporate the suggestions of its users, the CONSORT statement has indeed improved the quality of articles describing RCTs by encouraging more complete disclosures of critical trial design features. However, it should be noted that the CONSORT statement has not been able to fully compensate for the low quality of RCTs, since it applies only to the *reporting* of research trials, and not to their development or implementation. (What is true for the computer industry is doubly true for the medical profession: garbage in, garbage out.)

A review of the psychiatric literature reveals that RCT reports continue to fall far below CONSORT standards. Even the database held by the FDA (which is supposed to reflect *all* RCTs conducted by drug companies, including the 50% or more which are never published or publicly disclosed) reflects the same problem.[16] This makes it impossible for practitioners to access meaningful research results (such as raw data) and necessitates a critical appraisal of published material in order to compensate for methodological deficiencies.

Assumption #3: The RCT Improves Clinical Care

Despite the many arguments which supporters advance for Evidence Based Medicine and the hallowed RCT, it is not at all clear that their implementation leads predictably to improved patient care. Referring to an important observational (real world) study published in the *New England Journal of Medicine*, an Australian professor of cardiology illuminates why this is so.[17] Survivors of heart attacks treated with thrombolytic therapy (medication) rather than angioplasty (balloon inserted into coronary arteries) had better recovery rates, despite the fact that RCTs published in the same journal had consistently recommended angioplasty as the treatment of choice. This finding, not at all dissimilar from situations in the field of psychiatry, suggests a growing credibility gap between the world of the published RCT, and the world of the real clinical patient.

Deficiencies of the RCT: "Best Evidence" or Fraud?

From the moment a new drug is conceived, until the moment it enters the market, the costs of research and development average $100 million per product.[18] Following the submission of a new drug application to the FDA for final review – a process which typically spans one to three years – each day of the approval process costs the drug manufacturer a million dollars in lost revenue.[19] With stakes this high, there is enormous pressure upon researchers, publishers, and regulators to present the findings of RCTs in a way that consistently favors the latest product. This pressure fuels a volatile conflict between a corporate ethic of maximizing investment returns, and a medical ethic devoted to beneficence and non-harm. In the present climate of "win at all costs," it does not matter if the research is sponsored by private industry, academia, or the federal government.[20-24] The pharmaceutical industry pays the piper, and the pharmaceutical industry calls the tune. In the field of psychiatry, the tune has one lyric: drug therapies are effective, safe, and well tolerated. The newer the drug, the better.

How has the medical profession contributed to this situation? First, the results of negative trials (research finding no advantage for a new drug, when compared against rivals or placebo) have been intentionally suppressed. Concern about the concealment of unfavorable results has only recently reached such a critical mass that the American Medical Association itself has called for the creation of a comprehensive registry of *all* trials, with details of the investigations and all results to be filed in an electronic, publicly accessible database. Similarly, the editors of eleven major medical journals have called for the registration of all future trials to be featured in their pages.[25-26]

While all of these developments are laudable, it remains the case that no registry on earth will provide reliable or meaningful research results, if the methodologies of the trials themselves continue to reflect prejudicial manipulations and adjustments of the evidence. An appreciation of these distortions is essential for the development of a meaningful, informed consent to care.

Design and Reporting Deficiencies in Psychopharmacology Trials

Two informative overviews about psychopharmacology trial designs[27-28] are an excellent starting point for understanding the biases in published and unpublished (FDA reviews) research. Elements from these and other sources[29-31] provide important skills for identifying the critical deficiencies which invalidate the conclusions and recommendations of many RCTs.

Flaw #1: Selection bias

One of the strategies in drug studies is to select a narrowly defined group of subjects who are expected to respond well to the test drug. In psychiatry RCTs, it is common for investigators to exclude any or all of the following conditions:

➢ age below 18, age above 65

➢ comorbid illness (physical or mental condition other than that being studied)

➢ pregnancy

➢ hospitalization (inpatient or outpatient status, depending upon study)

> severe illness (active suicidal thoughts, psychosis, mania)

> poor response to previous treatment

Example: Jick Study on Antidepressants and Risk of Suicide[32]

In a recent and widely publicized study proclaiming the relative safety of serotonergic antidepressants such as fluoxetine (Prozac) relative to older drugs, the research team performed a restrospective case control study to "compare the risk of newly diagnosed suicidal behavior" in patients in the UK who had received one of four study drugs between 1993-1999:

generic name	U.S. trade name
fluoxetine	Prozac
sertraline	Zoloft
amitriptyline	Elavil
dothiepin	* a tricyclic antidepressant, not marketed in the US

After identifying all of the people in the UK (159,810) who had received at least one prescription for the four target drugs during the years of concern, the research team then *excluded from the cohort*:

cohort exclusions

■ anyone with less than two years of recorded history in the primary care database

■ anyone who turned 69 during the study period

■ anyone with a diagnosis of substance abuse (including alcohol)

Seeking to identify any *new cases of suicidal thought or suicide attempts* occurring within 90 days of receiving a prescription, the researchers then excluded:

suicidal act case exclusions

■ anyone who had a recorded prescription for another antidepressant, or anyone who had recorded prescriptions *for more than one study drug* prior to the onset of suicidality

The problem is that many of the patients in the population had received treatment with more than one antidepressant, and *all of these individuals were excluded from the analysis*:

"For users of amitriptyline and dothiepin, 19% and 20%, respectively, received at least one prescription for some other antidepressant either before or after their first prescription for the tricyclic antidepressant; for fluoxetine and paroxetine users, it was 28% and 34%, respectively. This indicates that persons who received the two study SSRIs were almost 50% more likely than those who received the tricyclic antidepressants to have required a change in antidepressant treatment, consistent with findings in our earlier studies."[33]

Given the fact that the most likely cause of a "change in antidepressant treatment" would be the emergence of suicidal thought or behavior, the Jick study excluded those subjects whose SSRI experiences most needed to be explained. In other words, the selection bias in the Jick study eliminated from discussion precisely those individuals whose drug treatments may have induced or exacerbated episodes of suicidal thought or self-injury. The findings, therefore, are not generalizable to the real world and the authors' conclusions are not supported due to the research design's deficiencies of cohort and case exclusions.

Another form of selection bias can occur at the time of randomization, when patients are supposed to be distributed equally (and by chance) to the different treatment arms of the study. A good example of selection bias due to *flawed randomization* occurred in the Treatment for Adolescents with Depression Study (TADS) which evaluated the efficacy and safety of fluoxetine (Prozac).[34] Patients were distributed to four different groups (Prozac with psychotherapy, psychotherapy alone, Prozac alone, or placebo). However, the distribution of patients relative to co-morbid (co-existing) conditions at baseline was disproportionate:

TADS Study – Randomization Bias

% of patients with	Prozac + CBT	CBT only	Prozac only	Placebo
dysthymia	10%	16%	6%	11%
anxiety disorder	28%	32%	24%	25%
obsessive compulsive/tic	4%	2%	2%	4%
*ADHD	13%	13%	12%	17%
Taking Stimulants	4%	4%	3%	9%

Because the TADS study sought to identify the most effective treatment for *depression*, the unequal distribution of dysthymic patients (subjects with chronic mild depression, poorly responsive to short-term interventions as conducted in this 12-week study) necessarily placed the **CBT group (16% dysthymic) at a disadvantage. Similarly, the percent of placebo subjects with ADHD (17%) were at higher risk for poor outcomes for two reasons: many ADHD symptoms, and many side effects induced by stimulant medications given to treat ADHD are identical to the symptoms targeted by the main assessment instruments used in this study (Children's Depression Rating Scale, Reynolds Adolescent Depression Scale).

Flaw #2: Non-equivalent dosing

The strategy of non-comparable dosing involves the use of non-equivalent doses of drugs in different treatment arms of a study. One of the best examples of this tactic occurs repeatedly in studies of olanzapine and other "atypical" (newer) antipsychotic drugs. The deception involves the administration of higher than needed doses (super doses) of an older drug, such as Haldol, relative to the new treatments.

There is a way to compare two drug treatments fairly, but this requires the administration of physiologically equivalent doses. Advocates of drug therapy for psychosis believe that it is necessary

---

*ADHD = Attention Deficit Hyperactivity Disorder

**cognitive behavioral therapy (CBT) - a form of psychotherapy emphasizing active interventions (such as exposure or desensitization), the teaching of social skills (assertiveness, communication), and regular homework assignments, all of which seek to identify and change maladaptive cognitions (automatic thoughts) or behaviors

to block 60-80% of the D2 receptors in the human brain. Beyond 80% blockade, the drug treatment commonly induces movement abnormalities (extrapyramidal symptoms or tardive dyskinesia) and/or cognitive and affective dysfunction.

In the Phase III studies of olanzapine (Zyprexa) submitted for FDA review, the investigators in one trial (HGAD) compared the following doses:[35]

	olanzapine (Zyprexa)	haloperidol (Haldol)
low dose	5 mg +/- 2.5 mg	10 – 20 mg
medium dose	10 mg +/- 2.5 mg	10 – 20 mg
high dose	15 mg +/- 2.5 mg	10 – 20 mg

Based upon comparable D2 blockade, the equivalent doses should have been 2 mg of haloperidol for every 10 mg of olanzapine:[36]

	olanzapine (Zyprexa)	haloperidol (Haldol)
low dose	2.5 mg – 7.5 mg	0.5 mg – 2.5 mg
medium dose	7.5 mg – 12.5 mg	1.5 mg – 2.5 mg
high dose	12.5 mg – 17.5 mg	2.5 mg – 3.5 mg

This suggests that haloperidol subjects were "overdosed" 4-6 times relative to the high dose olanzapine group; 7-8 times, relative to the medium dose group; and 8-20 times, relative to the low dose group. The same trial modification has been used repeatedly by drug companies to justify their claim that new antipsychotic drugs are more successful and safer than their predecessors. Although few researchers have been financed to conduct them, the limited studies which have compared equivalent doses of neuroleptics drugs have revealed no clear superiority for the new drugs, and disputable claims of greater safety.[37] A variant of non-comparable dosing involves the administration of unusual dosing *frequencies*, whereby a rival drug will be given in repeated doses throughout the day. Alternatively, a research team may increase the doses of a competing drug *more rapidly* than usual, in an effort to maximize side effects or drop-out rates in the control group.

Flaw #3: Concomitant medications

Although most trial protocols specifically prohibit the administration of concurrent drug treatments, there are many exceptions to this rule. Some treatments are continued for ethical reasons, as it would be dangerous to deprive patients of maintenance therapies required for the stabilization of a chronic condition (e.g., antihypertensive medication for control of blood pressure, insulin for control of diabetes). However, it is essential that investigators disclose and control for the precise nature of these treatments. Patient outcomes should be analyzed accordingly. This is particularly important in psychopharmacology research, where many drugs taken by patients for somatic conditions cross the blood brain barrier and exert active effects upon cognition, mood, and behavior.

In some cases, researchers will administer additional medications to compensate for side effects of the study drug. During the development of the antidepressant, fluoxetine (Prozac), it was widely known by German investigators that the drug frequently caused agitation, anxiety, and insomnia severe enough to require the concurrent prescription of a minor tranquilizer (such as a benzodiazepine).[38] The product label in that country, but not in the United States, was worded to reflect this practice. In other cases, researchers will permit the continuation of medications which a patient has been taking for "co-existing" psychiatric conditions. The TADS study, mentioned above, allowed children diagnosed with ADHD to continue their stimulant therapy. This may have introduced a significant bias, because stimulants commonly induce dysphoria, poor appetite, insomnia, and restricted activity – many of the key features of depression.

Flaw #4: Placebo washout

Most psychiatric drug trials begin with a seven to ten day preliminary phase called "placebo washout" (or placebo "lead-in"). There are two key features to this trial design. The "washout" refers to the fact that all subjects who have agreed to participate in the trial are taken off their previous medications. This abrupt discontinuation of previous therapies is performed in the interest of "washing out"

30

any chemical in the brain, so that the study will not be confounded by the effects of substances other than the test drug.

The "placebo" term in "placebo washout" refers to the fact that all subjects receive the same "dummy pill" that will be used during the actual study. When the lead-in period expires, subjects randomized to the placebo group will continue to receive the dummy pill, while subjects randomized to the active treatment group will be switched to the investigational drug.

There is a second meaning of "washout" in the placebo washout design. Any patients who respond "too well" during this introductory stage are removed from the study before it even begins. This practice is supported by the drug companies and the FDA, who believe it would be unethical to prejudice the trial by retaining placebo responders. By removing anyone who reacts favorably to a sugar pill before the study gets rolling, they believe that they enhance the integrity of the findings. According to their philosophy, anyone who responds to placebo is either not sick enough to continue in the study, or has reached the natural end of their acute illness, since they are improving without any "real" treatment. The placebo washout introduces significant bias into all psychotropic drug trials for several reasons. First, it inappropriately discards individuals who are demonstrating a favorable response to the healing or research experience. The reason why this is inappropriate is because it is impossible to discount the presence of the same *placebo effect* (influence of expectations, hopefulness, healing relationship, etc.) in the subjects who go on to receive the active drug. As the placebo effect is necessarily a part of *all* healing rituals, it is logically inconsistent to remove some subjects from a study, simply because they manifest this response "too quickly."

Drug companies understand the importance of the placebo washout design, because their own studies have demonstrated that patients who respond favorably to the placebo during the "lead-in" phase *maintain* that response throughout the course of the trial.[39] Thus, these patients *must* be removed, in order to inflate or protect the perceived benefits of the active drug treatment. (If the placebo subjects do too well, the trial fails, because the RCT demands the detection of a significant difference or discrepancy between the active drug and placebo.)

31

Second, the abrupt discontinuation of previous therapies places many individuals at a distinct disadvantage by inducing a state of drug withdrawal. Just as chronic alcoholics experience physiological changes when their beverage of choice is abruptly removed, so too, do psychiatric patients experience bodily changes when their medications are rapidly withdrawn. Thus, all psychiatric trials which begin with a placebo washout phase introduce a bias against the subjects who advance to the placebo arm. Rather than comparing the effects of a new drug against placebo in the treatment of a specific *underlying condition*, these trials compare the efficacy of a new drug versus placebo in *halting or reversing the symptoms of drug withdrawal*. It is no surprise, then, that most subjects receiving an active drug outperform subjects on placebo, since only the former patients have a chance of receiving a specific chemical intervention which might rapidly eclipse a drug withdrawal syndrome.

Flaw #5: LOCF analysis

The LOCF (Last Observation Carried Forward) refers to a statistical technique for reporting the results of trial drop-outs. When a subject departs from a study before its designated endpoint, a decision must be made by the investigators about how to record outcomes for that individual. Using LOCF, the research team decides to take the *last recorded assessment*, and to carry it forward week by week as though the subject had remained in the study without further change. The problem here is the assumption of "non-change." When drugs are stopped during the placebo lead-in phase of a trial, subjects may experience symptoms of withdrawal which are usually more severe in the *first weeks of the study period*. If their withdrawal syndromes are uncomfortable enough, many subjects decide to quit the trial. LOCF picks up the last observation of these individuals, potentially capturing the climax (most uncomfortable point) of these subjects' withdrawal phenomena. It then carries these scores forward to the end of the study for the final round of assessments. This places the placebo group at a profound disadvantage, because of the inclusion of scores from subjects who leave the study before investigators can detect a trend of gradual recovery.

Flaw #6: Unblinding

Proponents of the double-blinded study design believe that more objective (more valid) outcomes are obtained when no one in an experiment knows the true identity of the treatment which each subject receives. The goal is to eliminate, if possible, the influence of the power of suggestion. In reality, very few trials in medicine are conducted in which the participants fail to "penetrate" the blind.[40-44] The phenomenon of "unblinding" occurs for several reasons. Patients and clinicians are keenly aware of the side effects produced by active chemicals. In some cases, they may be sensitive to odors or tastes which are absent from the placebo condition but present in the active pill or capsule. Unblinding is particularly problematic in psychiatric research because of the fact that there are no objective means of determining a patient's progress. The assessment scales which are commonly used to validate treatment efficacy can be strongly influenced by the expectations of clinicians and patients, most of whom clearly recognize when an active drug is being administered or withheld.

Flaw #7: Omission of data

One of the fundamental ethics in scientific research is the faithful reporting of all data from an experiment. This also requires investigators to reveal the outcomes for all of the subjects who enter a study – even if they do not successfully complete the trial. Two studies conducted by a team of epidemiologists who requested FDA summary reports for seven antidepressants and three antipsychotics approved between 1987 and 1997 reflect a failure in the reporting or disclosure of full information. Data for completed suicides and suicide attempts were not available for fluoxetine (Prozac). Suicide data for venlafaxine (Effexor) were not clearly explained.[45] In the antipsychotic drug reviews, data for suicide attempts were not provided for quetiapine (Seroquel) or olanzapine (Zyprexa).[46] These omissions have made it difficult for researchers to retrospectively calculate the risks or benefits of medications in regards to self-harm.

The author's own analysis of the FDA summary report for olanzapine[47] detected a stunning exclusion of data from an *entire subset* of patients. In one trial (HGAP) which compared a very low dose of olanzapine (1.0 mg) against a higher dose (10.0 mg) and placebo, the FDA omitted results from all *fifty-one 1.0 mg patients* in the primary safety database. The justification appears to have been an assumption that 1.0 mg constitutes a pharmacodynamically "inactive" dose of the drug treatment. Nonetheless, scientific integrity would demand an objective analysis of *all* outcomes, if for no other reason than to corroborate the assertion that a 1.0 mg dose has no physiological effects.

Flaw #8: Biased assessment

The self-serving use of measurement scales can lead to inappropriate evaluations of a drug's efficacy and safety. Researchers commonly rely upon assessment instruments which are seldom seen in the clinical setting of the real world (e.g., the Brief Psychiatric Rating Scale, the Clinical Global Impression Scale, the Young Mania Rating Scale). An example of a particularly arbitrary rating instrument is the "worst EPS scale" (EPS = extrapyramidal symptoms) used by some researchers to stretch conclusions about the side effect profile of risperidone (Risperdal). In one study, investigators compared the effects of 2-6 mg of risperidone to placebo in the treatment of chronically medicated schizophrenics. Following a washout period, patients in the placebo condition understandably experienced the onset or worsening of Parkinsonian features, as a part of a neuroleptic discontinuation syndrome. This inflated their scores on the "worst EPS scale." (At the same time, the use of risperidone in doses below 8 mg per day helped to improve the EPS ratings in other subjects.) The investigators then concluded that risperidone poses no significant risk of movement abnormalities, relative to placebo.[48]

Another way in which investigators introduce bias is through the use of particular *kinds* of assessment scales. These questionnaires come in two forms: direct response by patients themselves (the Beck Depression Inventory, the Zung Depression Scale), or symptom checklists which are completed by the clinician (the Hamilton Rating Scale for Depression, the Positive and Negative Syndrome Scale in Schizophrenia, the Abnormal Involuntary Movement Scale) family members, or school officials (e.g., the Conners' Rating Scales for ADHD). A disparity frequently emerges in these assessments based upon the identity of the evaluator. This can introduce significant bias, because patients may inflate their response to treatment in order to obtain discharge from the hospital or the discontinuation of forced treatment. Investigators may inflate the response to treatment, in a conscious or unconscious effort to demonstrate the efficacy of a new drug or their prowess as a clinician.

The safety profile of drugs can also be exaggerated by intentionally omitting questions from a patient interview or symptom checklist. For example, the Barkley Side Effects Rating Scale (SERS) used in ADHD research omits questions about unusual behavior or hallucinations.[49] This is a vital oversight, given the fact that psychosis may be a far more common side effect of stimulant therapy than many clinicians realize. Selective sampling of adverse reactions contributes to an incomplete picture of drug risks and may encourage a cavalier attitude in prescribing.

In a similar fashion, investigators who evaluate the side effects of antidepressants – particularly, the serotonin reuptake inhibitors like fluoxetine (Prozac) – conceal the rate of drug-induced sexual dysfunction by failing to ask direct questions about changes in libido or orgasm. Not surprisingly, this tendency for selective sampling has resulted in a stark bias in drug-company literature (2-5% rate of sexual dysfunction in pamphlets prepared for patients and professionals) versus direct observational studies in the real world (60-90% of patients acknowledging sexual side effects).[50]

Flaw #9: Post hoc selection of endpoints

A critical aspect of research design involves the explicit communication of expected endpoints *before* the trial begins. The most common method of reporting results in psychiatric research is the "mean difference" between groups, using a particular assessment scale. For example, one of the most common instruments for evaluating depression is the Hamilton Rating Scale. This is a clinician-scored questionnaire which assigns a value from 0 (absent) to 4 (serious) on a variety of symptoms, such as:

- Depressed mood

- Feelings of guilt

- Suicide

- Insomnia

- Agitation

- Anxiety

- Appetite

- Libido

Researchers define their criteria for treatment efficacy in terms of the *percent improvement* which patients demonstrate when their baseline scores are compared with their final scores at the end of a study. The outcomes are reported in both absolute terms and proportions (i.e., 50% reduction in total score by completion of trial). One of the criticisms which is raised about psychiatric research is the inherent subjectivity of these definitions. In one study, investigators may require a 50% reduction in total score, as measured by the primary rating tool. In another study, they may decide to use a 30% reduction to define "treatment success." What investigators are *not* supposed to do is define the criteria of success after the trial has been completed (post hoc selection of endpoints).

In most drug trials, psychiatric researchers employ two or more measurement scales to track the progress of subjects. One scale is called the primary or main outcome measure. The other scales are called secondary measures. When different rating scales yield contradictory findings (for example: when patient-rated scores vary significantly from clinician-rated scores), investigators generally emphasize the results which are most favorable to the experimental drug treatment. (Critics refer to this process of sifting through multiple analyses as "data dredging" – symbolic of the efforts to dig up findings which suggest that a drug actually "works.")

Assessment scales can also introduce misleading conclusions about psychiatric drugs because the criteria for defining efficacy may overestimate patient improvement. In other words, even though a drug may reduce symptoms in a given patient by 20% or more, that patient may continue to experience significant impairment in daily functioning. Thus, the definition of drug efficacy in the research setting, and the definition of patient recovery in the real world, may differ substantially.

Post hoc (after the fact) selection of endpoints may also involve the reported *duration* of a trial. In this sense, "data dredging" refers to a strategy of highlighting outcomes from an arbitrary endpoint, different from (earlier than) the actual completion date. An example of this occurred in the FDA's deliberation of a Phase III trial that led to the approval of olanzapine (Zyprexa). In one pivotal study (HGAP), patients dropped out of the trial in such high rates that the study fell below the number of subjects (power) required for valid statistical inferences. As a result, what was intended to be a six-week investigation was retrospectively converted to a four-week trial by the FDA, in order to prevent the study from becoming underpowered. Had the regulatory officials based their analyses on the intended six-week outcomes (observed case data, rather than LOCF), as shown in the following chart, it is unlikely that they would have found a clinically substantial difference between the olanzapine and placebo completers:[51]

Olanzapine HGAP Trial

Brief Psychiatric Rating Scale Total Score Change from Baseline by Visit
Mean Change in BPRS

	Baseline BPRS score	Week 1 mean change	Week 4 mean change	Week 6 mean change
Placebo	36.78	-2.39	-2.12	-10.78
Olz 1.0 mg	39.57	-2.86	-2.83	-13.08
Olz 10.0 mg	37.43	-3.49	-7.48	-15.58

Flaw #10: Redundant publication

The phenomenon of redundant publication refers to the process of "publishing or attempting to publish substantially the same work more than once." Redundant publication violates the rules of most medical journals, which require that all papers represent original work. Nonetheless, it is estimated that 13% of all papers published are duplicate or redundant works.[52]

Drug companies are motivated to publish the same findings of a trial repeatedly, in order to inflate the perceived value of their drugs. Recent examples in psychiatry[53] include a series of overlapping papers prepared by a team of writers at Eli Lilly, each of which re-packaged the same trial data in order to magnify the public perception of olanzapine's superiority to haloperidol. Another example is the series of studies sponsored by Glaxo Smith Kline, the maker of sustained release bupropion (Wellbutrin SR) in order to magnify public awareness of the sexual side effects associated with rival anidepressants (i.e., the selective serotonin reuptake inhibitors). Redundant publication is considered to be an ethics violation within medical research, because it adds superfluous information to an extensive body of data which some might say is already excessive. Furthermore, it distorts the foundation of evidence-based medicine by introducing a retrieval bias. This occurs whenever meta-analyses include data from the same trial, without realizing that the same patient events have been counted repeatedly.

Flaw #11: Selective emphasis of findings

Many professionals make a habit of skimming the abstracts which appear in journals as an efficient way of keeping current with the latest research. For this reason, many investigators selectively emphasize certain findings in their abstracts, in order to inflate the value of a particular therapy. An excellent example of selective reporting occurred in a pivotal study which compared an herbal therapy (St. John's wort) to sertraline (Zoloft) and placebo in the treatment of moderately severe depression. Despite the finding that 32% of the placebo subjects demonstrated a full response to treatment (compared to 24% of the St. John's wort and 25% of the sertraline subjects), the research team (and the news media) emphasized the following conclusion: St. John's wort is ineffective for depression. The poor performance of sertraline – never mentioned in the abstract or press reports – was attributed in the text of the article to "low assay sensitivity," even though the same rationale was not used to defend the performance of the herbal product.[54]

Flaw #12: Industrial sponsorship

The pharmaceutical industry's stranglehold over medical research is a topic which exceeds the scope of this book. However, no outline of methodological deficiencies would be complete without acknowledging the extensive conflicts of interest which now pervade the medical profession. It has been suggested that 25% of biomedical researchers, 50% of medical school faculty, and 66% of academic institutions have extensive financial ties to the drug industry.[55] Almost 90% of the physicians who prepare clinical practice guidelines have ties to the pharmaceutical industry, with more than a third serving as consultants or direct employees of the companies whose products are most strongly endorsed.[56]

In 2002, the *New England Journal of Medicine* relaxed its policy about financial conflicts of interest, largely because it had become so difficult to find professionals who lacked them.[57-58] An equally conspicuous example of industry control is illustrated by the phenomenon of ghost writing,[59-60] whereby professionals are paid to lend their names to articles which the drug companies have produced. In many situations, this practice of cloaked sponsorship only comes to light when "lead authors" let it slip that they have "never seen the raw data" upon which their research reports are based. According to a deputy editor of *JAMA*:[61]

"The practice is well-known, scandalous, and outrageous. It is a perfect illustration of deceptive authorship practices for commercial reasons."

The existence of industrial sponsorship need not, by itself, undermine the credibility of medical research. However, industrial sponsorship tends to influence the way in which clinical trials are designed and reported, leading to the prevalent occurrence that industry sponsored trials inevitably find greater benefits for the sponsor's product, relative to competitors.[62]

Flaw #13:
Publication bias (suppression of negative results)

Publication bias refers to the process whereby research findings – especially, negative findings – are censored. The concealment of negative data has several origins. First, it has become widely known through litigation that the drug manufacturers themselves have regularly concealed unfavorable data from the public and the FDA. Although drug manufacturers are required to submit all trial data to the FDA in the process of seeking product approval, the FDA (with few exceptions) is not compelled to disclose any information about a drug until it has reached the market. (Even then, the FDA does not divulge the raw data which have been used in its clinical efficacy and safety reviews.)

Second, many researchers are silenced by non-disclosure agreements which limit their capacity to issue statements about safety or efficacy concerns which may be discovered in the testing of drug products. Researchers also find that their funding may be abruptly terminated when a trial fails to produce the desired results. Such was the case in a panic disorder study which compared the efficacy of a minor tranquilizer (Xanax) against a variety of non-pharmacological approaches. When it became clear that the most effective treatment was a combination of exposure therapy and relaxation techniques:

> **"monitoring and support stopped abruptly... Thereafter, Upjohn's response was to invite professionals to critique the study they had nurtured so carefully before."**[63]

Third, medical journals themselves have a longstanding tradition which favors the publication of positive research results. This trend has presumably been compounded by the financial conflicts of editors and peer reviewers, who may not act impartially in deciding the content and timing of the articles which they agree to print.

With an estimated 50% of all research findings unreported or suppressed,[64] medical professionals have good reason to doubt the credibility of the published literature in terms of its completeness. In addition to this concern, they must also consider the methodological deficiencies of the drug trials which *have* appeared in print. All of these developments have had devastating effects upon the integrity of clinical practice, necessitating additional sources of information as a corrective for what has clearly become a misinformed consent to care.

Chapter Five

A popular reference on psychiatric drug treatments suggests that:

> **"It is not at all necessary to know how psychiatric drugs work in order to take them safely and benefit from them."** [1]

While it may indeed be true that many health consumers consider the details of drug actions to be irrelevant or too complicated to understand, it is also possible that such a perspective underestimates their needs and abilities. Too limited a discussion of drug effects (how they "work") may undermine the principle of informed consent by failing to convey pertinent risks associated with *taking or stopping* a medication. Before any patient can fully appreciate the benefits or hazards of a proposed therapy, it is essential to consider the major target of that treatment: the human brain.

The Structure and Function of the Human Brain

The structure and function of the human brain can be appreciated on two levels. On a *macroscopic* scale (the "forest"), the brain appears to the naked eye as a grayish, wrinkled object, approximately the size of a coconut. Biologists and ethologists have described the brain in terms of its evolutionary features. Based upon comparisons to other species, the human nervous system is actually three brains in one (MacLean's "triune brain"):[2]

The Triune Model of the Human Brain

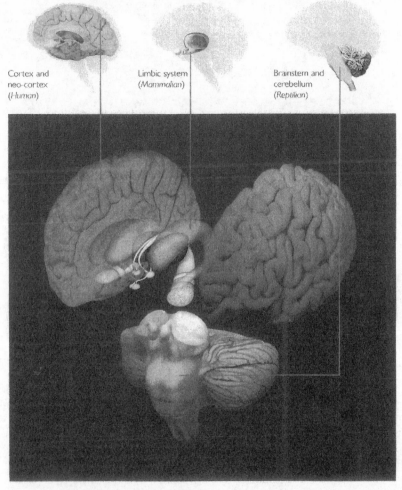

Cortex and
neo-cortex
(Human)

Limbic system
(Mammalian)

Brainstem and
cerebellum
(Reptilian)

Source: Rita Carter, *Mapping the Mind*, (Los Angeles: University of California Press, 1999), p. 33. Reproduced with permission of artist Malcolm Godwin.

a "reptilian brain" - referring to structures (brainstem, cerebellum, and spinal cord) which regulate reflexes and other automatic functions (such as breathing, blood pressure, and sleep)

a "mammalian brain" (limbic system) - referring to structures (cingulate and entorhinal cortices,

hippocampus, amygdala, thalamus, hypothalamus, mammillary body) which are responsible for emotion and memory (unconscious experience)

a "neomammalian brain" - referring to extensive cortical structures (especially frontal and temporal lobes) which enable language, planning, and consciousness

Because the structures of the human nervous system mature in a particular sequence - bottom to top, back to front - MacLean's "triune brain" captures the actual process of growth in the fetus, child, and young adult.   This phenomenon has given rise to the axiom: "ontogeny recapitulates phylogeny."   In other words, the structural development of each individual recapitulates, in sequence, the evolutionary processes which have shaped the defining features of the species.

On a *microscopic* scale (the "trees"), the structure of the human brain can be described in terms of its cellular components.[3] These elements - which can only be seen by dissecting the brain and examining tissue with the aid of special procedures and equipment - include 100 billion neurons (nerve cells), five to ten times as many glia (support cells), and an estimated 100 trillion synapses (connections) between them. Because the target of psychopharmacology is the individual brain cell, the study of drug effects begins with the appreciation of these structural units.

The Human Brain:
Macroscopic and Microscopic Perspectives

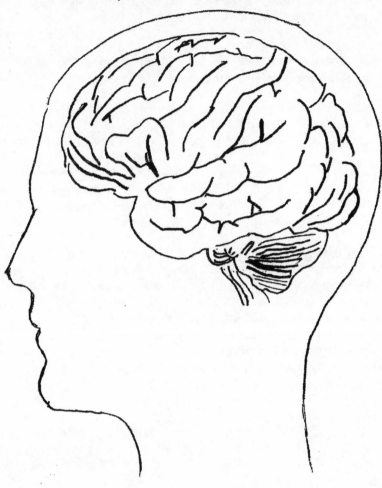

- ➢ 100 billion neurons
- ➢ 500 billion – 1 trillion glia
- ➢ 100 trillion synapses

The Glia

Glial cells (also called neuroglia) perform a variety of critical functions which vary according to cell type. Four kinds of glia have been characterized:

astrocytes - highly branched cells found in the white and grey matter. Their function includes the secretion of growth factors and the metabolic and structural support of neurons. (White matter refers to the portions of the brain that appear white because of their fatty insulation. Grey matter refers to the portions of the brain that appear dark because of the density of neuronal cell bodies.)

oligodendrocytes - myelinating oligodendrocytes form lipid (fatty acid) sheaths around axons in the brain and spinal cord; non-myelinating cells (called satellite cells) provide mechanical support to neuronal cell bodies

microglia - scavenger cells which respond to cell injury and death. These cells respond to infection and inflammation by clearing away debris and by secreting cytokines (small proteins) which attract other cells from the immune system.

ependymal cells - epithelial cells which line the ventricles of the brain and spinal cord. Some of these cells (called choroidal epithelial cells) produce the spinal fluid which bathes the brain. Ependymal cells also possess cilia (hairs) which contribute to the movement of the cerebrospinal fluid through the ventricles and the spinal canal.

Together, the glia participate in neuronal transmission by influencing the balance of neurotransmitters in the brain. For example, astrocytes play key roles in the uptake and secretion of amino acids (GABA and glutamate) and catecholamines (dopamine norepinephrine, epinephrine). The glia are also responsible for maintaining the electrolyte (salt) and pH (acid-base) balance of the fluids which surround neurons. Glial cells provide the structural framework for the migration of neurons in the developing fetus, and they contribute to the repair and regeneration of brain tissue after birth. Because psychopharmacology research has, until recently, emphasized the *neuron* as the target of chemical therapies, very little attention has been paid to the positive and negative effects of drugs upon the glia. (To say that this is concerning is an understatement, inasmuch as the glia constitute over half of the total volume of the brain.)

The Blood Brain Barrier

One final point about glial cells deserves to be emphasized at this juncture. Arguably the most important characteristic of the human nervous system is the fact that each brain cell (glia or neuron) is insulated from the environment by several layers of protection. The first layer is the human cranium – the protective shell of the skull. The second layer is the cushion of cerebrospinal fluid which bathes the brain. The third layer – the blood brain barrier – is a microscopic defense system, which prevents substances in the bloodstream from entering the brain tissue.

Ordinarily, the smallest blood vessels of the body – the capillaries – are lined by endothelial cells which permit the movement of chemicals in and out of the vascular spaces. However, the endothelial cells in the capillaries of the brain are glued tightly together – a process in which the glial cells (astrocytes) play a prominent role. The "blood brain barrier" prevents the penetration of large molecules, hydrophilic substances (water-liking, low fat soluble molecules), and/or any compound with a high electrical charge. The purpose of this barrier is to protect the central nervous system from toxins, infections, and other biochemical stressors in order to provide a stable environment for the brain. Perhaps the most significant aspect of psychopharmacology is the fact that each medication is a molecule which scientists have specifically designed in order to evade the blood brain barrier. *One would hope that this fact would encourage consumers and clinicians to reflect cautiously upon the use of psychoactive drugs, as they are all produced with the intention of eluding the body's natural defenses.*

The Neuron

The primary focus of clinical psychopharmacology is the *neuron,* the main communicator of the brain. Each neuron is composed of three elements:

the dendrite - a tentacle-like process which receives electrical and chemical impulses from other cells. Dendrites facilitate intercellular communication by extending to and from cell bodies, other dendrites, and axons to form synapses (connections) with other neurons.

the cell body (sometimes called perikaryon or soma) - the business center of the neuron, containing the nucleus with the cell's DNA blueprint for cell division and replication; and RNA for protein synthesis. The cell body produces enzymes and other components essential for the manufacture and storage of neurotransmitters.

the axon - the longest type of process, or extension, from a cell body. Axons can be short or long (the longest axons in the human body extend up to one meter in length). The function of axon is to conduct electrical impulses. The axon also transports enzymes and other products between the cell body (soma) and the nerve terminal (called the "bouton"). Neurotransmitters are synthesized in the cell body or in the bouton, and are then stored in sacs (synaptic vesicles) until an electrical stimulus arrives to trigger their release

The *function* of the brain is to send and receive electrochemical signals. The process begins when a nerve cell is excited by electrical or chemical stimuli. These stimuli can be received by any part of a neuron (either a dendrite, the cell body, or the axon). Stimulation leads to a change in cell membrane permeability and to the generation of small voltage changes, called EPSPs (excitatory post-synaptic potentials) or IPSPs (inhibitory post-synaptic potentials). If the sum of the EPSPs and IPSPs is sufficiently large, the result is an electrical impulse called an action potential. The action potential spreads over the neuron's surface until it reaches the end of the axon.

EPSPs (excitatory post-synatic potentials) prepare the neuron to initiate an action potential. The electrical impulse orginates at a special zone of the axon called the axon hillock. A myelinated axon is coated by a fatty layer of insulation. This accelerates the speed of transmission. When the action potential reaches the end of the axon, it triggers the release of neurotransmitters into the synaptic cleft (the gap) between two or more cells.

Once a neurotransmitter reaches the synaptic cleft, it undergoes one of many possible events:

> ➢ diffusion (travel) away from the synapse; this can involve travel via collateral axons all the way back to the cell body, or diffusion in the cerebrospinal fluid to interact with glia

> ➢ metabolism (breakdown) by chemicals that are present in the synaptic cleft

> ➢ reuptake into the original cell via special openings in the nerve terminal called transporters or reuptake pumps; once inside the nerve ending, it can be stored and recyled, or it can be broken down by enzymes

> ➢ fusion with a receptor on the surface of other neurons or glia, or with receptors on the nerve terminal from which it has just been released

As used in this superficial overview, the term *neurotransmitter* refers broadly to any kind of chemical substance which facilitates communication between cells of the brain. Current research suggests the existence of over sixty different neurotransmitters in the human nervous system. In reality, there may be well be hundreds of them, since new peptides and proteins are discovered every year. By convention, these chemicals are classified according to size, composition, and function:[4-5]

Examples of Neurotransmitters in the Human Brain

amino acids	nucleotides	neuropeptides	biogenic amines	hormones	gases
glycine	adenosine	substance P	acetylcholine	calcitonin	carbon monoxide
glutamate	ATP	cholecystokinin	serotonin	insulin	nitric oxide
GABA		somatostatin	histamine	parathryoid	
aspartate		gastrin	dopamine	hormone	
homocysteine		neurokinin A	norepinephrine	thyroid hormone	
taurine		neurokinin B	epinephrine	corticosterone	
		kassinin		aldosterone	
		eledoisin		testosterone	
		vasoactive intestinal		estradiol	
		peptide		progesterone	
		secretin		vitamin D	
		glucagon			
		growth hormone			
		releasing hormone			
		growth hormone			
		neuropeptide Y			
		angiotensin			
		B-endorphin			
		dynorphin			
		neoendorphin			
		leucine enkephalin			
		methionine enkephalin			
		grehlin			
		vasopressin			
		oxytocin			
		prolactin			
		motilin			
		neurotensin			
		substance K			
		FSH			
		LH			
		corticotropin releasing hormone			
		ACTH			
		alpha melanocyte stimulating hormone			
		bradykinin			
		atrial natriuretic factor			
		calcitonin gene related peptide			
		pancreatic polypeptide			
		galanin			

Although a portion of the communication in the brain occurs directly by the transfer of electrical impulses between cells, most neuronal activity is thought to arise from the interaction of chemical substances (the body's own neurotransmitters or the medications which mimic or compete with them). It is worth mentioning that many other cells of the body – including white blood cells, platelets, myocardial cells, and epithelial cells of the digestive tract – also possess receptors for the same transmitters which are active in the brain. This is the reason why psychiatric drugs exert widespread and diverse effects, both within and beyond the nervous system.

An understanding of receptor physiology is critical for clinicians who prescribe medications, because most drugs interact with a variety of receptors. It is the specific *combination* of receptors to which a drug binds, as well as the affinity (strength of binding) of a drug for each kind of receptor, which determines its unique effects in the human body. Consequently, it is not the neurotransmitter that determines the quality of cellular activity in the brain. Rather, it is the *cell receptor* that determines whether or not a particular chemical substance will produce excitatory (stimulatory) or inhibitory (non-stimulatory) effects. The diversity of receptor subtypes makes it possible for the same neurotransmitter to elicit a wide variety of cellular responses, depending upon the number, the location, and the kinds of receptors with which it interacts.

Examples of transmitters and receptor subtypes [6]

Norepinephrine	Dopamine	GABA	Acetylcholine	Serotonin
Alpha 1A	D1	GABA A	M1	5HT1A
Alpha 1B	D2	GABA B1a	M2	5HT1B * in rats
Alpha 1C	D3	GABA B1d	M3	5HT1D * in humans
Alpha 1D	D4	GABA B2	M4	5HT1E
	D5	GABA C	M5	5HT1F
Alpha 2A				
Alpha 2B				5HT2A
Alpha 2C				5HT2B
Alpha 2D				5HT2C
Beta 1				5HT3
Beta 2				5HT4
Beta 3				5HT5
				5HT6
				5HT7

Once a neurotransmitter or **psychiatric medication** - a *first messenger* - binds to a postsynaptic receptor, neuronal communication is amplified by a series of events within the next cell. These events include the activation of receptor "coupling factors," such as G-proteins and adenylyl cyclase. The coupling factors then recruit or activate *second messenger* systems: cAMP, cGMP, inositol trisphosphate, diacylglycerol, or a variety of enzymes known as protein kinases. The second messenger systems activate phosphorylated proteins (*third messengers*) which ultimately enhance or suppress the expression of DNA. The end result is the modulation of protein synthesis within the post-synaptic cell, leading to changes in neuronal and glial functions.

For the first twenty years of the modern psychopharmacology era (1950-1970), researchers studied the effects of medications upon neurotransmitter synthesis and turnover (i.e., the rates of production and metabolism). As a result, the biological theories of mental illness and treatment came to be based upon studies of chemicals in the urine, blood, and cerebrospinal fluid. The problem with this line of research was, and continues to be, a lack of consistent findings. Researchers have never been able to determine a "normal" baseline for comparing chemical concentrations in the brain.

The next phase of psychopharmacology research (1970s-1980s) saw the introduction of new technologies in molecular biology and radiology. This led scientists to distinguish the quality and quantity of cell membrane receptors in the brain. Medication effects came to be defined by receptor physiology and the behavioral effects of those interactions. Like the chemical studies which came before it, the "receptor era" also failed to produce a reliable standard or reference point against which brain dysfunction could be identified.

Continuing advances in molecular biology and neuroimaging techniques transformed the focus of psychopharmacology research – away from neurotransmitter levels, and away from ˙receptor-ligand interactions on each brain cell, to the level of the genome. Since 1990, research has shifted increasingly to the analysis and manipulation of signal transduction, DNA transcription, and RNA translation within the neurons and glia. When a clinician and a patient exchange a prescription for a psychiatric drug today, they should both be thinking about the following questions:

How will this drug modify the expression of DNA, alter protein synthesis, and create changes in the function and structure of brain cells ?

How might these changes present a chronic stress to the human body?

˙ligand – any ion or molecule that reacts to form a complex with another molecule;[7] in pharmacology research, a ligand is simply any substance which binds to a receptor. Ligands can be endogenous (made within the body, such as neurotransmitters) or exogenous (made outside the body, such as botanicals or synthetic medications).

Chapter Six

ALLOSTASIS AND THE PROBLEM OF ALLOSTATIC LOAD[1-4]

Coined in 1988 by Sterling and Eyer, the term *allostasis* refers to the collective adaptations made by the human organism in response to internal and external demands. In contrast to the earlier principle of homeostasis – which suggests that living systems maintain *stability through constancy* – the principle of allostasis predicts that *viability arises from change.*

Allostatic processes in the human body commonly involve the central nervous system (the spinal cord and brain), the endocrine system, and the immune system. Perhaps the best example of allostasis is the **hypothalamus-pituitary-adrenal axis** (HPA), which regulates the body's responses to stress. When an individual is faced with a threat, injury, or trauma, the central nervous system increases the activity of specific neurotransmitters called catecholamines (e.g., norepinephrine). These chemicals are a key part of body's "fight or flight" response (dilating the pupils, increasing the respiratory and pulse rates, and shunting blood away from the digestive tract to the muscles, lungs, and heart). Within the brain, catecholamines and circadian rhythms stimulate the **hypothalamus** to secrete corticotropin releasing hormone, or CRH. At the level of the **pituitary** gland, CRH triggers the release of adrenocorticotropic hormone (ACTH, also known as corticotropin). ACTH then travels through the bloodstream until it reaches the **adrenal** glands which sit atop the kidneys. There, it signals the production and release of cortisol.

The short term activation of this cascade represents the body's adaptive response to stress. This is an example of allostasis: *viability through change.* However, it is possible for the body's reactions to become overactive, underactive, or prolonged. As named by Dr. Bruce McEwen, this deleterious form of maladaptation is *allostatic load.*

Allostasis and Allostatic Load

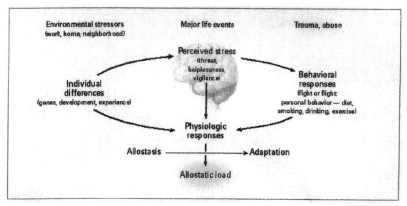

Source: Bruce S. McEwen, "Protective and Damaging Effects of Stress Mediators," *The New England Journal of Medicine* 338 (1998): 172. Reproduced with the permission of the New England Journal of Medicine.

The *stress response* in humans often begins with an individual's *perception* of stress in reaction to trauma, life events, or environmental factors (job, social network, culture). This perception then leads to the collective behavioral and physiological responses which constitute allostasis. At the point where adaptations become counter-productive, however, allostasis is replaced by *allostatic load* (negative or maladaptive change).

While McEwen does not explicitly identify *pharmacological agents* in his calculations of allostatic load, one should consider the potential for all foreign chemicals to act as environmental stressors in the model described above. *Because psychiatric drugs are a potential (though unintended) source of stress upon the human body, it is necessary to consider how these medications contribute to allostatic load.* McEwen envisions four possible mechanisms. For the sake of simplicity, I will refer to these as Types I, II, III, and IV.

Examples of Allostatic Load

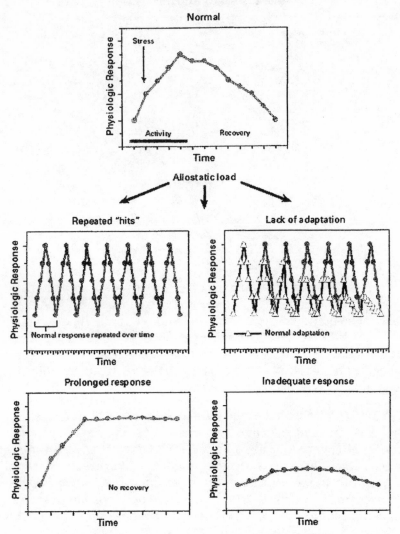

Source: Bruce S. McEwen, "Protective and Damaging Effects of Stress Mediators," *The New England Journal of Medicine* 338 (1998): 174. Reproduced with permission of the *NEJM*.

Allostatic Load - Type I: Repeated Responses to Repeated Hits

Example: toxic metabolites

The first possible mechanism of allostatic load involves frequent or repeated stress exposures. (This is represented in the diagram by the zig zag showing repeated hits.) Psychiatric drugs may cause trauma to the body through a process of repeated toxicity, similar to ionizing radiation. Type I load occurs with *repeated doses* of haloperidol, an antipsychotic drug which is converted by monoamine oxidase into pyridinium compounds similar to MPP+ (1-methyl-1-4-phenylpyridinium, the toxic metabolite of the synthetic opiate, MPTP). All of these chemicals damage or kill neurons by impairing cell membrane integrity and mitochondrial respiration.[5-8] By contributing to pathophysiological changes in many brain regions – particularly, the striatum – these metabolites are thought to play a prominent role in the etiology of Parkinsonian symptoms (shuffling gait, pill rolling tremor, ˙bradykinesia).

Type I load is also exemplified by the structural changes which occur in serotonin nerve fibers[9] following *repeated exposure* to SSRIs (selective serotonin reuptake inhibitors, such as Prozac and Zoloft). Although these changes have not been investigated in human subjects, the findings in animal specimens demonstrate that a number of antidepressants cause swelling and kinking in serotonin neurons. The clinical significance of these changes has not been determined, but they may be reflective of drug-induced injury, against which the brain must then mount an allostatic response (e.g., the production of growth factors for neuronal repair).

Allostatic Load - Type II: Lack of Adaptation (failure to habituate & sensitization)

Example: hyperprolactinemia, REM sleep suppression, addiction

McEwen gives public speaking as an example of Type II load. Most individuals experience nervousness immediately before making a speech or lecture, but over time, this anxiety subsides. This

---

˙bradykinesia – abnormal slowness of movement, or sluggishness of physical and mental responses

adjustment or adaptation is called habituation, referring to a form of learning whereby an organism stops responding to a particular stimulus after a period of repeated exposures. For about 10% of the population, though, the thought of speaking before an audience continues to evoke an intense stress response, characterized by a racing heart, dry mouth, sweaty palms, dizziness, and/or nausea. These individuals have failed to adapt or habituate to the environmental stressor of public speaking.

The adverse effects of psychiatric drugs are analogous to public speaking. Some patients experience physiological reactions which habituate over time. However, many drugs trigger bodily adaptations which fail to diminish over the course of therapy. Examples include the persistent elevation of prolactin levels which accompanies the use of many neuroleptics (antipsychotic drugs), including some of the newer drugs such as risperidone (Risperdal). This prolonged hormonal response can lead to osteoporosis, sexual dysfunction, amenorrhea, and heart disease.

Another example of Type II load is the suppression of REM sleep which occurs with many serotonergic antidepressants. Still another example is the growth suppression which occurs in prepubertal children exposed to stimulant medications, such as methylphenidate (Ritalin) and d-amphetamine (Dexedrine). Type II allostatic load is also exemplified by the phenomenon of sensitization, which refers to the process by which the human body becomes more sensitive (more responsive) to a given stimulus over time.   Both of these mechanisms (habituation and sensitization) are components of drug addiction.

As originally defined by the World Health Organization, *addiction* referred to:

> **"The repeated use of a psychoactive substance or substances, to the extent that the user is periodically or chronically intoxicated, shows a compulsion to take the preferred substance(s), and exhibits determination to obtain psychoactive substances by almost any means. Typically, tolerance is prominent, and a withdrawal syndrome frequently occurs when substance use is interrupted. The life of the addict may be dominated by substance use to the virtual exclusion of all other activities**

and responsibilities. The term addiction also conveys the sense that such substance use has a detrimental effect on society, as well as on the individual... From the 1920s to the 1960s attempts were made to differentiate between "addiction" and "habituation," a less severe form of psychological adaptation..."[10]

In 1964, the World Health Organization replaced addiction with the term *dependence*:

"In unqualified form, dependence refers to both physical and psychological elements. Psychological or psychic dependence refers to the experience of impaired control over drinking or drug use (craving, compulsion), while physiological or physical dependence refers to tolerance and withdrawal symptoms. In biologically-oriented discussion, dependence is often used to refer only to physical dependence. Dependence or physical dependence is also used in the psychopharmacological context in a still narrower sense, referring solely to the development of withdrawal symptoms on cessation of drug use."[11]

This re-definition ultimately became so dominant that psychiatric textbooks and the American Psychiatric Association's own nosology of mental disorders – the *DSM* – stopped defining or discussing the concept of addiction. Instead, the terms "dependence" and "abuse" came to be used (largely for political reasons) in order to explain the potential for any substance to induce intermittent or chronic patterns of compulsive consumption associated with negative consequences:[12]

Substance Abuse	Substance Dependence
A maladaptive pattern of use leading to clinically significant distress, with one of more of the following within a a 12-month period:	A maladaptive pattern of use leading to clinically significant distress, with three or more of the following within the same 12-month period:
recurrent substance use resulting in failure to fulfill major role obligations at work, school, or home	tolerance withdrawal
recurrent substance use in situations in which it is physically hazardous	substance taken in larger amounts or over longer period than was intended
recurrent substance-related legal problems	persistent desire or unsuccessful efforts to cut down
continued use despite persistent or recurrent social or interpersonal problems caused or exacerbated by the effects of the substance	great deal of time spent in activities necessary to obtain substance
	important social, occupational, or recreational activities given up or reduced because of the substance use
	substance use continued despite knowledge of having persistent or recurrent physical or psychological problem that is likely to have been caused or exacerbated by the substance

Two aspects of substance dependence are pertinent to the discussion of allostatic load. First, it is possible for psychiatric drugs to create physiological changes in the brain which are associated either with increased hedonic effects (more euphoria), or with increased motivation to use (drug seeking). To the extent that either of these *sensitization* processes emerge, one might speak of Type II allostatic load. Second, it is possible for the prolonged use of prescription or recreational drugs to induce *desensitization* in certain neural substrates of the brain, leading to tolerance and withdrawal (Type III allostatic load – see below). Since psychiatric medications are particularly prone to inducing these latter forms of change, they technically comply with the World Health Organization's revised definition of "addiction." What is generally minimized by the psychiatric profession, however, is the capacity for medications to sensitize the brain to *psychological* aspects of addiction (e.g., drug wanting), while desensitizing the brain to other aspects (physical or psychological) of drug dependence.[13]

A clear example of *sensitization* occurs with stimulant medications, such as d-amphetamine (Dexedrine) and methylphenidate (Ritalin). Like cocaine, both drugs inhibit the dopamine transporter. Also like cocaine, stimulant medications can sensitize the body to psychomotor and behavioral effects, such as restlessness, hyperactivity, tics, hallucinations, and paranoia. Some researchers have also documented sensitization (with low doses) to cardiovascular effects.[14] One of the curious aspects of chronic stimulant use, however, is a possible dissociation between euphoria and craving.[15] What this means is that compulsive users might experience diminished effects in terms of the drug's potential to induce pleasure (drug liking), while at the same time, they experience an increase in the desire to consume the drug (drug wanting). At first glance, this dissociation may seem illogical: if a substance no longer delivers a "drug high," why would a person still crave it? One possible answer lies in the "incentive-sensitization theory,"[16] according to which brain circuits responsible for motivation and reward deliver increasingly strong signals that a drug will provide the pleasurable sensations associated with its initial use. From a neuroanatomic and neurophysiologic perspective, this suggests that pathways in the nucleus accumbens presumably become sensitized over time, leading to an increased desire (conscious or even unconscious) to consume a particular substance or engage in a particular behavior. Simultaneously, pathways in other regions of the brain appear to become desensitized to the delivery or perception of euphoric sensations.

One final point about sensitization is worth emphasizing at this juncture. Although few physicians acknowledge the fact, there is considerable epidemiological and neuroscientific evidence to support the theory that psychiatric drugs sensitize the brain by altering neurotransmitter system reactivity and/or anatomic structures. **Because these changes may exacerbate the physiological processes which mediate the symptoms of many conditions,** *all* **psychiatric drugs have the potential to prolong or worsen the disorders for which they are prescribed.** The evidence for this profoundly disturbing phenomenon will be examined in the chapters which follow.

Allostatic Load – Type III:
Prolonged Response (after removal of stressor or medication)

Examples: Tolerance, Withdrawal

The third type of allostatic load defined by McEwen involves prolonged responses in the aftermath of a particular stressor. Using the example of "math anxiety" (the performance anxiety that accompanies math exams), McEwen describes how many individuals experience a rise in blood pressure during an exam which then persists even after the test period has ended. He attributes this state of prolonged arousal to the continuation of *allostatic responses which fail to shut off appropriately* when a stressful stimulus subsides.

Within the field of psychopharmacology, there are many examples of prolonged allostatic responses which prove to be maladaptive over time. Some of these adaptations influence the effectiveness of therapy *while medications are still being taken*. Some of these adaptations become visible only *when medication is interrupted or withdrawn*.

The phenomenon of *tolerance* refers to the effects of sustained or repeated drug exposure, leading to adaptive processes which reduce the acute effects of a drug. Eventually, it becomes necessary for the drug user to increase the dose or frequency of consumption, or to change the route of administration (e.g., intranasal or intravenous instead of oral) in order to reproduce effects of a given magnitude. Tolerance also refers to the process by which higher intensities of drug exposure result in decreased maximal effects.

The concept of *tolerance* can be depicted graphically in two ways. First, a dose-response curve which plots drug concentration (x-axis) against biological effects (y-axis) can be used to understand the kinds of changes which develop with chronic drug exposure. If the curve shifts to the right, *tolerance* (desensitization) has occurred because higher drug levels have become necessary to produce a biological effect that was seen previously at lower doses. (Conversely, a left shift represents sensitization, or an increased drug response, whereby bodily adaptations have resulted in greater effects at lower doses.) A second illustration of tolerance (not depicted below) would involve an overall *flattening* of the dose-response curve in order to demonstrate how equal drug concentrations would yield progressively smaller *maximal* effects:

Dose Response Curve

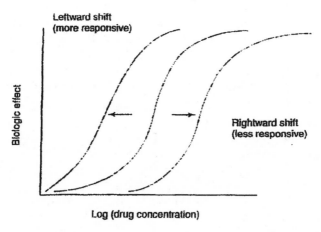

Log (drug concentration)

Source: Eric J. Nestler, Steven E. Hyman, Robert C. Malenka, *Molecular Neuropharmacology: A Foundation for Clinical Neuroscience*, (New York: The McGraw-Hill Companies, Inc., 2001), p. 11. Reproduced with permission of the McGraw-Hill Companies.

On a physiological level, there are many possible causes of drug tolerance. *Pharmacokinetic mechanisms* involve variablity in the *body's handling of a drug.* Changes in drug absorption, distribution, metabolism, and/or excretion can lead to diminishing drug effects over time. With the exception of medication effects upon the cytochrome P450 enzyme system of the liver, very little attention has been paid to the pharmacokinetic processes which accompany the chronic use of psychotropic drugs.

Pharmacodynamic mechanisms have received more attention. These processes refer to adaptations which occur *after a drug reaches its intended target.* In other words, nothing has changed in terms of drug absorption or delivery to the intended organ or cell type. Rather, pharmacodynamic tolerance implies that the body has experienced a change in sensitivity which reduces the former impact of the drug-target interaction.

Two models have been proposed to explain *pharmacodynamic tolerance*.[17] The first explanation, called the *decremental model*, suggests that tolerance results from a reduction in the intensity of the drug signal or stimulus. This may involve changes in receptor sensitivity (the affinity of the drug for the receptor, reflected by $^*K_d$) or changes in receptor density due to down-regulation (lower number of available receptors, reflected by $^{**}B_{max}$). The decremental model has been the dominant explanation for tolerance in the psychiatric literature. The second explanation of pharmacodynamic tolerance, called the *oppositional model*, suggests that signal intensity remains unchanged (the interaction between the drug and the receptors stays the same). However, the initial effects of the drug are ultimately counteracted by any of a number of physiologic or anatomic alterations:

- ➢ changes in the post-synaptic, signal transduction systems: 2nd and 3rd messengers, enzyme activity, and gene expression

- ➢ changes in neuronal and glial connections due to axonal and dendritic growth or degradation

- ➢ changes in neurotransmitter synthesis or degradation

- ➢ changes in the functioning of effector systems, such as the hypothalamus-pituitary-adrenal axis.

What is important about both the decremental and oppositional models of tolerance is the fact that they account for widespread occurrences in clinical practice. One such development is the phenomenon of drug 'poop-out,' whereby patients sense that their medications have "stopped working." This typically leads the prescriber to raise the dose or frequency of the drug, or to add still more drugs, beginning a vicious cycle that fails to address

---

$^*K_d$ - in biochemistry and pharmacology, the dissociation constant; K_d represents the concentration of neurotransmitter or drug at which half of the specific binding sites are occupied. The larger the Kd, the lower the affinity of a drug for the receptor and vice versa.

$^{**}B_{max}$ – the highest possible bound response; B_{max} represents maximal drug or neurotransmitter binding that can occur, based upon the total number of binding sites

the underlying cause of the problem. Similarly, many patients demonstrate a return of symptoms *during the maintenance phase of drug treatment*. Examples include the recurrence of mania during lithium therapy, the return of dysphoria (depressed mood) during antidepressant therapy, and the return of hallucinations during neuroleptic therapy.

Another widespread phenomenon is the condition of drug *withdrawal*, which refers generally to any of the symptoms which arise from physiological adaptations after a medication has been terminated. Some authors distinguish between *drug rebound* and *drug withdrawal*, using the former term to delineate the return or intensification of the underlying condition for which a drug was introduced; and reserving the latter term for the appearance of new symptoms which were not formerly apparent. Regardless of the terminology, the existence of drug discontinuation syndromes is of enormous importance in psychiatry for two reasons. First, the entire literature on prognosis and treatment has been confounded for over fifty years by the failure of researchers and clinicians to distinguish between drug rebound and withdrawal effects, and the alleged natural progression of psychiatric "disease." Second, the features of drug discontinuation syndromes have not been well explained to patients, nor widely appreciated by clinicians, with the frequently ruinous result that appropriate interventions have been delayed, neglected, or denied.

Unfortunately, the psychiatric profession has fallen into the habit of blaming the patient for tolerance and withdrawal symptoms, using the euphemism of "treatment refractoriness." The mendacity of this reflex has been exposed by the neuroscientific record. Far from reflecting "the faulty genes of the patient" or "the return of the underlying illness," withdrawal symptoms have been repeatedly investigated and explained by predictable, drug-induced transformations in the body – many of which persist for weeks or months.

Withdrawal and rebound phenomena can be understood in relation to the decremental and oppositional models of tolerance, for they represent the *processes that are left behind* whenever a psychiatric drug is no longer consumed. For example, withdrawal effects are explained by the *decremental model* in terms of changes in the number and/or affinity of drug receptors: if receptor density

63

increases, but the drug level drops, it becomes possible for more of the body's natural neurotransmitters to interact with the receptors without competition from the drug. Withdrawal effects are also explained by the *oppositional model* in terms of the additional systems – within or beyond the brain – which have been "recruited" by the body to oppose the effects of the drug. Once the drug is removed, these opposing systems remain active for some time until the body can again respond, leading to a new state of dynamic equilibrium (allostasis).

Examples of Drug Discontinuation Phenomena: Drug Rebound

Stimulant *Rebound*	Antidepressant *Rebound*
dopamine transporter levels (DAT) are reduced by drug treatment	during drug treatment, serotonin reuptake transporter (SERT) density falls, and cell body autoreceptors in the midbrain become desensitized
when drug levels fall or treatment is stopped, DAT density surges; less dopamine becomes available for neuronal transmission	when drug levels fall or treatment stops, SERT levels rise and autoreceptors become responsive again; less serotonin becomes available for neuronal transmission
this may result in worsening features of inattention, impulsivity, or hyperactivity	this may lead to suicidality, low mood, anxiety, fatigue, anergia, or sleep disturbance

Examples of Drug Discontinuation Phenomena: Drug Withdrawal

SSRI *Withdrawal* Syndrome	Neuroleptic *Withdrawal* Syndrome
shock-like sensations	shock-like sensations
diarrhea	diarrhea
nausea/vomiting	nausea/vomiting
tremor	tremor
gait instability	myalgia (muscle pain)
headache	diaphoresis (sweating)
visual disturbances	rhinorrhea (runny nose)
dizziness	
	also may include worsening features of *tardive dyskinesia and/or **tardive akathisia

---

*tardive dyskinesia (TD) – a condition marked by the delayed (tardy) onset of involuntary repetitive movements of the facial, buccal, oral, and cervical musculature. Usually induced by the long term use of antipsychotic agents, TD typically persists after the withdrawal of the inciting agent.

**tardive akathisia – a condition marked by the delayed onset of severe motor restlessness, or intense anxiety. Like TD, this can emerge after prolonged exposure to antipsychotic medications.

65

Allostatic Load - Type IV: Inadequate Response

Examples: antidepressant suppression of the HPA axis, antipsychotic suppression of the pleasure-reward/cognitive/motor systems

The fourth type of allostatic load characterized by McEwen involves an *inadequate stress response* by the body. McEwen gives the example of the hypothalamus-pituitary-adrenal axis (HPA). Normally, the hypothalamus of the brain responds to trauma, stress, or injury by delivering corticotropin releasing hormone (CRH) to the pituitary gland. As described above, this sets off a chain reaction which culminates in the release of cortisol. In the short run, this is not harmful. Cortisol promotes the breakdown of proteins and fats, and promotes the synthesis of sugar - all of which are fairly immediate forms of energy which can be used for mobility or for the repair of damaged tissue. However, the effects of *sustained* hypercortisolemia can have a variety of negative health consequences.

As one of the key stress hormones in the body, *prolonged elevations* of cortisol can adversely affect mood and cognition (inhibiting spatial memory, impairing the accuracy of contextual memory, and facilitating the development of anxiety and depression), metabolism (causing elevations in insulin and lipid levels, insulin resistance, and obesity), and immune function (decreasing the output of T-cells and antibodies from the lymph nodes and bone marrow). Because of these effects, the recent discovery that many classes of psychiatric medications appear to inhibit cortisol when they are consumed chronically has been met with enthusiasm. In fact, a growing area of neuroscience research focuses upon the development of novel drug agents designed specifically to diminish the activity of the HPA axis (e.g., the development of CRH antagonists). One would hope that scientists would think critically about the unintended consequences of these prospective inventions, for the following reasons.

First, if cortisol secretion does not increase in response to stress or trauma, the levels of chemicals which are usually inhibited by cortisol can become overactive. This can result in acute or chronic inflammation due to the proliferation of proteins (such as cytokines, histamine, bradykinin, prostaglandins, and leukotrienes) which increase vasodilation, capillary permeability, and white cell migration. McEwen lists fibromyalgia, chronic fatigue, and atopic dermatitis as possible products of a *hypoactive* HPA axis. It is possible that other conditions – such as asthma and rheumatoid arthritis – could be triggered or exacerbated by HPA suppression, as well.

Second, there may be good reason to worry about the chronic suppression of the body's stress response systems in terms of reducing an individual's capacity to react to *acute* stimuli. If the cortisol "thermostat" has been turned down low by the continued administration of antidepressants, neuroleptics, or stimulants, one must wonder about this adaptation's possible effects upon the ability of an individual to cope with new threats or injuries. In other words, while psychotropic drugs might dampen cortisol and relieve some of the effects of a prolonged stress response, they might also reduce the capacity of the body to repair damage arising from a fresh stressor.

Third, there is reason to worry about the allostatic load which can accompany the eventual *termination* of a hypoactive stress response (i.e., the *re-activation* of the HPA axis). When antidepressants or antipsychotic medications are reduced or stopped, it may be possible for cells and tissues in the neuroendocrine system to react in a *hypersensitive* or exaggerated fashion.[18] This explains why it is possible for an underlying condition (depression, anxiety, psychosis) to become worse each time a medication is started and stopped, as cortisol and other chemicals may surge (or dip) to levels which are potentially more harmful than those which existed prior to drug therapy.

One final example of Type IV load occurs with the chronic administration of antipsychotic drugs. As described in future pages, the neuroleptics have strong effects upon the behavioral, cognitive, and motor pathways of the brain. By blocking dopamine and other receptor subtypes in the midbrain, the neocortex, and the basal ganglia, antipsychotic drugs can precipitate dysphoria and cognitive slowing (called "neuroleptic induced deficit syndrome" or NIDS), akathisia (severe restlessness and agitation), and/or extrapyramidal symptoms (Parkinsonian features, as mentioned above). All of these examples demonstrate "inadequate" responses to therapy (Type IV load) since the assumed goal of treatment would be the restoration of each of these domains of functioning (i.e., cognitive, affective, motoric). Further examples of Type IV load are found in the compensatory behaviors (cigarette smoking, cocaine abuse) which many patients employ in an effort to counteract the physiological changes induced by antipsychotic medications.

Chapter Seven
ANTIDEPRESSANTS

The History of Antidepressants

Although few psychiatry textbooks include them, the earliest antidepressant drug treatments consisted of a variety of largely unregulated substances: in the 19th and early 20th centuries, opiates, alcohol, and cocaine; in the 1930s, amphetamines (Benzedrine) and other stimulants; in the 1940s and 1950s, a variety of sedatives (bromides, paraldehyde, barbiturates). From the lens of history, it is apparent that what has passed for an "antidepressant" has depended as much upon culture and the social construction of the targeted condition (melancholia, neurosis, neurasthenia)[1-2] as it has upon biological conceptualizations of abnormal brain processes awaiting chemical repair.

Despite this ambiguous tradition, the *formal* birth of antidepressant drug treatments[3] is generally attributed to the efforts of post-war scientists in Europe and North America. In the aftermath of World War II, chemists and pharmacologists analyzed and modified a variety of German products (dyes and rocket fuels) for possible applications in medicine. Among the earliest products synthesized were antihistamine derivatives (e.g., the phenothiazines) and antibiotics, many of which came to be tested by pioneering physicians who worked in some of the leading mental institutions of the day.

Overlooked by many historians (but one of the first drugs to be tested for *antidepressant* properties) was *Rauwolfia serpentina* (snakeroot) – a plant alkaloid that had been used in India for hundreds of years as a treatment for hypertension, snakebites, and insanity.[4] While working at New York's Rockland State Hospital in the early 1950s, psychiatrist Nathan Kline experimented with *Rauwolfia* and found it useful in controlling disruptive behaviors (e.g., his patients stopped breaking windows). At Kline's urging, CIBA (one of the four leading pharmaceutical companies at the time) isolated and then marketed the active ingredient of the plant (reserpine), giving birth to one of the first antipsychotic drugs in

America. Reserpine also gained popularity as a treatment for high blood pressure.

Shortly thereafter, there emerged in psychiatry the concept that antipsychotic drugs – which were being used in high doses to sedate patients with hallucinations and delusions – could be applied in lower doses for the treatment of anxiety or depression. Clinical drug trials with reserpine were conducted by Michael Shepherd, who compared the drug against placebo in depressed subjects. Although Shepherd's studies demonstrated that reserpine was efficacious as an antidepressant, it was never marketed for that purpose for a variety of reasons: 1) the drug was already successful as an antipsychotic; 2) there was no market at the time for antidepressants in the outpatient setting (depression was considered to be a serious illness, best treated by hospitalization and electroshock therapy); and 3) the drug – as a plant derivative – was not subject to patent exclusivity for any company.[5] An additional problem which eventually emerged was the potential for reserpine – in both psychiatric or non-psychiatric patients – to provoke akathisia, depression, and/or suicidality.

In 1955, Nathan Kline continued his investigations of reserpine. Noting the work of one researcher at the newly established National Institutes of Health (Steve Brodie), Kline was aware of animal studies with rabbits which showed that reserpine was very sedating. However, when the rabbits were pre-treated with an anti-tubercular drug called iproniazid, the administration of reserpine produced energizing effects. These findings inspired Kline to test the same combination of drugs in his patients. When Kline administered iproniazid (pre-treatment for reserpine) to several of the "neurotic" patients in his private practice, he was impressed by the results. By 1957, Kline was promoting the new drug a "psychic energizer." At the same time, physicians working on tuberculosis wards were noticing the mood-elevating properties of the new antibiotics (iproniazid and isoniazid) in their patients. Subsequently, researchers attributed the psychiatric properties of one of these drugs (iproniazid) to its ability to inhibit monoamine oxidase, an important enzyme in the breakdown of biogenic amines (e.g., dopamine, serotonin). This gave rise to a class of antidepressant drugs known as the monoamine oxidase inhibitors (or MAOIs). These antidepressants remained popular until physicians recognized their capacity to cause potentially lethal elevations in blood pressure when combined with certain foods or medications.

Concurrent with the discovery of these first antidepressants (reserpine, isoniazid, and the MAOIs), a Swiss psychiatrist named Roland Kuhn was experimenting with a new compound named imipramine (Tofranil). A modified antihistamine produced from a synthetic dye (summer blue), Kuhn found the drug to have energizing effects when he tested it in depressed patients. Due to its three ring structure, imipramine was the first drug in the class of tricyclic antidepressants (TCAs). These medications eventually became the dominant medication for depression until concerns arose about their lethality in overdose, their complex dosing requirements, and other troublesome side effects.

Perhaps the most important event in the history of antidepressants was a 1965 paper written by Joseph Schildkraut.[6] This announced the "catecholamine" hypothesis of depression, according to which depression was thought to be caused by low levels of norepinephrine in the central nervous system. The premise was a product of *ex juvantibus* reasoning. Although there was no convincing test for a norepinephrine imbalance in the brains of depressed patients, the fact that some individuals were responding to drugs (MAOIs, TCAs) which boosted norepinephrine was seen as proof that this specific neurotransmitter was the underlying cause of their disease.

Two years later, a Swiss psychiatrist named Paul Kielholz suggested that different tricyclic antidepressants seemed to produce very different effects: some of them, enhancing drive or motivation (e.g., desipramine); some of them, enhancing mood or emotions (clomipramine). His ideas encouraged a Swedish chemist, Arvid Carlsson, to develop and investigate the effects of drugs which would be more specific for the serotonin (rather than norepinephrine) system of the brain. The result was a medication called zimelidine (Zelmid), the first of the so-called "selective" serotonin reuptake inhibitors. Zelmid was patented in 1972 and was introduced in Europe in 1982. When it was discovered that Zelmid could cause

---

ex juvantibus – literally, "out of healing;" this refers to any argument which suggests the discovery of the cause of disease based solely upon a patient's response to treatment. The cause of illness is inferred from the treatment's mechanism of action.

a rare neurological condition known as Guillain-Barré syndrome, it was immediately withdrawn from the market.

Since 1982, a variety of SSRIs have been developed. These and other serotonergic agents (drugs with effects upon serotonin receptors or serotonin reuptake) have become the dominant drug treatments for a variety of conditions: major depression, obsessive-compulsive disorder, social anxiety, general anxiety, panic attacks, and post-traumatic stress, to name but a few. Initially touted for their alleged selectivity, safety, and tolerability, the story that has unfolded over two decades has contradicted every one of these original claims. Far from being selective for the serotonin reuptake transporter, the SSRIs have been found to interact with a complex variety of receptor subtypes:[7-10]

Prozac: 5HT2C receptor antagonist

Zoloft: dopamine reuptake inhibitor

Paxil: acetylcholine receptor antagonist

Moreover, the very concept that an antidepressant might be specific for one type of chemical (serotonin) has fallen by the wayside, as researchers have demonstrated the complex interactions which exist between and among the neurotransmitter systems of the brain. The claims to greater safety have been discredited by evidence of drug-induced violence occurring among SSRI patients at rates which greatly exceed older drugs and placebo. Many patients have found SSRIs difficult to tolerate, due to sexual side effects, akathisia and motor abnormalities,[11] withdrawal symptoms (sometimes protracted), and neuropsychiatric effects which have included insomnia, apathy, and mania.

Examples of Antidepressants

<u>Monoamine Oxidase Inhibitors</u>

iproniazid   (Marselid)   removed from market in 1950s due to liver toxicity

isocarboxazid   (Marplan)

phenelzine   (Nardil)

tranylcypromine   (Parnate)

<u>Heterocyclic Antidepressants</u>

amitryptiline   (Elavil)

clomipramine   (Anafranil)

desipramine   (Norpramin)

doxepin   (Sinequan)

imipramine   (Tofranil)

nortriptyline   (Pamelor)

Selective Serotonin Reuptake Inhibitors

zimelidine (Zelmid)   removed from European market in 1982 due to
                             neurotoxicity (Guillain-Barré syndrome)

indalpine   (Upstene)   removed from the European market in 1983 due to
                             bone marrow toxicity (neutropenia)

fluvoxamine (Luvox)

fluoxetine   (Prozac)

sertraline   (Zoloft)

paroxetine   (Paxil)

citalopram   (Celexa)

escitalopram (Lexapro)   the new version of citalopram (*s-enantiomer) based
                             upon stereochemical manipulation of the original
                             compound

---

*enantiomer chemistry: In nature, many substances assume a variety of chemical arrangements, called stereoisomers. When isomers of the same structure assume spatial orientations which are mirror images of each other, they are called "enantiomers." Enantiomers are identified according to a priority system which evaluates chemical subgroups surrounding the central carbon atom. If subgroup priority decreases in a clockwise direction, the spatial arrangement of the molecule is denoted by the letter "R" (from the Latin *rectus*, or right). If subgroup priority decreases in a counter-clockwise direction, the spatial arrangement is denoted by the letter "S" (from the Latin *sinister*, meaning left).

Pharmaceutical products are brought to the market as single isomers (Paxil, Zoloft) which lack a mirror image; or as racemic mixtures (Prozac, Celexa), which contain equal combinations of the R- and S-enantiomers. The current trend in drug development is the isolation of individual enantiomers from racemic mixtures (fluoxetine, citalopram) in order to distribute them as new and improved treatments (s-fluoxetine, s-citalopram). Supporters of this phenomenon believe that single isomers may possess fewer adverse effects, greater efficacy, and a diminished potential for drug-drug interactions. Critics of the "single isomer business" are skeptical about these assertions, noting that drug companies time the release of these new enantiomers perfectly in an effort to extend the patent exclusivity of the parent compounds.

<u>Serotonin Receptor Antagonists</u>

desyrel (Trazodone)   combined 5HT2, alpha 2 (noradrenergic) antagonist

nefazodone (Serzone)   combined 5HT2, alpha 2 (noradrenergic) antagonist;
                           removed from market in 2004 due to liver toxicity

<u>Selective Norepinephrine Reuptake Inhibitors</u>

reboxetine   not marketed in U.S. but available in Europe

tomoxetine   failed trials as antidepressant in 1980s but was released as ADHD
              treatment in U.S. in 2002 as atomoxetine = Strattera

<u>Other Antidepressants</u>

venlafaxine   (Effexor)   combined norepinephrine /serotonin reuptake inhibitor

duloxetine   (Cymbalta)   combined norepinephrine/serotonin reuptake inhibitor

bupropion   (Wellbutrin)   precise mechanism of action unknown
                              presumed to inhibit reuptake of dopamine and
                              norepinephrine

mirtazapine   (Remeron)   alpha-2 antagonist, 5HT2 and 5HT3 antagonist

Mechanisms of Action

The development of the first antidepressants occurred empirically (trial and error) rather than by reason, due to the fact that technology had not yet advanced far enough to permit the rational design of new treatments. While monoamine oxidase inhibitors and tricyclics were discovered serendipitously in the 1950s, it was not until the following decade that chemists (e.g., Julius Axelrod, Arvid Carlsson) ascertained the physiological effects of these substances in the laboratory. Such discoveries continue to be made, as demonstrated by recent publications declaring additional actions for the most famous SSRI, Prozac.[12-13]

The history of antidepressants has led some observers to propose a "universal mechanism of action," based upon a belief that efficacy arises from drug-induced elevations in several key neurotransmitters: serotonin, norepinephrine, or both.[14] In order to evaluate the validity of this claim, it is necessary to appreciate the enormous complexity of the neurotransmitter systems upon which antidepressants exert their effects.

The Serotonin System

> **"Serotonin is an enigma. It is at once implicated in virtually everything but responsible for nothing."**
> **- B.L. Jacobs, C.A. Formal**[15]

The neurotransmitter, serotonin, was first identified by Italian investigators in the 1800s. Named *enteramine* at that time, the chemical (an amine) was isolated from cells (enteric) of the intestine (enter + amine). The Italian researchers noted that the chemical caused constriction of the smooth muscle of the gut. One century later, scientists at the Cleveland Clinic purified and crystallized the same substance, renaming it "serotonin" (serum + tone) because of its vasoactive properties.[16] Technological advances by that time permitted the determination of the chemical nature of the molecule, revealing an indoleamine (5-hydroxy-tryptamine, or 5HT).

Although serotonin is now commonly thought of as a brain chemical, over 95% of it is produced by the enterochromaffin cells of the digestive tract. As blood passes through the stomach and intestines, it picks up serotonin and carries it throughout the body. Blood components - such as platelets and *mast cells - absorb serotonin through proteins (serotonin reuptake transporters = SERTs) identical to those which exist in the brain.

Because serotonin is too large a molecule to penetrate the blood brain barrier, the brain has to manufacture its own supply from smaller precursors, starting with the amino acid tryptophan.

---

* mast cell - a type of white blood cell which stores and releases chemical substances which are used by the body in the process of inflammation

Steps in the Brain's Production of Serotonin

➢ Tryptophan, contained within the bloodstream, penetrates the brain by crossing the blood brain barrier.

➢ Tryptophan enters specific populations of neurons in the midbrain, called the dorsal raphe nucleus and the median raphe nucleus.

➢ Within the neuronal cell bodies of these brainstem nuclei, serotonin is synthesized through a series of chemical reactions:

  o tryptophan is converted by tryptophan hydroxylase to form 5-hydroxy-tryptophan

  o 5-hydroxy-tryptophan is converted by AADC (amino acid decarboxylase) to form 5-hydroxy-tryptamine (5HT = serotonin)

➢ Once serotonin has been made within the cell bodies of the midbrain, it is transported along axons and dendrites for release throughout the brain.

Distribution of Serotonin

Although serotonin is produced by specific neurons in the midbrain (dorsal raphe nucleus, median raphe nucleus), the neurotransmitter has such an extensive distribution that some scientists speculate that "every neuron in the brain may be contacted by a serotonin fiber."[17] Some of these connections have been particularly well studied in animals and then corroborated with neuroimaging methods in humans:

Location of Serotonin Cell Bodies and Their Projections

dorsal raphe nucleus   frontal cortex, caudate, putamen,
projects to →   nucleus accumbens, substantia nigra,
                             ventral tegmentum, thalamus

median raphe nucleus   hippocampus, septum, other limbic structures
projects to →

Serotonin Distribution in the Human Brain

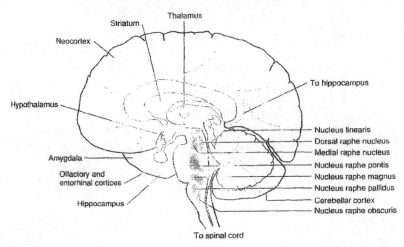

Source: Eric J. Nestler, Steven E. Hyman, and Robert C. Malenka, Molecular *Neuropharmacology: A Foundation for Clinical Neuroscience*, (New York: The McGraw-Hill Companies, Inc., 2001), p. 195. Reproduced with permission of the McGraw Hill Companies.

Storage and Metabolism of Serotonin

Once serotonin has been produced by the midbrain and distributed to other regions, it is stored within vesicles (sacs) or degraded by an enzyme called monoamine oxidase (specifically, monoamine oxidase A). When serotonin is released from the nerve terminal of a neuron (or from dendrites, or from swellings called varicosities), it undergoes several possible events:

> ➢ diffusion

➢ return to the nerve terminal via the serotonin reuptake transporter (SERT) These transporters are found in many regions of the brain. The activity of the SERT represents the primary mechanism by which serotonin is removed from the nerve synapse.

➢ binding to *pre-synaptic receptors* on the nerve terminal or cell body. 5HT1A receptors are located on the cell body. 5HT1D receptors are located on the nerve terminal. Stimulation of either of these receptors leads to a decrease in serotonin synthesis and release.

➢ binding to *post-synaptic receptors* on other neurons or glia. 14 post-synaptic receptor subtypes exist: 1A, 1B, 1D, 1E, 1F, 2A, 2B, 2C, 3, 4, 5A, 5B, 6, 7. The effects of serotonin binding to each of these receptors vary according to brain region. Many of these effects remain unstudied and unknown, particularly in human subjects.

Serotonin Receptors and Some of Their Locations in the Brain and Spinal Cord [18-19]

5HT1A	amygdala, entorhinal cortex, hippocampus, hypothalamus, raphe nuclei, septum
5HT1B	cranial vasculature (dural arteries)
5HT1D	basal ganglia, substantia nigra, superior colliculus, trigeminal sensory fibers
5HT1E	olfactory tubercle, parietal cortex, striatum
5HT1F	cortex, hippocampus, olfactory bulb, spinal cord, striatum, uterus
5HT2A	claustrum, cerebral cortex, nucleus accumbens, striatum,
5HT2B	amygdala, caudate, cerebellum, cortex, hypothalamus, olfactory tubercle, retina, substantia nigra, thalamus
5HT2C	choroid plexus, cortex, globus pallidus, hypothalamus, septum, spinal cord, substantia nigra
5HT3	amygdala, area postrema, entorhinal cortex, hippocampus, nucleus accumbens, spinal cord, trigeminal nerve
5HT4	hippocampus, olfactory tubercle, striatum, substantia nigra
5HT5A	astrocytes, cortical neurons
5HT5B	dorsal raphe nucleus, habenula, hippocampus
5HT6	cortex, hippocampus, nucleus accumbens, striatum
5HT7	frontal cortex astrocytes, smooth muscle cells in blood vessels

How Serotonergic Antidepressants "Work"

Many antidepressants target various elements of the serotonin system, either directly (e.g., by binding to the Serotonin Reuptake Transporter or serotonin receptors) or indirectly (by influencing other neurotransmitters in the brain). While it remains a mystery how or why these drugs produce changes in mood and behavior, most textbooks and advertisements focus narrowly upon immediate drug-receptor interactions. The situation is far more complicated, as the following analysis is intended to reveal.

Acute Effects

Drugs like fluoxetine (Prozac) are commonly described as binding "selectively" to the serotonin reuptake transporter (SERT). This binding action blocks the return of serotonin back into the nerve terminal from which it was released. As a result, more serotonin is permitted to linger in the synapse, awaiting diffusion to other cells or interaction with post-synaptic serotonin receptors in the vicinity. The early effects of SRIs (serotonin reuptake inhibitors) involve an increase in serotonin transmission, due to the prolonged availability of neurotransmitter in the nerve synapse. However, the story of SRI activity does not end here.

Some of the serotonin which is released by neurons of the midbrain travels back to the cell bodies for the purpose of autoregulation (self-regulation). Axon collaterals deliver serotonin to 5HT1A receptors on the dendrites or somas of the dorsal raphe nucleus, turning down the synthesis of serotonin via a negative feedback loop.

5HT1A somatodendritic autoreceptors: negative feedback loop

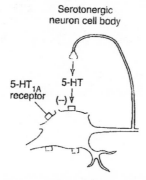

Source: Eric J. Nestler, Steven E. Hyman, and Robert C. Malenka, Molecular *Neuropharmacology: A Foundation for Clinical Neuroscience*, (New York: The McGraw-Hill Companies, Inc., 2001), p. 200. Reproduced with permission of the McGraw Hill Companies.

In other words, the brain has a built-in feedback system, or brake, which prevents the synthesis and release of too much serotonin. This feedback system causes a *decrease* in serotonin transmission, counter-acting the effects of reuptake inhibition at the synaptic cleft. Animal research suggests that this negative feedback loop remains functional for two to three weeks.[20]

After a period of several weeks, the 5HT1A receptors on the neurons in the dorsal raphe desensitize (become less responsive). This removes the brake on serotonin synthesis and release. As a result, serotonin transmission surges and remains elevated. Many researchers believe that this delayed cellular effect (known as the *5HT1A somatodendritic desensitization hypothesis*) is the reason why antidepressant medications often require several weeks to take effect.[21-23]

It should be noted that there is, to date, no direct evidence of these changes occurring in humans. Critics of the "desensitization hypothesis" of antidepressant efficacy raise the following objections:

> ➢ 1A receptors are located in many *post-synaptic* locations, and some of these receptors appear to desensitize, as well. To the extent that these post-synaptic receptors desensitize (become less responsive), antidepressant effects would be expected to diminish over time. Experimental evidence in animals suggests that post-synaptic 1A receptors desensitize in the hypothalamus, but remain unchanged in the hippocampus.

> ➢ Some researchers have found evidence of 1A downregulation in *untreated* depression.[24] If 1A downregulation is a cause of depression, antidepressants which induce 1A desensitization may exacerbate the condition which they are intended to treat.

> ➢ 1A antagonists have been administered to patients with depression, under the assumption that they might augment the quality and speed of antidepressant efficacy by blocking the negative feedback system in the midbrain. Results have been conflicting, leading some observers to wonder if 1A antagonism in post-synaptic locations (such as the

hippocampus) might be counter-productive rather than ameliorative.

Animal experiments have demonstrated several other adaptations occurring during the first weeks of antidepressant exposure. These changes have included the desensitization of *nerve terminal autoreceptors* (5HT1D) in the projection fields of midbrain neurons, leading to an enhanced release of serotonin.[25] Other studies have documented the downregulation of the *serotonin reuptake transporter* itself in the hippocampus and cortex.[26-28] This latter adaptation has been studied in sophisticated chemical and electrophysiological experiments. For example, researchers[29] examining the effects of sertraline (Zoloft) found that SERT density in the rat hippocampus was reduced by 15-30% after 4-10 days of treatment, and by 80% after 15 days of exposure. These changes persisted throughout treatment. The functional consequences were measured in vivo (by chronoamperometry), demonstrating that changes in SERT density contributed far more to enhanced serotonin transmission than the immediate effects of serotonin reuptake blockade. At least one study in humans[30] has duplicated these findings in the brainstem and diencephalon. Using ˙SPECT imaging technology in 17 healthy controls, researchers found that citalopram (Celexa) decreased the binding of a radiolabelled ligand for the serotonin reuptake transporter after 16 days of exposure. The same effects were found in depressed patients receiving paroxetine (Paxil), suggesting that SSRI exposure (rather than an underlying brain disorder) changes the sensitivity and/or number of serotonin reuptake transporters in the human brain.

While it is too soon to know whether these short-term adaptations are beneficial or deleterious, several studies have been performed which give reason for concern. In one investigation[31] involving mice, it was found that repeated social defeats resulted in the increased expression of genes coding for the serotonin reuptake transporter (SERT) and MAO (monoamine oxidase). The study suggests that the brain's stress response involves adaptations for removing or metabolizing serotonin, so as to prevent a serotonin excess. If humans are similar to mice, it is possible that

---

˙SPECT – single photon emission computed tomography; a fairly invasive neuroimaging technology which involves the introduction of radioactive substances to label target sites within the spinal cord and brain

antidepressants which cause a reduction in SERT density might be maladaptive rather than helpful. A neuroimaging study of human subjects[32] provides some support for this conjecture. In a study of *unmedicated* depressed patients diagnosed with the condition of "seasonal affective disorder," SPECT imaging revealed a reduction in SERT binding (reflecting a decrease in SERT density or sensitivity) in the diencephalon (thalamus and hypothalamus). This finding was consistent with earlier research, showing reductions in SERT binding in the midbrains of non-seasonally depressed subjects. *To the extent that SERT density is an important modulator of mood, antidepressants which reduce the number or responsivity of serotonin reuptake transporters may actually be inducing or exacerbating depressive symptoms.*

One unfortunate consequence of the monoamine theory of depression has been the recent hegemony of the opinion that low serotonin causes depression, anxiety, impulsivity, compulsions, and violence. While some studies have been produced which support this perspective,[33-34] there has never been a consistent body of evidence to demonstrate that low neurotransmitter levels (dopamine, norepinephrine, serotonin) *cause*, rather than *arise from*, changes in mood, behavior, and thought. In fact, during the 1970s and 1980s, the medical literature featured a number of studies which favored a "serotonin excess" theory of depression.[35-37] If it is possible for excessive serotonin transmission to contribute to psychological dysfunction, then antidepressants – both serotonergic and noradrenergic – could be quite harmful, since they all appear to induce *prolonged* elevations in the production and release of serotonin.

Long Term Effects of Antidepressants

In addition to the induction of brain adaptations which may be depressogenic (causing depression) and anxiogenic (causing anxiety) in the *short term*, antidepressants have also been linked to a variety of adaptations which may be chronically pathogenic. These long term effects include changes in gene expression, changes in cell function and structure, and changes in the homeostatic and allostatic capacities of the neuroendocrine system.

Persistent Changes in Gene Expression

Evidence that antidepressants modulate the expression of genes in the neurons and glia has been reflected in several animal experiments. For example, serotonin reuptake inhibitors administered to rodents have been shown to change levels of *mRNA for the serotonin reuptake transporter in a time-related and region-specific manner. SERT mRNA has usually been found to decline at the beginning of treatment, with a gradual recovery over several weeks.[38-41] However, when animal subjects have been subjected to antidepressant withdrawal, they have demonstrated a robust surge in SERT mRNA. It is not known to what degree this post-medication burst returns to "normal" (there is no reference level to even define "normal"). Researchers also do not know if the number of transporters eventually overshoots the original value present at baseline, resulting in a higher level of serotonin reuptake than existed before drug treatment. At the very least, the available animal models suggest that changes in SERT density correlate well with the timing of antidepressant withdrawal symptoms. This is consistent with the amine theory of depression and anxiety: a rapid increase in SERT density when drug therapy is reduced or stopped would be expected to induce an abrupt drop in serotonin transmission. Such a drop - if sufficiently large or rapid - correlates with the onset of distressing withdrawal symptoms. What remains unclear is the final homeostasis (equilibrium) of SERT availability and functionality, following the *continuation or termination* of drugs which have been consumed for months or years.

Persistent Changes in Cell Structure and Function: Evidence in Rodents and Humans

A significant body of research suggests that antidepressants may reduce the long term capacity of the brain to autoregulate (self-regulate) neurotransmitter systems. By using animal models, scientists have been able to administer medications at various

---

* mRNA - messenger RNA (ribonucleic acid), a single-stranded molecule in the nucleus of each cell which directs the synthesis of proteins. In this particular case, the mRNA directed the production of the serotonin reuptake transporter (SERT).

points in the lifespan, removing and analyzing brain tissue for cellular and genetic changes induced by drug exposure.

Animal studies investigating the consequences of *prenatal exposure* to antidepressants such as fluoxetine (Prozac) have revealed age-dependent reductions in the *serotonin content* of specific brain regions;[42] reductions in *5HT2A/2C density* in the hypothalamus;[43] and reductions in *SERT density* in several regions of the limbic system.[44-45]

A number of researchers have speculated that sustained antidepressant exposure in *infancy* may interfere with the development of the monoamine systems. **In rats, an exposure to clomipramine (Anafranil) - a tricyclic antidepressant which inhibits the serotonin and norepinephrine reuptake transporters - *during the first month of life* has been linked to significant dysregulation of sleep and behavior in adulthood.** Drug challenges presented to these same animals after maturity have revealed a desensitization of 5HT1A receptors in the *midbrain*.[46] A more recent study exposing neonatal rats to a selective serotonin reuptake inhibitor found evidence of disturbed behavioral responses at the age of four months.[47] This finding prompted investigators to conclude:

> "...treatment during neonatal life produces long-term changes... suggest[ing] that the central serotonergic system may be involved in a putative animal model of depression."[48]

Persistent drug-induced changes in *adult rodents* have been identified by at least one team of researchers.[49] Following a fourteen day period of exposure to fluoxetine (Prozac), male rats demonstrated prolonged desensitization of 5HT1A receptors in the hypothalamus. **This change in receptor responsiveness continued for several weeks (14 to 60 days) even after treatment had been withdrawn.**

Human Studies

Evidence that similar changes might occur in *humans* has been found by researchers using PET imaging (positron emission tomography) in previously medicated, depressed subjects.[50] Upon discovering a 17% decrease in 5HT1A binding throughout the cortex, these investigators speculated that low 1A activity might be a marker for "vulnerability to recurrent major depression." However, this change in 1A binding is a worrisome finding, in light of the animal studies presented above.

Some of the most important human research to date has involved deliberate efforts to manipulate the levels of biogenic amines in order to test for the behavioral effects of these interventions. In a series of investigations which have now given rise to the "revised monoamine theory of depression,"[51] subjects received special dietary supplements in order to reduce levels of specific neurotransmitters in the brain. A high amino acid drink was used to deplete brain levels of tryptophan (and hence, serotonin). AMPT (alpha-methyl-para-tyrosine) was administered in order to inhibit the synthesis of catecholamines (dopamine and norepinephrine). A variety of studies have been summarized by one team of researchers, allowing comparisons between healthy volunteers, actively depressed subjects (off medication for at least two weeks), recently recovered and formerly depressed (on or off medication) patients:

Results of Neurotransmitter Depletion Studies

> ➢ Healthy subjects experienced no depression in response to abrupt reductions in serotonin, dopamine, and norepinephrine. (At most, subjects experienced only mild dysphoria when tested by sensitive rating scales.)

> ➢ Unmedicated, currently depressed subjects exposed to serotonin and catecholamine depletion did not experience a worsening of symptoms.

> ➢ Recently remitted patients exposed to neurotransmitter depletion experienced a rapid return of symptoms.

> o A specific correlation was found between the nature of past or continuing pharmacotherapy, and the type of neurotransmitter depleted.

- o In one study involving *serotonin depletion*, 14 of 21 recently remitted patients experienced a rapid return of symptoms. Relapse sensitivity was highest among subjects who had received *serotonergic* antidepressants: 100% of the MAOI patients relapsed, 63% of the SSRI patients relapsed, but only 18% of the desipramine (a norepinephrine reuptake inhibitor) patients relapsed.

- o In another study involving *catecholamine depletion*, 8 of 19 recently remitted patients experienced a rapid return of symptoms. Relapse sensitivity was highest among those who had received *catecholamine reuptake inhibitors*: 90% of the CRI patients (8/9) vs. none of the SSRI patients (0/10) relapsed.

➢ Previously medicated, fully recovered patients (median remission of 30 weeks) exposed to serotonin depletion experienced an average increase (worsening) of 8 points on the Hamilton Depression Rating Scale. In comparison, healthy controls experienced an average increase of just 2 points on the same rating scale.

Note: While this particular depletion study did not intend to focus upon patients who had recovered *without* medication, 25% of the subjects had done so. In all of these cases, serotonin depletion had either no effect, or substantially smaller effects than those which occurred among patients with a history of drug treatment.

In discussing these findings, the research team concluded that "the evidence requires a revision of the monoamine hypothesis of depression."[52] Conceding that "monoamines may not be a direct regulator of mood in depressed patients and healthy individuals," they proposed that monoamine systems play a "necessary but not sufficient" role in the generation and maintenance of an *antidepressant response*. Unfortunately, the researchers did not seem to grasp an additional implication of their findings.

The depletion of monoamines in newly remitted, currently medicated patients led to a rapid relapse. *Serotonergic* drugs altered the equilibrium of the *serotonin* system. *Noradrenergic* drugs altered the equilibrium of the *norepinephrine* system. Among formerly depressed patients in extended remission, the depletion of serotonin also triggered a return of depressive symptoms. Given the fact that chemical challenge produced a lower *severity* of relapse (and no higher *rate* of relapse) in formerly *unmedicated* individuals, the available evidence suggests that antidepressants may induce persistent sensitivities in the brain which increase a patient's vulnerability to recurrent depression beyond that which would occur naturally.

Persistent Changes in the Neuroendocrine System

Despite the existence of serotonergic antidepressants for more than forty years, their potential effects upon the neuroendocrine system have only belatedly received attention. Until the weight loss medication, *fenfluramine, was removed from the market in 1997, it was commonly used in research to investigate the effects of serotonin upon the endocrine system. Fenfluramine was used to provoke elevations in stress hormones, such as prolactin and cortisol. A diminished response to "fenfluramine challenge" was sometimes observed in depressed patients, giving rise to the theory that a "blunted prolactin response" might be used as a marker for depression. Although this theory did not endure, the connection between serotonin and the hypothalamus-pituitary-axis (HPA) was strongly established. These neuroendocrine connections provide a number of possible mechanisms through which medications may induce adverse effects and maladaptive reactions (allostatic load) which lead to the relapse or prolongation of undesirable symptoms.

A review article on these neuroendocrine connections[53] summarizes a few of the hormones which are modulated by the interaction of serotonin with various post-synaptic receptors:

---

* a serotonin reuptake reverse inhibitor which binds to the reuptake transporter, enters the nerve terminal, and forces the release of serotonin back out through the transporter

ACTH (corticotropin)	prolactin	vasopressin	growth hormone
5HT1A	5HT2A	5HT2C	5HT1A
5HT2A	5HT2C		
	5HT3		

Antidepressants and Cortisol

Animal and human studies have revealed the chemical effects of antidepressants upon receptors in the hypothalamus. The acute administration of fluoxetine (Prozac), paroxetine (Paxil), and citalopram (Celexa) has been shown to raise cortisol levels in human subjects.[54-58] The administration of fluoxetine (Prozac) with 5-hydroxy-tryptophan (a serotonin precursor) has also been shown to increase cortisol in humans.[59-60] Given the fact that hypercortisolemia is associated with depression, weight gain, immune dysfunction, and memory decrements (largely due to cortisol-induced atrophy of the hippocampus), the possibility that antidepressants may contribute to prolonged elevations in cortisol is alarming.

While studies in rodents suggest that 1A receptors on the hypothalamus desensitize as antidepressants are chronically consumed (thereby decreasing the serotonin-induced secretion of cortisol and growth hormone), additional investigations suggest that 2A receptors become *more sensitive* over time.[61-62] Thus, a continued exposure to antidepressants may contribute to long-lasting increases in the secretion of ACTH. Such an increase (which may or may not be accompanied by a parallel rise in cortisol) has been linked to depressive features in at least one population of patients. In a study evaluating the effects of serotonin (5HT2A, 5HT2C) antagonists in the treatment of Cushing's syndrome (an endocrine disorder which results in high levels of cortisol, and which is commonly associated with major depression), researchers discovered a clinically significant decrease in cortisol and ACTH within the first week of antidepressant therapy.[63] However, by the end of one month, ACTH levels had again increased, accompanied by the return of symptoms. In some cases, the increase in ACTH exceeded levels which had existed prior to drug treatment. Noting that a prolonged favorable response was seen in only 3 of 11 patients, the researchers wondered if the long term use of the medications had recruited an ACTH-dependent process which opposed the initial benefits of the drugs. While no firm conclusions could be drawn, these investigators proposed that antidepressant-induced alterations in the HPA axis might have been responsible for the problems of tolerance and treatment resistance seen in these patients.

Antidepressants and Prolactin

As a stress hormone secreted by the anterior pituitary gland, prolactin plays important roles in reproduction and fertility, in maternal and grooming behaviors, and in food intake, anxiolysis, and immune function. However, serious health problems can arise when prolactin reaches excessive levels for sustained periods of time. This condition is called hyperprolactinemia.

While there are many hormones in the brain which regulate the activity of prolactin, serotonin is one of the primary chemicals with stimulatory effects. Several mechanisms have been proposed for this interaction.[64] One pathway involves the effects of serotonin upon the paraventricular nucleus (PVN) of the hypothalamus. Serotonin receptors (2A and 2C) in the PVN promote the activity of VIP and oxytocin. Those two hormones directly stimulate the pituitary to release prolactin. A second pathway involves the serotonergic inhibition of dopamine via the tuberoinfundibular pathway. Serotonin is thought to bind to 1A receptors on GABA (gamma-amino-butyric-acid) neurons in the hypothalamus, turning off the flow of dopamine and thereby enhancing the secretion of prolactin.

A concern of many clinicians is the potential for antidepressants to induce sustained states of hyperprolactinemia. For example, a recent study of eleven healthy volunteers[65] compared prolactin levels after several weeks of exposure to paroxetine (Paxil). After one week of treatment, prolactin levels were no higher than baseline. However, by the end of three weeks, prolactin levels were significantly elevated. Although this particular study did not progress past three weeks, the possibility that prolactin levels remain elevated in patients who are chronically medicated with serotonergic drugs (e.g., SSRIs and venlafaxine) has been reinforced by more than two dozen case reports and trials. Moreover, a study conducted by French epidemiologists (French Pharmacovigilance Database Study) revealed that 17% of all cases of drug-induced hyperprolactinemia in that country were associated with SSRIs.[66]

The significance of these findings lies in the physical consequences of hyperprolactinemia. In the short term, the clinical features of hyperprolactinemia include decreased libido, lactation (galactorrhea), anovulation, menstrual irregularity, and amenhorrea in women; decreased libido, erectile dysfunction, hypogonadism, and breast enlargement in men. While there is no consensus on the precise duration or intensity of hormonal change which is necessary to produce other pathologies, the *chronic effects* of hyperprolactinemia include:

> ➢ infertility

> ➢ decreased bone density (osteopenia/osteoporosis)

> ➢ breast cancer[67-69]

> ➢ cardiac disease[70-71]

> ➢ prostatic enlargement[72]

Of particular concern is the expanding use of antidepressants in children and teens. *Hyperprolactinemia in adolescents has been associated with persistent bone loss.*[73] Although many physicians reassure patients and families that "hormones will return to normal once medications are stopped," such advice fails to consider the issue of critical periods in the development of the human body. Researchers have found that the achievement of peak bone mass during adolescence represents an important protection against osteoporosis in adulthood.[74] Thus, the administration of antidepressant drugs to children may interfere with the attainment of maximal bone density, and this disruption may have long-lasting, detrimental effects. In adults, the occurrence of prolactin-related bone loss appears to persist, even after the resolution of hyperprolactinemia.[75]

The primary limitation in neuroendocrine research is the fact that few people have studied the consequences of sustained, subtle abnormalities in hormones. Even modest elevations of prolactin[76] have been known to cause infertility in females (perhaps by interfering with the pulsatile secretion of other hormones, such as GnRH and LH). It is possible, therefore, that the concentrations of prolactin, cortisol, and other chemicals might remain "normal" in terms of current lab standards (a reference range based on the *population*), but represent significant perturbations at the level of the *individual* – changes which may be significant enough to increase the risks of cancer, bone loss, and heart disease.

Persistent Changes in Brain Structure

In a study designed to investigate the *anatomic* effects of serotonergic compounds,[77] researchers at Thomas Jefferson University exposed male rats to four days of treatment with fluoxetine (Prozac), sertraline (Zoloft), sibutramine (a norepinephrine/serotonin reuptake inhibitor), and fenfluramine (a serotonin depleting agent). Each animal received one of two possible doses for a given drug: a low dose, 10x higher than that used in humans; and a high dose, 100x larger than that used in clinical settings. Following these exposures, the animals were divided into two groups. Half were sacrificed after a post-treatment phase lasting eighteen hours, and the other half were sacrificed after thirty days. Researchers then used a variety of techniques (immunocytochemistry and HPLC) to examine the serotonin content and the structural organization of each brain. Findings were significant for the following:

	serotonin content	structural changes after 18 hours of drug washout	structural changes after thirty days of drug washout
fluoxetine	trend towards decrease	high dose: swollen fibers in frontal and occipital cortex, hippocampus, superior and inferior colliculus *low dose: occasional swelling	no abnormalities
setraline	significant decrease with high dose	low and high dose: swollen and truncated axons, corkscrew profiles in cortex, hippocampus, superior and inferior colliculus	no abnormalities
sibutramine	increase with low and high doses	changes identical to fluoxetine	no abnormalities
d-fenfluramine	decrease seen with low and high dose	swollen axon terminals, thick axons, corkscrew like profiles cortex, hippocampus, sup. and inf. colliculus	no abnormalities

* Although the narrative portion of the published study did not mention it, a separate photograph (reference 77: figure 8, pg. 99) depicted serotonin nerve fiber swelling in the prefrontal cortex of rats exposed to a fluoxetine (Prozac) dose of 2.8 mg/kg per day x four days.

The investigators concluded that high dose, short-term exposure to serotonergic agents was sufficient to produce swelling and kinking in the serotonin nerve fibers. The brain appeared to compensate for these changes over time, as demonstrated by the resolution of abnormalities following a recovery period of thirty days.

The study raises important questions for human subjects. First, it is not known to what extent the *chronic exposure to low levels* of these same drugs might be sufficient to produce similar changes in the human brain. Second, although the doses administered to rats in this investigation were intended to be toxic (10-100x the human therapeutic levels), the *metabolic* differences between rats and humans recommend a careful interpretation of these findings. Given the fact that rats metabolize drugs two to ten times faster than humans, it is necessary to administer two to ten times more of a substance to produce comparable drug levels. Thus, the effects of the lower doses which rats received in this experiment (11.4 mg/kg of fluoxetine and 2.8 mg/kg) might very well approximate the effects of 60 mg and 20 mg doses of Prozac in humans.

Research performed by a different team of investigators[78] has also demonstrated drug-induced changes in brain structure. Juvenile rats (21 days old) were exposed to a variety of antidepressants (fluoxetine, fluvoxamine, desipramine) for one vs. twenty-one days of treatment. Following short (one day) and long (three weeks) recovery periods, brains were examined for changes in structure. Rats exposed to fluoxetine for three weeks demonstrated a reduction in dendritic length and dendritic spine density. **These changes did not reverse, even after a prolonged period of recovery.** The results were interpreted as suggesting that chronic exposure to fluoxetine may arrest the normal development of neurons.

The potential for antidepressants to effect structural changes in the dendrites and axons of serotonin nerve cells may represent an acute process of neurotoxicity which arises in the first weeks of treatment. If the same processes which have been detected in lab animals occur equally in humans, it is possible that a number of antidepressants induce lesions (destructive changes) which the brain must then attempt to repair. This might explain the "neurogenesis theory" of antidepressant action,[79-80] which has arisen from the discovery that chronically administered serotonergic agents have been associated with the emergence of new neurons in the hippocampus. At this point in time, research suggests that neurogenesis in some brain regions represents a natural process of cellular turnover[81-82] which is always active. Without knowing the background rates of this activity, it is possible that some of the changes in the hippocampus which have been identified experimentally have been mistakenly attributed to the action of antidepressants.

Furthermore, while a variety of environmental stimuli (including learning and exercise) have been found to promote neurogenesis in the hippocampus, it is also true that several kinds of brain injury (such as ischemia and seizures) have been found to stimulate identical processes of renewed growth. Equally perplexing is the finding that neurotrophic factors, such as *BDNF, are not uniformly favorable. Research in animal models of epilepsy, for example, suggests that the induction of growth factors can actually increase the intensity of the underlying condition, by enhancing the vulnerability to seizures. Thus, it seems premature to form conclusions about the cause, consequences, or value of hippocampal changes which arise during antidepressant therapy. Based upon animal studies, it is possible that the "neurogenesis theory of antidepressant action" reflects a process of medication-induced injury, in response to which certain brain regions secrete proteins during a compensatory process of attempted repair.[83-88]

Tissue Sequestration

One long term effect of antidepressants pertains to their distribution within the brain and body. The use of magnetic resonance spectroscopy (MRS) has been particularly valuable in tracking the concentrations and localization of *fluorinated* compounds, including several neuroleptics (fluphenazine and trifluoperazine) and the antidepressants fluoxetine (Prozac) and fluvoxamine (Luvox). Because the fluorine-19 nucleus is a natural, stable, and non-radioactive label, medications which contain fluorine atoms have been susceptible to study by nuclear magnetic imaging techniques. This fortuitous occurrence has yielded several important results.

First, researchers have documented large dissociations between plasma and brain levels of psychiatric drugs.[89] In one such study, the plasma (blood) vs. brain concentrations of medications were compared in twelve subjects who had been treated with antidepressants for one month to a year. For fluovoxamine

---

* BDNF - brain derived neurotrophic factor; a hormone which stimulates neuronal development

(Luvox), the brain:plasma concentration ranged from 6 to 14. For fluoxetine (Prozac), the brain:plasma concentration ranged from 6 to 18. Following an abrupt cessation of drug treatment in six of these subjects, Luvox washout times in the brain were twice as long as washout times in blood (4 vs. 2 days). This research finding is important, because it reveals the longer persistence of medication in brain tissue relative to the bloodstream.

Second, the monitoring of brain levels – even by an advanced technology, such as magnetic resonance spectroscopy – may fail to detect the true quantities of medication which persist in brain tissue.[90] When chemicals like fluoxetine (Prozac) are consumed, they become heavily bound to brain proteins. This "protein bound" pool remains invisible to MRS, requiring special methodologies for detection (i.e., magnetization transfer). The chronicity and consequences of this Prozac reservoir remain unknown, but one must wonder about the potential for metabolic changes to facilitate drug dissociation (un-binding) from brain proteins over an extended period of time. This could lead to an unanticipated resurgence or prolongation of medication effects and delayed drug washout.

Third, the application of magnetic resonance spectroscopy has confirmed the persistence of fluorinated compounds within non-brain compartments. In the same group of subjects mentioned above (four Luvox, two Prozac patients), researchers performed fluorine MRS recordings of the brain and lower extremities during active treatment and medication withdrawal. **Following the cessation of drug treatment, and even after plasma levels had reached zero, a fluorine signal was still detected in peripheral tissues for one to ninety-one days.** Researchers concluded that the imaging scans were consistent with drug (or drug metabolite) sequestration within the bone marrow of the legs.[91] They also observed that these changes appeared to be the result of chronic exposure, as the same kinds of effects were not detected in other subjects who had just initiated drug therapy. Although no hematologic abnormalities were seen in these patients, the eventual consequences of bone marrow drug accumulation (for example, effects upon bone growth or blood cells) remain unknown.

Efficacy & Effectiveness

From their inception, antidepressants have plagued manufacturers, reviewing authorities, and clinicians with an ambiguous record of clinical utility, accentuated by the following features:[92-94]

> ➢ ineffectiveness in treating inpatients and outpatients with *severe* depression and atypical (delusional) depression

> ➢ questionable superiority to placebo in the management of *mild* and *moderate* depression

> ➢ inability to reduce risks of suicide (even among the severely depressed)

The indistinguishability of antidepressants from placebos has been problematic for three essential reasons. First, because antidepressants are frequently no more beneficial than inert substances, the adverse effects associated with their use have been difficult to justify according to assessments of clinical utility (benefits vs. risks). Second, the application of novel imaging technologies has produced scientific evidence for the biological legitimacy of placebos: namely, that patient expectations of benefit have real physiological effects. Whether these effects are direct or indirect, it is now clear that placebo interventions provoke detectable changes in the brain,[95-96] some of which replicate the changes associated with medication. Third, the evidence of long term drug effectiveness – a topic which has never been a part of the FDA approval process, and which has seldom been a part of psychiatric research agendas – has been contradicted by an accumulating body of research. In fact, based upon long term outcomes, the allostatic load precipitated by antidepressant drugs argues against their use in favor of safer alternatives.

Prozac for Adults

The dubious efficacy of antidepressants is well illustrated by fluoxetine (Prozac), a drug which many observers consider to be the most successful medication in the history of psychiatry. During the FDA approval process of Prozac, three placebo controlled trials were submitted for regulatory review.[97] The first trial was a negative study which failed to demonstrate product efficacy. The second trial (Protocol 27) was a multi-site investigation involving six different facilities. At the request of the FDA, data from one of these centers was specifically removed from the portfolio submitted for review. Data from the remaining five facilities were combined. Even with this selective pooling of results, Protocol 27 revealed that fluoxetine was inferior to an older drug (imipramine), with no significant advantages versus placebo on many of the efficacy rating scales. A third trial (Fabre) was a small investigation of limited duration: four weeks in length, with only *eleven* trial completers. When the Fabre study was combined with Protocol 27, the FDA determined that Prozac had met the regulatory threshold of "two trials" showing superiority to placebo. However, if one considers the individual trial *components,* the evidence of Prozac's antidepressant potency was far from impressive:

four studies in favor

four studies against

Even this estimation may be unnecessarily generous, due to the methodological deficiencies employed in the trials (e.g., concomitant use of benzodiazepines, placebo washout, high rates of attrition, and use of multiple rating scales for post-hoc "data dredging"). While the approval of Prozac for the treatment of adult depression has attracted the attention of keen observers for years, recent regulatory decisions have recalled and repeated aspects of this troubled history. In January 2003, the FDA approved Prozac as the first (and only) antidepressant with "proven" efficacy for depression in children and teens. Because Prozac has since been elevated by FDA leaders[98] to the status of *gold standard* for the treatment of pediatric depression, it is worth examining the details of the pivotal trial upon which efficacy in children has been proclaimed.

Prozac for Kids

The definitive investigation[99] which led to the approval of Prozac for children and teens was a nine-week study enrolling 219 participants at fifteen hospitals and research clinics throughout the U.S. Subjects ranged in age from eight to eighteen years. Entry criteria included

99

a diagnosis of moderate to severe depression, no serious risk of suicide, and no concurrent diagnoses of substance abuse (active within the past six months), psychosis, or mania.

An extended evaluation phase was conducted on a weekly basis for three weeks. At the third visit, all subjects were placed on placebo. Patients retained in the study were then randomly assigned to Prozac or placebo, receiving daily treatment over a period of eight weeks. The clinical progress of each subject was monitored with a variety of clinician- and patient-rated instruments:

| Clinician Rated | Patient Rated |

Childhood Depression Rating Score-Revised (CDRS-R)
a seven item scale, scored 1 through 5
possible score: 17-85
developed in 1996 by Poznanski and Mokros

Beck Depression Inventory (BDI)
a scale assessing symptoms
of depression
possible score: 0-62
developed by Beck in 1984

Clinician's Global Impression (CGI) – Severity
a seven point scale measuring the severity
of symptoms
developed by Guy in 1976

Children's Depression Inventory (CDI)
a scale measuring the severity of
depression in children
possible score: 0-54
developed by Kovacs in 1985

Clinician's Global Impression (CGI) – Improvement
a seven point scale for measuring change in global
condition from baseline

Hamilton Anxiety Rating Scale (HAM-A)
a fourteen-item scale, scored 0-4 on each item
possible score: 0-56
developed by Hamilton in 1959

Montgomery-Asberg Depression Rating Scale (MADRS)
a scale for assessing depressive symptoms;
not commonly used in children or teens
developed by Montgomery & Asberg in 1979

Global Assessment of Functioning (GAF)
an instrument for assessing the highest current level of
functioning
scores range from 1 – 90
(90 = excellent functioning in
all areas of life)
developed by Endicott in 1976

The primary rating scale for establishing efficacy was the CDRS. All other instruments were secondary measures. The goal of the study was to detect a 20% difference between *response rates* in patients receiving 20 mg of Prozac or placebo. *Response* was defined as a 30% (or more) reduction in CDRS from week three (placebo lead-in) through week nine (eighth week of active Prozac vs. placebo).

Remission was defined as an endpoint (last visit) CDRS score less than, or equal to 28.

The childhood Prozac study assumed the following structure:

Weeks 1 & 2:   diagnostic evaluation

To be eligible for study, baseline CDRS had to be = or > 40, CGI-severity had to be = or > 4 (moderate or severe depression).

no psychoactive medication consumed for at least two weeks

Week 3:   continuing evaluation

All subjects were placed on placebo for 1-week "placebo lead-in."

Eight placebo responders were removed from the study during this phase.

Week 4:   true starting point of the study

Subjects were randomized to Prozac vs. placebo for **eight weeks** of treatment.

Prozac (n = 109)	Placebo (n = 110)
10 mg of prozac per day during week 4	daily placebo capsules
20 mg of prozac per day from weeks 5-12	throughout weeks 4-12

Several features of the trial introduced methodological biases in favor of Prozac. *First, the prevalence of at least one co-morbid disorder was disproportionate among placebo and Prozac participants.* Approximately 15% of placebo subjects met threshold or subthreshold criteria for conduct disorder, compared to 5% for Prozac. This difference was statistically significant (p = 0.02). This randomization bias may have influenced overall responses to treatment, as well as trial completion rates: 42 dropouts (38%) occurred in the placebo group, versus 19 dropouts (17%) for Prozac. *Second, more than 20% of the subjects in each arm of the study had experienced a prior episode of depression.* Although details of past medication exposure were not provided in the published study, it seems likely that many of these subjects would have had earlier exposure to psychotropic medication. Such experience may have rendered these patients especially sensitive to the detection of antidepressant side effects (sexual dysfunction, insomnia, diarrhea), quickly dissolving the double blind in the study and confounding outcomes with expectancy effects. ***Third, the researchers did not control for the effects of previous medications or drug discontinuation syndromes (especially among the placebo subjects).*** Given the fact that fluorinated compounds have now been demonstrated in the bone marrow of patients several months after stopping drug treatment; and given the fact that these and other medications have protracted clearance times from the brain (4-17 days or more), it is possible that this trial's restrictions on prior drug use (no centrally acting medications within the two weeks before entry into the trial) may not have been long enough to exclude individuals whose symptoms represented drug withdrawal or drug rebound. The use of Last Observation Carried Forward (LOCF) data to characterize mean change in CDRS may have disadvantaged the overall outcome for placebo due to the impact of attrition: individuals experiencing the physical and/or psychological discomfort of drug cessation would presumably have swelled the ranks of the placebo subjects who departed the trial early due to adverse events (9 subjects), lack of efficacy (12 subjects), or personal decision (11 subjects). ***Fourth, the primary determination of efficacy (response rate) was biased in favor of Prozac, because the investigators omitted the results of any Prozac subject who exited trial in the first 2 weeks of drug treatment (i.e., weeks #4-5).*** Meanwhile, the assessment scores of **all** placebo subjects were recorded and carried forward, regardless of attrition. Given the fact that five Prozac subjects dropped out for lack of efficacy, five for adverse events, and three more for personal reasons; and given the possibility that some or all of these drop-outs occurred during the earliest phase of drug therapy, ***these exclusions may have removed efficacy data for more than 10% of the Prozac subjects.*** Such an exclusion could have made a substantial difference in the final outcomes and conclusions of the trial.

Even *with* these biases in study design and interpretation, the investigators failed to achieve their stated goal of detecting a 20% difference in response rate (CDRS) between Prozac and placebo. This failure was apparent, using two different methods to determine treatment response:

Calculation Method for Response Rate	Definition of Response	% Responding Fluoxetine	% Responding Placebo	p
[Baseline CDRS – Endpoint CDRS] Baseline CDRS	30% improvement	65%	54%	0.093
	50% improvement	34%	17%	0.007
[(Baseline CDRS – 17) – (Endpoint CDRS – 17)] Baseline CDRS - 17				
	30% improvement	79%	61%	0.006
	50% improvement	58%	41%	0.014

According to the first equation (change from baseline to endpoint), 54% of placebo subjects experienced a 30% reduction in symptoms compared to 65% for Prozac (an 11% difference in response rate). This finding did not quite reach statistical significance (p = 0.093). When treatment response was defined in terms of a 50% reduction in symptoms, there was a 17% difference between Prozac and placebo (17% response rate for placebo vs. 34% for Prozac). Using a second method to calculate response (compensating for the non-zero baseline of the CDRS rating scale, which begins at 17), the difference in response rates was still below 20%. It is important to appreciate the fact that **this efficacy failure occurred even with the post-hoc exclusion of data from Prozac drop-outs (failures) occurring in the first two weeks of the trial.**

On the primary outcome measure (CDRS), the difference in mean change (placebo mean change - Prozac mean change) was a mere 7 points (on an assessment scale which ranges from 17 to 85 points). Two of the secondary outcome measures revealed small differences which were of doubtful clinical significance: on the MADRS, the difference in mean change was 2.8 points (p = 0.023); on the Hamilton Anxiety scale, the difference in mean change was 1.2 points (p = 0.115). A third outcome measure– the Global Assessment of Functioning – revealed **mean changes in favor of placebo.** Data from the patient-rated scales (BDI for adolescents; CDI for children 8-13) were not divulged, but the investigators lamented in their discussion section the dissociation between patient and clinician evaluations, attributing the low scores (lower levels of distress) reported by the placebo subjects to "difficulties in reading" and "symptoms of ADHD" (Attention Deficit Hyperactivity Disorder).

The Emperor's New Drugs

The example of Prozac – in children, teens, and adults -- is neither an exception, nor an aberration in the history of antidepressant development. A carefully designed meta-analysis[100] of the FDA dataset for six of the most recent antidepressants approved between 1987 and 1999 revealed a variety of methodological biases, including: 1) the use of concurrent psychoactive medications in addition to the study drug (25 of 47 trials, or 53%); 2) the replacement of patients who failed to improve after two weeks of treatment (3 out of 5 Prozac studies, 3 of 7 Zoloft studies); and 3) the removal of participants who improved more than 20% during the 1-2 week placebo lead-in phase. **Despite these and other manipulations, 57% of the trials funded by the pharmaceutical industry failed to demonstrate a significant difference between active drugs and placebo.**[101]

In conducting their meta-analysis, the research team reviewed findings of 47 short-term RCTs (5 Prozac, 16 Paxil, 7 Zoloft, 6 Effexor, 8 Serzone, and 5 Celexa). All of these trials lasted four to eight weeks in duration. Only four achieved the FDA's target completion rate of at least 70%, with attrition rates generally equal (40%) between active drug and placebo. After discarding trials (9 of 47) for which the FDA dataset failed to report complete information (i.e., the mean difference in outcomes as measured by the Hamilton Depression Rating Scale), the research team calculated the degree to which the placebo condition duplicated improvements associated with each active drug condition. For those trials which featured comparisons of several fixed doses, the researchers also performed a separate analysis of medication dose (low vs. high) and treatment response. Findings were remarkable for the following:

> ➢ 80-90% of the antidepressant response was consistently duplicated by placebo based upon the formula:

placebo duplication percent = $\dfrac{\text{placebo response rate}}{\text{active drug response rate}}$ x 100

> ➢ the drug vs. placebo difference appeared to be negligible for most patients; in the majority of studies (moderate to severe depression in outpatient

settings), the mean difference in improvement scores (mean change in Hamilton Depresssion Rating Scale) for active drug – placebo was just two points; this two point difference was of doubtful clinical significance

➢ a 10-20% difference in response rates (active drug vs. placebo) was fairly consistent; this difference was small enough to have arisen from methodological artifact[102]

➢ two dose-response studies for Prozac were submitted to the FDA; one trial (mild depression) found no difference in treatment response between low and high doses; the second trial (moderate to severe depression) found lower doses to be significantly *more effective* than higher doses

➢ three trials were conducted among severely depressed, hospitalized inpatients; two of these studies failed to detect a significant difference between active medication and placebo.

In reviewing these findings from the FDA dataset, researchers critiqued the assumption used in the drug approval process: namely, that drug response – placebo response = true drug effect. To the extent that pharmacological and placebo (positive expectancy) effects are additive, these data suggest that unique actions of antidepressant drugs are very small indeed – small enough to be clinically insignificant in most patients. While antidepressant enthusiasts maintain that drugs are indispensable in the treatment of severe depression, the FDA database contradicts their assertion. **Two-thirds of the trials conducted among hospitalized patients revealed a placebo response equal to active drug treatments. Similarly, the FDA database fails to support the argument that higher doses produce superior outcomes.**

The therapeutic value of antidepressants has been even less clear when researchers have employed study designs using active placebos. In such trials, non-inert substances have enhanced expectancy effects in placebo subjects by producing physiological changes associated with potent therapies. Under these conditions, the efficacy of real study drugs has been difficult to discern.[103] The abysmal trial performance of antidepressants has occurred with such regularity that mindful observers refer to it as psychiatry's "dirty little secret."[104] In the face of this dilemma, governmental regulators themselves have not known what to conclude:

> **"How do we interpret... two positive results in the context of several more studies that fail to demonstrate that effect? I am not sure I have an answer to that but I am not sure that the law requires me to have an answer to that - fortunately or unfortunately. That would mean, in a sense, that the sponsor could just do studies until the cows come home until he gets two of them that are statistically significant by chance alone, walks them out and says that he has met the criteria."[105]**

Long Term Effectiveness

Antidepressant enthusiasts have been quick to assert that short term trials are "not long enough" to reveal the true advantages of pharmacotherapy. While *efficacy* (short term) studies typically focus upon rates of *treatment response* (the proportion of patients who reach an arbitrarily defined improvement level, such as a 50% reduction in symptoms) or rates of *treatment remission* (the proportion of patients whose symptoms abate completely, or whose symptoms meet a pre-defined level of recovery), *effectiveness* (long term) studies focus more heavily upon two kinds of outcomes:

> **relapse rate - the proportion of treatment responders who experience a worsening of symptoms prior to achieving remission (remission being the total or partial resolution of symptoms necessary for the return of adequate functioning)**

> **recurrence rate - the proportion of treatment remitters who experience a return of symptoms following recovery.**

Methodological deficiencies apply equally to effectiveness as to efficacy trials. *Relapse prevention trials* typically feature two different designs. In one model, active drug responders (patients who have done well in an acute *efficacy* trial) are randomly assigned to receive placebo or medication for a period of extended treatment. In another model, treatment responders from the efficacy trial are permitted to remain on their original therapy (active drug *or* placebo) for a period of continued monitoring. The issue here is an inherent bias against placebo. Both study designs begin with the enrollment of placebo failures, based upon the earlier elimination of all subjects who responded "too well" during the placebo lead-in phase of the efficacy trial. By selecting the active drug responders for the extension phase, these studies focus upon a pool of individuals whose histories predict a poor ability to tolerate *withdrawal effects* (discontinuation syndromes) when half of them are abruptly switched to placebo for continued monitoring.

A major problem within the psychiatric literature is a more than fifty-year history of methodological confounds in relapse research, whereby investigators have misidentified the origin of symptoms which arise from the physiological effects of drug cessation. These confounds have had a critical impact upon the pronouncement of long term prognosis associated with a variety of conditions (not just depression). Moreover, the misattribution of drug withdrawal symptoms to underlying "disorders" has been manipulated skillfully by the pharmaceutical industry. Using opinion leaders in the mental health field to orchestrate treatment guidelines which mandate the chronic use of medication, the drug companies and professional organizations have suppressed publicity about drug withdrawal phenomena;[106] encouraged the misidentification of iatrogenic syndromes as proof of relapse or recurrence; and promoted the continuation of drug treatment for increasingly extended periods of time. Resultingly, almost half of all Americans[107] treated with antidepressants have remained on medication for more than a year. The epidemiological observation that most episodes of depression end at three to six months has been obscured.[108] Psychiatric textbooks themselves have been revised over the past decade, replacing descriptions of depression as an episodic phenomenon with intimations that depression is a lifelong disease – perhaps because pharmacotherapy has helped to make it so.

Turning Short Term Suffering Into Long Term Misery

A growing body of research supports the hypothesis that antidepressants worsen the chronicity, if not severity, of depressive features in many subjects. One unintended consequence of pharmacotherapy appears to be the induction of protracted allostatic load (i.e., long-lasting changes in cell receptor function, effector system activity, and gene expression). These maladaptive responses contribute to the persistence of minor symptoms, more sustained episodes of illness, and more frequent relapses.

In a naturalistic study conducted by the National Institute of Mental Health,[109] 122 patients were monitored during and after treatment for a first episode of major depression. Researchers evaluated the status of participants at regular intervals (every six months for five years, then annually) for an average of nine years. Patients were divided retrospectively into two groups: a "residual symptoms" group (26 subjects) who experienced continuing but subthreshold features of depression following their first episode of significant impairment; and a "symptom free" group (70 subjects) who remained asymptomatic for more than 80% of the follow-up period. The two recovery groups did not differ with respect to age, gender, marital status, duration of 1st episode, worst global assessment of severity (GAS) score, or mean length of follow-up. What **did** distinguish the two groups was exposure to aggressive treatments: 85% of the residual symptom group received inpatient treatment at intake (first episode) vs. 57% of the asymptomatic group. **Patients with residual symptoms also received significantly higher levels of weekly antidepressant therapy during their first recovery interval.** Over the nine to twelve year period of follow-up, recurrent depression occurred **three to twelve times faster among subjects with residual symptoms.** Only 8% of the residual symptom group failed to relapse into a second episode of depression, compared to 34% of the asymptomatic (and less intensively medicated) group.

A British team of researchers investigated the long term outcomes of 115 patients initially evaluated within 6 months of the onset or relapse of a depressive episode.[110] After a mean interval of four months, the patients were re-evaluated for their response to treatment. At the start of the trial, 33% of the participants were experiencing a first episode of major depression, while 67% were experiencing a relapse. Recovery rates for both groups varied according to treatment. Although there were no significant associations between the kinds of treatment rendered (medication vs. non-medication), and the *severity* of the *initial* episode or the *duration* of the *current* episode, **antidepressant therapy was associated with poorest outcomes.** Of 44 patients who began the study in an unmedicated condition, 16 received antidepressants; 28 received no drugs or alternative medical (non-antidepressant) therapies. Of the patients who received antidepressants, 30% recovered. Of the patients who did *not* receive antidepressants, 50% recovered. Even after controlling for treatment compliance, and after controlling for the severity, duration, and type of depression (e.g., endogenous or neurotic), antidepressants were still associated with the worst clinical results.

A large, retrospective study[111] in the Netherlands involved an analysis of treatment records from more than 12,000 patients with the goal of identifying *first episodes of depression* diagnosed before 1985. After locating 222 subjects in four primary care practices, the researchers examined the relationship between treatment and 10-year outcomes. Antidepressant exposure was associated with poorer long term results. Of the 222 subjects in the starting pool, 134 (60%) experienced only one episode of depression with no further recurrence. Of these "one episode" patients, 50% received *no antidepressants* during or following the initial episode; 19% received *no psychotropic medications* at all. This contrasted sharply with the medication experience of 88 subjects who *did* relapse on one or more occasions over a period of ten years: 72-79% of the relapsing patients received *antidepressants* in the initial episode; 6% received *no psychotropics* at all.

Number of subjects identified with first episodes of depression = 222

---

134 subjects with 1 episode only	88 subjects with recurrent episodes
50% received antidepressants in the first episode	72-79% received antidepressants in the first episode
19% received no psychotropics	6% received no psychotropics

Netherlands Study

N = 222

	# of patients with only 1 episode of depression	# of patients experiencing recurrent depression
# of patients receiving an antidepressant in 1st episode	67	70
# of patients receiving no antidepressant in 1st episode	67	18
	134	88

62% of the subjects received an AD in the first episode of depression.

Of the patients who received an AD in the 1st episode: 51% relapsed

Of the patients who did not receive an AD in the 1st episode: 21% relapsed

A major limitation of the study was the failure of the investigators to stratify outcomes according to the severity of the initial condition (e.g., relapsing subjects might have been those patients whose starting symptoms were more prolonged or most severe). Nonetheless, their findings corroborate the hypothesis that psychoactive medications might change the brain in ways which either enhance, or fail to diminish, the vulnerability of many individuals to the return of depressive symptoms.

Concerns about the overall utility of antidepressants have recently been echoed by researchers in Iceland.[112] A retrospective analysis of medication use (based upon Ministry of Health records of antidepressant sales, in terms of daily defined doses per 1000 inhabitants), psychiatric hospital admissions, disability pensions, and suicides revealed the following trends:

Medication Trends in Iceland: 1989 - 2000

➢ 48% increase in total quantity of medication sales

➢ 92% increase in non-antidepressant psychotropic sales

➢ 387% increase in antidepressant sales

Between 1981 and 1985, antidepressant sales increased, then stabilized through 1990 at a rate of 15 daily defined doses per 1000 inhabitants per day. Following the emergence of SSRIs (e.g., Prozac, Zoloft) in the late 1980s, antidepressant use soared to 73 daily defined doses per 1000 inhabitants per day. An estimated 8.7% of the population (over age 15) received an antidepressant in 2000. Despite the exponential rise in the sales (and presumed consumption) of antidepressants, suicide rates in Iceland have remained largely unchanged (11/100,000 inhabitants per year); admission rates for inpatient psychiatric treatment have increased (after correcting for increases in the population, each patient was hospitalized more often); and the proportion of inhabitants claiming disability for depressive or anxiety disorders has not declined (13% of all disability pensions awarded for medical or psychological reasons). Commenting upon the aggressive marketing of new pharmacological agents and the development of treatment guidelines which advocate their use, the Icelandic researchers concluded that the public health impact of antidepressants has been limited, while the "costs to society" have not been favorably or significantly reduced.

Safety

Suicide

The possibility that medications designed to alleviate depression and thoughts of suicide might paradoxically induce them, has been known by the medical profession, the pharmaceutical industry, and the Food and Drug Administration for more than forty years. When reserpine was tested as a treatment for psychosis and depression in the 1950s, clinicians noticed that many patients experienced the worsening of symptoms – sometimes accompanied by the emergence of self-harm.[113] This phenomenon of drug-induced suicidality was legitimized only when cardiologists began to notice the same kinds of side effects in their patients to whom reserpine was being administered for the control of hypertension. Not surprisingly, reserpine fell out of favor and other medications took its place.

Although antidepressant-related violence was intermittently recorded over the intervening years – including misconduct associated with tricyclics and monoamine inhibitors – such behavior was generally attributed to the patient instead of the treatment. It was not until 1991 that the issue of iatrogenic suicide began to receive significant public attention. In September of that year, the Food and Drug Administration convened a meeting of its Psychopharmacologic Drug Advisory Committee (PDAC) to hear testimony regarding the safety of fluoxetine (Prozac). Already the market leader and rising to the status of sociocultural icon, a number of case reports had nonetheless appeared in leading medical journals linking Lilly's SSRI to the "sudden emergence" of akathisia and suicide. The 1991 hearing might have been an important venue for the deliberation of critical public health question, had it not been handicapped by a number of crucial limitations:

> the FDA's refusal to hear evidence about antidepressants other than Prozac

> the committee chair's refusal to allow a non-industry sponsored presentation of pertinent trial data, showing a threefold higher risk of suicide for Prozac versus older drugs

> the FDA's unwillingness to acknowledge multiple biases in the drug manufacturer's evidence, including:

  o the concurrent administration of benzodiazepines to many subjects in Phase III trials, in order to allay drug-induced agitation

  o the miscoding of suicidal and homicidal acts with euphemistic labels (i.e., suicide attempts coded as "emotional lability" or "non-accidental overdose;" homicide attempts coded as "hostility")

o the manipulation of suicide data, prejudicing findings in favor of Prozac (i.e., the misattribution of suicidality to placebo when these behaviors occurred during the lead-in phase of a trial, or in some cases when these events occurred months after the end of the trial).

These deficiencies notwithstanding, an FDA leader did admit some concerns about the information divulged at the meeting:

"The anecdotes that are most evocative are not the ones where people who have a 20-year history of suicidal ideation finally do it... but where [people] assert that there has never been anything in their minds like that before and yet now they have suddenly become excessively concerned with suicide and may even do it."[114]

While some support did exist in 1991 for stronger warnings on the package label (as voted by a full third of the committee members, most of whom had received waivers to participate in the hearing because of considerable financial ties to the pharmaceutical industry), the FDA concluded that the evidence for drug-related suicide was ambiguous.[115] This was a shocking announcement in light of the fact that the FDA had met the previous year with Eli Lilly and with an early antidepressant watchdog (*Dr. Martin Teicher) in order to devise a special suicidal ideation rating scale, and in order to design *CDR protocols specifically *because* of its

---

*Teicher – a Harvard psychiatrist and neuropharmacologist, and author of several of the early papers which set off alarms about Prozac and akathisia. Teicher ultimately disappeared from the antidepressant safety debate. When he reappeared, it was as the lead investigator at a new drug development firm called Sepracor, where he oversaw the synthesis of enantiomeric versions of Lilly's fluoxetine.[116-118] Teicher ultimately served as a spokesman for Lilly during patent fraud disputes involving Zalutria (R-fluoxetine) – a product which was never brought to market. Some observers believe that Zalutria was shelved because its patent blatantly acknowledged the risks of violence associated with the drug (racemic fluoxetine) which it was designed to replace.

*CDR – challenge, rechallenge, dechallenge. CDR experiments test for drug effects by introducing, discontinuing, and then re-introducing the treatment.

concern about drug-potentiated suicide. Although there appeared to be a plan emerging for investigations of fluoxetine's behavioral toxicity, no such research was ultimately financed or performed. Instead, U.S. regulatory officials adopted a risky public health position, gambling that specific warnings about antidepressant lethality would paradoxically evoke *more* deaths by deterring psychiatric consultations and squelching patient enthusiasm for pharmacotherapy. (The fact that Prozac had seldom performed well in the few studies where it *had* been tested in suicidally depressed patients was apparently dismissed or overlooked.)

The issue of antidepressant-related violence was quickly suppressed by the drug companies, minimized by the federal government, and overlooked by most members of the mental health profession. What changed over the course of the next decade was the gradual unveiling of incriminating evidence. This included occasional (and court limited) references to privileged material discovered by expert witnesses and attorneys in the course of product liability cases. It also included information detected by journalists in their investigations of new studies which had been pursued for two reasons: first, to extend the *patents of existing drugs; second,

*patent extensions[119] – In 1997, Congress passed the FDA Modernization Act (FDAMA) which provided incentives to drug companies to conduct pediatric clinical trials. Under FDAMA, the FDA was authorized to grant additional patent (marketing) exclusivity to manufacturers who agreed to conduct child studies in support of a new drug application or supplemental application for an existing drug. Patent exclusivity was to be granted merely for the performance of these additional trials, rather than on the basis of outcomes. Furthermore, trial information was not to be publicly disclosed by the FDA unless it was a part of a drug application that was ultimately approved. In other words, FDAMA permitted the makers of antidepressants to obtain patent extensions regardless of the efficacy or safety of drugs when they were tested specifically in the "pediatric market." In 2002, Congress renewed the pediatric exclusivity authority in the Best Pharmaceuticals for Children Act (BPCA). Under BCPA, the FDA has been required to release summaries of its medical and clinical pharmacology reviews of all child trials within six months of their submission, irrespective of the final regulatory decision (approval or non-approval). Unfortunately, a variety of antidepressants qualified for patent extensions under FDAMA, rather than BCPA. The data from those trials have been concealed from the public and the medical profession, partly because the FDA has been restrained from sharing that material according to provisions of federal law.

115

to comply with regulators' specific requests for trials within the pediatric population. Conducted at various intervals throughout the 1990s (for example, Paxil protocol 329 ran from 1993-1996), these child studies demonstrated an appalling lack of efficacy for the serotonergic drugs, along with a high rate of psychiatric side effects.

The watershed event occurred in October 2002 when the BBC (British Broadcasting Corporation) aired a *documentary entitled "The Secrets of Seroxat." Highlighting the problems of antidepressant dependence and withdrawal, the program generated a record number of phone calls and e-mails to the producers, and incited a groundswell of public attention to the problems of drug safety and regulation. In their background research for a follow-up production, BBC reporters unearthed evidence of a true marketing scandal. An internal document obtained from Glaxo Smith Kline (the maker of Seroxat) revealed that the company had first concealed and then whitewashed a number of findings from pediatric investigations, in order to minimize any "negative commercial impact."[120]

According to one authority on the subject, such secrecy now appears to have been the rule rather than the exception in the process of antidepressant development. By June 2003, it was clear to industry critics that a majority of the Phase I (healthy volunteer) studies had **never** been released by drug companies for publication. This included 41 studies on Prozac; 21 studies on Paxil; and 28 studies on Zoloft.[121] By 2004, it was also clear that the FDA itself had remained in the dark, as litigators and their expert consultants discovered that Phase III trial results (e.g., Paxil protocols 511 and 716) had not been surrendered by drug companies to governmental regulators as required by law.

Following the BBC broadcasts of 2002, the British equivalent of the FDA (the Medicines and Healthcare Products Regulatory Agency – MHRA) requested further material from Glaxo Smith Kline in order to clarify the issue of suicide miscoding (i.e., the practice of minimizing the true nature of serious adverse events). In response to the information which it received, the MHRA collaborated with National Health Service (Department of Health) in issuing

---

* Seroxat – the trade name of Paxil (paroxetine) in the U.K.

stern warnings to clinicians in the U.K. On June 10th of 2003, the government disseminated a press release which included the following statements:

> **"SEROXAT MUST NOT BE USED FOR TREATMENT OF CHILDREN...**
>
> **"New data, received within the last two weeks, has been evaluated and considered by the Committee on Safety of Medicines, (CSM) and its Expert Working Group on SSRIs. It shows that there is an increase in the rate of self harm and potentially suicidal behavior in this age group, when Seroxat is used for depressive illness. It has become clear that the benefits of Seroxat in children, for the treatment of depressive illness, do not outweigh these risks."**[122]

One week later, the manufacturer of Seroxat (Paxil) distributed a letter in the U.K., updating providers about several changes on the package insert. Wording was removed which had previously denied the habit-forming potential of the drug. Wording was added, in order to acknowledge the drug's potential to induce akathisia and gastrointestinal bleeding, and to emphasize sharply the contra-indication in children:

> **"Seroxat should not be used in the treatment of major depression and adolescents under 18 years of age."**[123]

Across the Atlantic, however, the situation proceeded quite differently. Although the FDA had also met with key individuals in October of 2002 about the issue of adverse event coding, the U.S. regulators continued to believe that no label changes or advisories were necessary. Instead, they assigned to epidemiologist Dr. Andrew Mosholder the task of reviewing the FDA antidepressant database for evidence of a drug-suicide connection *in children*. Interestingly, while all of this research was occurring behind the scenes, the manufacturer of one of these drugs – Wyeth Pharmaceuticals – came forward in August 2003 with a voluntary letter addressed to professionals:

> **"Wyeth wishes to inform you about an update to the prescribing information for Effexor (venlafaxine HCl) Tablets and Effexor XR Extended-Release Capsules**

to reflect important safety information on the use of venlafaxine in children and adolescents...Safety and effectiveness in pediatric patients (individuals below 18 years of age) have not been established. *In pediatric clinical trials, there were increased reports of hostility and, especially in Major Depressive Disorder, suicide-related adverse events such as suicidal ideation and self-harm.*"[124]

Four months later, the British Committee on Safety of Medicines acted to restrict the use of *almost all* SSRIs in children and adolescents:

"Paroxetine, venlafaxine, sertraline, citalopram and escitalopram are now contraindicated in paediatric MDD [major depressive disorder] in the under 18s." [125]

Although Prozac escaped the list of proscribed agents, it was notable that Eli Lilly itself distributed a product update throughout the U.K. in December of 2003. In a letter to healthcare professionals, Lilly announced that its Prozac SPC (Summary of Product Characteristics) in European countries would no longer include an authorization for the treatment of pre-menstrual dysphoric disorder (PMDD). An abbreviated prescribing information sheet enclosed with the letter[126] may have been overlooked by most recipients, but the **dosage and administration section** featured the following language:

"Children: Not recommended."

In the United States, Dr. Mosholder's review of pediatric trial data was also emerging in December of 2003. Media attention had by this time reached a true roar, and questions were being raised by many parties about the glaring differences assumed by regulatory authorities on two sides of the same ocean. When the FDA convened its second hearing on antidepressant safety on Feburary 2nd 2004, Dr. Mosholder was allowed to observe the proceedings, but he was not permitted to present his findings or conclusions:

"Given the strength of the association shown by the present data, the clinical importance of the apparent effect (i.e., an estimated excess of one additional serious suicide-related event per 12 patient-years of active treatment), and the fact that the additional analyses are likely to take several more months to complete

while considerable numbers of pediatric patients are being exposed to these drugs, I favor an interim risk management plan regarding the use of these drugs in the pediatric population...Specifically, I propose a risk management strategy directed at discouraging off-label pediatric use of antidepressant drugs [...]"[127]

Arguing that Mosholder's report was unreliable because of the questionable validity of the classification of adverse events, the FDA leadership adjourned the February hearing with a decision that "further research was needed." Only after the hearing did the story emerge that Mosholder himself had become the target of an internal investigation, involving allegations by FDA officials that he had inappropriately revealed the existence and results of his research to individuals outside the agency. This turn of events stimulated a Congressional inquiry into conflicts of interest and misconduct within the FDA. Meanwhile, a research team at Columbia University had been given the assignment of re-analyzing the same dataset which had formed the basis of the Mosholder report, in preparation for a third penultimate hearing about antidepressant safety. In the interim, the FDA issued a Public Health Advisory (March 22, 2004) urging physicians to closely monitor their patients on antidepressants for "worsening depression and the emergence of suicidality," and asking the manufacturers of ten medications to add stronger precautionary language to their product labels.

On September 12-13th of 2004, the Psychopharmacologic Drug Advisory Committee and the Pediatric Advisory Committee joined together for the FDA's third hearing on the topic of antidepressants and suicide. The non-public testimony, as crafted specifically by the FDA, focused heavily upon two studies (Jick and TADS, discussed in chapter four) whose late summer appearance in the *Journal of the American Medical Association* (*JAMA*) seemed to have been coordinated perfectly for the approaching hearing. Because of the timing of those publications and the press releases which accompanied them - all of which loudly denied a causal connection between suicide and serotonergic drugs - the FDA advisory panel seemed primed to repeat their past performances. Amazingly, not a single member of the advisory panel expressed concern about the methodological confounds of the two studies which the FDA chose to emphasize. Only the evidence presented by the Columbia

University researchers (whose summary vindicated the conclusions reached by Dr. Mosholder some twelve months before) appeared to change the direction and tone of the meeting, convincing a majority of the committee members to acknowledge (albeit weakly) a causal association between suicidal behavior and antidepressants.

Thirteen years and thousands of *excess* suicides[128] after the first antidepressant safety hearing, FDA leaders informed the press that "two to three children out of every hundred" could be expected to develop suicidal thoughts or actions *as a result of antidepressant therapy.*[129] Unlike the regulators in England, no bans or restrictions were promulgated by the American bureaucrats. However, the FDA did vote for sterner measures. On October 15th, 2004, the agency required the makers of **all** antidepressants to add a Black Box Warning to their product labels, instructing physicians to communicate the risk of drug-related suicidality and to balance this risk with the "clinical need" for medication.

While the belated actions of governmental authorities were welcomed by some observers, others believed they represented far too little, too late. This was especially true for discerning critics who perceived a larger problem involving *faulty methodologies* which were still likely to be employed by drug companies, and still likely to be accepted by drug regulators in their calculations of treatment-related adverse events. One of these faulty methodologies has involved the use of Patient Years of Exposure (PYEs) rather than Events Per Treatment Group in reporting serious drug side effects. A fictional example may serve to illustrate the important difference between these two techniques.

Imagine a drug trial involving 100 subjects. Fifty participants receive Prozac, and fifty receive placebo. After 6 months of treatment, five Prozac subjects attempt suicide and leave the study. The remaining Prozac patients (45) complete two years of treatment. Suppose that one placebo subject attempts suicide at 6 months, but forty-nine placebo subjects remain non-suicidal. All of the placebo subjects quit the trial at six months. The suicide data from such a study could be reported in two ways:

Suicide Events Per Treatment Group:

5 suicide attempts divided by 50 subjects on Prozac   = 10%
1 suicide attempt divided by 50 subjects on placebo   = 2%

Suicide Events Per Patient Years of Exposure:

Prozac   Placebo

5 events divided by   1 event divided by
(5×0.5 years) + (45×2 years)   (50×0.5 years)
= 5 events per 92.5 yrs of exposure   = 1 event per 25 years of exposure
= 0.05 events per year of exposure   = 0.04 events per year of exposure

The problem with the use of PYEs to report suicides is the fact that it leads to an inflation of drug safety, due to the fact that poor treatment responders frequently depart studies much earlier than their fellow participants. The significance of the terminators' experiences is then diluted by the time factor (denominator). The drug ends up looking much safer than it really is, because the number of bad outcomes is concealed by the exposure years contributed by those who can tolerate the medication for extended periods of time.

A second methodology which has contributed to mischaracterizations of antidepressant safety has been the misattribution of suicidality to placebo, when those actions have occurred during lead-in or extension phases of clinical trials. At least one forensic consultant has called attention to this practice of miscoding adverse events to favor active drug treatments.[130] One approach employed by the drug companies (including the makers of Prozac, Paxil, and Zoloft) and recognized but not corrected by the FDA has involved the identification of adverse events occurring in the "lead-in" phase of a trial as belonging to the placebo arm of the active study. A second approach has attributed to placebo any adverse event which occurs in non-medicated subjects during the weeks or months *after* the acute phase of a trial has ended.

While it will hopefully be obvious to the reader why post-trial tampering with placebo statistics is inappropriate, it may be less clear why suicide events occurring in the lead-in phase should not be assigned to placebo. There are two reasons why the placebo lead-in manipulation is improper. First, the lead-in phase of any trial is not a part of the active study. Although many trials *do* begin by placing all subjects onto placebo (while previous medications are abruptly stopped), not all lead-in phases include the administration of an inert drug. Second, in those trials which *do* administer a placebo pill to all subjects during the 1-2 week lead-in phase, the FDA and the drug companies fail to adjust the denominators (n = *all* subjects participating in the lead-in phase) which are then used in reporting summary statistics.

When **adult** antidepressant trial data have been re-analyzed to compensate for these erroneous methodologies, the SSRIs have consistently revealed a risk of suicide (completed or attempted) that is **two to four times higher than placebo**. When **pediatric* trial data have been similarly reviewed, the risk of suicide events for patients receiving SSRIs and other serotonergic drugs has been **three times higher than placebo**.[131-132] Similar findings have occurred in studies involving the use of serotonergic drugs in the treatment of non-depressive (anxiety) conditions. Because none of these statistics have received adequate attention from the news media, the government, or the medical profession, the public remains largely unaware of the fact that the safest "drug" in antidepressant clinical trials has consistently been the placebo.

The Rollback Phenomenon

Now that regulatory officials in the U.K. and U.S. have acknowledged the existence of a real signal between antidepressants and suicide,

---

*pediatric trials - Unpublished trial data for venlafaxine have reportedly shown even higher risks of suicidality among children: **nine to fourteen times greater risk of violence or suicidal thought compared to placebo**. Presumably, it was these research findings which prompted Wyeth to voluntarily convey a warning to physicians in August of 2003. Wyeth conceded not only a drug-related association between venlafaxine and hostility, suicidal ideation, and self-harm in children, but also the lack of evidence for efficacy in children. According to the *Wall Street Journal*, the FDA subsequently contacted Wyeth and forced the company to downplay its warning, in order to bring the venlafaxine product label into line with revisions which the FDA was about to recommend to other drug companies.[133-135]

it has become increasingly common to find interviews of psychiatric opinion leaders who speak of "rollback" as the source of harmful behaviors emerging during pharmacotherapy. As described by Detre and Jarecki in 1971, rollback was a term which entered psychiatry's lexicon as a way of explaining suicidal behaviors (or other symptoms) which appeared during treatment:

> "For example, if an illness begins with occasional anxiety attacks that are superseded some weeks later by depressive symptoms which then become progressively more severe until after several months the patient develops total insomnia and confusion, the symptoms tend, as the condition improves, to remit in reverse order, the confusion and insomnia diminishing first, and the depressed mood next [...].[136]

> "In some cases, however, [a depressed patient's] illness progresses so rapidly that he loses the initiative, energy, and organizational ability needed to carry out his plan, while retaining his intention of doing so. As his depression lifts, and his retardation diminishes, he may regain the initiative and energy that suicide requires...This kind of sequence is another example of the *rollback phenomenon* [...]".[137]

There are many problems with the arguments advanced by FDA officials and practicing clinicians who attribute drug-related suicide to rollback. First, it is difficult to imagine how anergia (a lack of sufficient energy) would prevent depressed patients from executing one of the most common suicidal behaviors: the medication overdose.

Supporters of the rollback theory of suicide ask others to believe that a patient who retains sufficient energy to swallow the usual number of pills generally *lacks* the energy needed to swallow an *excess* number of pills. The rollback phenomenon of "sudden energy for suicide" simply does not hold up under close inspection.

Second, the rollback theory ignores the fact that suicidal thoughts and behaviors have emerged in *non-depressed* subjects, including healthy volunteers in Phase I trials and patients receiving antidepressants for symptoms associated with Lyme disease, migraine headaches, and insomnia. In all of these cases, there have been no symptoms of depression to which the consumers of medication were *rolling back*.

Third, the rollback phenomenon as described by its original proponents was an event which commonly emerged after many *months*, as it referred to a phase of recovery which coincided with a patient's exit from depression. This is quite different from the pattern associated with serotonergic treatments, where violent events have commonly emerged early in the course of drug therapy.

Fourth, the rollback phenomenon is never mentioned in the *DSM* (the psychiatric profession's manual of disorders), nor is it mentioned in other major medical references – including the prestigious *Textbook of Psychiatry*[138] published by the American Psychiatric Press (otherwise known as the "Red Book") and *The Harvard Guide to Psychiatry*.[139] In the author's own experience, neither medical school, nor internship, nor residency curricula alluded to the rollback phenomenon or its historical origins.

The only serious consideration of rollback as an explanation for drug-associated suicide has appeared in the transcripts of FDA hearings and media interviews, wherein agency officials and prominent names in psychiatry have suddenly embraced rollback as the most likely cause of suicide in patients receiving psychoactive drugs.

Rather than identifying an underlying psychiatric condition as the origin of suicidality, it might be more appropriate to consider rollback as an iatrogenic phenomenon in medicated subjects. The time course (first several weeks of treatment) corresponds perfectly to the adaptive brain changes which the drug company scientists have explained:

> **first, an initial burst of serotonin as the reuptake transporter is blocked. Next, a plunge in serotonin levels as autoreceptors in the midbrain are stimulated, leading to the suppression of neurotransmitter synthesis and release. Third, a reduction in autoreceptor sensitivity and serotonin transporter density, leading to yet another burst in serotonin transmission.**

Given the fact that low and high serotonin levels have been linked to impulsivity, anxiety, and depression, it is difficult to know which of these changes play the most important role in treatment emergent violence. It is possible that all three of these changes contribute to drug-related suicidality. It is also possible that the etiological factor is not the direction of change (too much or too little) in the activity of serotonin or other neurotransmitters, so much as the *rapidity of change* (i.e., sudden shift in neurotransmission, or change per unit of time) to which some patients' central nervous systems may be particularly sensitive.

Mechanisms of Antidepressant-Induced Suicide

Several theories have been advanced to explain the biological underpinnings of antidepressant-related suicide. One of the most obvious explanations is the connection between psychoactive drugs and akathisia - the latter term referring to the condition of inner restlessness or severe agitation, usually associated with antipsychotic agents. The potential for akathisia to induce aggression and suicide has long been recognized by the mental health profession and research teams. In fact, akathisia-related violence receives specific attention[140] in the pages of the *DSM* (*Diagnostic and Statistical Manual of Mental Disorders*). All that remains to complete this theory of iatrogenic suicide, therefore, is a biochemical connection between serotonergic antidepressants and akathisia.

Akathisia >>> suicide/violence

Antidepressants >>> akathisia

Ergo: antidepressants >>> suicide/violence

Such a model has been constructed, based upon pharmacological, anatomical, and electrophysiological studies in animals. The "four neuron model of the extrapyramidal motor system" postulates a chain of connections, beginning with cells in the raphe nuclei.[141] According to this model, serotonergic fibers project from the midbrain to dopamine neurons in the substantia nigra of the forebrain. There, serotonin transmission inhibits dopaminergic cells which would usually exert a negative effect upon GABAnergic interneurons in the same region. The result is the disinhibition of these GABA neurons.   Now activated, these GABA cells communicate with a second population of dopamine cells located in the striatum (caudate & putamen). This GABA activity impairs voluntary movement.

The four neuron model explains a sequence of events which leads to bradykinesia (slow movement, difficulty initiating movement) and akathisia (inner restlessness, pacing, intense agitation), otherwise known as extrapyramidal side effects and usually associated with Parkinson's disease or antipsychotic medications.   Although some observers have downplayed the significance of extrapyramidal side effects arising from serotonin reuptake inhibition, suggesting that its occurrence is quite rare,[142] others have found these problems to be disturbingly common and severe – enough so, that they have prompted at least one psychiatrist to pose the following question: must we now consider SRIs (serotonin reuptake inhibitors) to be *neuroleptics?[143]

A second possible mechanism of antidepressant-related suicide involves the impairment of activity within the frontal lobes. These brain regions are believed to be the critical centers of personality, impulse control, and executive functioning. Several teams of clinicians[144-146] have been trailblazers in documenting the appearance of a reversible, amotivational syndrome in both adults and children treated with SSRIs. Ultimately recognized by the prestigious *Textbook of Psychiatry*, the apathy syndrome refers to the delayed manifestation of behavioral changes in patients receiving serotonergic drugs, whose symptoms include apathy, flat affect, diminished motivation, and disinhibited actions. These features suggest a **frontal lobe syndrome** occurring eight weeks or more after the initiation of pharmacotherapy, or in many patients, after an increase in dose.   One team of investigators[147] corroborated the syndrome using neuroimaging studies in a 23-year-old patient who was treated with fluoxetine (Prozac) for obsessive compulsive disorder. In their research, the findings from SPECT scans obtained before and after four months of daily medication revealed a 108% reduction in frontal lobe blood flow. These changes in blood flow paralleled reductions in motivation, attention, and memory, as well as decrements on neuropsychological tests designed to measure

---

* neuroleptics – the antipsychotic drugs

frontal lobe functions (e.g., problems with perseveration, poor self-monitoring, difficulty in organizing material).

Additional theories have been advanced as possible mechanisms of antidepressant-related violence. These include synergistic actions between alcohol and medication, whereby the disinhibiting effects of both substances hinder impulse control. Others have noted the potential for antidepressant therapy to provoke a wide variety of psychiatric symptoms, including mania, paranoia, hallucinations, panic attacks, or obsessive ruminations – all of which may contribute to suicidal and/or homicidal behaviors.

Psychiatric Side Effects

It would be difficult to identify an area of medicine outside of psychiatry in which pharmacotherapies so frequently provoke or exacerbate the symptoms which they are intended to cure. The best studied phenomenon of this type is manic-depression: a behavioral syndrome typically characterized by alternating episodes of high and low mood. From their inception, antidepressants and other somatic therapies were recognized as having a worrisome capacity to incite changes (switches) between episodes of *depression* (characterized by dysphoria, insomnia, low energy, poor concentration, reduced appetite, and diminished libido) and episodes of *mania* (characterized by euphoria, increased activity, rapid speech, racing thoughts, diminished need for sleep, hypersexuality, and diminished impulse control). As early as 1938,[148] Plattner described *hypomanic states in patients receiving insulin and cardiazol shock therapies. In 1949, von Baeyer referred to these treatment-related phenomena as **"transitional syndromes of organic genesis."** By 1950 and 1961, Plogg and Fink, respectively, had identified the emergence of manic syndromes in up to 50% of subjects receiving electroconvulsive (electroshock) treatment, otherwise known as ECT.

Given these precedents, it was not surprising to early observers that antidepressant medications could also provoke mania in

---

*hypomanic – referring to hypomania; a milder form of mania distinguished by an absence of psychotic features, an absence of marked disruptions in work or social relationships, and an absence of need for hospitalization

many patients. Unfortunately, the hegemony of pharmacotherapy eventually fueled a profession-wide denial of this manic potential.

Biopsychiatry has grown disturbingly fond of blaming the patient rather than the cure, as demonstrated by the now standard invocation that psychotropic drugs have merely "unmasked" a latent bipolar condition whenever treatment coincides with the onset of manic or hypomanic symptoms. One can only wonder how long this behavior would be tolerated in another specialty of medicine: if an antacid caused a patient's heart to stop, the medical profession would consider it an abomination for gastroenterologists to claim that treatment had merely unmasked a latent dysrhythmia.

Currently, no clear consensus exists about the *prevalence* of antidepressant-associated mania (or, for that matter, the prevalence of antidepressant-induced depression). Similarly, there is no consensus about the potential of antidepressants to *cause* manic symptoms, rather than to "simply" accelerate their appearance in patients presumed to be at risk for mania *naturally*, as part of an alleged brain disease. However, this lack of consensus ignores an impressive body of research. Evidence from case reports, population studies, and clinical trials has consistently suggested that antidepressant drugs do as much as to incite, as to "unmask," the clinical entity of bipolarity or manic-depression.

One particularly ambitious project was conducted in the 1980s by Swiss researchers[149] who sought to identify the spontaneous rate of switching between depression and mania. The study involved a retrospective review of records from inpatient admissions to the Psychiatric University Hospital in Zurich (the famous Burgholzli Hospital) from the years 1920 through 1982. Between 100 and 300 patients were randomly selected from the admissions logs in each decade. Cases were included if the admission diagnosis was endogenous depression or the depressive phase of a manic-depressive condition. The research team tracked the progress of each patient, noting the final diagnosis at the time of discharge, or the last recorded diagnosis in the case of rehospitalization. These constituted the before and after points used to establish the presence or absence of switching.

Several findings from this study are remarkable. First, the rates of *first admissions* decreased over time: from 65% of depressive admissions in the 1920s and 1930s, to 30% of the depressive admissions between 1969-1982. While it is possible that this change reflects a trend away from long-term confinement in general, it is also possible that it reflects an increase in the chronicity of distress, accompanied by an increased frequency of rehospitalization. Second, the rate of diagnosed bipolar disorder increased substantially from 1959 onward. This is important, because 1959 was the year in which tricyclic antidepressants became the primary treatment of depression in this particular setting.

Zurich Burgholzli Study of Admissions for Depression: 1920 – 1982[150]

	Major Treatments	Percent of All Admissions	
		Unipolar Depression	Bipolar Depression
1920-1929	*psychoanalysis	77%	8%
1930-1939	*insulin & cardiazol shock	78%	2%
1940-1952	ECT	89%	6%
1953-1957	neuroleptics	84%	6%
1959-1963	tricyclic antidepressants	66%	12%
1969-1973	tricyclic and heterocyclic antidepressants	70%	26%
1980-1982	tricyclic and heterocyclic antidepressants	73%	21%

*Treatments for these two decades were not specifically assigned by the Swiss researchers in their published paper. However, historical information suggests that the major treatment was talk therapy (psychoanalytic / psychodynamic approaches). Beginning in the late 1920s and 1930s, medications such as bromides, paraldehyde, barbiturates, and stimulants (Benzedrine) were increasingly employed in the asylums of Europe and North America as adjunctive therapies to Freud's talking cure. Additional treatments were used for psychosis, including sex hormones, thyroid hormones, and leucotomy.[151] Malarial treatment was used briefly for the treatment of neurosyphilis until penicillin (discovered by Fleming in 1928) replaced it in 1943.

Following the introduction and widespread use of antidepressants in the late 1950s, the rates of bipolar admissions increased approximately two- to threefold (from 2-8%, to 12-26%). Third, the change in rehospitalization rates paralleled the rise in the number of patients suffering multiple episodes (either multiple episodes of depression, multiple episodes of mania, or both):

Zurich Burgholzli Study of Admissions for Depression: 1920 – 1982[152]

	Major Treatments	Percent of All Admissions		
		1 episode	2-3 episodes	> 3 episodes
1920-1929	psychoanalysis	57%	28%	15%
1930-1939	insulin & cardiazol shock	43%	35%	22%
1940-1952	ECT	40%	40%	20%
1953-1957	neuroleptics	34%	45%	21%
1959-1963	tricyclic antidepressants	8%	20%	**72%**
1969-1973	tricyclic and heterocyclic antidepressants	16%	30%	**54%**
1980-1982	tricyclic and heterocyclic antidepressants	20%	25%	**55%**

The data from hospital admissions reveal a trend towards increased periodicity in affective illness, following the introduction of antidepressants. From 1959 on, fewer patients admitted for the treatment of depression were experiencing their first episode; more patients were experiencing 3 or more episodes; and more patients were diagnosed (either at admission or discharge) with bipolar disorder. Finally, the *switch rates* (percent of hospitalized depressed patients *switching* to mania) increased from 2-7% between 1920-1957, to 9-25% of patients admitted after 1959.

Although American researchers have failed to duplicate the Swiss efforts (in terms of a cross-decade analysis of diagnosis and switch rates), several short-term studies have corroborated the European findings. In one U.S. investigation,[153] 74 patients (mean age 23) hospitalized initially for unipolar or non-cycling depression were followed prospectively for 15 years. By the end of the observation period, 26% of the patients had experienced one or more periods of hypomania; 15% had experienced at least one episode of mania; and 7% had experienced episodes of both. The cumulative proportion of polarity conversion (unipolar >> bipolar) was 45% over 15 years.

131

Researchers attributed almost half of these switches to the unambiguous effects of antidepressant therapy. (Of those who converted to mania or hypomania, 47% received antidepressants during follow-up, compared to 32% of those who remained unipolar. Unfortunately, no analysis was offered for lifetime exposure to pharmacotherapy or treatments received in the initial episodes of depression.)

The risks of antidepressant-induced cycling (i.e., increased periodicity of depression, mania, or both) are not limited to adults. In fact, children and adolescents appear to be especially vulnerable to the effects of antidepressant medications. Researchers at Yale University[154] examined a national computerized database to identify manic conversion rates among mental health users aged 5 through 29. After identifying all subjects with an initial diagnosis of anxiety or non-manic mood disorder, records were evaluated for the appearance of bipolarity emerging in a four-year period (1997 through 2001). Results were then correlated to treatment. Findings were significant for a 5% rate of conversion (4786 patients, median follow-up: 41 weeks). **Compared to patients who received no antidepressant drug treatment, exposure to tricyclics and other non-SSRIs was associated with a fourfold risk of manic conversion, and exposure to SSRIs was associated with a twofold risk of conversion.** The highest rate of emergent bipolarity occurred among children aged 10-14. In a similar investigation, researchers at the University of Louisville[155] examined pediatric hospitalizations for bipolar disorder and correlated these admissions to medication histories. Children exposed to antidepressants or stimulants were diagnosed as bipolar approximately two years earlier (mean age: 10.7) than their unmedicated peers (mean age: 12.7 years). A research team in Los Angeles[156] followed the longitudinal course of 51 bipolar patients who developed resistance to drug treatment. Antidepressant-induced mania occurred in 35% of these adult patients. The risk of cycle acceleration (present in 26% of the sample) was predicted by *younger age at the time of first treatment.*

The complications of antidepressant exposure in childhood have also received attention from a team of Harvard investigators.[157] In a chart review of 82 pediatric outpatients receiving an SSRI (paroxetine, fluoxetine, sertraline, fluvoxamine, citalopram) for

132

anxiety (obsessive-compulsive disorder) or depression, the following psychiatric side effects were observed:

Psychiatric Side Effect	Percent of Patients Reporting Problem
sleep distubance	35%
irritability	15%
anxiety	10%
psychosis	10%
depression	9%
mania	6%

The researchers observed *psychiatric adverse events* in a full 22% of their SSRI patients.

Although surprisingly large, this statistic probably underestimated treatment effects for several reasons: 1) the data were based on voluntary rather than solicited complaints; 2) many subjects experiencing drug-related adverse effects may have dropped out of treatment and been lost to follow-up; and 3) many children were receiving combinations of drug therapy, including medications that may have diminished the usual kinds of adverse events (anxiety, insomnia, mania) associated with SSRIs. Interestingly, while many of these psychiatric symptoms emerged early in the course of treatment, half of the children developed them *after* three months of drug exposure. For most children, these symptoms subsided completely when antidepressant therapy was withdrawn – a fact which reinforced the researchers' impressions that these had truly been medication-induced.

Sleep Disruption

Two of the most important effects of antidepressants involve REM sleep. First, a number of serotonergic drugs (SSRIs, TCAs) cause *qualitative* disturbances within REM sleep. Second, the majority of antidepressants (MAOIs, TCAs, mirtazapine, venlafaxine, trazodone) create a *quantitative* disturbance, by reducing the *amount* of REM sleep. In order to appreciate the significance of these effects, it is necessary to understand the role of REM and the role it is believed to play in the health of humans.

Discovered by University of Chicago researchers in 1953, REM refers to a specific form of brain activity during sleep which is characterized by **R**apid **E**ye **M**ovements (hence, **REM**), muscle paralysis (atonia), and dreaming.[158] Cycles of REM activity repeat at 90 minute intervals throughout the night, alternating with a qualitatively different form of brain activity identified (logically enough) as non-REM. While the quality and quantity of sleep diminishes with age, REM sleep is particularly prone to shortening. In healthy humans, REM activity constitutes 80% of the fetal sleep cycle, 50% of the infant sleep cycle, but only 25% of the adult sleep cycle.

Over the past five decades, neuroscientists have made many discoveries about the anatomy and physiology of sleep. According to Harvard psychiatrist and sleep expert, Dr. J. Allan Hobson,[159] the brain can be understood in reference to three features: 1) its level of activation; 2) its apparent source of stimuli (internal or external); and 3) its dominant mode of chemical activity (i.e., monoamines, GABA, acetylcholine). When organized by these criteria, it is possible to compare various kinds of human consciousness according to associated brain features:

Hobson's Integrated Model of Brain-Mind State[160]

	Awake	REM sleep	non-REM sleep
Level of Activation	high	high	moderate
Source of Input (stimuli)	high external	high internal	intermediate between external and internal
Dominant Chemicals	monoamines	ACH	monoamines
	*high level of NE and 5HT relative to ACH	low level of amines relative to ACH	moderate level of amines relative to to ACH

What is particularly unusual about REM sleep is the fact that it incorporates a state of hyperarousal or excitation in the cortex (due to the activity of the reticular formation in the pons), along with a state of inhibition through parts of the spinal cord (due to the activity of the reticular formation in the medulla). During REM sleep, the sensory and motor control centers of the brain appear to be as active as they are during waking. These internally driven stimuli are believed by some researchers to form the basis of dream images and plots. At the same time, the peripheral motor circuits (i.e., legs and arms) are shut down. This evening paralysis is believed to serve a protective function, by preventing an overly aroused sleeper from acting out the events of a dream. One of the potential hazards of antidepressant drug therapy pertains to its effects upon REM sleep paralysis.

Under the influence of certain medications (SSRIs, tricyclic antidepressants), some patients have developed an otherwise rare sleep disturbance known as RBD (REM sleep behavior disorder). Their motor systems have **not** turned off during REM, leading to a phenomenon called "wakeful dreaming." RBD is a drug side effect which has the potential for tragic events, as it has been known

*NE – norepinephrine

5HT – 5-hydroxytryptamine, or serotonin

ACH – acetylcholine

to contribute to violent behaviors performed by patients who remained asleep.[161-164]

A far more common effect of antidepressants is the suppression of REM sleep, which often persists throughout treatment.[165] In other words, the human brain does not desensitize to this particular drug effect. While some researchers have suggested that REM sleep suppression is a marker for the therapeutic benefits of antidepressant drug treatment, and that an increase in REM density is a pathophysiological sign of depression itself, several findings from research contradict both of these claims. First, it should be noted that some antidepressant medications (such as bupropion) are associated with an *increase* in REM density which has corresponded to symptomatic improvement.[166-167] This fact argues against the necessity of suppressing REM sleep in order to produce antidepressant effects. Second, an increase in REM density has been observed in the sleep patterns of experienced practitioners of meditation.[168] In these individuals, increased REM has been a correlate of elevated consciousness and spiritual transcendence rather than depression. In the context of these realities, the suppression of REM by many antidepressants raises several legitimate concerns.

The findings of neuroscientists and ethologists suggest that REM sleep is a behavioral instinct essential for mammalian survival. In the 1960s, for example, the experiments of Dr. Allan Rechtshaffen demonstrated that prolonged sleep deprivation in rats resulted in death within four weeks. Follow-up studies revealed that REM sleep, in particular, was needed by lab animals for the maintenance of proper cognitive functioning. Similar studies were soon performed in humans, including experiments that focused upon reducing certain kinds of sleep (REM vs. non-REM). Some of these studies revealed psychological effects emerging from REM sleep deprivation, including irritability and psychosis.[169-171]

These early explorations, and the studies which followed, have stimulated many tentative hypotheses about the importance of REM sleep. As explained by Hobson, the purpose of REM involves two main functions:[172] ***homeostasis** (balance) and

---

*homeostasis – the tendency of an organism to maintain stability among normal physiological states

*heteroplasticity (change). The homeostatic role is achieved by *energy conservation*. This involves a variety of mechanisms, including the shut down of both motor and sensory inputs from the external world; the shut down of brainstem (medullary) outputs to the peripheral motor system (paralysis); and the reduction of monoamine transmitter release (e.g., serotonin and norepinephrine) from the raphe nuclei and the pons. The heteroplastic role is achieved by information processing. During REM sleep, internally driven signals (e.g., pontine-geniculo-occipital waves) are thought to participate in the strengthening of synapses. (Alternatively, it is conceivable that REM activity contributes equally to synaptic pruning.) The end result is that REM sleep is believed to play a major role in learning – particularly, in the transfer of new material from localized areas into more distributed neural networks which may form the basis of long-term memory. In related research, Australian investigators have speculated that REM sleep deficits may contribute to the progression of Alzheimer's dementia.[173] This makes intuitive sense, given the fact that recent therapies for Alzheimer's disease are drugs which increase acetylcholine and REM sleep.

Another heteroplastic function of REM sleep is the production of dreams, the purpose of which has long occupied the center of scholarly debate. According to philosophical materialists, (who generally regard the mind as limited to, and wholly explained by physical processes) the dream function of REM sleep reflects little more than the brain's monitoring of its own nocturnal activities. Such a mechanistic view conceptualizes the dream as a random occurrence, lacking in special relevance. In contrast, philosophical idealists (whose ranks include psychoanalysts, depth psychologists, and shamans) perceive dreams to be uniquely *meaningful* phenomena. According to these metaphysical perspectives, each dream represents an intentional process, through which the Psyche or Soul presents information to the Self. For these non-materialists, the dream content – whether it reflects a simple replay of the day's experiences, or a representation of remote memories triggered by recent events – is felt to convey *purposeful* material. While pre-

---

*heteroplasticity – the tendency to adapt to changes, injury, or stress through change.

modern societies commonly embrace the dream-time as a pathway to other dimensions of knowing, modern and post-modern societies typically reject such notions as the products of fantasy, delusion, or religion. Nevertheless, it is notable that no less a scientist than Dr. Sigmund Freud regarded the dream to be the "royal road to the Unconscious," through which hidden aspects of the Self could percolate into conscious awareness. When recalled and examined in the waking state, Freud and others believed that these nocturnally derived messages could be integrated into the personal narrative (autonoesis), leading to positive changes in character, behavior, and health. The point of this discussion is not to establish the veridical purpose of dreams, but to explore a range of ideas across time and culture. These perspectives may shape an individual's opinion about the relative hazards of medications which impede the neuronal activities through which dreams are currently thought to be expressed.

In review, the possible hazards of REM sleep suppression include the impairment of energy-conserving processes; the production of psychological disturbances, including psychosis; and the obstruction of learning and memory. To the extent that all psychotherapeutic endeavors are processes of *learning*, the negative impact of antidepressants upon REM sleep should raise concerns about the prudence of combined treatment (talk therapy + drugs). Finally, for those who attribute to dreams a transcendental value – specifically, through the interpretation of dream symbols and themes in the context of a larger life story – the suppression of REM sleep diminishes a vital process that can be used for self-knowledge and growth.

Endocrine Effects

The endocrine risks of antidepressant medications include hyperprolactinemia, growth hormone disturbances, and hyponatremia. By stimulating prolonged elevations in prolactin (as described above), serotonergic drugs may interfere with the pulsatile secretion of GnRH (gonadotropin releasing hormone) and impede the release of sex hormones. If severe enough, these changes may contribute to lactation (milk secretion, even in males), anovulation, amenorrhea, diminished libido, erectile and ejaculatory dysfunction, and hypogonadism. Hyperprolactinemia has also been identified as a risk factor for breast cancer – a fact which lends support to the epidemiological studies connecting antidepressants to the same malignancy, particularly when culprit medications (TCAs, SSRIs) are consumed for extended periods of time.[174] Interestingly, this risk applies to both genders, as surgeons in the U.K.[175] have reported three cases of neoplastic (cancerous) or pre-neoplastic changes in males who were previously exposed to SSRIs. Hyperprolactinemia has been associated by some researchers with an increased risk of heart disease, and substantial evidence connects hyperprolactinemia to the problem of reduced bone mass in males and females, regardless of age.

Researchers have only recently discovered negative growth effects of antidepressant therapies. A team of endocrinologists[176] reported their observations of four children receiving SSRIs, all of whom experienced significant growth suppression at a time when pubertal growth spurts should have occurred. These patients, who ranged in age from 12 to 14 at the time of their endocrine consultations, had been treated with antidepressants (Luvox or Prozac) for 6 months to five years. Lab tests conducted throughout the period of observation demonstrated reductions in growth hormone secretion, as well as diminished growth hormone responses to chemical stimulation tests. As soon as the antidepressant therapies were halted, hormonal responses normalized and growth resumed.

More recently, the manufacturer of Prozac (Eli Lilly) was asked by the FDA to undertake Phase IV, post-marketing studies in children, in recognition of the growth-impairing effects of SSRIs. In a 19-month study[177] involving subchronic treatment in children and teens (aged 8-18), investigators compared the efficacy and safety of Prozac against placebo. Limitations of the study included a high drop-out rate (55% of the Prozac subjects, 57% of the placebo subjects); high use of concomitant medications (84% of the Prozac subjects, 72% of the placebo subjects); a failure to standardize height measurements; and a failure to report results of chemical tests which might have been used to confirm endocrine abnormalities. Despite these failings, however, the Lilly team confirmed a statistically significant association between Prozac and growth deficits in children and teens. Over the course of 19 weeks, Prozac recipients gained less height and less weight (1.0 cm in height, 1.2 kg in weight) than placebo controls (2.1 cm in height, 2.3 kg in weight), leading the investigators to concede that "the clinical significance of fluoxetine's effect on growth rate requires further investigation."[178]

Another endocrine effect of SSRIs is the induction of SIADH, otherwise known as the Syndrome of Inappropriate Antidiuretic Hormone.[179] Normally produced and secreted by the posterior pituitary gland in response to high levels of sodium, antidiuretic hormone (ADH, or vasopressin) regulates the body's balance of fluid. When ADH is erroneously released, it can trigger a dangerous lowering of the sodium concentration in the human bloodstream (hyponatremia) leading to seizures, coma, or death. The condition of antidepressant-induced SIADH appears more commonly among older than younger patients, and usually in the first weeks of treatment. Proposed etiologies include direct stimulation of vasopressin release via 5HT1C or 5HT2C serotonin receptors in the hypothalamus; indirect stimulation of vasopressin release, via the inhibition of dopamine; peripheral effects on the kidney (renal medulla) which lead to excessive water retention; or the re-setting of the hypothalamic osmostat (a set of specialized neurons which sense the concentration of dissolved substances in the blood and generate signals to maintain proper fluid balance).

Serotonin Syndrome

Serotonin syndrome refers to a potentially fatal reaction to medications which (alone or in combination) increase the serotonergic tone of the central nervous system. The syndrome includes behavioral, neurological, autonomic, and gastrointestinal disturbances:[180-182]

<u>Symptoms of Serotonin Syndrome</u>

Behavioral	Neurological	Autonomic	Other
insomnia	confusion	rapid heart rate	nausea
agitation	obtundation	hypertension	vomiting
mania	hyperreflexia	fever	diarrhea
mutism	myoclonus	profuse sweating	elevated creatine kinase
hallucinations	tremors	tachypnea	elevated white blood cells
	ataxia	shivering	
	akathisia	mydriasis (dilated pupils)	
	seizures		
	coma		

Proposed mechanisms for serotonin syndrome include the over-stimulation of 5HT1A receptors in the brain (medulla) and spinal cord; the over-stimulation of central 5HT2 receptors; and chemical disruptions (such as over-activity of dopamine, or high ratios of tryptamine relative to serotonin).

Due to the presence of mental status changes (i.e, confusion), autonomic dysfunction (changes in blood pressure, heart rate, and temperature), and neuromuscular abnormalities, serotonin syndrome appears to be a mild variant of NMS (Neuroleptic Malignant Syndrome) – the latter condition, a potentially lethal effect of antipsychotic medications. The identification of the appropriate syndrome is sometimes difficult for physicians to make, not only because of the overlapping symptoms, but also because many patients in current treatment settings are recipients of both kinds of drugs (antidepressants + neuroleptics). Nevertheless, NMS can usually be distinguished by its features of high fever, muscular rigidity (cogwheeling), leukocytosis (high white blood cell count), and muscle breakdown (reflected by elevations in creatine kinase). Treatment for both conditions begins with the immediate cessation of the inciting drug(s), but additional interventions must be made with caution. Some of the therapies suggested for NMS (bromocriptine, dantrolene) have been known to worsen serotonin syndrome, presumably by increasing serotonin levels in the brain. Although serotonin syndrome usually responds to supportive measures (withdrawal of precipitating agent, IV fluids, cooling beds, mechanical ventilation, benzodiazepines, and/or antihypertensives) within 24 to 72 hours, some patients have experienced residual symptoms lasting for weeks; severe cases have resulted in death.

Antidepressant Withdrawal Syndrome

The existence of syndromes, or clusters of symptoms, emerging upon the termination of antidepressant therapy has been documented since 1959.[183-184] Despite this historical record, professional acknowledgement of these conditions (euphemistically named discontinuation syndromes) has been strikingly poor. An excellent illustration of this trend is demonstrated in the results of a U.K. survey[185] which involved 100 psychiatrists and 100 general practitioners (50% and 53% responding, respectively):

	Psychiatrists	GPs
confident awareness of antidepressant discontinuation syndromes	72%	30%
awareness of withdrawal syndromes associated with:		
SSRIs	94%	68%
MAOIs	78%	47%
TCAs	74%	58%
direct experience treating patients for withdrawal associated with:		
SSRIs	66%	42%
MAOIs	34%	6%
TCAs	42%	38%

A surprisingly large percentage of psychiatrists (28%), and an alarming majority of GPs (70%) reported a lack of familiarity with antidepressant withdrawal effects. This was particularly true when providers were questioned about older classes of medication. Even fewer clinicians reported direct experience in managing patients who may have presented with these treatment-related conditions. When queried specifically about communication styles, the U.K. respondents revealed the following:

	Psychiatrists	GPs
always or usually advise patients about drug withdrawal effects	52%	51%
would report events to national surveillance agency	40%	49%
would write a letter to professional journal	3%	0%

A sizable percentage of specialists and general physicians conveyed limited or no knowledge about adverse events arising directly from antidepressant withdrawal. Among the few clinicians who did report a confident awareness of these phenomena, most expressed disinterest in communicating this information to patients, health surveillance authorities (e.g., MHRA or World Health Organization), or peers (via journal letters).

Given the surprisingly high rate of ignorance or silence among clinicians, it seems likely that many patients have been misinformed about the fact antidepressant discontinuation can result in the emergence of physical and psychological symptoms. It was only in May 2003,[186] for example – a full twelve years after product approval – that the Irish Medicines Board required the manufacturer of Seroxat (paroxetine) to remove language on its patient leaflets describing the drug as non-addictive. This remarkable development was presumably assisted by the efforts of industry watchdogs, some of whom repeatedly called attention to international registries of adverse events. Those databases have consistently revealed the potential of serotonergic therapies to produce problems associated with drug withdrawal:

Numbers of Spontaneously Reported Withdrawal Reactions[187]

	U.K. Medicines Control Agency	World Health Organization	Uppsala Monitoring Center
Paroxetine/Paxil SSRI	1281	2003	2380
Venlafaxine/ Effexor SNRI	272	1058	1185
Sertraline/Zoloft SSRI	81	585	631
Fluoxetine/Prozac SSRI	91	402	419

Despite the existence of these datasets, and largely in denial of therapeutic drug dependence, medical professionals have only rarely acknowledged the existence of these phenomena. In 1987, Dilsaver[188] proposed five categories of features appearing after treatment with tricyclic antidepressants. Six years later, Dilsaver teamed with Halle[189] to document similar syndromes in patients withdrawing from the monoamine oxidase inhibitor, tranylcypromine (Parnate). More recently, teams of clinicians have convened for the purpose of identifying unique features of "discontinuation syndromes" associated with SSRIs and other inhibitors of serotonin reuptake.[190-191]

Antidepressant Withdrawal Syndromes

TCAs tricyclic antidepressants	MAOIs monoamine oxidase inhibitors	SSRIs/SNRIs serotonin & norepinephrine reuptake inhibitors
(Dilsaver's categories)		
somatic/anxiety:	delirium	flu-like symptoms:
anorexia	thought disorganization	runny nose
nausea	depression	muscle aches
vomiting	mania	malaise
diarrhea	hypomania	nausea
sweating	irritability	vomiting
headache	aggression	diarrhea
chills	agitation	shaking chills
lethargy	insomnia	
	myoclonic jerks	neurological symptoms:
sleep disturbances:	paranoid delusions	dizziness
insomnia	hallucinations	headache
vivid dreams		electric shocks
		burning/tingling
movement disorders:		insomnia
akathisia		vertigo
parkinsonism		dystonias
		dyskinesias
behavioral activation:		memory problems
mania		gait disturbances
hypomania		confusion
panic attacks		tremor
delirium		
		behavioral symptoms:
other:		mania
cardiac arrythmias		suicidality
		"spaced out"
		"buzzed"
		nightmares
		vivid dreams
		hallucinations
		irritability
		aggression
		impulsivity
		lack of energy
		weakness
		crying spells
		anxiety

The incidence of antidepressant withdrawal syndromes in controlled studies (RCTs) has varied from an astounding rate of 0% for Prozac subjects in a study which compared SSRIs against each other,[192] to 100% in a study of patients withdrawing from imipramine.[193]

Most published trials and epidemiological reviews, however, have reported withdrawal events among 20-80% of all subjects when antidepressant therapy was interrupted or removed. This broad range is presumably reflective of different research methodologies, including disparate reporting techniques (spontaneous vs. solicited) and/or varying thresholds in defining the condition of drug withdrawal.

One of the most concerning features of the antidepressant literature has been the intentional manipulation of these clinical realities. Through their influence upon the content and dissemination of treatment guidelines, journal supplements, CME (continuing medical education) symposia, and public announcements, pharmaceutical companies have promoted the misinterpretation of withdrawal symptoms as evidence of relapse for which the resumption of pharmacotherapy has been strongly endorsed. Because of these efforts, old and new generations of psychiatrists and patients have been led to believe that depression is a chronic disease for which patients require ever longer periods of medication.

Several papers have revealed the pharmaceutical companies' awareness of this problem. In a study sponsored by Eli Lilly (maker of Prozac), 192 medicated subjects in remission from an episode of depression were exposed to a brief period (5 to 8 days) of interrupted drug therapy.[194] Approximately one-third of the patients who were abruptly withdrawn from Paxil or Zoloft experienced a return of symptoms *"to a level generally associated with a major depressive episode."* These features were unambiguously identified by the researchers as a rapidly emerging *withdrawal depression*, based upon specific assessments of dysphoria, diminished motivation, anhedonia, thoughts of death, and hopelessness. In contrast, the Prozac subjects were reported to display no symptoms associated with drug cessation. This led the research team to conclude that Prozac poses no risk of a withdrawal or discontinuation syndrome. However, a close inspection of the study design casts doubts about the validity of that conclusion. First, an unknown number of subjects were allowed to consume concomitant medication for insomnia (either chloral hydrate or zolpidem). Second, the drug-interruption period was limited to just eight days. This was far too brief an interval to induce effects of Prozac withdrawal, due to the drug's long half-life (7-14 days), delayed brain washout (13-17 days or more), and sequestration in surprise locations (i.e., bone marrow of the legs for up to 90 days).

According to a second team of researchers (also sponsored by Eli Lilly to examine the effects of SSRI interruption), antidepressant withdrawal syndromes:

> "...can include features of the illness for which for the drug was administered, but are not generally thought to reflect relapse of the underlying condition...

> "Discontinuation symptoms can include prominent psychological manifestations, and patients who experience discontinuation symptoms after stopping medication could be misdiagnosed as having relapsed, and as a result have therapy reinstated prematurely. Similarly, a body of data suggests that many patients have gaps in medication compliance or stop medication spontaneously, and our results suggest that some patients...will develop interruption-related symptoms that may be viewed as breakthrough depressive symptoms or some other condition (e.g., influenza). The degree to which such problems actually result in inappropriate or unnecessary treatment, however, is not known."[195]

The significance of these revelations cannot be overstated, for at least three reasons. First, the current standard in psychiatric drug trials has emphasized the use of a seven to ten day placebo lead-in or "drug washout" phase, during which previously medicated participants have been abruptly withdrawn from their earlier treatments. Given the documented association between antidepressant-withdrawal and the *rapid appearance* of depression, anxiety, and/or suicidality, the FDA's acceptance of existing research methodologies has contributed to a sham approval process. Due to the existence of drug-withdrawal phenomena, placebo subjects in all such protocols have been disadvantaged. Efficacy and safety findings have necessarily favored subjects receiving active drug therapies, as their withdrawal syndromes have presumably been more quickly and effectively eclipsed.

Second, although antidepressant-withdrawal syndromes have generally been mild and short-lived (seldom lasting more than 14-30 days), many patients have experienced severely disabling symptoms (e.g., suicide, dystonia, vertigo, ataxia). For some, these problems have not abated even after the removal of drug therapy for months or years. Although many psychopharmacologists would recommend the reinstatement of previous drug therapies in such cases, the prospects of permanent treatment are no less problematic as they include protracted sexual dysfunction, akathisia, apathy, or weight gain.

Third, the existence of antidepressant-withdrawal symptoms has been used by the pharmaceutical industry to construct a mythology of chronic disease, based upon the experience of patients who repeatedly develop depressive (or manic) features whenever their medications are stopped. Many clinicians have embraced the "prophylactic efficacy" argument for pharmacotherapy, according to which long-term treatment has been recommended to patients as the best means of relapse prevention:

> **"Since depression is a recurrent illness, long-term maintenance therapy should be considered for anyone who has had three or more serious depressive episodes or two episodes in the past five years."[196]**

The problem with these guidelines is the failure to acknowledge the timing, intensity, and ubiquity of drug-withdrawal effects. Stripped to its essence, the treatment philosophy of contemporary biopsychiatry has assumed the following form:

Antidepressant withdrawal causes antidepressant-withdrawal effects.

To avoid antidepressant-withdrawal effects, antidepressants must not be withdrawn.

Regrettably, the tautology of the prevalent Zeitgeist presents an enigma which many providers seem perpetually determined to ignore.

Alternatives to Antidepressant Drugs

A number of studies have been conducted which document the effectiveness of psychotherapies in the treatment and prevention of depression. The first multi-site study of this kind to be conducted by the National Institute of Mental Health was the Treatment of Depression Collaborative Research Program (TDCRP), which compared the responses of 250 patients seeking treatment for non-bipolar, non-psychotic depression.[197-198]

Seventy percent of the participants had prior histories of treatment for depression; 28% had previously received medication. After a 7 to 14 day drug washout period, subjects were randomly assigned to one of four conditions for a sixteen-week duration of treatment: antidepressant medication (imipramine), *interpersonal therapy (IPT), **cognitive behavioral therapy (CBT), or ***placebo. Medication (active drug or placebo) was administered *daily*, along with weekly supportive sessions lasting 20 to 30 minutes for the evaluation of progress and/or side effects. Antidepressant doses were titrated for effect. By contrast, psychotherapy was administered in weekly, fifty-minute sessions conducted by individuals who had received special instruction in each of the manualized programs of care. At the end of the acute treatment period, a primary analysis (using a variety of clinical assessment tools) revealed very few significant differences between the four interventions. When data from all study *completers* were compared at sixteen weeks, there was no evidence that either psychotherapy was more or less effective than the tricyclic antidepressant. Recovery rates (defined as Hamilton Depression Rating Scale scores of six or less; or Beck Depression

---

*cognitive behavioral therapy – a form of psychotherapy emphasizing active interventions (such as exposure or desensitization), the teaching of social skills (assertiveness, communication), and regular homework assignments, all of which seek to identify and change maladaptive cognitions or behaviors; in this particular study, the CBT techniques developed by Aaron Beck were employed

**interpersonal therapy – a form of psychotherapy developed by Gerald Klerman and Myrna Weissman, in which the therapist seeks to help the patient identify and understand interpersonal problems and conflicts, and to develop more adaptive ways of relating to others (not to be confused with the interpersonal tradition of psychodynamic therapy attributed to Harry Stack Sullivan)

***placebo – although an inert substance was administered to these subjects, the placebo condition was actually a "supportive therapy" condition *with* placebo, due to the provision of feedback and advice in the context of a weekly psychotherapeutic relationship

Inventory scores of 9 or less) for imipramine and the two forms of psychotherapy were essentially indistinguishable:

16 Week Recovery Rates for All Study Completers

imipramine	57%
IPT	55%
CBT	51%
Placebo	29%

Nonetheless, this therapeutic equivalence was not the result which psychiatrists or the NIMH chose to emphasize. Rather, by stratifying patients retrospectively according to initial symptom severity (and by ignoring the Observed Cases, or "completer" data, as discussed in chapter four), the investigators demonstrated strong evidence of efficacy for imipramine, and moderate evidence of efficacy for IPT. (Interestingly, the researchers openly acknowledged that study dropouts had poorer scores at termination. What they did not seem to appreciate was the manner in which high attrition rates exerted a disproportionate influence upon LOCF or endpoint data, leading to a deflation of mean improvement among the non-medicated participants in the study).

Despite the methodological biases and statistical manipulations which led to an early proclamation of antidepressant superiority, the NIMH team continued to analyze outcomes at intervals of 6, 12, and 18 months. During this extended phase of monitoring, antidepressants were resumed by 33% of the original imipramine subjects, and were initiated by 14% of IPT, 13% of placebo, and 9% of CBT participants. When rates of *remission and **relapse were compared at 18 months, long term outcomes demonstrated a clear advantage for psychotherapy:

---

*remission rate - percent of patients experiencing 8 weeks of minimal or no symptoms following the end of treatment

**relapse rate - percent of patients experiencing a return of disabling depressive symptoms for at least two weeks

Remission Rates		Relapse Rates	
30%	CBT	50%	imipramine
26%	IPT	36%	CBT
20%	placebo	33%	IPT
19%	imipramine	33%	placebo

Long term outcomes were also analyzed according to the severity of each patient's initial condition. Relapse rates for subjects with severe depression (GAS < 50) were essentially equal among the four treatment groups: 76% for CBT, 77% for imipramine, 81% for placebo, and 82% for IPT. Among patients with milder symptoms of depression (GAS > 50), the use of medication in the initial period of treatment appeared to be detrimental, with 85% of the imipramine subjects relapsing, compared to 68% and 66% of the IPT and CBT subjects, respectively. Finally, time to relapse was *shorter*, and duration of recurrent symptoms was *longer*, for those subjects who had initially received antidepressant medication:

Mean Survival Time

(Weeks Until Relapse or Resumption of Treatment)

47 weeks for imipramine
54 weeks for IPT
63 weeks for placebo
66 weeks for CBT

Mean Number of Weeks Without Symptoms

53 weeks for imipramine
63 weeks for IPT
67 weeks for CBT
67 weeks for placebo

The example of the NIMH study is hardly an aberration in the history of depression. Other research groups have corroborated similar findings, with psychotherapeutic interventions demonstrating equal or superior effectiveness to medication in the acute management of symptoms for adults and younger patients.[199-205]

Non-pharmacological approaches, including aerobic exercise,[206-208] have been especially impressive in the prevention of relapse and recurrence.[209-210] Moreover, the potency of psychotherapy has been repeatedly established even in the treatment of patients with severe depression and suicidality, despite the vociferous claims of many health care providers who erroneously believe that serious symptoms demand the use of medication.[211-213]

Several studies have demonstrated that combined treatments (medication + psychotherapy, exercise + medication) produce inferior results when compared to non-drug modalities administered alone.[214-216] The failure of these combined approaches ("drugs plus") is entirely predictable when one considers the counter-productive effects of invasive chemical interventions (e.g., suppression of REM sleep, elevation of cortisol, induction of mania), all of which have been discussed above.

Whether by ignorance or design, the mental health profession remains largely oblivious to this tragedy of its own making:

> **"Some investigators have argued that the relatively high relapse rate after drug treatment indicates that depression should be treated like a chronic medical disease requiring ongoing, long-term, high-dose medication treatment indefinitely. This logic appears tautological: Drug treatment results in a higher relapse rate than cognitive-behavioral therapy; therefore, the patients should be maintained on drugs to prevent relapse."[217]**

The history of antidepressants illustrates the potential of drugs to induce allostatic load, ultimately condemning many patients to a lifetime of recurrent or chronic symptoms. Unfortunately, as the next chapters will reveal, this feature is by no means limited to the antidepressants.

Chapter Eight

The History of Antipsychotics[1-3]

Throughout the history of psychopharmacology, the notion that *specific* drug therapies might have *specific* disease effects has been determined as much by sociocultural and economic forces as by science.[4] Nowhere has this phenomenon been more clearly exemplified than in the story of antipsychotic drugs – medications which, rightly or wrongly, have come to be associated with salutary effects upon hallucinations, *delusions, and disordered thought.

Although most textbooks of psychiatry overlook its role in history, the first chemical treatment for psychosis may have been the snakeroot plant, *Rauwolfia serpentina*: an alkaloid used for centuries by healers in India for the treatment of insanity, insomnia, and snake bites. Following the 1931 (in India) and 1952 (in Germany) isolation of *Rauwolfia*'s active ingredient, reserpine, the drug became a popular treatment for high blood pressure, psychosis, and depression. Not until the 1960s did reserpine fall from favor, when a variety of side effects – including akathisia, depression, and suicide – led to its replacement by alternative therapies. Within psychiatry, these early substitutes consisted of antihistamine compounds derived from the synthetic dye industry.

The emergence of the "first generation" of antipsychotics was very much a serendipitous event, building upon previous discoveries in organic chemistry. In the late 19th century, dyes such as methylene blue had permitted the identification of distinct microorganisms by biologists, who used the new compounds to stain bacteria and examine discrete cellular structures with light microscopy. This practice gave rise to the hypothesis that the same chemicals absorbed by bacterial cell walls might be effective in treating infections. Although the dreams of an antibiotic dye did not pan out, further testing of the phenothiazine nucleus in methylene blue was shown (by the chemist Daniel Bovet) to have antihistamine

---

* delusion – a false, fixed belief despite evidence to the contrary

properties. The potential utility of Bovet's discovery attracted the attention of physicians who believed that histamine played a powerful role in the body's stress response. An innovative French military surgeon, Henri Laborit, proposed that cooling procedures (artificial hibernation) might be used before operations to reduce surgical shock.

In perceiving a role for the new antihistamines (as a chemical adjunct to the ice bath), it was Laborit who is generally credited with the discovery of clinical applications for chlorpromazine (Thorazine) - the phenothiazine antihistamine, produced by Rhone Poulenc in 1950. When Laborit administered chlorpromazine to his patients, he was particularly captivated by the tendency of the drug to produce a curious form of calming without sedation, or "psychic indifference." Laborit was not alone. Several other prominent clinicians (Delay, Deniker, Winkelman, Anton-Stephens) commented upon the same result, equating the effects of the new drug to a chemical lobotomy.[5-6] The same phenomenon was noticed by chemists at Rhone Poulenc. In testing the compound in rats,[7] they had observed the product's capacity to induce a lack of responsiveness to aversive stimuli. Rodents exposed to chlorpromazine failed to display their usual escape behaviors in reaction to electric shock. Wondering about possible psychiatric applications - particularly, for agitated or delirious patients - Laborit shared his new discovery with a psychiatrist friend named Cornelia Quarti. As was commonly done at the time, Quarti sampled chlorpromazine directly and recorded the following effects:

> **"At thirteen hours...the painful feeling of imminent death gives way to a euphoric calm. I still feel I am dying, but this leaves me indifferent...At fifteen hours,...my speech has become painful, dysarthric, I can't find my words...In the evening, I am still very tired and must stay in bed...The speech difficulty continues...The lassitude and speech disorders persist for a few days to disappear progressively."[8]**

Ultimately, chlorpromazine was tested and developed by two competing teams of psychiatrists in France: one affiliated with St. Anne Hospital (Delay, Deniker, Pichot, Thullier) and another affiliated with the Val de Grace military hospital (Hamon, Paraire, and Velluz). To some observers, the drug appeared to have a magical capacity to *awaken patients who had been catatonic or psychotically withdrawn for years.

Because there was, at the time, no particular market for a reserpine rival, and no particular concept of an "antipsychotic" drug, chlorpromazine was licensed in the United States in 1955 as an anti-emetic. Nevertheless, it soon became the most widely used drug in American asylums, finding applications in the treatment of delirium, mania, agitation, aggression, and psychosis. The success of chlorpromazine ushered in an era of chemical modification (mostly of antihistamines) and rapid testing, as a variety of companies vied for their share of the emerging market in psychopharmaceuticals.

A critical feature in the early development of antipsychotic drugs was the theory of efficacy which guided their use. Although its chemical and cellular mechanisms of action were not established for more than twenty years, chlorpromazine's capacity to induce Parkinsonian or **extrapyramidal symptoms (rigidity, tremor, shuffling gait, masked face) was quickly acknowledged. Practitioners in France and Germany regarded these effects as a necessary pre-requisite for the onset of anti-psychotic action. In fact, doses of the new drugs were given at sufficiently high levels to guarantee the appearance of movement abnormalities. In 1955, Delay and Deniker named chlorpromazine a *neuroleptic* because of the drug's capacity to "seize" (leptic) the brain (neuro) in the

---

* In this sense, these early reports about chlorpromazine bear a striking resemblance to Dr. Oliver Sacks' experiences with L-dopa (levodopa, a precursor to the neurotransmitter dopamine). Sacks, of course, had administered that anti-parkinsonian agent to catatonic survivors of encephalitis lethargica (EL), noting a series of awakenings which eventually gave rise to a book and movie of the same name. It is possible that chlorpromazine's "awakenings" occurred through similar neurological mechanisms (an increase in dopamine synthesis and release) in the same subset of patients, as many European asylum residents in the 1950s were presumably experiencing the residual effects of EL.

**extrapyramidal[9] – a functional, rather than anatomic, unit of the central nervous system comprising the nuclei and fibers involved in motor activities; it includes the striatum, subthalamic nucleus, substantia nigra, and the red nucleus, along with their connections to the reticular formation, the cerebellum, and the cerebral cortex

same manner as several neurological disorders which had already been identified.

That the intentional infliction of brain damage was seen as ameliorative may seem bizarre from today's perspective, but it is important to recognize the historical precedent for this belief: the flu pandemic which had ravaged Europe in the early 1900s. Many survivors of the viral infection known as *encephalitis lethargica* (an inflammation of the brain tissue which resulted in lethargy) ultimately developed long-lasting, extrapyramidal effects after recovering from the acute stages of illness. Some of the psychiatric patients in the asylums of Europe had demonstrated an interesting progression of symptoms during the active infection, characterized by an improvement in hallucinations and delusions just as movement abnormalities and akathisia emerged. It was this phenomenon which led Delay and Deniker to propose a common action for the new drugs, speculating that a specific action upon the *basal ganglia of the brain must be responsible for beneficial effects in the treatment of agitation, excitement, and psychosis.[10]

Because of the perspective that extrapyramidal symptoms were essential for the production of antipsychotic effects, the practice of megadosing the neuroleptics dominated psychiatry for more than 20 years. Increasing doses of chlorpromazine – as much as 5000 milligrams per day – were administered to patients. Similarly, following the successful introduction of haloperidol (Haldol) in 1956, psychiatrists extended this treatment philosophy with the practice of neuroleptic narcosis. This was an intense form of therapy involving the intravenous administration of Haldol at doses of 10 mg per hour – a practice which would be considered overtly toxic by today's standards.

These early assumptions and treatment patterns yielded slowly under the influence of scientific advances (e.g., the discovery of dopamine as an important neurotransmitter, the identification of specific dopamine receptors, and the recognition that adverse motor effects were not essential for therapeutic action), and a variety of social and legal events. Most notably, the psychiatric profession

---

* basal ganglia – discrete gray matter structures located deep within the cerebral hemispheres and the brainstem, responsible for the coordination of movement

remained remarkably tolerant of movement abnormalities until the discovery that many patients came to experience these problems in a *persistent form* which did not reverse – even, or especially, when the medications were stopped. It was not until the 1960s that the American psychiatric profession acknowledged *tardive dyskinesia as an iatrogenic condition,[11] and it was not until 1974 that the first product liability case was successfully litigated in this regard. By the late 1980s, a substantial body of research in animals and humans had resulted in published papers which recommended the use of the "lowest effective dose" and which, collectively, repudiated the historical tragedy of the neuroleptic megadose as both unnecessary and unacceptably hazardous.[12]

An enduring legacy of this neuroleptic tradition has been the classification of antipsychotic drugs in reference to the earliest compounds, without an appropriate consideration of the excessive dosing patterns which characterized the first decades of their use. Accordingly, the label of **conventional** or **typical** antipsychotic has come to refer to any agent which reliably provokes Parkinsonian side effects and/or tardive phenomena. The notion of an **"atypical"** antipsychotic has been applied to agents less likely to induce these undesirable features.

The tragedy of this system of classification has been the ascendance of a myopic perspective of efficacy and safety. By underestimating the iatrogenic consequences of administering toxic levels of the neuroleptics (as occurred regularly with first generation antipsychotics), the advantages of newer compounds (second and third generation antipsychotics) have frequently been overstated. Furthermore, by constructing an entire theory of psychosis around the chemical (dopamine) effects of the earliest compounds, such as chlorpromazine, the psychiatric profession has overlooked the record of a wide variety of substances which displayed significant clinical utility in the treatment of psychosis prior to the arrival of phenothiazines. When, by the 1970s and 1980s, North American researchers decided that D2 antagonism was the *sine qua non* of antipsychotic efficacy, the successful trials of pure antihistamines,

---

*tardive dyskinesia[13] – involuntary, repetitive movements of the facial, buccal, oral, and cervical musculature, commonly induced by the long term use of antipsychotic agents, which may persist after withdrawal of the agent

tricyclic compounds, monoamine oxidase inhibitors, barbiturates, and even placebos[14] were relegated to the annals of history, instead of the textbooks of psychiatry and psychopharmacology.

The Myth of Atypicality

The term neuroleptic gradually assumed a pejorative connotation because of its association with extrapyramidal symptoms and tardive dyskinesia. As a consequence of this transformation, new products targeting hallucinations and delusions have been identified as atypical antipsychotics on the basis of one or more of the following properties:

➤ behavioral effects

  o a reduced probability of inducing extrapyramidal symptoms and tardive phenomena

  o in animal models: a capacity to block *stereotypies associated with the administration of aopmorphine or amphetamine, without inducing **catalepsy

  o superior efficacy in improving the cognitive features of schizophrenia (poverty of speech, poverty of thought)

➤ biochemical effects

  o a reduced tendency to produce elevations in prolactin relative to first generation neuroleptics

---

* stereotypies – repetitive, apparently purposeless movements of body parts or the entire organism; these are believed to represent overactivity in the dopamine system; in lab rodents, examples include gnawing and sniffing

**catalepsy – a form of paralysis, used as an animal model for Parkinson's disease. Chemicals which produce catalepsy in rodents are predicted to cause extrapyramidal symptoms in humans.

➤ molecular effects

- ○ a lower affinity for the D2 receptor (particularly in the striatum) when compared to first generation neuroleptics

- ○ a high affinity for the serotonin 5HT2 receptor (especially in the frontal cortex)

- ○ a high 5HT2/D2 binding ratio

- ○ a high rate of dissociation ("fast off") from the D2 receptor (a putative feature of clozapine and quetiapine)

Many of these attributions of atypicality have turned out to be false (olanzapine and risperidone induce catalepsy in rodents; risperidone is associated with protracted elevations in prolactin; and clozapine has been shown to cause akathisia and tardive dyskinesia in many patients). Furthermore, the notion of atypicality has been used inappropriately to advance claims about enhanced product efficacy and safety – assertions which will be considered in detail in later sections of the present chapter. The point to be made at this juncture, however, is the arbitrary nature of antipsychotic classification. First, the concept of **atypicality** did not become an issue for the pharmaceutical industry or the psychiatric profession until there was an awareness of tardive dyskinesia, the irreversible movement disorder commonly associated with (but not limited to) the neuroleptics.

While current textbooks refer to clozapine (Clozaril) as the prototype of atypicality, this simplistic designation overlooks that drug's complicated history. Created in 1958, and first tested in European patients in 1961, *clozapine was not welcomed by most clinicians as an "atypical" treatment for psychosis.* On the one hand, leading psychopharmacologists were quite satisified with chlorpromazine and haloperidol, both of which were regarded as equally effective in combating the *positive and negative features of schizophrenia. On the other hand, a number of early trials convinced psychiatrists that

---

*positive and negative – the concept of "positive" and "negative" symptoms began with Swiss psychiatrist, Eugen Bleuler. (cont'd-next page)

clozapine was ineffective and far too dangerous to warrant further use. In Switzerland, Hanns Heimann had noted an aggravation of psychosis in many of his clozapine patients. In Paris, Pierre Deniker's group administered the medication to nineteen patients. This resulted in four deaths.[15] Heimann and Deniker explicitly opposed further testing and development of the product.

Claims about clozapine's "atypical efficacy" did not appear until the 1970s, and only after the psychiatric profession had decided how to handle the drug's toxicity. In 1975, Finnish regulators removed clozapine from the market following the deaths of eight patients from complications related to agranulocytosis, a bone marrow abnormality involving the suppression of infection fighting white blood cells.[16-17] In reaction to the Finnish tragedy, a number of other countries halted their efforts to license and distribute the drug. This sparked a heated debate within the psychiatric community. A committed group of clozapine defenders (Hippius, Battegay, Angst) in Germany and Switzerland convinced the manufacturer (first Sandoz, then CIBA, now Novartis) to keep the drug on the market. Among the arguments presented by the clozapine camp was a belief that the drug had special efficacy in patients who had failed to respond to other treatments; and a concern that the withdrawal of clozapine would precipitate a rapidly emerging, severe worsening of psychotic symptoms in patients who had already been exposed to the new compound. (Not considered was the possibility that the reason clozapine appeared to be so impressive in some refractory patients was the fact that their previous treatments had made

---

*positive and negative (continued) – According to Bleuler, schizophrenia was a psychological disorder characterized primarily by negative symptoms (emotional dullness, social withdrawal, apathy, avolition). Positive features (+) such as hallucinations, delusions, bizarre behaviors were so-named because of their blatancy, and the fact that they were seen as something added to the usual background of negativity. Following the introduction of neuroleptics in 1952, Bleuler's characterization of schizophrenia as an essentially cognitive and affective disorder was gradually reversed. Positive symptoms came to occupy the center of attention. At least one historian has suggested that this reversal originated in the psychiatric profession's attempts to downplay the behavioral toxicity of the neuroleptics, which was recognized even in the 1950s because of the drugs' capacity to induce or exacerbate the "negative" symptoms which Bleuler had carefully described. For more on this interesting history, see Healy's *The Creation of Psychopharmacology*.

them unresponsive, due to the brain changes induced by the administration of neuroleptics in truly poisonous quantities.)

The "save clozapine" campaign was successful. Over time, it was discovered that clozapine had the potential to reverse or improve tardive dyskinesia in some cases. This fact, as much as any other, restored the drug to good graces. Testing and licensure resumed around the world in the 1980s, aided by the inception of the *Clozaril Patient Monitoring Service (CPMS) – a mandatory blood testing program established by the manufacturer and implemented by many countries, in order to prevent epidemics of death like the one which had transpired in Finland in 1974.

Following a twenty-year drought in antipsychotic development (attributed by some observers to "litigation anxiety" in the aftermath of the first tardive settlements), Janssen Pharmaceuticals successfully revisited earlier attempts to produce a single pill with combined effects upon serotonin and dopamine. The result was the 1984 creation of risperidone (Risperdal). Shortly thereafter, the first American trials of clozapine were completed. In 1989, the FDA approved clozapine as a treatment for refractory schizophrenia, with the expectation that its use would be heavily restricted because of its potential lethality. When risperidone received FDA approval in 1994, the era of the "SDA" (serotonin dopamine antagonist) was firmly established. Each of the new treatments – and even one old one (clozapine) – was defined in terms of its differential affinities (binding potential) for various dopamine and serotonin receptor subtypes. A new mythology was engendered, as mental health professionals and the public were assured that the "second" and "third" generation antipsychotics would be indisputably more effective, less hazardous, and better tolerated than their progenitors.

---

*CPMS - the CPMS continues today, with clozapine prescribers obliged to obtain blood specimens at regular intervals: weekly for the first six months of treatment, and biweekly thereafter. The goal is to detect blood cell and platelet abnormalities before life threatening emergencies arise.

Examples of Neuroleptics[18]

First Generation	Second Generation	Third Generation
Butyrophenones	Benzisoxazole	Dihydrocarbostyril
haloperidol (Haldol) droperidol (Inapsine)	risperidone (Risperdal)	aripiprazole (Abilify)
Dibenzodiazepines	Benzothiazolylpiperazine	
*clozapine (Clozaril)	ziprasidone (Geodon)	
Dibenzoxapine	Dibenzothiazepine	
loxapine (Loxitane)	quetiapine (Seroquel)	
Dihydroindolone	Thienobenzodiazepine	
molindone (Moban)	olanzapine (Zyprexa)	

Phenothiazines

chlorpromazine (Thorazine)
fluphenazine (Prolixin)
perphenazine (Trilafon)
trifluoperazine (Stelazine)
thioridazine (Mellaril)

Thioxanthenes

thiothixene (Navane)

* Historically speaking, Clozaril emerged at the same time as the first generation neuroleptics. Only after 1975 did the pharmaceutical industry and psychiatric profession emphasize an "atypical" action for clozapine. In the 1990s, due to its late approval in the USA, clozapine was received as a second generation antipsychotic drug.

Other *Antipsychotics[19]

antihistamines
barbiturates
benzodiazepines
monoamine oxidase inhibitors   (e.g., iproniazid)
placebo
reserpine
tricyclic antidepressants   (e.g., trimipramine)

*Although their role has been neglected by most textbooks of psychopharmacology, it is important to appreciate the clinical utility of a wide variety of medications which were tested in the 1950s and 1960s. It was the "dopamine theory of schizophrenia" that ultimately led to the rejection of these non-dopamine-receptor antagonists as a primary therapy for the treatment of hallucinations, delusions, or catatonia. They are included here for the sake of historical accuracy, even though few clinicians appreciate the value which these treatments demonstrated in trials that were conducted more than forty years ago.

The Dopamine Hypothesis of Schizophrenia

The alleged utility of reserpine and chlorpromazine in moderating the symptoms of schizophrenia was a serendipitious discovery, arising from the empirical testing of new compounds in a captive audience: the residents of European and American asylums. As noted previously, many of these denizens had been suffering from the persistent effects of infectious diseases, such as encephalitis lethargica and neurosyphilis. Because the earliest concept of a neuroleptic attributed the ameliorative properties of each drug to the production of Parkinsonian symptoms (tremor, shuffling gait, difficulty initiating movement), dopamine became a major focus of antipsychotic drug research. Several historical events were responsible for this development.

In 1817, the London physician James Parkinson identified the "shaking palsy" which eventually bore his name. In the aftermath of this achievement, anatomic dissections of Parkinsonian patients revealed characteristic abnormalities (lack of pigmentation) in discrete regions (substantia nigra) of their brains. Interestingly, it was not until 1958 that dopamine was recognized as an important neurotransmitter in the central nervous system. Two years later, the Viennese pharmacologist, Oleh Horneykiewicz, connected the presumptive chemical cause of Parkinson's disease (dopamine deficiency) with the anatomical regions noted previously. By measuring dopamine levels in the nigrostriatal tissue taken from deceased patients, Horneykiewicz noted an 80% depletion of dopamine in Parkinson's disease.[20]

The relevance of these discoveries for the field of psychiatry emerged in the 1960s and 1970s, when investigators proposed the dopamine hypothesis of schizophrenia. The idea was advanced that a dopamine excess was responsible for hallucinations and delusions.

The examples of reserpine and chlorpromazine inspired researchers to identify common properties in the drugs' mechanisms of action, based upon a belief that shared features would provide an explanation for both the cause and treatment of psychosis. Until the advent of molecular biology and associated technologies in the 1970s, these first investigations were limited to the analysis of *chemical changes*. In the 1950s, reserpine was shown to *deplete* neurons of their stored neurotransmitters; specifically, serotonin, norepinephrine, and dopamine. In 1962, Arvid Carlsson demonstrated that chlorpromazine and other neuroleptics caused a significant *increase* in dopamine metabolites. Carlsson associated these changes with a drug-induced acceleration of cell firing (increased electrical activity in the dopamine cells), leading to the synthesis and release of more dopamine. Perplexed by the apparent contradiction in these mechanisms of action – reserpine, depleting dopamine and chlorpromazine, increasing it – Carlsson proposed a theory that non-reserpine neuroleptics might be exerting their effects by blocking *post-synaptic receptors*. Such a blockade, he reasoned, might send a signal back to the dopamine-producing neuron, accelerating neurotransmitter production and release.

In 1975, Carlsson's ideas were validated by two separate teams of neuroscientists.Researchers at Johns Hopkins University (Snyder, Burt, Creese) and the University of Toronto (Seeman) identified the first subtypes of dopamine receptors (D1 and D2) using techniques of autoradiography and biochemistry. According to these theorists, the antipsychotic effects of neuroleptics depended upon the antagonism of post-synaptic D2 receptors. More specifically, the potency of a given drug's effects (i.e., the intensity of clinical benefit) was linked to the drug's affinity (strength of binding) for the D2 receptor. While these views have subsequently been *challenged and revised – even by some of their original proponents[21-22] – they have nonetheless remained the foundation of research and development in the field of antipsychotic pharmacotherapy. Consequently, the proper starting point in the discussion of antipsychotic drug effects is a review of dopamine and its functions within the human body.

*Challenges to the Dopamine Hypothesis of Schizophrenia[23-24]

selective D2 antagonists (amisulpride, sulpiride, remoxipride) have been developed and used for the treatment of psychosis, but their efficacy has not been particularly impressive

L-dopa (a dopamine precursor) administered to Parkinsonian patients does not consistently worsen psychotic symptoms in individuals experiencing movement abnormalities along with hallucinations or delusions

amphetamines (which increase dopamine transmission indirectly, by causing catecholamines to be released from intraneuronal storage sites) do not consistently provoke psychotic symptoms

fifty years of research have failed to confirm the existence of any pre-medication dopamine "imbalance" in the serum, urine, or cerebrospinal fluid of individuals experiencing psychosis

Dopamine: Sources and Function

Dopamine is both a neurotransmitter and a peripheral hormone, produced by cells of the the **central nervous system, the ***sympathetic

---

**central nervous system – the brain and spinal cord

***sympathetic ganglia – groups of cell bodies arranged in a chainlike fashion on either side of the spinal cord; these cells release norepinephrine and regulate the processes of the central nervous system pertaining to "fight or flight" (dilation of the pupils, racing heart, increased respiration, sweating, activity of the skeletal muscles)

ganglia, and the *adrenal medulla. As a neurotransmitter, dopamine plays prominent roles in cognition (attention, learning, memory); motor events (the coordination of voluntary and involuntary movement); mood (pleasure, fear); and behavior (compulsions, stereotypies, addictions, desires). As a hormone, dopamine participates in the regulation of blood pressure, heart rate, cardiac output, fluid and sodium balance, gastric motility, lactation, fertility, and bone strength.

Because of its extensive distribution throughout the body, serum and urinary levels of dopamine and its metabolites cannot be used to estimate its activities in the brain. Furthermore, the existence of key metabolic enzymes (catecholamine-o-methyltransferase or COMT, and monoamine oxidase or MAO) in the liver and gut compromises the direct control of dopamine via dietary intake. As a result, the pharmacological manipulation of dopamine *neurotransmission* depends upon the use of chemical agents which affect its synthesis, breakdown, and receptor interactions within the brain.

Steps in the Synthesis, Release, & Metabolism of Dopamine[25-28]

The production of dopamine occurs in specific regions of the brain. The starting ingredient is tyrosine, a non-essential amino acid which is consumed in the diet or made within the body from phenylalanine. Tyrosine crosses the blood brain barrier and enters neurons, where it is used in the production of several neurotransmitters. When an appropriate stimulus is received by a dopamine-producing brain cell, tyrosine is converted to dopamine through a series of chemical reactions:

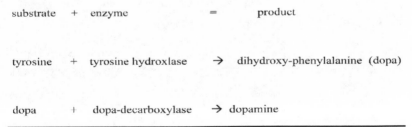

substrate	+	enzyme	=	product
tyrosine	+	tyrosine hydroxlase	→	dihydroxy-phenylalanine (dopa)
dopa	+	dopa-decarboxylase	→	dopamine

---

*adrenal medulla – a section of the adrenal gland, which is a small organ atop each kidney; the medulla synthesizes and secretes catecholamines, thereby performing a major role in homeostasis (e.g., cardiac and renal functions)

Inside each dopamine-producing neuron, there exist three discrete mechanisms for the control of cellular events: an impulse flow mechanism, through which electrical changes in the cell body stimulate the synthesis and secretion of dopamine; and two chemical mechanisms – one for synthesis, and one for release. These last two processes reflect the activity of autoreceptors (usually D2 receptors) which are located on the cell body, the dendrites, and the axon. When stimulated, these autoreceptors signal the neuron to stop or reduce the manufacture and release of dopamine.

Once dopamine has been synthesized inside the neuron, it is temporarily stored in special reservoirs. Within the nerve terminal, the storage sites consist of spherical bodies called vesicles. Dopamine enters these reservoirs through a special portal called the VMAT (vesicular monoamine transporter – more specifically, VMAT2). Inside the cell body and dendrites, however, dopamine is stored in a specialized cell component known as the smooth endoplasmic reticulum. The neurotransmitter remains inside these storage sites until the arrival of an electrical signal (the action potential – see chapter five). This sets off chemical changes, resulting in the release of dopamine from the neuron.

Following its release, the neurotransmitter undergoes a variety of physiological processes:

> **reuptake** into the pre-synaptic neuron (via the dopamine transporter, called DAT);

> **diffusion** to nearby cells and fluid reservoirs (bloodstream or CSF)

> **enzymatic degradation** inside or outside of neurons and glia; MAO and COMT catabolize dopamine into a primary metabolite called homovanillic acid (HVA), and into smaller amounts of dihydryoxyphenylacetic acid (DOPAC) and 3-methoxytyramine (3-MT).

> **receptor interaction** (pre-synaptic and post-synaptic); dopamine interacts with autoreceptors (D2, D3) on the pre-synaptic cell to modulate impulse flow, synthesis, and release; and with post-synaptic receptors (D1 – D5) on the surfaces of non-dopaminergic cells throughout the body

The Dopamine Neuron

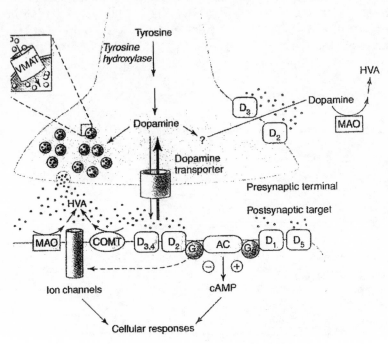

Source of picture: Eric J. Nestler, Steven E. Hyman, and Robert C. Malenka, *Molecular Neuropharmacology: A Foundation for Clinical Neuroscience*, (New York: The McGraw-Hill Companies, Inc., 2001), p. 177. Reproduced with permission of the McGraw Hill Companies.

This drawing depicts the nerve terminal of a dopamine-synthesizing neuron making contact with a post-synaptic neuron. These cells could be located in many regions of the brain: the retina, the olfactory bulb, the striatum, the cortex, or the hypothalamus. VMAT (top left) refers to the transporter protein through which dopamine is taken up into storage vesicles within the nerve terminal. D2 and D3 receptors are shown on the pre-synaptic neuron, where they function as autoreceptors to turn off or reduce the production and release of the neurotransmitter. Post-synaptic receptors (D1 through D5) are shown on the membrane (surface) of a second cell. This membrane might be located on a cell body, on a dendrite, or on the axon of another neuron. Once dopamine binds a post-synaptic receptor, it triggers a complex chain of events inside the next cell. The end result varies (more or less movement, attention, appetite, memory) depending upon the unique properties and location of the target neuron.

The net effects of dopamine depend upon many factors. These include the electrochemical events which arise from the stimulation or antagonism (blockade) of each dopamine receptor subtype (e.g., the activation or inhibition of 2nd and 3rd messenger systems, gene expression, and protein synthesis); the reciprocal interactions between dopamine and other neurotransmitters; and the locations where each of these processes occur. Part of the complexity of the dopamine system is revealed by its heterogeneous population of receptors, which are variably distributed throughout the body:

Dopamine Receptors and Their Location [*] [29-32]

	central nervous system	peripheral nervous system / somatic tissue
D1	hippocampus, neocortex nucleus accumbens, olfactory tubercle, retina, striatum, substantia nigra	kidney (nephron), parathyroid gland, vascular smooth muscle in kidneys &gut
D2	nucleus accumbens pituitary, retina, striatum, substantia nigra, ventral tegmentum, zona incerta	adrenal and pituitary glands sympathetic nerve terminals
D3	hippocampus, hypothalamus, nucleus accumbens, olfactory tubercle	
D4	amygdala, basal ganglia, frontal cortex, hippocampus, medulla, midbrain, striatum	heart, kidney
D5	hippocampus, hypothalamus, thalamus (parafascicular nucleus) other limbic structures	kidney

*Most of these locations are based upon research in rats. Studies in non-human primates have revealed only small amounts of D2 or D3 mRNA in the ventral tegmentum of the midbrain. Although human research on dopamine receptors in cardiac, renal, and other non-neural tissues has been limited, animal studies have detected D2 receptors on the heart muscle and coronary blood vessels. Their role has not yet been determined.

Dopamine Systems in the Brain

While the previous discussion has emphasized the molecular properties of the dopamine neuron (i.e., the "trees"), it is important to appreciate the larger systems through which these cells interact (i.e., the "forest"). Researchers have conducted extensive investigations in lab animals (mostly rats), subsequently confirming their findings in humans as relevant technologies have appeared (e.g., autoradiography and neuroimaging). Based upon this body of evidence, **four major pathways** of dopamine have been classified according to size (intermediate, and long), location, and cell type:

ultra-short pathways >>>>	associated cell populations
retina	inner and outer plexiform layers of the retina
olfactory bulb	periglomerular cells

intermediate pathways >>>>	associated cell populations
tubero-hypophyseal or "tubero-infundibular" (TIDA)	arcuate and periventricular nuclei of the hypothalamus, which connect to the median eminence and the pituitary gland
*incerto-hypothalamic	various regions within the hypothalamus, and hypothalamic projections to the lateral septal nuclei
*medullary periventricular	cells in the medulla, located in the nucleus tractus solitarius, the perimeter of of vagus nerve, and the periaqueductal gray

long pathways >>>>	associated cell populations
nigrostriatal	striatum (caudate, putamen), substantia nigra
mesolimbic	cells of the ventral tegmentum (VTA) communicate with various regions of the limbic system: amygdala, nucleus accumbens, olfactory tubercle, piriform complex, septum
mesocortical	cells of the ventral tegmentum (VTA) communicate with various regions of of the frontal and cingulate cortices

---

*ultra-short & intermediate pathways - (continued on next page)

Dopamine Distribution in the Human Brain

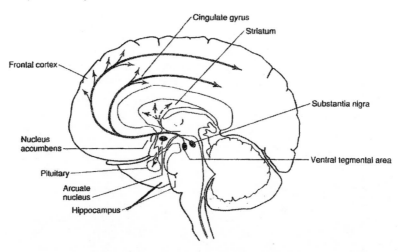

Source of picture: Eric J. Nestler, Steven E. Hyman, and Robert C. Malenka, *Molecular Neuropharmacology: A Foundation for Clinical Neuroscience,* (New York: The McGraw-Hill Companies, Inc., 2001), pp. 176. Reproduced with permission of the McGraw Hill Companies.

An understanding of the location and function of dopamine pathways in the brain is essential for the study of antipsychotic drugs, all of which affect dopamine receptors throughout the body. This picture shows the major pathways of the dopamine system in the human brain: the **nigrostriatal** pathway, the **mesolimbic** pathway, the **mesocortical** pathway, and the **tuberoinfundibular** pathway. Not shown are the ultra-short pathways in the retina or the olfactory bulb, nor the intermediate pathways of the hypothalamus and brainstem (medulla).

(continued from previous page) most textbooks of psychopharmacology do not mention these specific pathways; nevertheless, the effects of dopamine antagonists upon these regions of the central nervous system are important and not always benign

Like all medications, the actions of antipsychotic drugs depend upon their affinity for specific proteins (receptors). Although the first neuroleptics were characterized by their diverse behavioral effects (e.g., chlorpromazine received the name "Largactil" in Europe), advances in technology ultimately led to the characterization of drugs according to their ability to bind specific receptors. Most neuroleptics – typical and atypical – interact with such a broad range of receptors that it is difficult to predict the mechanisms which are responsible for clinical efficacy or adverse events:

Effects of Antipsychotics on Neurotransmitters/Receptors

Effects of Antipsychotics on Neurotransmitters/Receptors*

	Chlorpro-mazine	Methotrim-eprazine	Triflupro-mazine	Mesori-dazine	Pericya-zine	Pipota-zine	Thiorida-zine	Fluphe-nazine	Perphe-nazine	Thioprop-erazine	Trifluo-perazine	Zipra-sidone
Blockade D_1	+++	?	++	+++	?	?	+++	+++	+++	?	++	++
Blockade D_2	+++	+++	++++	++++	++++	+++++	++++	+++++	+++	+++++	+++++	++++
Blockade D_3	++++	?	?	?	?	+++++	++++	+++++	?	+++++	?	+++
Blockade D_4	++++	?	?	?	?	?	+++	++++	?	?	?	+++
Blockade H_1	+++	+++++	+++	++++	?	?	++++	+++	++++	+++	++	+++
Blockade M_1	+++	?	+++	+++	?	?	++++	+	+++	?	+	++++
Blockade α_1	+++	?	++++	+++	+	?	++++	+	+++	?	+++	++
Blockade α_2	++	?	?	+	?	?	+	+	+	?	+	+
Blockade $5\text{-}HT_{1A}$	+	+++	+	++	?	++	+	++++	++	+?	+	+++
Blockade $5\text{-}HT_{2A}$	++++	++++	++++	+++	?	+++	++++	+++	++++	++	+++	++++
DA reuptake	+	?	?	?	?	?	+	+	+	?	?	?

	Haloperidol	Loxapine	Molin-done	Pimozide	Flupen-thixol	Thiothi-xene	Zuclo-penthixol	Cloza-pine	Risperi-done	Olanza-pine	Quetia-pine
Blockade D_1	+++	+++	+	++	+++	+++	+++	+++	+++	+++	+
Blockade D_2	+++++	++++	+++	++++	++++	++++	++++	+++	++++	+++	++
Blockade D_3	+++	?	?	+++	+++	?	?	++	++	+++	++
Blockade D_4	+++++	++++	+	+++	+++	?	++++	++++	++++	++++	+
Blockade H_1	+	+++	–	+	+++	++	++	+++	+++	++++	+++
Blockade M_1	+	++	–	+	+++	+	?	++++	–	++++	+++
Blockade α_1	+++	+++	+	+++	+++	++	++	++++	+++	++++	+++
Blockade α_2	+	+	+	?	+	+	+	+++	+++	++	++
Blockade $5\text{-}HT_{1A}$	+	+	+	+	+	+	?	?	++	+	?
Blockade $5\text{-}HT_{2A}$	++	+++	+	+++	++++	+++	+++	++++	+++++	+++	++
DA reuptake	+	?	?	++	++	+	++	+	+	?	?

* The ratio of K_i values between various neurotransmitters/receptors determines the pharmacological profile for any one drug.
Key: K_i (nM) > 100,000 = –; 10,000–100,000 = +/–; 1000–10,000 = +; 100–1000 = ++; 10–100 = +++; 1–10 = ++++; 0.1–1 = +++++
$1/K_i$ < 0.001 = –; .001–.01 = +/–; .1–1 = +; 1–10 = ++; 10–100 = +++; 100–1000 = ++++; 1000–1000 = +++++
See p. 87 for Pharmacological Effects on Neurotransmitters.

Source: Kalnya Z. Bezchlibnyk-Butler and J. Joel Jeffries, *Clinical Handbook of Psychotropic Drugs*, 13th Revised Edition, (Cambridge, Massachusetts: Hogrefe & Huber, 2003), p. 98. Reproduced with permission of Hogrefe & Huber.

173

Mechanisms of Action

Cellular Effects

Despite this enormously complex array of drug-receptor interactions, most textbooks of pharmacology discuss the therapeutic actions of antipsychotic drugs in terms of dopamine and dopamine receptor blockade. **During the acute phase of treatment (hours to days), antipsychotic medications increase the synthesis and release of dopamine.** Researchers believe that the underlying mechanism for this effect is the blockade of autoreceptors (D2) located on the cell body, the dendrites, or the nerve terminals of cells which produce dopamine. By blocking these receptors, the antipsychotics turn off a negative (inhibitory) feedback loop.

One of the difficulties in studying the effects of medications which influence dopamine, however, is the fact that D2 receptors are located pre-synaptically (autoreceptor function on dopamine neurons) and post-synaptically (heteroreceptor function on non-dopamine neurons). The net effect of any dopamine-modulating therapy depends upon which part of the dopamine circuit prevails. For example, when dopamine antagonists are administered in low doses, studies have demonstrated a predominant pre-synaptic effect which leads to an *increase* in the synthesis and release of dopamine. At higher doses, however, post-synaptic effects become predominant. This leads to an overall *reduction* in dopamine transmission (based upon the effects within the post-synaptic neurons).

As drug therapy continues, the receptors themselves begin to change. Prolonged dopamine blockade induces an increase in the production of dopamine receptors. This has been demonstrated most consistently for the D2 receptor. (In fact, the upregulation of the D2 receptor has been by offered by some theorists as a possible cause of tardive phenomena and drug withdrawal effects.) To the extent that autoreceptors themselves become more numerous with extended treatment, dopamine may interact with these sites to restore negative feedback activity (in other words, to inhibit dopamine transmission).

Superimposed on all of these chemical changes (pre-synaptic vs. post-synaptic) are the electrophysiological events which arise from drug therapy. Animal studies suggest that the **prolonged**

administration of antipsychotics (dopamine antagonists) **induces a state of depolarization block.** This refers to an intracellular condition marked by the inability of new stimuli to trigger the conduction of electrical impulses. In other words, following prolonged treatment with an antipsychotic drug, certain cells of the brain experience a kind of electrical paralysis: action potentials cease to conduct.

While staying mindful of the limitations inherent in these hypotheses (i.e., findings limited to studies of rodents), it is possible to summarize the presumed effects of antipsychotic drug therapies: *with acute or short term therapy*, antipsychotics appear to exert a net increase in the transmission of dopamine by stimulating the synthesis and release of the neurotransmitter. *With chronic therapy*, however, electrical and chemical events reverse. Dopamine transmission declines. Exceptions[33] are thought to exist in specific areas of the brain (e.g., the frontal and cingulate cortices), where antipsychotics may produce a prolonged enhancement of dopamine activity – a result, according to some theorists, of a lack of depolarization blockade, or an absence of significant autoreceptor activity in the neurons which project to these cortical zones. Although some investigators speculate that the neocortex is relatively immune to the effects of antipsychotic medications for these reasons, such assertions have not been verified in human subjects. Furthermore, the consequences of sustained, artificial elevations in dopamine release have been neither well studied, nor explained.

The Effect of Drugs Upon the Dopamine Pathways of the Brain

Because the prevailing consensus in psychiatry asserts that antipsychotic efficacy depends upon the antagonism of the dopamine receptor (specifically, the D2 subtype), it is important to examine the effects of medications upon each dopamine pathway in the brain.

Mesocortical and Mesolimbic Pathways

Following the demise of the "Parkinsonian theory" of therapeutic action, pharmacologists came to ascribe the efficacy of antipsychotic drugs to dopamine blockade within the **mesolimbic** and **mesocortical** circuits of the brain. The **mesocortical** pathway refers to connections between the *midbrain* (ventral tegmental area) and the *cortex* (frontal cortex, cingulate gyrus, entorhinal cortex, and other areas). Cortical functions include attention, consciousness, planning, impulse control, and many aspects of learning and memory (e.g, working, long term or remote, and episodic). Antipsychotics which augment dopamine activity within these networks are believed to improve cognition, mood, behavior, and mood.

The term **mesolimbic** refers to connections between cells of the *midbrain* (**meso-** for *middle*) and the *limbic system*. Limbic (from the Latin limbus, meaning border) refers to a variety structures which surround the brainstem, including the amygdala, fornix, hippocampus, hypothalamus, mamillary bodies, nucleus accumbens, and septal nuclei. Together, these brain structures coordinate human emotions, drives (instincts), and moods, as well as many aspects of learning and memory (e.g., autobiographical and emotional).

Within the mesolimbic pathway, the nucleus accumbens has received prominent attention. Often termed the "reward" center of the brain, the nucleus accumbens is regarded as a key locus for motivation, appetite, addiction, learning (conditioning), and survival (fight or flight response under conditions of severe stress). Recently, a prominent researcher at the University of Toronto has proposed that antipsychotic effects (anti-hallucination, anti-delusion) might be understood in terms of a dampening or reduction of inappropriate attention. According to this theory, psychosis arises from "aberrant motivational salience." This means that the person experiencing psychosis has come to attach an inappropriate significance to external objects or internal representations.[34] According to this view, antipsychotics are ameliorative when they create a state of psychic indifference (i.e., the chemical lobotomy first noted by Laborit and his contemporaries), dissipating the organism's attention to an object which has assumed a contextually inordinate degree of value.

> **"Symptom resolution may have much in common with the mechanisms whereby all humans give up on cherished beliefs or frightening dreads, and it may**

involve processes of extinction, encapsulation, and belief
transformation – fundamentally psychological concepts.
Thus, antipsychotics do not excise symptoms; rather,
they attenuate the salience of the distressing ideas and
percepts, allowing patients to reach their own private
resolution of these matters."[35]

If this hypothesis is correct, it predicts several problems attending
the current drug therapies – none of which possesses the ability
to *selectively* restrict the salience of stimuli. In other words, if it
is possible for an antipsychotic medication to blunt the salience
of hallucinations and delusions, it is equally possible for the same
drug to blunt the salience of *enjoyable* stimuli (such as sex, food,
exercise, or non-medicinal drugs). The heavy smoking behaviors
of many patients diagnosed with schizophrenia might well reflect
their attempts to restore the hedonic (pleasurable) effects of
those pursuits, by stimulating nicotine receptors in the nucleus
accumbens.

It is no less certain that a medication which blunts the salience of
psychotic features would avoid blunting the salience of painful or
aversive stimuli. To the extent that this is true, psychiatrists should
probably contemplate the prevalence of "silent ischemia" and other
masked pathologies among their medicated patients. It is possible
that the abnormal findings on EKGs (electrocardiographs) which
frequently arise during antipsychotic therapy are far too quickly
dismissed as clinically irrelevant whenever a patient is deemed
asymptomatic. Indeed, most published reviews on the subject of
drug-induced abnormalities specifically *encourage* psychiatrists to
ignore such changes, based upon a patient's denial of subjective
discomfort. Such professional apathy might well contribute to
the excess morbidity and mortality which has been demonstrated
among patients receiving chronic antipsychotic drug therapy (see
below). Since the absence of pain can reflect a central or peripheral
neuropathy (i.e., an abnormality in a nerve's ability to transmit
messages) or a defect in the central processing of pain signals (e.g.,
the effects of dopamine blockade in the nucleus accumbens, the
putamen, or the thalamus), it is entirely possible that antipsychotic
medications directly compromise perceptions of pain or other
somatic problems. By doing so, the drug treatments potentially
undermine survival strategies which might otherwise be used by

patients to alert their health care providers to the presence of underlying pathologies.[36-39]

Nigrostriatal and Tuberoinfundibular Pathways

The **nigrostriatal** pathway refers to the projections from the **substantia nigra** (another midbrain structure) to the **striatum** (deep, subcortical structures, called the caudate and the putamen). A number of adverse side effects are believed to arise from the blockade of D2 receptors in these locations, including drug-induced parkinsonism (tremor, slowness of movement, shuffling gait, reduced emotional expression) and the persistent abnormalities of tardive dyskinesia or TD (see below). Although the precise mechanisms for these disturbances have not been clarified, what has improved is the scientific appreciation of the complexity of the nigrostriatal system. Where, previously, this pathway was felt to be limited to the control of voluntary movement, contemporary discoveries have expanded its list of functions. Based partly upon the identification of connections between the striatum and various regions of the cortex (e.g., the visual cortex and the association cortices), and based also upon research in behavioral neurology (suggesting the striatum's involvement in procedural memory), it now seems appropriate to incorporate the basal ganglia into neuroscience models of cognitive functioning.[40]

The **tuberoinfundibular** pathway refers to the connections between specific regions of the hypothalamus (i.e., the arcuate and the periventricular nuclei) and the anterior pituitary gland. Under ordinary conditions, dopamine is released by specific neurons of the hypothalamus, traveling to the median eminence (also a hypothalamic structure). Dopamine then enters the portal circulation and travels through the bloodstream to the anterior pituitary. By binding to receptors on specific pituitary cells (lactotrophs), dopamine suppresses the release of prolactin. Antipsychotic drugs reverse this sequence of events, leading to the sustained release of prolactin (hyperprolactinemia) and many associated physiological difficulties (see below).

"Minor" Dopamine Pathways

Omitted from the textbooks of pharmacology are discussions of the peripheral effects of dopamine antagonism upon the kidneys and heart. Also omitted are the effects of antipsychotics upon the *so-called minor pathways* of dopamine in the brain, such as the short systems within the retina, the hypothalamus, and the medulla. Furthermore, although the mesolimbic system receives abundant attention, few writings refer to the extensive signals which reach one part of it – the hypothalamus – from the midbrain, the striatum, and the cortex. To put it simply, large networks of neurophysiology are consistently neglected in the discussion of medication effects, leading to a pervasive disregard of many problems which are associated with antipsychotic drug therapies: visual disturbances (retinopathies and photosensitivity – especially with first generation neuroleptics); metabolic irregularities (weight gain, thirst, hyperglycemia, and malignant hyperthermia); and autonomic dysfunction (respiratory dyskinesias, hemodynamic instability, hiccoughs, incontinence, and vomiting). With few exceptions, these lesser pathways have been ignored, much to the peril of the quality and quantity of patients' lives.

Long Term Structural Changes in the Brain

No discussion of antipsychotic effects would be complete without mentioning the *structural changes* which accompany prolonged treatment. As neuroscientists have only recently emphasized, drug therapies alter not only the function but also the **anatomy** of the human brain. This rather startling realization has inspired two prevalent reactions by the psychiatric profession: first, a tendency to applaud the drugs ("chemically induced neural plasticity") whenever such changes are perceived to be helpful; second, a tendency to blame the patient (an underlying "disease process") whenever structural changes are regarded as harmful. While it is premature to comment upon the theories and consequences of neural plasticity (do synaptic changes reflect the brain's response to injury? if synapses are constantly undergoing repair, how does one isolate the unique effects of drugs? is neural plasticity uniformly beneficial?), a substantial volume of research supports the concern that antipsychotic medications are potentially very toxic to the brain.

Anatomical Changes in Lab Animals

Animal research has permitted the manipulation and observation of drug-induced changes in neuroanatomy, without the confounding influence of pre-existing neuropsychiatric conditions. **Based upon cellular analyses of tissue samples from monkeys and rats, antipsychotics have been repeatedly shown to alter the size, density, and properties of the neurons and glia.** Following chronic exposure to neuroleptics, rat brains have shown consistent *reductions in neuronal density within the striatum* (due to neuronal loss or striatal enlargement), as well as *alterations in the structure and properties of synapses within the striatum and the frontal cortex.* Some, but not all, of these changes have persisted even after medication consumption stopped. While fewer studies have been conducted in primates, architectural changes have been noted there, as well. In a study of rhesus monkeys which examined cellular changes after six months of exposure to antipsychotic drugs (typical and atypical), glial cells were found to proliferate, and the prefrontal cortex became significantly enlarged.[41]

Anatomical Changes in Humans

The psychiatric profession has been reluctant to acknowledge anatomical changes arising from pharmacotherapy in humans. Structural changes in the brains of medicated patients have been attributed either to the presence of an underlying neurological disorder (by those who believe that schizophrenia is a disease of aberrant maturation or cell connectivity), or to a neurodegenerative disease (by those who believe that schizophrenia represents a pathological condition which necessarily deteriorates over time). Both of these perspectives remain contestable for several reasons: 1) a lack of *consistent* findings to distinguish the brains of "schizophrenics" from "normal" controls; 2) a lack of *robust* findings (e.g., the small effect sizes in neuroimaging studies raise doubts about their clinical significance) to distinguish schizophrenics from normal controls; and 3) a lack of *normative standards* (some studies have found no differences between previously unmedicated patients and their healthy relatives or other healthy controls).[42-43]

Because of these limitations, it has become increasingly important to note areas of correspondence between inter-species research, and between different levels of inquiry (macroscopic studies, using neuroimaging or gross anatomical inspection; and microscopic studies, using the tools of dissection, immunocytochemistry, and electron microscopy). By synthesizing research findings in this way, a more coherent picture of drug effects begins to emerge. *At the very best*, the available evidence suggests that antipsychotic medications (old and new) fail to reverse the structural abnormalities which many theorists associate with schizophrenia. *At the very worst*, the evidence suggests that current drug therapies actually precipitate or potentiate the anatomical features which are linked to cognitive, behavioral, and social dysfunction.

In what may be the only published study to compare brain tissue from medicated and unmedicated subjects, Jellinger[44] reported the neuropathological findings of 56 individuals who had been diagnosed with schizophrenia. Post-mortem analyses revealed significant **enlargement and scarring in the caudate** of the chronically neuroleptized (89% with gliosis and swelling in large neurons) versus 4% of the subjects who had avoided treatment with antipsychotic drugs. Today, such a study would be impossible to conduct, due to the fact that the non-pharmacological management of psychiatric conditions (at least within the United States) has lost institutional support. The closest substitute for this kind of analysis has become the neuroimaging study in which "first-episode" or new "psychotics" are compared to patients who have received previous or continuing drug treatment:

Neuroimaging Studies and Frontal Lobe Changes[45-48]

Gur et. al.   MRI study of 20 first-episode and 20 previously treated schizophrenics
                 compared to 17 healthy controls. Scans were obtained at two points
                 in time (follow-up scan occurred 2 to 3 years later). Findings were
                 significant for smaller frontal and temporal lobes in patients, relative to
                 controls. **Reductions in frontal and temporal lobe volumes progressed**
                 in patients, despite continued treatment with antipsychotic therapy.
                 Temporal lobe reductions were also seen in healthy controls. In first-
                 episode patients, higher neuroleptic dose was correlated with greater
                 reduction in frontal and temporal lobe volumes, smaller improvement on
                 some symptoms (affect, alogia, avolition, bizarre behavior), and relative
                 worsening on neuropsychological functioning. Previously treated patients
                 did not show clear correlations between brain volume reductions and
                 neuropsychological change.

Ho et. al.   Longitudinal MRI study of 73 recent onset schizophrenic patients and
                 23 controls, followed-up at three years (mean duration of follow-up).
                 Patients displayed progressive reduction in frontal lobe white
                 matter *which correlated with greater negative symptoms.* **Frontal**
                 lobe reductions worsened over three years, despite active
                 treatment with antipsychotic drug therapy.

Madsen   Prospective CT study of 21 first episode schizophrenics and 19
et. al.   controls (10 with other psychiatric disorders, 9 healthy volunteers).
                 Head scans were performed at first hospitalization, and again
                 five years later. Sulcal enlargement was noted at the time of
                 first treatment. **Frontal and central brain atrophy progressed in**
                 schizophrenic patients, regardless of response to treatment. Atrophy
                 was positively correlated to lifetime dose of neuroleptics, with
                 estimated risk of atrophy increasing 6.4% per 10 grams of neuroleptic
                 consumed.

Neuroimaging Studies and Nigrostriatal Changes[49-52]

Chakos et. al.	MRI study of 29 first-episode schizophrenic patients, studied over eighteen months. Patients received typical neuroleptics. **Caudate volumes increased approximately 6%.** Higher amounts of medication were positively correlated with striatal enlargement.
Corson et. al.	MRI study of 23 male patients with schizophrenia spectrum disorders followed for period of two years. Patients were retrospectively divided into two groups according to predominant treatment. **Mean basal ganglia volume of patients receiving neuroleptics increased over two years;** basal ganglia volume in patients receiving atypicals declined. Study design did not permit answer about cause of shrinkage (result of withdrawal from first-generation antipsychotic, or direct effect of atypical drugs).
Lang et. al.	MRI study involving 37 patients with schizophrenia and 23 healthy volunteers. **Basal ganglia volumes at baseline were larger in patients (chronically medicated) compared to controls.** After transition to olanzapine (atypical antipsychotic), patients were re-scanned. Volumes in the basal ganglia (putamen and globus pallidus) declined.
Scheepers et. al.	MRI study of 28 patients who had failed treatment with typical antipsychotics. Twenty-two subjects completed study, involving transition to clozapine for one year. **Left caudate volume decreased in 16 patients who responded to treatment** (response defined as 20% improvement in clinician rated symptom scale). No changes were seen in 6 patients who remained unresponsive to treatment.

It is quite likely that the inconsistencies which have plagued the field of psychiatric neuroimaging will continue indefinitely, either because the methods themselves are inherently unreliable (e.g., different investigators may be defining and measuring brain regions differently); or because the suppositions about the existence of radiographically identifiable and identical neuropathologies are, themselves, erroneous.

"Indeed, the literature on progressive volumetric brain changes during the longitudinal course of schizophrenia seems to be conflicting...'no [two] (longitudinal) studies have found the same pattern of changes across all of these measures, and each study seems to have its own unique combination of results.'"[53]

It may be that histological and biochemical investigations will continue to generate the clearest insights into antipsychotic mechanisms of action. In the area of drug toxicity, this certainly appears to be true.

Approximately forty years after its market introduction, neuroscientists discovered that haloperidol (Haldol) is metabolized by the liver and brain into pyridinium metabolites (HPP+ and RHPP+). The importance of this finding lies in the structural similarity between the breakdown products of the neuroleptic, and the breakdown product of a street drug called MPTP (methyl-phenyl-tetrahydropyridine). A synthetic opiate, MPTP achieved fame in the summer of 1982, following an epidemic of what appeared to be Parkinson's disease among young heroin addicts.[54] In time, animal studies revealed that the street drug was a pro-toxin for dopamine neurons. Researchers determined that MPTP enters the brain where it undergoes conversion to the pyridinium metabolite MPP+. (This transition has been shown to occur in the astrocytes of non-human primates.) Further research revealed that MPP+ binds to the dopamine transporter, enters the nerve terminal, and kicks off a sequence of events (via reactive oxygen species) culminating in the death of the dopamine neuron.[55] Because the cells of the substantia nigra are particularly sensitive to MPP+, the synthetic heroin users experienced symptoms identical to Parkinson's disease. With the discovery of HPP+ (the pyridinium metabolite) in the plasma, urine, and brain tissue of haloperidol patients; and with the further recognition that the levels of this metabolite have often corresponded to the severity of Parkinsonian symptoms, neuroscientists have proposed the existence of a similar process in the basal ganglia of patients exposed to the neuroleptic.[56-60]

Reactive Oxygen Species & Oxidative Damage

The potential neurotoxicity of *all* antipsychotic drugs has been a taboo subject for psychiatry. Although the phenomenon of *oxidative stress *has* been mentioned in the professional literature,

---

*oxidative stress – a term for the collective effects of *reactive oxygen species* or *ROS* (e.g., the superoxide radical, the hydroxyl radical, hydrogen peroxide, nitric oxide, singlet oxygen), all of which impair energy production, cell membrane integrity,...(continued on next page)

discussions there have been limited to the basal ganglia and the problem of TD (tardive dyskinesia). One must wonder, though, about the existence of these same toxic processes in other regions of the brain.

Oxidative damage arising from neuroleptic therapy has been demonstrated in animal tissue and cell cultures for at least ten years.[61-63] It has also been *suggested by findings in human consumers of antipsychotic drugs. For example, in a study of 20 subjects[64] who had been medicated chronically for schizophrenia, researchers analyzed the spinal fluid for biochemical markers of oxidative stress. All of the patients demonstrated higher levels of excitatory amino acids (e.g., aspartate and glutamate) and lower levels of protective antioxidants (e.g., superoxide dismutase), relative to a group of healthy controls. These chemical features corresponded to the severity of the patients' movement abnormalities, prompting the investigators to propose a role for oxidative damage in the pathogenesis of TD (tardive dyskinesia).

Oxidative damage has been demonstrated more directly in post-mortem analyses of brain tissue. In a study of ten elderly patients diagnosed with "poor outcome" schizophrenia, researchers found evidence of oxidized DNA in cells of the hippocampus.[65] Although each patient's history of medical therapy was not emphasized in this investigation, the results were nonetheless important for the identification of a cytotoxic process in a location (temporal lobe) that is not typically reviewed.

(contined from previous page)...and/or the structure and function of DNA. Oxidative stress in the body accelerates with ageing, due to the accumulation of oxidizing agents (ROS) and a reduced capacity to neutralize their effects through the activity of *antioxidants* (superoxide dismuatase, glutathione peroxidase, catalase). The end result is tissue damage via necrosis (degeneration) or apoptosis (programmed cell death).

* suggested – many studies in human subjects fail to control for the effects of smoking, which introduces reactive oxygen species of its own. However, animal studies clearly demonstrate the capacity of phenothiazines, butyrophenones, and most of the newer drugs to induce pro-oxidant species, albeit in variable distributions of the brain. These findings cannot be attributed to cigarettes, since they have occurred in non-smoking rats.

The potential for antipsychotic drugs to incite diffuse injury throughout the brain (or at least, beyond the basal ganglia) has been suggested by a variety of laboratory investigations. In one such study,[66] researchers detected reactive oxygen species in the brains of rats following exposure to both typical *and* atypical antipsychotic drugs. Of particular note was the induction of oxidative changes in the striatum (haloperidol) and also in the hippocampus (haloperidol and clozapine). Similarly, *in vitro* analyses of cell lines (tissue cultures) have documented the capacity of many antipsychotics (haloperidol, chlorpromazine, thiothixene and clozapine) to impede cellular respiration, due to the impact of reactive oxygen species upon the mitochondrial electron transport chain.[67] Given the established relationship between oxidative free radicals, tissue damage (particularly, in the heart and brain), and reduced longevity,[68] the cytotoxic profile of any pharmacological therapy would have understandably significant effects upon treatment efficacy and safety. Unfortunately, these toxicities have been largely ignored in the training of psychiatrists. As a consequence, they have not been discussed with the average health care consumer.

Efficacy and Effectiveness

According to the American Psychiatric Association's *Textbook of Psychiatry*, "antipsychotic medications are effective agents for the treatment of a variety of psychotic symptoms, such as hallucinations, delusions, and thought disorder, regardless of etiology....The most common indications for the use of antipsychotic drugs are in the treatment of acute psychosis and the maintenance of a remission of psychotic symptoms in patients with schizophrenia. ...The atypical antipsychotics – clozapine, risperidone, and olanzapine – appear to be at least as effective as the older medications for the treatment of positive symptoms and more efficacious for the treatment of negative symptoms of schizophrenia."[69] A similar enthusiasm is conveyed by the *Massachusetts General Hospital Handbook of General Hospital Psychiatry*: "We are currently in the midst of a remarkable period in antipsychotic drug development, with superior efficacy for psychotic symptoms well established for the atypical agent, clozapine, and impressive evidence mounting for the therapeutic advantages offered by olanzapine, risperidone, and several new agents that are at various stages in premarketing trials...Psychotic symptoms usually improve with antipsychotic medication, regardless of cause...Negative symptoms (apathy, flat affect, social isolation, and poverty of speech) generally are less responsive than psychotic symptoms, although modest improvement is quite common, particularly with atypical agents."[70] A third leading text – this one, specializing in psychopharmacology – tells readers that "the relocation of treatment from chronic hospital settings to outpatient community mental health centers [was], in great part, due to the efficacy of antipsychotics. Naturalistic studies done before the era of psychotropics revealed that 2/3 of psychotic patients spent most of their lives in state asylums. After the introduction of antipsychotics, there was a marked reduction in those hospitalized for various psychoses. While the antipsychotics have not been a panacea, they [have made] community based care a reality for many who would otherwise have remained chronically institutionalized."[71] In addition to the fiction that psychiatric drugs were responsible for the emptying of the world's asylums, such paeans to antipsychotic efficacy have inspired the dissemination of other mythologies, including:

> ➤ the belief that unmedicated psychosis is somehow injurious to the brain

> *Refuted by the lack of an association between "duration of untreated psychosis," neurocognitive and neuropsychological functioning, and brain appearance in neuroimaging studies.*[72-76]

> ➤ the belief that delayed drug therapy impedes recovery and complicates a patient's overall clinical course

> *Refuted by the efficacy of psychotherapy in many patients who avoid or postpone exposure to antipsychotic drugs.*[77-79]

> ➤ the belief that schizophrenia is a progressive, deteriorating brain disease requiring lifelong medical (pharmacological) therapy

> *Refuted by long term outcome studies in Europe and Vermont, and by the recovery rates in undeveloped countries (World Health Organization research)*

> *wherein half to two-thirds of all patients diagnosed with schizophrenia experience full or significant recoveries.*[80-83]

Promulgated by the opinion leaders in the field of industrialized psychiatry, and echoed at every opportunity by their sycophants in the lecture halls, the professional journals, and the news media, each of these notions has now attained the force of cultural credo. If this misinformation campaign has succeeded at anything, it has been the perpetuation of biopsychiatry's already long history of "bad science, bad medicine, and the enduring mistreatment of the mentally ill."[84]

In contrast to the assertion that "antipsychotic drugs emptied the asylums," the historical record demonstrates that these changes occurred globally[85] for a variety of reasons. While pharmacological discoveries may have improved symptoms in some patients, encouraging their caretakers to consider the termination of lengthy confinements, it was the complex interplay of economic, social, and medical forces which led to the experiment of deinstitutionalization. In the United Kingdom, the census of the state hospitals decreased well before the appearance of chlorpromazine, peaking at about one million residents in 1930 and declining steadily through 1954. On the continent of Europe, however, the arrival of the neuroleptic coincided with a two-decade rise in the inpatient census in Spain (1960-1975). Similarly, the number of psychiatric beds (a marker for admissions) increased in many other countries between 1950 and 1975:[86]

Percent Increase in Psychiatric Beds

Belgium	38%	(1951-1960)
Czechoslavakia	27%	(1953-1963)
East Germany	21%	(1962-1974)
Finland	115%	(1951-1975)
Italy	28%	(1954-1961)
Norway	53%	(1951-1962)
Sweden	15%	(1952-1962)
West Germany	10%	(1953-1963)

Within the United States, while it is true that the state hospital census declined between 1955 and 1960 (558,000 vs. 528,800), it would be hyperbole to suggest that this 5% change amounted to an "emptying" of the wards. Changes in the American system of mental health care were primarily an outgrowth of social and economic reforms, rather than a reflection of miracle drug cures. In the 1950s, the profession of social work took the lead in the monitoring and case management of discharged patients, many of whom had experienced short-term hospitalizations within the Veterans Administration following the Second World War. By providing continuity of care in the areas of individual and family psychotherapy, vocational and social rehabilitation, and the coordination of housing, legal, medical, and transportation needs, it was the social workers who demonstrated that community treatment models could succeed.[87] Although the influence of the social work profession is generally unacknowledged in the textbooks of psychiatry, it is doubtful that deinstitutionalization could have advanced without it. In 1963, the U.S. federal government offered to assume financial responsibility for the mentally ill who were no longer housed within state hospitals. This provided a substantial incentive for local governments to release patients to nursing homes, shelters, or other alternative facilities.[88] Next, the anti-psychiatry and social psychiatry movements took hold in the 1960s, fueling a temporary interest in experimental treatment milieus (such as halfway houses) and also engendering the creation of community health clinics. Finally, in 1972, an amendment to the Social Security Act[89] authorized disability payments to the mentally ill. It was the collective effect of these and later forces which led to collapse of state hospitals within America, although some observers have astutely commented that it was the psychiatrists, and not the patients, who were ultimately deinstitutionalized.[90] While the neuroleptics may have hastened the pace of community transfers for some individuals, the drugs were seldom able to restore former asylum residents to a level of independent social or occupational functioning. Subsequently, as the funding of vocational and other rehabilitative programs was systematically dismantled by a series of unenlightened politicians, America's mentally ill fell through the cracks and into a new kind of institutionalization: the correctional system.

Just as political and cultural institutions have failed the mentally ill, so too, have professional opinions about the kinds of interventions which appear to be most helpful. The efficacy and effectiveness of antipsychotic medications continue to be mischaracterized by many practitioners in the mental health field, and by those who do not appreciate the scope of these distortions. A contributing factor to this confusion has been the failure of most commentators to attend to the distinction between *efficacy*, which refers to short-term evidence of *some kind* of effect (the FDA's notion of efficacy being "proof in principle" that a psychotropic drug actually works); and *effectiveness*, which refers to long-term improvements or, ideally, to full recovery. For more than fifty years, the clinical trial literature on antipsychotic utility has emphasized *efficacy*, to the near total exclusion of drug *effectiveness*. A 1998 report prepared by researchers in the U.K. analyzed the features of 2000 controlled trials conducted over the preceding five decades, all focusing upon the treatment of schizophrenia and other non-affective psychoses.[91] Research methodologies were rated according to the quality of randomization, blinding procedures, and the handling of patient attrition (early termination, loss to follow-up). Findings were remarkable for the following:

> ➤ overall quality of reporting was low; 4% of the trials described methods of treatment allocation (i.e., how patients were assigned to the experimental vs. control groups); 22% of the trials described blinding procedures; 42% of the trials described treatment withdrawals

> ➤ trial size was generally small (65 patients or less) raising concerns about the statistical power of each study

> ➤ duration of each trial was limited; 54% lasting six weeks or less; 19% lasting six months or more

> ➤ pharmacotherapy was emphasized; 86% of the trials evaluated the effects of 437 different drugs

> ➤ assessment techniques were inconsistent; 25% of the trials did not use rating scales; of the 75% of the trials which did use rating scales, more than 600 different instruments were employed

When, on rare occasion, the results of long-term (or catamnestic) outcome studies have appeared, the research has consistently supported the view that antipsychotics do more to impede, rather than facilitate, the recovery and longevity of many patients. Moreover, the low quality of the clinical trials which have pervaded the psychiatric literature has contributed to a body of evidence (evidence *biased* psychiatry) whose validity and clinical relevance remain contestable.

In the face of such professional ambiguity, it is difficult to determine the best way of discerning the "true" benefits of antipsychotic drug therapy. Consumers and providers are left with the task of critically assessing the available evidence, despite its flaws and limitations. This demands close attention to the ways in which drugs have traditionally been appraised:

1) by their capacity to remove or blunt the symptoms of psychosis and schizophrenia, otherwise known as syndromal recovery

2) by their capacity to prevent relapse, once symptomatic improvement has been achieved;

3) by their capacity to produce *functional repair, such as social and occupational competence.

Each of these three elements – syndromal improvement, relapse prevention, and functional change – has been discussed in the research literature **quantitatively**, in terms of the numbers of patients who respond to a particular drug therapy, or in terms of the overall size or intensity of the response; and **qualitatively**, in terms of the kinds of patients who appear to respond (i.e., patients with first episode psychosis or early schizophrenia vs. patients with chronic or relapsing symptoms) and the timing of the response (i.e., efficacy = immediate or short-term capacity to achieve a symptomatic response; effectiveness = immediate or delayed capacity to deliver a sustained and/or full response). *As the following section will elaborate, the antipsychotic drugs have demonstrated a moderate but uneven record of treatment efficacy, but a poor record of clinical effectiveness.*

Historically, the quantitative evaluation of antipsychotic drug efficacy has involved the use of specific rating scales, completed by clinicians in the conduct of clinical trials in order to rank the intensity of symptoms over time. These assessment instruments, which are seldom seen or employed by clinicians outside of research settings, include:[92-96]

---

*The concept of *functional recovery* has received very little attention since the 1970s. This is probably a reflection of two developments within American psychiatry following the adoption of *DSM-III*: first, a tendency to emphasize things transient and superficial (symptoms and neuron receptors) rather than lasting and profound (functionality and psychosocial context); second, a tendency to adopt a neo-**Kraepelin**ian attitude of therapeutic pessimism, emulating the German neuropsychiatrist who claimed that recovery from psychosis was highly unlikely.

the BPRS
(Brief Psychiatric Rating Scale):

an 18 or 24 item rating scale, scored from 0 to 6 (some researchers convert the scale to 1 to 7, in order to simplify statistical calculations) 0 = not present, 1 = very mild, 2 = mild, 3 = moderate, 4 = moderately severe, 5 = severe, 6 = extremely severe. Items include: somatic concern, anxiety, emotional withdrawal, mannerisms, grandiosity, depressive mood, motor retardation, blunted affect, disorientation, self-neglect, motor hyperactivity

the PANSS
(the Positive and Negative Syndrome Scale):

a thirty symptom checklist scored from 1 to 7 (1 = absent, 7 = extreme). Symptoms include aggression, thought disturbance, depression, delusions, hallucinations, excitement, grandiosity, suspiciousness

the SANS
(Scale for the Assessment of Negative Symptoms):

a survey instrument which assesses five symptom complexes scored from 0 to 5 (0 = not at all, 5 = severe). Complexes include affective blunting, alogia (impoverished speech), avolition/apathy, anhedonia/asociality, disturbance of attention

the CGI
(Clinical Global Impression):

A three item scale used to assess overall treatment response in psychiatric patients; items include Severity of Illness (scored from 1 = normal to 7 = extremely ill); Global Improvement (1 = very much improved, 7 = very much worse); and Efficacy Index (four point scale, 1 = no therapeutic effect)

Having defined the major dimensions and rating instruments which have been used to appraise the treatment effects of antipsychotic medications , it is now possible to address the following question: how successful are they?

Dimension #1:
Syndromal or Symptomatic Improvement

The Neuroleptics: Conventional Antipsychotics

The conventional or "typical" antipsychotics were approved for the market before the existence of a regulatory standard which required new drugs to outperform placebo in at least two randomized controlled trials (RCTs). Although the first studies performed by Deniker and others in Europe proclaimed magical effects for chlorpromazine in the treatment of the chronically ill (including an unknown number of patients with tertiary syphilis and the residual symptoms of encephalitis lethargica), subsequent studies were less convincing. In the early 1950s, research conducted at a California state mental hospital and a large public asylum in Washington, D.C. (St. Elizabeth's) demonstrated no difference in release rates between patients receiving the new drug treatments, relative to their unmedicated peers.[97] For some observers, these findings suggested that the neuroleptics possessed a limited ability to modulate the course of chronic or severe psychosis.

In reaction to these early disappointments, researchers turned their attention to the testing of neuroleptics in younger populations, whose prospects for successful rehabilitation were believed to be more promising. In April of 1961, the National Institute of Mental Health sponsored one such study: a nine-hospital investigation of phenothiazines in the treatment of acutely ill schizophrenics.[98] Perhaps the first large scale, *blinded trial to randomize treatment

---

*blinded - the integrity of the blind was most likely compromised by the nature of the participants' side effects and their previous treatment experiences: only 9% of the placebo subjects received anticholinergic medications for Parkinsonian symptoms, compared to 16% of the thioridazine (Mellaril), 37% of the chlorpromazine (Thorazine), and 44% of the fluphenazine (Prolixin) subjects. Furthermore, this differential exposure to anticholinergic medication – rather than the neuroleptics, per se – may have contributed to some of the therapeutic benefits which the investigators attributed to the effects of dopamine blockade.

(patients were randomly assigned to receive chlorpromazine, perphenazine, thioridazine, or placebo) in a multi-drug study, the project monitored the progress of 344 newly admitted patients (average age: 28 years) over a period of six weeks. It is significant that fifty-two percent of the subjects had experienced a previous psychotic episode, and 40% had experienced a previous hospitalization, **suggesting that this was largely an investigation of psychotic relapse.** (Regrettably, the published report does not convey the prior treatment histories of these patients, making it impossible to discern the impact of earlier medication exposure and abrupt withdrawal.) Despite the methodological limitations, almost 50% of the placebo subjects experienced clinical improvement (20% were unchanged). Although the phenothiazines had no discernible effects upon delusions of grandeur, pressured speech, guilt, sadness, delirium, derealization, or memory deficits, the researchers found them to be "superior to placebo" on the basis of categorical rating scales, according to which 95% of the medicated subjects were said to have improved. In terms of specific symptoms, however, only 46% of the medicated patients achieved significant remission. On the basis of this six-week study, *in which treatment compliance and blindedness were never assessed,* the NIMH team concluded that the phenothiazines should be regarded as "antischizophrenic in a broad sense," effective in a large number of patients, relatively safe, and easy to use.[99]

Typicals vs. Atypicals

Even under the best of circumstances, the conventional neuroleptics have demonstrated a capacity to facilitate acute remission (i.e., few or no lingering psychotic symptoms) in only 30-50% of the patients who consume them. Against this background, the atypicals (second and third generation antipsychotics) were welcomed as a "breakthrough" in the treatment of schizophrenia and other psychoses, but a close inspection of the published data reveals wide variability in efficacy. Negative trials have generally been dismissed or overlooked by the medical profession. Positive trials have featured non-comparable dosing strategies and other tricks (see chapter four) prejudicing short-term outcomes in favor of the newest and most expensive chemical therapies. Each of these developments has raised legitimate concerns about the claims of those who tout the superiority of the atypicals.

Historically, the trail-blazing "atypical" trial in the United States was Study #30, a multi-center investigation of clozapine which was published in 1988.[100-101] Conducted at sixteen different treatment facilities, the investigation enrolled 319 schizophrenics who had failed at least three periods of neuroleptic therapy (at least two different classes of drugs) over the preceding five years. Inclusion criteria called for a moderate severity of illness (CGI score of 4); a BPRS total score (18 item scale) of at least 45; and moderately severe scores on at least two of the following symptoms: conceptual disorganization, hallucinatory behavior, suspiciousness, and unusual thought content. All patients received haloperidol (up to 60 mg per day or more) and benztropine (Cogentin, 6 mg per day) for a period of six weeks, in order to confirm the continued status of treatment refractoriness. (Anyone responding to Haldol was removed from the study. This resulted in the departure of four patients.) Three hundred and five subjects were then advanced to a one-week placebo washout. Although this was hardly enough time to "wash" the remaining Haldol out of these patients' systems, due to the fact that the drug lingers in the brain tissue for weeks to months,[102] the investigators appeared as oblivious to this confound in the late 1980's as subsequent investigators have been ever since. Following the alleged washout period, then, the remaining participants were randomly assigned to receive clozapine (136 subjects, consuming up to 900 mg per day) or chlorpromazine (142 subjects, consuming up to 1800 mg per day) for a period of six weeks. The latter drug – but not clozapine – was administered with Cogentin, in order to prevent the emergence of Parkinsonian symptoms.

At the completion of the trial, 30% of the clozapine patients were pronounced "treatment responders," compared to 4% of the patients who had received chlorpromazine. However, two enormous confounds were not observed. First, the investigators failed to appreciate the fact that their study amounted to a comparison of clozapine + haldoperidol versus chlorpromazine + haloperidol, in light of the fact that all patients had consumed high doses of haloperidol therapy in the early weeks of the investigation. Second, there existed in 1988 very little awareness of the obfuscating effects of extrapyramidal symptoms. Thus, deficiencies on the BPRS (such as anergia, apathy, avolition, affective blunting, and motor retardation) were as likely to be a reflection of drug-induced difficulties as they were a reflection of an unremitting illness.

While Study #30 was accepted by the FDA as the definitive trial "proving" clozapine's efficacy in treatment-resistant schizophrenia, there was no recognition by the regulatory agency of the manner in which the deck was stacked against the non-clozapine subjects. Those patients were exposed to not just one, but two neuroleptics (haloperidol + chlorpromazine) administered in doses that were high enough to compromise both safety and therapeutic utility.

Since the publication of Study #30, the fervor surrounding clozapine has intensified, fueling an epidemic of goodwill towards this and other atypicals. Kasper's 2000 report on quetiapine (Seroquel) featured a trial in which 29% of the patients receiving that drug were classified as responders, with average symptom scores on the BPRS falling from 47 to 38.[103] **While 29% of the patients met the *a priori* criteria for treatment response (arbitrarily defined as a 40% or more reduction on the BPRS), most of the quetiapine subjects continued to experience psychosis in the moderate to severe range of intensity.** These findings are hardly impressive, yet they resonate with the results of the two privotal trials upon which the FDA based its approval of olanzapine (Zyprexa) – to date, the most financially successful atypical antipsychotic in the world.[104]

In the first FDA approval trial (for simplicity, I shall refer to this as olanzapine **Trial #1**), 164 patients meeting *DSM-IIIR* criteria for schizophrenia were enrolled in twelve treatment facilities throughout the United States. Patients began the trial in a hospitalized status, based upon the presence of psychotic symptoms which were rated with the BPRS as moderately severe or worse. They were transitioned to outpatient status as their clinical conditions improved. The study consisted of a 4-9 day placebo washout period, after which 152 patients were randomized to one of three treatment groups for six weeks of therapy and monitoring: placebo (hence, an antipsychotic withdrawal group), 1.0 mg of olanzapine, and 10.0 mg of olanzapine.

In the second FDA approval trial (olanzapine **Trial #2**), 419 patients meeting *DSM-IIIR* criteria for schizophrenia were enrolled in twenty-three different study sites throughout the United States and Canada. Again, the subjects began the investigation in the hospital, transitioning to outpatient care as their conditions improved. Following a 4-9 day placebo washout (**during which 85 subjects,** or 20% of the original starting pool, were removed from the study because they responded too well to milieu therapy), 355 patients were randomized into one of three groups for six weeks of treatment: placebo, various doses of olanzapine (5mg , 10mg, or 15 mg = low dose, medium dose, and high dose), or a fixed dose of haloperidol (15 mg per day). The findings in both of these trials were remarkable for overwhelming rates of attrition (early dropouts, particularly in Trial #1), and a consistently poor outcome for olanzapine, in terms of the drug's potential to achieve the pre-defined "response" threshold of a 40% reduction on the BPRS, or a final score of 18 or less:

Attrition Rates by Treatment Group [105]

Percentage of Patients Unable to Complete Six Weeks of Therapy

Olanzapine Trial #1		Olanzapine Trial #2	
olanzapine 1.0 mg	77%	olanzapine low	59%
olanzapine 10.0 mg	62%	olanzapine medium	59%
placebo	80%	olanzapine high	51%
		placebo	68%

Response Rates in the Olanzapine Trials [106]

Olanzapine Trial #1		Olanzapine Trial #2	
olanzapine 10.0 mg	27.9%	olanzapine high	49.2%
placebo	9.5%	*placebo	33.9%

In a specific analysis of attrition according to the reasons for early termination, the FDA's review of the olanzapine efficacy trials revealed the following:

---

*This omits the data from the 85 subjects who improved too much during the placebo washout.

Reason for Early Termination[107]

	% of Terminators Quitting for Adverse Event	% of Terminators Quitting for Lack of Efficacy
Trial #1		
placebo	0%	74%
olanzapine 10.0 mg	4%	56%
Trial #2		
placebo	10%	47%
olanzapine low	8%	34%
olanzapine medium	2%	38%
olanzapine high	6%	26%
haloperidol	9%	28%

Several points are worth highlighting. First, these statistics were taken directly from the pages of the FDA's approval package, reflecting that agency's summary of the raw clinical trial data submitted by the manufacturer (Eli Lilly). These were the data which formed the basis of the FDA's decision to approve olanzapine in September of 1996. Second, it is remarkable that 50-60% of the olanzapine subjects were unable to tolerate the drug, even for six weeks. Third, the short-term response rates of just 30-50% are consistent with -- and in no way superior to -- the results of efficacy trials for clozapine and the phenothiazines, as demonstrated by many years of published research.

Presumably, few providers have had the time or opportunity to review the FDA product approval packages for each of the atypicals. Nevertheless, summary assessments of published trials have been made available by several teams of researchers, and at least one clinician[108] has offered his reaction to this work. Writing in 2002 on the 50th Canadian anniversary of chlorpromazine, Dr. Emmanuel Stip questioned the general effectiveness of antipsychotics, based upon the legacy of abysmal trial design and the continuing picture of dubious clinical utility. Among the research which Stip highlighted was: 1) a study by Leucht,[109] which commented specifically about the ambiguous efficacy of the new drugs due to the difficulty of establishing their effects upon primary (underlying) versus secondary (drug-induced) negative symptoms; and 2) a meta-analysis by the Cochrane Schizophrenia Group in the U.K., which found no differences in efficacy between clozapine and other atypicals. Two additional studies identified by Stip warrant further discussion because of their implications for clinical research and future practice.

In 2001, Chakos et. al.[110] assessed the comparative value of the second generation antipsychotics in ten trials which involved the treatment of "refractory" schizophrenia. Four studies found no differences between the old and new agents, particularly when comparable dosing strategies were employed. Among seven trials which focused upon clozapine, two failed to reveal superior efficacy for that drug – even when clozapine was compared against high doses of conventional neuroleptics (e.g., 1200 mg of chlorpromazine, 18.5 mg of haloperidol).

Three findings of the Chakos meta-analysis are particularly striking. First, the team identified a positive association between trial duration (length of follow-up) and apparent drug efficacy, with longer periods of observation (1-2 year follow-ups) eroding the differences between conventional and atypical antipsychotics. Over time, the new drugs and the old drugs grow more and more alike. Second, the response rates to clozapine have been 30-40% in most trials, accompanied by great variability in the magnitude of clinical effect (usually, a BPRS reduction on the order of 5-30%). Third, in the few trials which have compared them, there has been very little difference between the efficacy of clozapine and other atypicals, such as risperidone (response rates in published trials of 30-67%, BPRS changes on the order of 25%). Each of these findings supports a far more cautious attitude about the atypical antipsychotics than is generally heard, particularly in light of the clinical realities which Chakos' own research team explicitly conveyed:

> **"...The introduction of the phenothiazines between 1953 and 1980 both raised expectations that were never fully realized and prompted policies of deinstitutionalization that were not very successful and have had considerable adverse social ramifications."[111]**

A cautious tone is also found in the 2000 report by Geddes et. al., who published the findings of a meta-analysis involving 52 randomized trials which compared typical and atypical antipsychotic drugs in more than 12,000 patients.[112] Significant heterogeneity was observed, but most trials contradicted the notion that the newer drugs were superior in terms of efficacy or patient compliance. Furthermore, in a secondary analysis which controlled for the influence of neuroleptic dose, the research team found that excessive amounts of conventional agents (such as haloperidol and chlorpromazine) were associated with reduced efficacy and tolerability. Thus, while it is true that atypicals have generally been associated with fewer Parkinsonian side effects, it is also true that conventional neuroleptics have been no less efficacious than the newer agents when administered in comparable doses (i.e., in doses which produce similar levels of D2 receptor blockade).

Because meta-analyses are often criticized for methodological reasons, leading some to reject their claims, it is significant that the conclusions of Geddes' team have been validated by the clinical research of others. A prospective, 12-month trial was undertaken between June of 1998 and June of 2000 at seventeen Veterans Administration Medical Centers in the United States.[113] The purpose of that study was to compare the efficacy, safety, and costs of olanzapine (Zyprexa) and haloperidol (Haldol), in an attempt to respond to the debate about the alleged superiority of the newer drugs. The investigation enrolled 309 patients diagnosed with schizophrenia or schizoaffective disorder (*DSM-IV*), who met the following criteria: 1) serious dysfunction for the previous two years, with significant occupational and social limitations; 2) active symptoms of psychosis (BPRS score of 36 or more); and 3) inpatient status for less than one year (as the study progressed, patients could be enrolled as outpatients).

The V.A. Medical Center trial assigned 159 subjects to olanzapine (5-20 mg/day) and 150 subjects to haloperidol (5-20 mg/day), for a period of treatment lasting one year. Concomitant medications were allowed, but no patient was permitted to take any antipsychotic other than the assigned study drug. Haloperidol patients were administered benztropine (Cogentin) prophylactically, in order to prevent the emergence of Parkinsonian symptoms. Efficacy was measured with several rating scales (e.g., the PANSS, the CGI, the Quality of Life Scale), and side effects were evaluated with similar instruments (the Abnormal Involuntary Movement Scale, the Simpson Angus scale for Extrapyramidal Symptoms, the Barnes scale for akathisia). In addition, neurocognitive status was monitored with a variety of tests (such as the Wisconsin Card Sorting Test, Trail-Making Test B, and the Grooved Pegboard) designed to assess learning, memory, recognition, and motor and executive functions.

As the study population was culled from the V.A., most participants were male (96%), African-American (51%-52% of each treatment group), disabled (92% of the olanzapine and 89% of the haloperidol subjects receiving disability payments), and suffering from co-morbid addictions (56-65% with alcohol abuse or dependence, 30-35% with cocaine abuse). The average patient age was 46-47. Most patients had been diagnosed with a schizophrenic condition at age 24.

By the end of one year, 57% of the patients had stopped taking their assigned treatment ahead of schedule. The investigators made a committed effort to follow-up with all participants, successfully contacting 27% of the olanzapine and 32% of the haloperidol drop-outs. No significant differences were found between the two study drugs on any of the efficacy rating scales, including assessments on specific subscales (such as "negative" or "positive" symptoms of schizophrenia). Haloperidol patients were only slightly more likely than their olanzapine counterparts to quit taking their drug due to adverse effects (10% of haloperidol vs. 4% of olanzapine). While neurocognitive improvements were noted among olanzapine subjects on tests of motor function and memory, these were modest in nature and of insufficient magnitude to improve the overall quality of life, interpersonal relationships, or employment earnings. If olanzapine demonstrated any benefits, they included a lower incidence of akathisia (6% of olanzapine vs. 10% for haloperidol) and TD, but these risks were felt to be mitigated by a higher incidence of weight gain, a greater risk of diabetes, and higher treatment costs (four to five times the costs of haloperidol). In summarizing their findings, the V.A. research team concluded:

> "...olanzapine does not demonstrate advantages compared with haloperidol (in combination with prophylactic benztropine) in compliance, [psychotic] symptoms, extrapyramidal symptoms, or overall quality of life, and its benefits in reducing akathisia and improving cognition must be balanced with the problems of weight gain and higher cost."[114]

Medication enthusiasts may be tempted to dismiss the above findings as artifacts of research conducted among the "overly sick," the chronically ill, or the ageing. Emerging evidence might encourage them to think again. Until recently, few studies had compared the comparative benefits of new and old treatments in the acutely ill. In 2003, an international team of investigators responded to just this research challenge, publishing the first results (**12 week outcomes**) of a multi-center trial of olanzapine and haloperidol in the treatment of early schizophrenic conditions.[115]

The study involved the participation of both inpatients and outpatients ranging in age from 16 to 40; with active psychotic features of at least moderate severity, lasting from one month to five years in duration. Two-hundred sixty three patients met the inclusion criteria, most of whom were male (82%), Caucasian (53%), young (mean age: 24), and early in the course of illness (mean duration of symptoms: 1 year and 2 months). Although three-quarters of the subjects reported prior exposure to antipsychotic therapy, the doses and durations of those treatments were neither reported, nor objectively confirmed. After a 2-14 day drug washout (to clear the systems of those patients who had recently consumed other medications), patients were randomly assigned to olanzapine (5-10 mg per day for the first six weeks, increasing to a maximum of 20 mg per day) or haloperidol (2-6 mg per day for the first six weeks, increasing to a maximum of 20 mg per day). Antiparkinsonian medications were not administered prophylactically, but a variety of agents were available when significant side effects emerged.

Additionally, the study protocol permitted the use of sedatives (chloral hydrate, lorazepam, or diazepam) for the management of agitation, behavioral disturbances, or insomnia. These sedatives were permitted for a total of twenty-one days. The primary outcome measure was the PANSS (Positive and Negative Syndrome Scale for schizophrenia). Treatment response was pre-defined as a 30% reduction in symptoms along with significant improvements on specific PANSS items, and a CGI (Clinical Global Impression) severity of illness score that was moderate or lower.

Despite the presence of significant methodological confounds (including the liberal use of sedatives among olanzapine subjects, and the withholding of antiparkinsonian medications until the onset of movement abnormalities), **the researchers failed to detect** any significant differences in efficacy between olanzapine and haloperidol in first episode schizophrenia. Findings were otherwise remarkable for moderate attrition rates (32% of olanzapine, 46% of haloperidol of subjects unable to complete the twelve week course of therapy); limited response rates (46% for haloperidol, 55% for olanzapine); poor modification of negative symptom scores; and, perhaps surprisingly, a significant rate of extrapyramidal side effects among the consumers of olanzapine (26% with parkinsonism, 12% with akathisia).

Dimension #2: Relapse Prevention

A second dimension of treatment efficacy is the capacity of drug therapy to prevent the return or worsening of psychotic features. Relapse prevention studies involving antipsychotics (and other drugs) have contributed to exaggerated ideas about the need for lifelong medication, largely because the psychiatric profession has failed to appreciate the problem of allostatic load. In 1997, this situation might have changed if physicians had paid attention to the concept of *pharmacological stress factors – a term which was briefly used by Baldessarini and Viguera to describe "neural adaptations that accompany long term drug treatment which may have downstream effects on the disease process or other aspects of cerebral functioning."[116] Such stress factors (i.e., allostatic load) – whether they involve changes in the number or sensitivity of dopamine receptors, changes in the expression and synthesis of neuronal gene products, or changes in the structure of the brain – have contributed to the onset and severity of relapsing symptoms, separate and apart from the natural course of any underlying "disease."

For more than fifty years, the published literature on antipsychotics (old and new) has overlooked the phenomenon of *therapeutic drug dependence, confusing the symptoms of medication withdrawal with the return of a pre-existing disease. While it may be politically and economically convenient for the psychiatric profession to

---

*pharmacological stress factors – undesirable or harmful symptoms arising from the body's adaptations to drug therapy; while these symptoms may appear in the course of continued treatment, they typically emerge or intensify when a medication is reduced in dose or withdrawn (cont'd.)

blame the return of psychosis upon the patient rather than the effects of previous treatments, such a perspective is scientifically unsupportable. Evidence that the termination of dopamine antagonists can, itself, be pathogenic has been documented for decades: most impressively, among the non-mentally ill. In a creative review on the subject, Tranter and Healy[117] have summarized five examples from history which illustrate the reality of the neuroleptic discontinuation syndrome:

Neuroleptic Discontinuation Syndrome: Five Lines of Evidence

1) anti-emetic withdrawal

> Many patients who have received medications to prevent nausea and vomiting have not realized the effects of those drugs - such as metoclopramide and prochlorperazine - upon the dopamine receptors of the brain. (The anti-emetics block D2 receptors, although not as potently as the neuroleptics.) Dozens of case reports appear in the medical literature documenting the symptoms of non-psychiatric patients who have stopped taking anti-emetic compounds. Withdrawal of these dopamine antagonists in the non-mentally ill has produced a a variety of symptoms, including akathisia, rigidity, irritability, anxiety, reduced libido, impaired concentration, memory disturbance, sweating, and paresthesias. In some cases, anti-emetic discontinuation symptoms have persisted for a year more after the termination of drug therapy.

---

*therapeutic drug dependence - the potential of prescription medications to cause physiological dependence (tolerance or habituation while continuing a drug; withdrawal symptoms upon stopping) was the topic of a 1966 conference of the CINP, the International College of Neuropharmacologists. Reacting to patient experiences with barbiturates, benzodiazepines, and other agents, the CINP members accepted the reality of **"dependence of a non-addictive type."** The notion subsequently vanished before emerging political pressures. The psychiatric profession has worked hard to separate the notion of "therapeutic" from "recreational" drug use, ultimately introducing the distinction that a drug can only be called addictive if it causes cravings in the user. For more on this history, see Healy's *The Creation of Psychopharmacology.*

2) chlorpromazine withdrawal in pulmonary patients

In the late 1950s, chlorpromazine (Thorazine) was discovered to impede the growth and reproduction of the bacterium which causes tuberculosis. As a result, chlorpromazine was administered to 17 patients for six months in a double blinded trial. When it was discovered that the neuroleptic had no efficacy in treating the patients' pulmonary infections, the drug was abruptly withdrawn. Five of the 17 patients experienced nausea, vomiting, restlessness, and insomnia.

3) neuroleptic withdrawal in mood disorders

In the 1970s, several antidepressants and neuroleptics were combined in the same pill for the treatment of mood disorders. Examples include Tryptafen (a combination of amitryptiline and perphenazine) and Parstelin (a combination of the monoamine oxidase inhibitor, tranylcypromine; and trifluoperazine). The maker of Parstelin (Smith Kline Beacham) recommended that physicians taper their patients off the drug slowly – over weeks – in order to minimize the potential for a wide range withdrawal symptoms: hallucinations, agitation, nightmares, insomnia, fatigue, sweating, paresthesias, and weakness. Furthermore, it was recognized that these withdrawal symptoms could be quickly relieved by resuming Parstelin.

4) tardive dyskinesia

Although the problem of tardive dyskinesia is not limited to the cessation of antipsychotic drug treatment – since tardive can arise during the continuation of therapy – its appearance is typically triggered by reductions in dose or drug termination. In addition to the problems of dyskinesia (involving repetitive, disfiguring, involuntary movements of the face, tongue, neck, limbs, and trunk), other tardive features may appear. These include akathisia, respiratory disturbances, and long-lasting changes in affect or mood (i.e., tardive dysmentia).

5) discontinuation studies in schizophrenia

A series of studies conducted in the 1960s suggested that neuroleptic discontinuation was responsible for the emergence of distinct symptoms, clearly separable from the conditions receiving treatment. For example, Battegay withdrew neuroleptics from 81 patients in a double-blind experiment. Fifty-five of the patients experienced the rapid onset of sweating, vertigo, nausea, vomiting, insomnia, and dyskinesia. Most of these patients were so distressed that neuroleptics had to be resumed within one week. Several other research teams replicated these findings independently between 1964 and 1966.

Because of the prevalence of therapeutic drug dependence and discontinuation syndromes, there is no shortage of publications which report high rates of psychotic relapse among patients who have stopped taking their medications, or among patients in clinical trials who have been abruptly transitioned onto placebo. The problem is that most investigators have confused these examples of allostatic load with the pathophysiological processes of a recurring "disease." By expecting medication withdrawal to mimic the patterns which are common to street drugs (e.g., alcohol, which is associated with a maximum withdrawal period of 1 to 10 days), many physicians have unwittingly overlooked neuroleptic discontinuation syndromes. Few textbooks or curricula instruct clinicians about the evolving and persistent nature of these clinical phenomena (as long as six months, according to Viguera). At this point in time, there is simply no way of knowing how much of the psychiatric literature has been confounded by this oversight. The words of Tranter and Healy are especially pertinent in this regard:

"...where prophylactic benefits have been calculated on the basis of emergence of difficulties on the withdrawal of treatment, these may have been overestimated. There are, furthermore, implications for clinical trial

207

designs that would infer efficacy from relapse on halting treatment."[118]

Clinical trial designs which have committed this error are abundant. In fact, they are predominant. Examples include Greenblatt's (1965) hospital study, which randomly assigned previously medicated chronic schizophrenics to drug or non-drug treatment groups, with or without social therapy.[119] After six months, the unmedicated subjects were switched back to neuroleptics. When they still displayed the poorest outcomes, the researchers concluded that the drug-free period had produced "negative carryover effects." Another example is the study by Hogarty and Goldberg published in 1973, involving 374 schizophrenic outpatients assigned randomly to chlorpromazine or placebo.[120] At the end of one year, placebo subjects relapsed at rate of 63-73%, compared to 26-33% of those on neuroleptics. Still another example is the 1980 publication by Davis[121] which compared relapse rates in over 3500 patients, reporting relapse to be "more than three times as likely" among the subjects transitioned onto placebo (55%) than among subjects whose antipsychotics had been maintained (19%).

The fallacy of "inferring efficacy from relapse upon halting treatment" was particularly florid in Gilbert's 1995 meta-analysis of schizophrenia drug trials,[122] summarizing the data from 66 different studies involving 5600 patients who received treatment between 1958 and 1993. Ignoring the methodological confounds of the investigation (for example: the lack of diagnostic details in about one-third of the studies; the lack of consensus on the definition and criteria of relapse; the short duration of follow-up in most studies; and the unclear reporting of the duration and dose of previous drug treatments), Gilbert's team found that neuroleptic withdrawal was, on average, associated with a cumulative relapse rate of 53% over a follow-up period of ten months. By contrast, the relapse rate for patients maintained on neuroleptics was found to be 16%. When the same data were re-examined by an outside team of researchers, sensitive to the problem of pharmacological stress (allostatic load), they added several important qualifications: namely, that the risk of psychotic relapse varies by *time*, by *dose*, and by the *speed of drug taper*.[123]

First, the risk of relapse after stopping a neuroleptic was non-linearly distributed, arising primarily in the first three months.

Fifty percent of the unmedicated patients who relapsed did so within the first ninety days of follow-up, compared to four percent of those who remained on drug therapy. For the unmedicated patients, the risk of relapse declined after twelve months, while it increased for those who remained on drug therapy.

Second, studies outside of the Gilbert meta-analysis have demonstrated a correlation between relapse risk and the dose of medication from which a patient is withdrawn. One such investigation[124] was conducted by the National Institute of Mental Health in the 1970s. Among patients whose neuroleptics were discontinued, six-month rates of relapse were positively associated with the previous daily dose of chlorpromazine: 65% of the patients relapsed when withdrawn from 500 mg (or more); 54% upon withdrawal from 300-500 mg; and 23% upon withdrawal from 300 mg or less.

Third, the risk of relapse appears to vary according to the rate of neuroleptic discontinuation. Writing in 1993, Green and colleagues documented a considerable difference in the six-month rate of relapse among a small group of psychotic patients whose drug therapies were tapered rapidly or slowly.[125] Four of eight patients (50%) relapsed when their drugs were withdrawn over fourteen days, but only one of thirteen patients (8%) relapsed when drug therapy was progressively reduced over two months.

When Baldessarini and Viguera re-examined the Gilbert data using this last criterion, they discovered that 33 studies had employed abrupt withdrawal (<1-14 days), compared to 13 studies which removed medication over a period of two weeks or more.[126] Monthly relapse rates varied *threefold*: 15% of patients relapsed after abrupt drug cessation, compared to 5% whose treatments were gradually withdrawn. The importance of this last point cannot be overstated, because it suggests that **the risk of psychotic relapse (5% per month) when medications are carefully and slowly withdrawn is no greater than the risk of relapse when medications are chronically maintained.**

A substantial body of evidence serves to illustrate this essential point. In a paper dedicated to examining the economic burden of schizophrenia,[127] Weiden and Olson estimated the direct costs associated with one-year relapse. The research team divided the patient population into three groups for the purpose of predicting outcomes: 1) an optimal dose medication group, consisting of patients maintained on depot (injected) neuroleptics; 2) a medication withdrawal group, consisting of patients whose drug therapies were removed under physician supervision; and 3) a noncompliant group, consisting of patients who stopped taking their drug therapies against medical advice. Synthesizing a wide variety of studies, the investigators proposed an average relapse rate of 3.5% per month among patients maintained on neuroleptics; a relapse rate of 8% per month, among patients whose doctors withdrew drug therapy; and a relapse rate of 11% per month, among patients who grew non-compliant (presumably, stopping their drugs abruptly). A close inspection of several component studies, however, demonstrates significant overlap between the outcomes of medicated and unmedicated subjects:

Monthly Relapse Rates for Patients Maintained on Depot Neuroleptics[128]

Study	Year	# of Patients	Duration of Study	Monthly Relapse Rate
Crawford	1974	66	9.5 months	3.6%
Del Guidice	1975	30	16 months	4.9%
Falloon	1978	21	12 months	4.2%
Knights	1979	40	6 months	6.9%

Monthly Relapse Rates for Patients With Physician Withdrawal of Medication[129]

Study	Year	# of Patients	Duration of Study	Monthly Relapse Rate
Engelhardt	1967	56	6 months	5.5%
Hirsch	1973	38	12 months	3.1%
Johnson	1979	71	24 months	4.9%
Capshick	1980	59	24 months	6.5%

Based upon the published literature on relapse rates, Weiden and Olfson predicted that 50% of previously admitted schizophrenics would require rehospitalization within one year, while another 30% would require readmission within two. Furthermore, based upon the rates of relapse occurring among compliant and noncompliant patients, they concluded that 70% of the first-year relapse risk was attributable to the loss of neuroleptic efficacy (drug tolerance or habituation), while only 30% was attributable to noncompliance. After twelve months, these risks appeared to become equal (i.e., risk of relapsing on drug therapy due to loss of efficacy = risk of relapsing from non-compliance).

While it may seem tedious to belabor the issues of relapse prevention and neuroleptic discontinuation syndrome, several key points are worth re-emphasizing:

> ➢ relapse prevention studies have generally ignored the existence of pharmacological stress factors (allostatic load), such as neural adaptations which occur in the brain in response to chronic drug therapy

> ➢ neuroleptic withdrawal syndromes may persist for much longer periods of time than most clinicians appreciate, leading to inappropriate interpretations about the causes of recurring symptoms

> ➢ relapse rates among patients maintained on antipsychotic drugs are frequently no different than relapse rates among patients whose drugs have been gradually withdrawn

> ➢ recommendations for lifelong pharmacotherapy may needlessly expose patients to the risks of drug toxicity, while decreasing their chances for a full recovery due to allostatic load

Dimension #3: Functional Recovery

Since the invention of the neuroleptic and its chemical successors, few studies on the treatment of psychosis have addressed the impact of drug therapies upon social and occupational recovery. In response to the void in this area, a team of American researchers examined the two-year outcomes for 219 patients diagnosed with affective psychosis.[130] Hoping to maximize treatment response rates by limiting participation to the non-chronically ill, the investigators enrolled in the study only those patients who were experiencing a first hospitalization (1989-1996) for bipolar disorder or depression accompanied by psychotic features. Patients were excluded if they had suffered symptoms for more than a year; if they had undergone previous psychiatric hospitalizations; or if they had received specific drug treatments (antipsychotics or mood stabilizers) for more than three months. Clinical outcomes were evaluated with a variety of assessment instruments. Symptomatic or syndromal recovery was defined in terms of improvements using the *DSM-IV* and the CGI (Clinical Global Impression rating scale). Functional recovery was evaluated in terms of occupational and social change, using the Modified Vocational Status Index and the Modified Location Code Index. At two-year follow-up, 98% (199 of 219) of the patients had achieved symptomatic recovery. However, among the patients evaluated for *functional* recovery, only 37.6% (68 of 181) had achieved significant improvements in terms of work status and the capacity for independent living. A short length of hospitalization was positively correlated with both types of recovery. Among the psychotically depressed, syndromal recovery was delayed the more that drug treatment intensified:

Number of Medications	Syndromal Recovery
1 drug	50% recovered by 7 weeks
2 to 4 drugs	50% recovered by 15 weeks
5 or more drugs	50% recovered by 31 weeks

Whether drug exposure was a cause or effect of these findings, a similar trend was observed among bipolar and depressed subjects with good functional outcomes: patients who resumed prior levels of occupational and social activity tended to receive fewer medications than those who remained chronically impaired.

The failure of antipsychotic medications to ameliorate the functional deficits of psychosis has received scant publicity for years. While it was hoped that the atypicals would prove to be new *and* improved in comparison to their predecessors, such dreams have not been actualized in terms of occupational and interpersonal rehabilitation. Perhaps because of these limitations, the concept of functional recovery has generally been ignored in many studies. An exception to this trend was the recently published (2004) six-month, double-blind trial comparing clozapine and risperidone in patients labeled as schizophrenic.[131]

Investigators recruited 107 patients with moderately severe symptoms (or worse), administering up to 800 mg of clozapine or 16 mg of risperidone per day for a period of 29 weeks. Social skills were evaluated using the Maryland Assessment of Social Competence. Cognition was evaluated with the Wisconsin Card Sorting Test, a popular instrument for assessing working memory, problem solving ability, and the capacity to shift sets (apply new rules). By the end of the study period, risperidone patients displayed no changes in their social skills. Clozapine patients showed a small but significant decline in their verbal skills. In terms of cognitive ability, clozapine patients had deteriorated in executive functions (*negative* effect sizes on the Wisconsin Card Sort), while risperidone patients displayed only minor improvements (clinically insignificant) which diminished by week 29. Summarizing these findings at the end of the investigation, the research team drew the following conclusions:

"Clozapine and risperidone both had significant effects on symptoms, but neither had an appreciable impact on either social skill or problem-solving ability. These findings are consistent with a prior study we conducted comparing clozapine and haloperidol and underscore the independence of social role performance from symptoms."[132]

Many historians, clinicians, and epidemiologists have asked the question: has the course of schizophrenia been favorably altered since the advent of neuroleptic? While it is seemingly impossible to control for all of the factors – sociocultural, economic, political, biological – which have had a bearing on long term prognosis, a 1994 meta-analysis on the subject was not entirely encouraging.[133] Researchers reviewed the status of more than 51,000 patients in 320 studies conducted between 1895 and 1991. Studies were selected according to precise inclusion criteria, such as mean follow-up of at least one year; diagnoses limited to schizophrenia or dementia praecox; availability of data explaining clinical, social, and vocational outcomes; and details of the interventions. The investigators evaluated patient prognoses by decade, seeking to identify the impact of treatments and the diagnostic systems employed. Between 1956 and 1985, approximately 49% of schizophrenic patients demonstrated significant clinical improvement. After

1985, however, favorable outcomes dropped to a rate of 36%, identical to the outcomes of the 1930s. Surprised by these results, the investigators offered the following interpretation:

> "...despite routine use of neuroleptics and other contemporary therapies, reported average clinical outcomes have deteriorated in the past decade. We propose that diagnostic changes have had an important impact on outcome...since the introduction of *DSM-III*, with its return to a more Kraepelinian emphasis on duration and course of illness for diagnosis. Additional factors that may contribute to the recent downward trend in average rates of favorable outcome include...[declining] responsiveness to treatment or ...evolving changes in the organization or financing of psychiatric services."[134]

Declining responsiveness to treatment will remain a problem for psychiatry, as long as the profession continues to emphasize drug therapies at the expense of allostatic load.

Safety

With the possible exception of the chemotherapies used in the treatment of cancer, it would be difficult to identify a class of medications as toxic as the antipsychotics. Whether one considers the effects of dopamine antagonists upon the central nervous system or beyond, their proven harmfulness has been an iatrogenic tragedy too often minimized or denied. While the following section does not presume to present a full overview of antipsychotic drug toxicities (indeed, these are still emerging), it will present some of the prominent hazards associated with dopamine blockade.

Cognitive Toxicity

The conventional notion of drug toxicity suggests that undesirable effects arise only in conjunction with excessive exposure (i.e., excessive dose or duration of therapy), but this premise is often irrelevant for psychopharmacology. A curious distinction of all brain-altering substances – whether synthetic or botanical, medicinal or recreational – is the tenuous threshold which exists between therapeutic or desirable effects, on the one hand, and toxic or adverse effects, on the other.[135]   Nowhere is this phenomenon better illustrated than by the antipsychotic medications:

> **"Rather than improving cognitive deficits, conventional antipsychotics may instead contribute to the impairment seen in many patients with schizophrenia. These damaging effects on cognition might be expected not only when antipsychotic drugs with intrinsic anticholinergic properties are used but also when anticholinergic drugs are prescribed for the relief of treatment-emergent extrapyramidal symptoms."[136]**

Such concessions have generally appeared belatedly or begrudgingly, and only then, in the guise of marketing campaigns touting the superiority of the latest chemical therapies. In the context of this record of professional deception, therefore, it may be startling to know that the cognitive risks of dopamine blockade have long been recognized.   Indeed, the neurological hazards of chlorpromazine were overtly characterized by Delay and Deniker in 1957, when they listed the five defining features of all drugs worthy of being classified as a *neuroleptic*:[137]

> ➤ the creation of psychic indifference

> ➤ efficacy in sedating agitation, excitation, or mania

> ➤ the gradual reduction of psychotic symptoms

> ➤ the production of extrapyramidal syndromes

> ➤ dominant subcortical effects

It was the chemically lobotomizing effects – indifference, sedation, and the induction of Parkinsonian symptoms – rather than antipsychotic effects which drew the attention of asylum physicians in the 1950s. In this regard, the words of the Canadian psychiatrist, Heinz Lehmann, are particularly revealing:

> **"'In 1956, ...I introduced the term 'antipsychotic' apologetically, and more as a metaphor than a designation.'"[138]**

Ignorant of this history, it is only at rare intervals that mental health professionals have announced their surprise about the cognitive (and behavioral) toxicity of the dopamine antagonists. Although the American Psychiatric Association issued its first guidelines for the management of tardive dyskinesia in 1975, it was not until the 1980s that independent researchers published papers about the existence of *other tardive conditions*, including cortical deficiencies, such as anosognosia (*tardive dementia*); affective instability (*tardive dysmentia*);[139-141] and delusional or hallucinatory phenomena (*tardive psychosis*).[142] In 1993, many of these concerns were evident as clinicians convened in Scandinavia for the first (and apparently only) symposium addressing similar problems, this time under the euphemism of Neuroleptic Induced Deficit Syndrome,[143-145] or NIDS. To the detriment of patients and clinicians alike, each of these alarms has been unheralded and short lived.

Awareness about the neurotoxicity of antipsychotic drugs has been hampered by the poor quality of research in this area. In a 1999 review on the subject,[146] Keefe et. al. outlined a number of quality standards for research on the neurocognitive impact of antipsychotic drugs. Eight features were identified as essential components of an adequate study, including the careful description of each patient's treatment status prior to the administration of the study drug; randomized assignment of patients to multiple treatment arms (i.e., placebo vs. active medications); double-blind design; clinically appropriate dosing strategies (i.e, no unfair advantages by using non-comparable doses); and *discrimination between cognitive improvements arising from treatment of the underlying condition, versus improvements arising from changes in drug side effects.*

Keefe's research team then reviewed articles published between 1990 and 1998, identifying fifteen studies which focused on atypical antipsychotics and their effects upon cognitive function in patients with schizophrenia. None of the fifteen studies met all of the quality standards for research methodology. Moreover, none of the studies were large enough to detect small or medium effect sizes; only three studies (20%) employed a double-blind design; four studies (27%) employed multiple study arms with randomization; and only nine studies (60%) examined some aspect of the relationship between cognitive changes and clinical symptoms, particularly with respect to drug side effects (extrapyramidal symptoms).

Despite the inherent biases introduced by these methodological deficiencies, Keefe's meta-analysis was not uniformly favorable. Five atypical antipsychotics were compared (clozapine, risperidone, zotepine, ziprasidone, aripiprazole) to conventional neuroleptics in terms of their effects upon several categories of cognitive ability: attention, executive function (i.e., sorting, planning, sequencing), working memory (a form of short-term memory, similar to RAM on a computer), visuospatial analysis, verbal fluency, digit symbol substitution, fine motor function, and learning and memory. Based upon their findings, the investigators concluded that *conventional* neuroleptics compromised fine motor function, performance on timed tests of cognitive ability (due to the presence of Parkinsonian symptoms), and ability to improve test performance through practice. Although the *atypical* antipsychotics seemed more effective in improving attention, executive function, motor skills, and verbal fluency, no specific pattern of cognitive change was noted for any particular medication. **Six studies found no evidence of neurocognitive improvement among patients receiving the new therapies, and no studies found evidence of drug efficacy resulting in cognitive functions that were equal to normal controls.** Similar to the conventional neuroleptics, the atypical antipsychotics demonstrated a poor capacity to ameliorate deficits in learning and memory. The fact that seven of the fifteen studies lasted for twelve weeks or less raises further doubts about the efficacy of the newer agents, since the detection of certain cognitive toxicities may require more extended periods of observation.

Other investigators have also expressed concerns about the cognitive effects of antipsychotics. By correlating the findings from animal and human research, they have constructed hypotheses about potential mechanisms of drug-induced toxicity. It is possible to organize this body of evidence in two ways: first, by examining specific neurotransmitter systems; second, by inspecting specific cognitive domains for evidence of therapeutic or deleterious drug effects.

Acetylcholine Effects

Medications which block acetylcholine receptors (specifically, the muscarinic subtype) have consistently demonstrated the ability to impair cognitive functioning in animals and humans. These anticholinergic effects (so named, because the drugs block acetylcholine) have been shown to disrupt associated learning (conditioning) in rabbits; episodic visual memory in monkeys; and working memory in rats. Similar limitations have been documented in humans, including decrements in tests of verbal memory (specifically, the encoding of new information from word lists) and learning.[147]

A 2004 study conducted by researchers in California[148] evaluated the association between anticholinergic load (defined in terms of *benztropine equivalents), the severity of psychotic symptoms, and neurocognitive functioning in 106 outpatients diagnosed with schizophrenia. The research team asked clinicians to prepare a rating scale for the anticholinergic load presented by various antipsychotic medications. A *pharmacological* index was prepared based upon the affinity of antipsychotics for various muscarinic receptors, and a *clinical* index was prepared, based also upon the potential of each drug to produce anticholinergic side effects (such as dry mouth, blurred vision, constipation). The patients were then evaluated in terms of these two indices, and cognitive functions were assessed by a variety of neuropsychological screening tools.

Patients were compared to fifty healthy controls, with the latter group providing reference values on the tests of cognitive capacity. Compared to healthy volunteers, patients performed worse on every measure of the neuropsychological battery except one (visual span forward). Over half of the variability in cognitive functioning was due to differences in visual attention, general intelligence, and short-term declarative memory. Each of the two anticholinergic indices (pharmacological and clinical) was significantly related to performance on tests of verbal learning, immediate and delayed facial memory, delayed recall and copying of complex figure designs, color naming, and certain aspects of executive function (such as Trails B). After controlling for the influence of symptom severity and global functioning (PANSS and GAF, respectively), no significant relationship was noted between psychopathology and

---

*benzotropine (Cogentin) – an anticholinergic medication commonly used to counteract Parkinsonian symptoms; benztropine "equivalents" refer to the doses of other anticholinergic medications which must be given to produce similar effects

cognitive ability. This suggested that the impact of anticholinergic load was independent of illness effects.

Anticholinergic load was found to account for 10% of the difference between patients and controls on measures of divided attention and declarative memory, and between 1/3 to 2/3 of the cognitive deficits associated with schizophrenia. Commenting upon the implications of their findings, the researchers concluded that their indices of anticholinergic activity provided useful estimates of cognitive toxicity:

> "...[I]n routine clinical practice, the intrinsic anticholinergic activity of psychiatric medications (such as tricyclic antidepressants, paroxetine, and olanzapine) is often not considered when adding an antiparkinsonian medication to the regimen. Therefore, the effective anticholinergic load probably exceeds the level recognized by many clinicians, as [others have] found in geriatric medicine...In patients with schizophrenia, central cholinergic antagonism is associated with selective impairments of memory and recall, as well as certain complex attentional functions. This is quite consistent with animal research demonstrating roles of forebrain ascending cholinergic subsystems in memory and divided attention. Routine increases in anticholinergic load may impair verbal memory by as much as 1.7 standard deviations...the anticholinergic load of common medication regimens may have a significant clinical impact - sufficient to shift memory performance, for example, from the normal to the impaired range."[149]

Dopamine Effects

Healthy volunteer studies have demonstrated the capacity of haloperidol (a D1 and D2 antagonist) to impair performance on tests of attention and working memory, such as the Wisconsin Card Sort Test and the Tower of Toronto.[150-151] These findings are consistent with animal studies in monkeys and rats, where high doses of D1 receptor agonists and all doses of D1 antagonists appear to impair spatial working memory. Similarly, investigations of D2 antagonism in *psychotic patients and normal controls* have revealed a wide

219

variety of drug-induced impairments, including deficits in the following domains:

> executive function & working memory[152-156]

> sustained attention and arousal[157-158]

> reaction times[159]

> information processing[160]

> fine motor coordination[161]

> temporal processing (ability to estimate or perceive passage of time)[162-163]

> latent inhibition (ability to ignore irrelevant stimuli)[164]

> declarative memory[165]

> procedural learning[166-167] and

> driving ability.[168-169]

Serotonin

Drugs which bind to serotonin receptors have demonstrated variable effects upon cognitive functioning. Because of the enormous complexity of the serotonin system (fourteen different types of receptors: 1A, 1B, 1D, 1E, 1F, 2A, 2B, 2C, 3, 4, 5A, 5B, 6, 7), the cognitive and behavioral consequences of many drug-receptor interactions have not yet been investigated in humans. Animal studies have shown that 5HT1A agonists impair spatial learning and memory, based upon experiments involving the direct infusion of specific chemicals (such as OH-DPAT) in the hippocampus. Similar studies have been conducted with 2A and 2C antagonists, revealing drug-induced deficits in aversive conditioning (conditioned fear, or the learning of conditioned avoidance responses) and complex learning (the ability to learn complex mazes) in rats; deficits in the conditioned eye blink response in rabbits; and deficits in the working memory of monkeys.[170-172] While the human correlates of these findings remain uncertain, there is evidence which suggests that 2A/2C antagonism may impair several domains of learning and memory. A recent study performed in the United Kingdom compared the effects of several atypical antispsychotics (clozapine, olanzapine, risperidone, quetiapine, and amisulpride) in 44 patients diagnosed with schizophrenia.[173] Patients received treatment for 18 months, along with neuropsychological assessments after nine and eighteen months of treatment. When subjects were grouped according to the 5HT2A affinity of their medications, the patients experiencing the highest 2A antagonism displayed decrements in visual memory and planning.

Norepinephrine

The cognitive effects of norepinephrine are mediated by a variety of adrenergic receptors. While alpha-2 antagonists have been shown to impair working memory in non-human primates,[174-175] experiments in humans have borne ambiguous results. Nevertheless, it is significant that the stimulation of post-synaptic noradrenergic receptors by alpha agonists (such as clonidine or guanfacine) has consistently improved human performance on tests of memory. Thus, the blockade of these same receptors by antipsychotics suggests a possible mechanism through which medications may facilitate cognitive decline.[176-178]

Glutamate

At the turn of the millennium, the "glutamate theory of schizophrenia" achieved celebrity in the field of neuropharmacology. Based upon the finding that hallucinogenic and dissociative drugs, such as ketamine and PCP (angel dust) antagonize the NMDA glutamate receptor in the brain, the notion was advanced that deficient glutamate activity might be a cause of psychosis. Treatments to boost glutamate were proposed, despite the potential hazards of those therapies. As the major excitatory peptide in the nervous system, excessive glutamate has been linked to neuronal degeneration, and to changes in anatomy and function associated with Alzheimer's disease, stroke, epilepsy, and head injury.[179] Thus, it appears that glutamate modulates a wide array of behaviors, but possibly within a precarious range of safety.

221

Because of the importance of glutamate in the homeostasis (and allostasis) of the brain, researchers have begun to investigate medication effects upon this neurotransmitter system. Animal studies of atypical antipsychotics, such as clozapine, have demonstrated a variety of effects, including the desensitization of NMDA receptors in the medial prefrontal cortex;[180] the inhibition of NMDA 2A and 2B receptors in vitro;[181] and the downregulation of NMDA 2B receptors in the hippocampus.[182-183] The latter finding is particularly significant, since similar changes in NMDA 2B density have been found to correlate with the progression of dementia in Alzheimer's disease.[184] Moreover, the subchronic administration (21 days) of clozapine in rats has revealed suppression of LTP, or long term potentiation, in the prefrontal cortex.[185] Since LTP is a glutamate-mediated mechanism through which synapses are believed to be strengthened, and through which long term memory is believed to be formed,[186] its drug-induced suppression may account for the observations of Hoff and others who have demonstrated the negative effects which atypical antipsychotics (such as clozapine) exert upon visual memory and executive functions.[187]

Animal studies have documented the potential of NMDA antagonists to induce neuronal degeneration throughout the limbic system, including the cingulate, entorhinal, and piriform cortices; and the hippocampus.[188-189] Such findings are consistent with the behavioral effects of NMDA antagonists in humans. Studies of NMDA blockade in healthy volunteers have also shown decrements in learning (spatial and verbal information) and deficits in working[190] and declarative memory[191] (the latter process, involving long term verbal memory and recognition of objects). While the verdict is still out on the net effect of antipsychotics with regard to NMDA activity, a growing body of evidence suggests that typicals and atypicals decrease the number and responsivity of many NMDA receptor subtypes. Thus, legitimate questions remain about the potential for these drugs to induce neuronal changes which eventuate in psychotic symptoms or cognitive decay.

Do Newer Drugs Improve Cognition?

Current marketing campaigns suggest that the atypical antipsychotics are particularly effective in improving cognition. Mindful of the extensive impairments associated with the extrapyramidal side effects of the neuroleptics, more than a few clinicians have expressed a more cautious assessment of the latest drug therapies. Due to the fact that cognitive research has generally examined new medications in previously neuroleptized patients, it has been difficult to discern their true properties. The cognitive improvements which have emerged in some patients upon the transition to atypicals may well reflect the dissipation of previous treatments. In other words, it might not be the case that the newer drugs are such potent cognitive restorers, as much as it is the case that the older drugs are so cognitively toxic.

Evidence to this effect has been demonstrated most clearly in studies of first-episode psychosis. For example, a Danish team of investigators randomly assigned 25 drug-naïve (previously unmedicated) schizophrenics to the treatment conditions of a conventional (zuclopenthixol) or atypical (risperidone) antipsychotic.[192] A comprehensive neuropsychological battery was used to assess cognitive abilities before treatment and again after thirteen weeks of therapy. The same tests were also administered at similar intervals to healthy volunteers. After controlling for extrapyramidal side effects and anticholinergic medication (both of which were more frequent among the subjects receiving zuclopenthixol), *neither drug showed efficacy in improving cognitive functions.* Performance changes in the medicated subjects were indistinguishable from the retest changes which occurred among the healthy controls.

No discussion about the alleged cognitive superiority of the atypicals would be complete without reference to clozapine. Praised by some psychiatrists in the 1960s as a cognitive "brightener" responsible for patient "awakenings," a substantial body of research has emerged which challenges this stereotype. In an eight-month investigation of clozapine's effects upon the speed and accuracy of information processing,[193] Galletly et. al. found only limited improvements in cognitive functioning. In multiple studies of psychosis, Goldberg et. al.[194-195] demonstrated clozapine-induced improvements in attention, response speed, and verbal fluency. Simultaneously, however, decrements occurred in visual memory and some executive functions. Social and vocational adjustments remained poor. In a seven-month comparison between haloperidol and clozapine involving 71 "treatment refractory" subjects, Kane et.al.[196] found no differences between treatment groups in the improvement of negative symptoms. Laker et. al.[197] conducted a five-year study of psychiatric inpatients hospitalized in the U.K. between 1990-1995. After 35% of the subjects had become non-compliant with clozapine therapy, the research team analyzed patient outcomes according to drug status. Three-year rates of discharge were no different for the patients who remained on clozapine versus those who no longer received it.

It is tempting to attribute at least some of these outcomes to the electrophysiological effects of clozapine. In fact, a Finnish observer has suggested that clozapine's primary effect appears to be the induction of a soporific condition in which patients experience the ability to "sleep while awake."[198] Such a premise finds support in the research of Freudenreich et.al., who correlated clozapine blood levels with EEG changes in 50 state hospital patients.[199] Abnormal slowing was identified in 53% of the subjects, and epileptic changes (spikes) in 13%. Similarly, Treves and Neufeld[200] demonstrated EEG abnormalities in 11 of 15 clozapine patients (64%), even though the subjects were maintained on a fixed, low dose of the medication (300 mg per day). The cognitive consequences of EEG slowing have been explored by others. In a study of vigilance and memory, Adler et. al.[201] demonstrated a dose-dependent impairment of cognitive functions in seventeen subjects with schizophrenia. In Adler's investigation, neurocognitive deficits were directly related to clozapine's suppression of high frequency EEG activity.

Behavioral Toxicity

Since the introduction of neuroleptics in the 1950s, a minority of concerned professionals have broached the possibility that dopamine antagonists might induce iatrogenic injury in terms of affect and behavior, in addition to the more widely recognized damages to cognition (described above) and movement (explored below). The behavioral toxicity inflicted by antipsychotic drugs has been explained in terms of acute and chronic processes.

In a 2004 review on the subject of neuroleptic *dysphoria,[202] a team of Canadian researchers explained the historical classification of anhedonia, apathy, and cognitive deficits arising from dopamine blockade. On the one hand, many observers have subsumed the phenomenon of drug-induced dysphoria under the category of Parkinsonian side effects, based upon the similarities observed in psychiatric patients and individuals diagnosed with basal ganglia disease. On the other hand, some clinicians have emphasized the potential independence of psychological and neurological features, suggesting that neuroleptic dysphoria need not be a variant of parkinsonism. In other words, it is entirely possible for antipsychotic drugs – old and new – to exert negative effects upon mood and behavior, while sparing the motor centers of the brain.

Evidence for both premises has emerged, due to technological advances in experiments which use chemical probes and neuroimaging. In studies involving the administration of AMPT (alpha-methyl-paratyrosine), in order to create temporary depletions of brain dopamine, researchers have performed biological and psychological assessments within 48 hours of the chemical manipulation.[203] Findings have been significant for a reduction in dopamine synthesis and release (as demonstrated by lower levels of homovanillic acid, and higher levels of available D2 receptors), accompanied by a distinctive pattern of adverse effects: loss of pleasure, social withdrawal, and psychomotor slowing within six hours; akathisia at 24 to 36 hours; and movement abnormalities (rigidity, tremor) around 48 hours post-treatment. These observations correspond to the time-course of antipsychotic drug reactions, in which a similar progression of side effects and receptor changes commonly occur.[204-205]

A number of neuroimaging studies have demonstrated significant associations between D2 receptor blockade and the induction or worsening of depressive features.[206-207] For example, Fujita et. al. found a correlation between mood and D2 occupancy in the temporal lobe of healthy controls exposed to AMPT. De Haan et.al. demonstrated a correspondence between dysphoria and striatal D2 blockade in 22 schizophrenics who received treatment with the atypical antipsychotics, olanzapine and risperidone. As the drug

---

*dysphoria – a subjective feeling of unpleasantness or discomfort; malaise

225

occupancy of D2 receptors increased, so too, did the patient scores on rating scales of depression and negativity (based upon the PANSS). *These affective changes were seen, even in the absence of extrapyramidal symptoms.*[208]

Animal experiments have employed anatomical lesioning, electrical stimulation, immunocytochemistry, and autoradiography to study specific dopamine networks in the brain, and to correlate the manipulation of these tracts with behavioral changes. For many years, neuropsychologists have regarded the frontal cortex as the major locus of executive functions (planning, sequencing, choosing, intending); the limbic system as the center of emotionality; and the nigrostriatal system as the center of motor control. Only recently has this consensus been challenged, based upon the realization that the functions of the central nervous system are not nearly as compartmentalized as researchers have previously believed.[209-210] The integrated nature of neuronal activity has had important repercussions for psychiatry.

In the 1950s and 1960s, researchers attributed the antipsychotic action of neuroleptics to the same neural processes responsible for movement abnormalities (parkinsonism). Over time, this theory was gradually refined and the "psychotic center" of the brain was moved away from the striatum, into the limbic system and the neocortex. Along with these changes, the therapeutic value of an antipsychotic came to be defined by its affinity for non-striatal regions of the brain. While it remains unclear if these revised hypotheses about psychosis are any more accurate than the ideas which came before them, they do provide new mechanisms through which neuroleptic dysphoria might be explained.

One potential theory is based upon the research evidence which has identified the nucleus accumbens (a subcortical, basal forebrain, limbic structure) as the key region in the brain's system of pleasure and reward. All antipsychotics – typical and atypical – antagonize the dopamine receptors of midbrain neurons which communicate with the nucleus accumbens. As mentioned earlier, the resulting changes have been advanced by Kapur[211] as the cause of a medication-induced state whereby "aberrant salience" becomes blunted. According to Kapur, hallucinations arise when patients attach an inappropriate level of meaning to external stimuli or internal representations. Delusions occur when patients exert cognitive effort in an attempt to make sense of these "aberrantly salient" events. Antipsychotics are presumed to work by dampening the "motivational salience" which a person attaches to these internal events:

"In particular, the mesolimbic dopamine system is seen as the critical component in the 'attribution of salience,' a process whereby events and thoughts come to grab attention, drive action, and influence goal-directed behavior because of their association with reward or punishment. This role of dopamine ...provides an interface whereby the hedonic subjective pleasure, the ability to predict reward, and the learning mechanisms allow the organism to focus its efforts on what it deems valuable and allows for the seamless conversion of motivation into action [...]."[212]

For the student of history, Kapur's theory is a neurophysiologically sophisticated version of the psychic indifference which was first noted by Delay, Deniker, and the other phenothiazine pioneers.

"The concept of dampening salience can trace its conceptual origins to the very first behavioral studies of antipsychotics in animals...In pivotal experiments in 1956, which are relevant to this day, Courvoisier observed that rats who had come to associate the ringing of a bell with a shock would try to avoid the mere sound of the bell. However, when these rats received an antipsychotic they stopped avoiding the bell, even though they were motorically capable of doing so and still responded to the shock."[213]

Kapur has suggested that the value of antipsychotic drugs lies in their ability to decrease the significance of stimuli, be they aversive or agreeable. What is surprising, perhaps, is his enthusiasm for dopamine antagonists despite an open acknowledgement of the following:

"Neither normal volunteers nor patients find antipsychotics pleasant; in both populations they are associated with a plethora of unpleasant subjective effects, captured under the rubric of 'neuroleptic-induced dysphoria,'...or 'neuroleptic-induced deficit state'... It is

quite conceivable that the same mechanism...that takes the fire out of the symptoms also dampens the drives of life's normal motivations, desires, and pleasures."[214]

Equally disturbing is the implication that this dampening effect of antipsychotics may underlie the tendency of so many patients to increase their use of *nicotine, alcohol, or other drugs, in an effort to compensate for the suppression of dopamine neurotransmission - particularly, within the nucleus accumbens.[215-218]

Supersensitivity Psychosis and Other Behavioral Syndromes

At rare intervals, clinicians have published case reports and essays, expressing concern about the potential of antipsychotic therapy to gradually, and perhaps irreversibly, induce changes in perception and affect.   In the late 1970s and 1980s, Chouinard and Jones introduced the concept of "neuroleptic induced supersensitivity psychosis" (or SSP) as a possible explanation for two phenomena: first, the return or worsening of psychotic symptoms *during* drug treatment (habituation or tolerance, compelling an increase in dose to regain symptom stability); second, the emergence or progression of symptoms *following* the termination of drug treatment.[219-220] At that point in time, the leading theory of TD (tardive dyskinesia) suggested that "super sensitive" D2 receptors in the striatum were the most likely source of involuntary repetitive movements. Knowing this, Chouinard and others advanced the notion that a similar process of receptor change (either higher in number, higher in sensitivity, or both) might very well occur within the limbic

---

*nicotine - based largely upon findings in animal research, many theories have been proposed to explain the high rates of smoking by schizophrenics. Experiments suggest that: 1) nicotine boosts dopamine activity in the nucleus accumbens, perhaps offsetting the dysphoric effects of D2 blockade in the mesolimbic system; 2) nicotine boosts dopamine transmission in the striatum and reduces D2 receptor up-regulation, possibly reducing extrapyramidal symptoms and TD; 3) components of tobacco *smoke* inhibit monoamine oxidase, raising catecholamine activity throughout the brain; and 4) smoking increases the metabolism of medications in the liver, thereby reducing the plasma level of antipsychotics and diminishing the intensity of their undesirable effects.[221-226]

system. Some observers came to call this phenomenon tardive psychosis.[227-228]

Although tardive psychosis is seldom discussed by contemporary practitioners, it is significant that the intervening years of research have provided support for Chouinard's initial premise. Neuroimaging technologies have suggested that typical *and* atypical antipsychotics increase the number of D2 receptors in the human striatum. While it is apparent that these changes are not, in and of themselves, sufficient to produce dyskinetic features in all patients, it remains possible that they are a necessary precursor to tardive conditions, particularly upon dose reduction or the removal of drug therapy.[229]

Furthermore, it remains possible that non-receptor changes – perhaps in 2nd and 3rd messenger systems, or in the expression of specific gene products – result in functional or structural modifications, such as those detected by MRI (e.g., enlargement of the caudate, atrophy of the frontal lobes). To the extent that this is true, the old research which emphasized receptor supersensitivity may be largely irrelevant. Tardive psychosis, if or when it occurs, may find expression through processes which existing technologies are simply unable to detect or explain.

Perhaps the strongest line of evidence for supersensitivity psychosis is found in studies of the non-mentally ill, who have developed hallucinations or delusions following the removal of medications which reduce dopamine activity in the brain. The importance of this research lies in the fact that drug withdrawal has repeatedly been shown to provoke psychotic symptoms in patients with no prior history of psychiatric "disease." Kent and Wilber[230] reported the experiences of an elderly female who had been treated for twenty years with the dopamine-depleting agent, reserpine, as a treatment for hypertension. Three days following the discontinuation of reserpine, the patient developed sleeplessness, euphoria, loud and rapid speech, and visual hallucinations. Reserpine was immediately resumed. Within one week, the patient's psychiatric symptoms had fully resolved. The authors concluded that the chronic use of reserpine had created conditions of highly sensitive catecholamine receptors (similar to that detected in animals following denervation). Upon the withdrawal of reserpine, dopamine and norepinephrine levels were presumed to have surged, flooding the up-regulated receptors and producing the features of mania and psychosis.

More recently, clinicians in Taiwan published two case reports involving patients who had received chronic therapy with metoclopramide (Reglan), a D2 receptor antagonist commonly used as a treatment for heartburn and bloating (e.g., esophageal reflux, dyspepsia, and gastroparesis).[231] In both cases, the patients lacked any history of mental illness. Following the improvement of gastrointestinal symptoms, metclopramide therapy was withdrawn. Within twelve to thirty-six hours, the subjects experienced the emergence of anxiety, agitation, tremors, restlessness, visual or auditory hallucinations, and persecutory delusions. When their symptoms persisted for several days, psychiatric consultations were obtained. Under the impression that both cases involved a metclopramide-induced "supersensitivity psychosis," the patients were treated briefly with a low dose of an atypical antipsychotic (six week taper), after which no further withdrawal symptoms appeared.

It is important to appreciate the fact that tardive changes may occur in any region of the brain, including the neocortex. The potential of chronic antipsychotic therapy to produce changes in the frontal lobes has been noted by several teams of researchers. In 1983, Wilson et. al. proposed the existence of a **tardive dysmentia**, characterized by changes in affect, activation level, and interpersonal interactions following chronic dopamine blockade.[232] Acknowledging the changed phenomenology of schizophrenia since the appearance of neuroleptics, Wilson commented upon the increasing prevalence of phasic (relapsing-regressing) psychotic episodes, marked by mood symptoms. He wondered if these affective changes might represent the behavioral equivalent of tardive *dyskinesia*. In order to test this hypothesis, Wilson and his colleagues reviewed the records of 29 chronically hospitalized psychotic patients, correlating the presence or severity of movement abnormalities with progressive changes in behavior and mood. Findings were significant for a correlation between AIMS scores (an assessment of dyskinetic features) and behavioral attributes (unstable mood, loud speech, and social intrusiveness). Cumulative exposure to drug therapy was also associated with mood changes, leading the researchers to conclude that neuroleptics are capable of inducing changes in brain regions concerned with emotions and thought.

Expanding upon these observations, Goldberg in 1985 proposed the existence of two discrete forms of tardive dysmentia: one, involving reductions in speech, motivation, energy, and spontaneous activity; the other, involving mood lability, disinhibiton, hostility, loud speech, and social intrusiveness.[233] Goldberg proposed that these phenomena were two variants of a frontal lobe syndrome induced by chronic drug therapy. Based upon findings from neurology (e.g., stroke survivors) and neuroscience research, the condition of aspontaneity was attributed to iatrogenic injury in the dorsolateral prefrontal cortex. Hyperactivity was attributed to drug-induced changes in the orbitofrontal and mesiobasal cortex. Goldberg's paper was additionally significant for exposing the possibility of these damages in the chronically medicated, *even in the absence of TD* (tardive dyskinesia).

Possibly the last mainstream commentary on tardive *dysmentia* appeared in 1986, when Myslobodsky[234] proposed the existence of dementia-like symptoms in many patients with TD. At the time, Myslobodsky was unique in suggesting the existence of *tardive dementia*, emphasizing the delayed appearance or exacerbation of neocortical deficits in the chronically neuroleptized. The notion of asymmetric disturbances in the frontal lobes was suggested by Myslobodsky as a possible explanation for the predominantly right-sided deficits displayed by so many patients with TD, such as anosognosia (the failure to recognize aspects of one's own body, including faciolingual movements), oscillations in emotional reactivity, and disprosody (scanning speech). At the same time, Myslobodsky was quick to identify the inconsistency of research purporting the existence of hemispherically specific abnormalities. This conclusion, in addition to the research which has followed, suggests that tardive dementia is best conceptualized as a more global process of drug-induced, cognitive debilitation.

Nigrostriatal Disorders: (see footnote pg. 232) Extrapyramidal Side Effects and TD

The historical precedent of encephalitis lethargica (EL) became the basis of a decades-long debate within psychiatry in which the boundary between therapeutic and toxic effects of drug therapy was tragically blurred. Based upon the belief that the induction of basal ganglia damage was "necessary" for the remediation of schizophrenic features, neuroleptic therapies were administered for many years in high doses, with the explicit intention of creating movement abnormalities in the drug recipient. In France, Belgium, and Italy, the majority of psychiatrists regarded extrapyramidal symptoms as a necessary phase in the process of clinical improvement. This consensus was slow to change. By 1959, Freyhan recognized that the alleviation of Parkinsonian side effects with anticholinergic medication did not reduce the benefits of neuroleptic therapy in some patients.[235] Goldman drew the same conclusion two years later, noting that more than 4000 patients had improved clinically without the emergence of Parkinsonian features.[236] By 1965, several more teams of investigators had added to the research exploring the alleged link between clinical efficacy and extrapyramidal side effects, concluding that the production of motor disturbances was clearly unnecessary and unwarranted.[237]

Today, textbooks and curricula unambiguously refer to the nigrostriatal effects of antipsychotic medications as deleterious rather than healing. Acute effects include **dystonias** (episodic contractions or spasms in the muscles of the limbs, neck, back, or face); **akathisia** (severe motor restlessness and agitation), and **parkinsonism**, named for the features of Parkinson's disease (tremor, slow movement, reduced facial expression, shuffling gait). Delayed effects – sometimes emerging after months of treatment, and often irreversible – are described as **"tardive"** conditions. They include tardive dystonia, tardive akathisia, tardive parkinsonism, and **tardive dyskinesia (TD)**. The latter is a unique syndrome characterized by repetitive, involuntary movements of the face, lips, tongue, limbs, or trunk. Some clinicians also include among TD the phenomena of respiratory and esophageal dysmotility. These conditions are believed to arise from chronic dopamine blockade in the brain centers which innervate the digestive tract, the diaphragm, the larynx, and the tongue. Respiratory dyskinesia, for example,

---

* nigrostriatal – pertaining to the neurons (and other elements) involved in the control of voluntary movement; the nigrostriatal system refers to the cells of the substantia nigra and the striatum (caudate and putamen), as well as the connections to and from these regions of the brain

232

is characterized by symptoms of hyperventilation, abnormal vocalizations or grunting, and forcible contractions of the chest wall – sometimes resulting in rib fractures.[238-239] Possible etiologies include dopamine supersensitivity in the striatum, leading to over-stimulation of the autonomic breathing system in the medulla; or neuronal damage in the pontine reticular formation, as seen in Shy-Drager syndrome.[240]

Despite the use of antipsychotic therapies for more than fifty years, and despite the existence of a large body of research exploring the epidemiology and physiology of extrapyramidal side effects, the precise etiology of these motor disturbances remains unknown. Parkinsonian features are *presumed* to arise from a relative increase in acetylcholine neurotransmission, which develops in reaction to the blockade of D2 receptors in the striatum.   Tardive syndromes, on the other hand, are *presumed* to arise from a number of possible pathophysiologies, including: structural changes in the brain, due to oxidative damage to the basal ganglia[241] or due to depletion of cholinergic neurons in the striatum;[242] supersensitivity of dopamine receptors; and imbalances (hypofunction or hyperfunction) in the activity of neurons which produce and release specific neurotransmitters (such as GABA and norepinephrine).[243-245]

Misinformed Consumers

The risks of extrapyramidal side effects have often been concealed by drug companies and clinicians due to avarice, ignorance, or fear. Manufacturers of antipsychotic medications have downplayed the hazards of their wares in an effort to maximize profits and sales. Health care professionals have failed to recognize iatrogenic injuries or have minimized adverse effects, in order to avoid "scaring" patients into treatment non-compliance. As late as the 1980s, for example, one major drug company claimed that tardive dyskinesia was a rare phenomenon, occurring in just 3% to 6% of all patients maintained on antipsychotic drugs.[246]   Misinformation of this kind has stretched beyond the communiqués of the pharmaceutical corporations, however. A 1992 survey of more than 500 American psychiatrists[247] revealed that half of the respondents acknowledged a routine failure to educate patients about the risk of developing TD. These "failures to inform" are particularly salient in light of the high prevalence of movement abnormalities, *even among patients who receive antipsychotics in low doses, for short durations, or in the form of the latest, supposedly less injurious chemical agents.*

Prevalence of Extrapyramidal Side Effects and TD

In his 2000 review on extrapyramidal side effects, TD, and the concept of atypical antipsychotics,[248] Glazer summarized the findings of a number of critical investigations. Chief among them was the Yale study on TD, in which he and his colleagues followed a cohort of 362 chronic schizophrenics prospectively for a period of five years:

Yale TD Study

cumulative duration of neuroleptic therapy	percent of patients with TD
0-5 years	32%
5-10 years	49%
10-15 years	57%
15-20 years	65%
20-25 years	68%

These findings resonate with the discoveries of other research teams, in which the risk of TD during neuroleptic therapy has been 3-5% per year of continuous drug exposure. In his comprehensive review of the movement disorders, Glazer also mentioned the Nithsdale schizophrenia survey (published in 1992), in which 271 patients were followed for ten years. By the end of that study, extrapyramidal side effects had emerged in 56% of the subjects: 29% had developed TD, 27% had developed parkinsonism, and 23% had experienced akathisia at some point in the period of treatment.

The risk of TD appears to be even higher among certain subgroups of patients. In 1999, Jeste et. al.[249] published their research on 307 older outpatients (mean age: 66) whose previous lifetime exposure to neuroleptics had been limited to five years or less. Patients were treated with relatively low doses of conventional antipsychotics. Multiple assessments for movement abnormalities (AIMS test) were performed over the course of one year. Among patients with limited or no previous neuroleptic exposure, the cumulative incidence of TD at 12 months was 22%-25%. Among patients with at least one month of previous neuroleptization, the cumulative incidence of TD at one year was 37%. Interpreting these outcomes, the researchers concluded that the duration of neuroleptic exposure was indeed a significant risk factor for TD. Furthermore, their study documented the onset of dyskinesia in older patients within a remarkably short period of time (i.e, within the first month of drug therapy).

Similar results have been conveyed by other researchers. In a 2003 report, a team of South African investigators summarized the effects of low dose haloperidol in 57 patients (aged 16-55) experiencing a first episode of psychosis.[250] None of the patients exhibited movement abnormalities at baseline, and none of the patients had received previous treatment with antipsychotics for longer than one month. Patients were followed prospectively for one year. At the end of twelve months, 65% of the patients remained on drug therapy. For most of these patients (81%), only a miniscule dose of haloperidol (1.7 mg per day) was consumed. Despite this limited exposure, a full 12% of the patients met the study team's criteria for TD, and another 5% satisfied criteria for "probable" TD (defined as the onset of dyskinetic symptoms by the end of one year). *This study is particularly significant, because it demonstrates the capacity of even small doses of Haldol (small by American convention) to induce dyskinetic features in young patients (mean age: 28), and within an extraordinarily short period of time (one year).*

Blaming the Patient

A number of researchers minimize the role of antipsychotics in the etiology of movement abnormalities among medicated patients. Prominent voices in psychiatry have suggested that TD is part and parcel of an underlying brain disease, with psychotropic medication simply "unmasking" a pre-existing neuropathology.[251] The evidence against this claim of "spontaneous" dyskinesia includes hundreds of animal experiments, in which rats and monkeys have consistently developed motor dysfunction in response to dopamine blockade. Further evidence is found in the case histories of non-mentally ill human subjects, who have experienced TD in response to metclopramide (or other dopamine antagonists) prescribed for the treatment of somatic rather than psychiatric symptoms.[252]

Although it has become common for neuroleptic enthusiasts to cite the writings of Kraepelin and Bleuler, who commented upon movement disorders in their psychotic patients prior to the advent of neuroleptics, neither Kraepelin nor Bleuler distinguished the possible confound of post-encephalitic changes in the basal ganglia of their European asylum populations.[253-255] An unknown number of patients survived the flu pandemic of the early 20th century, only to develop psychosis and/or dyskinesia as long term sequelae of their viral disease. This historical precedent undermines the credibility of the research which offers this subset of patients as "proof" that schizophrenia, rather than medication, is the cause of TD. More recent research, emphasizing the rates of dyskinesia among patients in undeveloped countries, has been offered to justify the claim that schizophrenia itself is the cause of TD. The limitations of this research include the failures of the investigators to control for the influence of environmental confounds such as nutritional deficiencies (e.g., cobalamine, thiamine, iron) and toxins (e.g., heavy metals, organophosphates) - all of which have been linked to neuropathological changes associated with movement disorders.[256-261] Even within developed countries, however, speculations about the cause of TD have been compromised by significant misjudgments, including inadequate consideration of the neurological effects of convulsive therapies, infectious disease, and addictions. In one analysis, for example, investigators concluded that schizophrenia itself must be the cause of movement abnormalities among a cohort of chronically hospitalized patients, based upon similar rates of dyskinesia in subjects exposed for years to convulsive or chemical treatments.[261]

New and Improved?

The so-called atypical antipsychotics have gained their notoriety on the basis of reduced risks of extrapyramidal side effects. However, a close inspection of the emerging evidence suggests that this claim is not incontrovertible. A growing body of research has revealed a dose-response relationship between many atypicals (such as risperidone and olanzapine) and the induction of Parkinsonian symptoms.[262-264] Given the fact that sufficiently low doses of conventional neuroleptics carry the same risks of extrapyramidal side effects, the hype surrounding the newest agents has often reflected the chicanery of non-comparable dosing strategies. Moreover, physicians have been encouraged to prescribe the atypicals based largely upon the contention that they produce antipsychotic effects *without* binding to high levels of D2 receptors in the striatum. Although many textbooks ignore them, it is important to acknowledge the laboratory investigations conducted by Seeman and Kapur, who have repeatedly demonstrated the *artifactual nature of these claims.[265-267] When administered in clinically "effective" doses, both atypical and typical antipsychotics have been shown to bind high numbers of dopamine receptors in the striatum. What appears to distinguish medications from one another is the dissociation constant (K value) of each compound, which refers to each chemical's affinity for specific receptors in the absence of competitors. In this regard, it appears that clozapine (Clozaril) and quetiapine (Seroquel) may be unique among the atypicals due to the fact that they appear to associate with D2 receptors more weakly than endogenous dopamine and experimental ligands, relative to other antipsychotic drugs.

Many psychiatrists fail to appreciate the complexity of the methodologies employed in the research on antipsychotic medications and their nigrostriatal effects. It may behoove them to recognize the deficiencies in this area. By understanding even a few of the ambiguities and limitations which persist, it is hoped that more clinicians might realize why it is still premature to pass judgment on the severity, the prevalence, and the prognosis of movement abnormalities associated with the atypical (second and third generation) antipsychotics:

> ➤ Neuroscientists have no way of measuring synaptic dopamine levels in a living human brain (a fact which makes the determination of dissociation constants speculative).[268]

---

*artifactual – neuroimaging studies of receptor occupancy employ radioactive chemicals (ligands) to "light up" available receptors on PET or SPECT scans of the brain. Ligands are injected into the bloodstream of each research subject. The ligands travel into the brain, ultimately arriving at neurons and glia where they compete with other chemicals (such as medications and neurotransmitters) for available receptors on each cell. The apparent affinity of a medication for a specific receptor subtype depends upon the ability (continued – next page)

➢ *In vitro* studies of dopamine receptors cannot replicate *in vivo* conditions, in which receptors fluctuate between low-affinity and high-affinity conformations.[269] This is another fact which makes the determination of dissociation constants and binding rates speculative.

➢ New ligands are continuously being discovered and employed. These compounds permit the study of receptors (such as D2) in brain regions where their density has traditionally been too low to detect. For clinicians, this suggests that existing theories about medications and psychopathology will need to be revised.

➢ Neuroscientists have no way to control for the simultaneous effects of multiple substances – such as endogenous neurotransmitters, radiolabelled ligands, and previously administered medications -- when they *compete* for the same kinds of receptors.[270] The theories purporting antipsychotic efficacy and safety on the basis of D2 receptor binding ratios may very well be incorrect with respect to the true workings of the human brain.

In summation, the extrapyramidal advantages of the newer agents have frequently been exaggerated or erroneously described. All of the antipsychotics bind D2 receptors in the movement centers of the brain, and at apparently high ratios – a finding which is presumed to be the basis of extrapyramidal side effects and TD. The fact that some antipsychotics bind to dopamine receptors more weakly than others (either due to "slow-on" or "fast-off" pharmacodynamics)

---

*artifactual (continued) – of the injected ligand to displace it from receptors. Ligands that have high tissue/buffer partition coefficients are particularly lipophilic (lipid-liking). Such ligands are particularly good at displacing medications from receptors in the brain, producing the illusion that the medications do not bind in certain brain regions. Receptor occupancy studies fail to acknowledge the artifactual confound which is introduced by the use of high-affinity ligands (such as raclopride). For more information on this important concept, see Seeman and Kapur as cited above (refs. 265-267).

may account for their reduced rates of parkinsonism.[271-272] **While research suggests that extrapyramidal side effects occur among 50-90% of patients on the conventional neuroleptics, the risks of the same symptoms have in no way been eradicated by the newer therapies.**[273] Some investigators have documented extrapyramidal side effects in as many as 20-50% of their patients exposed to atypical antipsychotics.[274-275] High rates of akathisia (30% or more) have been documented even for clozapine, which remains the "gold standard" for atypicality.[276-277]

Many psychopharmacologists have predicted that TD will be an unlikely problem with the newest therapies. Cautious observers have suggested that this conclusion may be premature. First, it is worth remembering that it took psychiatry 25 years to acknowledge TD in association with the *first* generation of neuroleptics. Second, although clozapine and quetiapine have been touted as possible treatments for TD,[278] achieving remission in 10-30% of the patients in some studies, it remains unclear to what extent these remission rates have reflected spontaneous improvements rather than atypical drug effects. What is clear at this juncture is the fact that tardive dyskinesia *has* been documented among recipients of each of the new antipsychotics, and the case report literature on this problem continues to expand.[279-284]

Neuroendocrine Effects

Hyperprolactinemia

Prolactin is a polypeptide hormone which plays important roles in reproduction and fertility, maternal and grooming behaviors, food intake, stress response, and immunity. In both males and females, serious health problems may arise when prolactin levels become excessively high, resulting in the clinical condition of *hyperprolactinemia*. Antipsychotic drugs have the capacity to produce prolactin imbalances directly, by blocking D2 receptors on cells of the anterior pituitary gland. All of the conventional neuroleptics, and at least one of the so-called "atypicals" (risperidone) have been shown to induce sustained, abnormal elevations in prolactin which persist throughout the course of drug therapy. Other antipsychotic medications – such as olanzapine, clozapine, and quetiapine – have been shown to induce transient elevations in prolactin characterized by rapid hormonal shifts at the time of each dose.[285] These risks appear to be even greater in children and adolescents.[286]

Although drug makers and the FDA minimize the potential hazards of these intermittent fluctuations – particularly, when they remain below the usual threshold for hyperprolactinemia (<25 ng/mL) – it is concerning that patients exposed to atypical antipsychotics commonly display a rise in prolactin which is twice as high as their baseline.[287] Such endocrine perturbations are not displayed by patients who remain unmedicated. Furthermore, the medical profession as a whole does not dismiss these kinds of changes as irrelevant. Researchers in obstetrics and gynecology, for example, have acknowledged the fact that even intermittent, subthreshold (normal but elevated) changes in prolactin can be sufficient to cause infertility.[288-289] Moreover, endocrinologists have long appreciated the fact that population-based references, while helpful, can sometimes detract from adequate regard for intra-individual variations.[290] To the extent that all antipsychotic drugs introduce disruptions in the homeostasis (and allostasis) of prolactin, patients and providers should beware of the potential consequences of these disturbances (see previous discussion of long term effects in this chapter and again in chapter seven).[291-292]

Hyperglycemia, Hyperlipidemia, and Weight Gain

Disturbances in the regulation of glucose and lipids have long been noticed in patients diagnosed with schizophrenia. Some clinicians have been quick to attribute these abnormalities to an underlying physiological condition, based upon the assumption that genetic aberrations predispose individuals equally to psychosis and metabolic dysfunction. While this theory of shared susceptibility remains possible, a more parsimonious explanation may be found in other variables, including lifestyle, substance abuse, diet, obesity, and age. Given the likelihood that derangements of glucose and lipid metabolism are multifactorially determined, it is reasonable to attempt to control the agents which cause them. It is in this context that the potential hazards of antipsychotic medications warrant review.

Beginning with the phenothiazines in the 1950s, a number of astute clinicians attempted to alert their peers about an association between neuroleptic therapy and the appearance of diabetes.[293-295] In the decades which followed, however, haloperidol came to dominate the market. Because haloperidol carried a uniquely low risk of glucose dysregulation, the metabolic effects of the neuroleptics as a drug class receded into the background. Not until the 1990s, and after the FDA approval of clozapine and olanzapine (in 1989 and 1996, respectively), did the medical literature return to this important subject.

American regulators lagged behind the rest of the *world, belatedly acknowledging the connection between the serotonin-dopamine antagonists and endocrine anomalies such as hyperglycemia, insulin resistance, weight gain, and elevated lipids (especially triglycerides). Following a fifty-year blackout of the scope and severity of the metabolic toxicity of **antipsychotics, an appreciable body of research has ultimately emerged. Although large scale, epidemiological investigations are still lacking, more limited analyses have occurred. In one such study, researchers identified the point prevalence of glucose abnormalities among consumers of clozapine, documenting a 12% rate of diabetes and an additional 10% rate of impaired glucose tolerance.[296] In another analysis,[298] researchers performed a retrospective chart review of eighty-two patients (mean age: 36) exposed to clozapine for five years. Over half of the subjects manifested abnormal blood sugar levels at some point in therapy and 31% were diagnosed with type 2 diabetes, unrelated to cholesterol, body weight, or BMI (body mass index). These findings are consistent with even more stringent studies of clozapine and olanzapine, in which strict diagnostic criteria have identified new-onset diabetes among 6-35% of the patients.[299] It appears that some atypicals may have lower risks of endocrine dysfunction when compared to the thieno-& dibenzodiazepines

---

*Japanese authorities required the re-labeling of olanzapine in 2000, in order to alert practitioners and consumers to the high risk of glucose dysregulation and weight gain.[297] In contrast, the Food and Drug Administration remained silent on this issue until March of 2004. Following the issuance of public health alerts and the placement of new warnings on package inserts in the U.S., opinion leaders in American psychiatry were engaged by the manufacturer of at least one antipsychotic drug to participate in a high profile educational campaign. This effort emphasized *schizophrenia* as the most likely cause of diabetes.

(continued on next page)

(olanzapine, clozapine). Nevertheless, all of the atypicals carry some risk of metabolic derangement, as a growing case literature now reveals.

Proposed Mechanisms of Metabolic Abnormalities

The causes of these drug-induced disturbances remain tentative, but several mechanisms have been proposed. Speculative processes include:[300-301]

> ➤ the induction of insulin resistance via increased synthesis and secretion of insulin and c-peptide, changes in insulin receptor density or sensitivity, or changes in post-receptor physiology (signal transduction, phosphorylation)

> ➤ the inhibition of glucose transporter proteins, leading to decreased cellular uptake of glucose from the blood

> ➤ the induction of leptin (a hormone made by fat cells) which regulates appetite, food intake, and body weight

> ➤ the induction of neurotensin via D2 blockade, leading to diabetic changes

> ➤ the antagonism of 5HT2C serotonin receptors, leading to weight gain, obesity, and diabetes

---

Although clozapine was introduced in Europe in 1961, it took forty years for the psychiatric profession to acknowledge its side effects of obesity, high lipids, and diabetes. This history is all the more disturbing when one considers the fact that clozapine consumers have been precisely those patients whose medical needs should have been most apparent. Since its implementation in the 1970s, the Clozapine Patient Monitoring System has required weekly or biweekly blood draws for the early detection of white blood cell deficiencies. The fact that endocrine disturbances were ignored for so long – even with all of these lab tests -- only underscores biopsychiatry's enduring mistreatment of the mentally ill.

> ➤ the inhibition of IGF-1 (insulin-like growth factor) activity, used in the uptake of amino acids by skeletal muscles for the synthesis of proteins

> ➤ the elevation of free fatty acids, leading to impaired glucose transport into skeletal muscle

> ➤ the destruction of beta islet cells in the pancreas, via directly toxic effects.

A concerning outcome of this research has been the revelation that diabetes, high lipids, and weight gain can emerge quickly in the consumers of antipsychotics, even among those who lack risk factors for endocrine disease. The fact that medication is the cause of these problems has been proven most convincingly by case reports and controlled studies which employ a CDR (challenge-dechallenge-rechallenge) protocol, in which glucose and lipid abnormalities appear during treatment, resolve upon drug cessation, and recur upon the resumption of drug therapy. Research has also shown that weight again itself is not a necessary cause of these disturbances. According to one review, as many as 15% of the case reports of diabetes and hyperglycemia; and as many as 25% of the cases of *DKA have emerged among patients in the *absence* of weight gain.[302]

Sexual and Reproductive Side Effects

No discussion about neuroendocrine effects would be complete without mentioning the deleterious impact of antipsychotics upon sexual functioning. While the consequences of hyperprolactinemia have already been discussed in some detail, it is important to recognize the fact the sexual side effects of antipsychotic medications arise through a variety of pathways, in addition to the dopamine-prolactin system. Sexual side effects are often ignored by clinicians, since they are usually not medical emergencies. Many clinicians also presume that psychotic patients are asexual. For consumers, however, it is often the case that the sexual effects of drug treatment diminish life quality, self-image, and recovery

---

* DKA – diabetic ketoacidosis, a potentially fatal emergency involving a drop in blood pH, associated with nausea, vomiting, anorexia, lethargy, and confusion

from *psychosis. Motivated by many of these concerns, a team of investigators in Spain conducted a survey among consumers (mean age: 32-41) of antipsychotic medications. They documented significant rates of sexual and reproductive dysfunction, even among recipients of atypical agents:[303]

EIRE Study: Sexual and Reproductive Side Effects in Spain

% of Patients Experiencing Side Effect

	haloperidol	risperidone	olanzapine	*quetiapine
males				
decreased libido	31%	38%	38%	21%
erectile dysfunction	31%	32%	26%	17%
ejaculatory dysfunction	28%	33%	20%	11%
gynecomastia	3%	4%	3%	0%
females				
decreased libido	24%	41%	34%	6%
amenorrhea	14%	28%	11%	6%

*Note: Quetiapine results reflect treatment exposure of 12 weeks or less. For all other drug therapies, 85-92% of the patients were exposed to these medications for more than 12 weeks.

Implications: Mortality and Morbidity

The implications of endocrine abnormalities are significant, for many of the aforementioned side effects - obesity, diabetes, and hyperlipidemia - increase the risks of microvascular and macrovascular disease. The former category includes disorders of the kidneys, retina, and nerves. The latter category includes

---

*psychosis - psychiatry, as a profession, seldom acknowledges the psychological impact of drug side effects. For example, one looks in vain across the medical literature for papers which discuss the impact of retrograde ejaculation. This common side effect of antipsychotic medications (which results in ejaculate flowing into the bladder, rather than outwards through the urethra) can easily lead to somatic delusions, body dysmorphic disorder, heightened anxiety, paranoia or mistrust.

damage to the heart and brain (i.e., heart attack and stroke). What is particularly concerning about these metabolic hazards is the fact that they often intensify the effects of risk factors which are already present in many patients (such as smoking, drug abuse, and a sedentary lifestyle).

The medical morbidities introduced by drug treatments must figure prominently in calculations of therapeutic utility. Considerations of just this kind prompted a New England team of investigators to estimate the health effects of antipsychotic-associated weight gain.[304] Based upon expected rates of impaired glucose tolerance and high blood pressure, the researchers predicted the impact of clozapine over a ten-year period of time. For every 100,000 schizophrenic patients treated over the upcoming decade, 492 suicides were felt to be preventable. At the same time, 416 additional deaths were believed to be likely as a result of medical conditions related to weight gain.

Other Forms of Antipsychotic Lethality

Omitted from the previous research group's projections were deaths from myocarditis, cardiomyopathy, agranulocytosis, seizures, pulmonary embolism, and other potentially lethal side effects of clozapine. Also omitted were projections of NMS, or neuroleptic malignant syndrome, a condition which can be caused by all antipsychotics through their blockade of dopamine receptors in the hypothalamus. First recognized by Jean Delay in 1961, NMS is characterized by fever, altered mentation (confusion, delirium), elevated white blood cell count, severe rigidity (sometimes with muscle breakdown, leading to elevated CPK and myoglobinuria), and autonomic dysfunction. Although the incidence of NMS has been estimated to range from 1-3%, the condition represents a true medical emergency which is fatal in about 10% of the cases.[305]

It is significant that mortality rates among patients with schizophrenia have been rising since the introduction of antipsychotic drug therapies. A recent mortality study performed in Sweden[306] monitored observed versus expected death rates among patients first hospitalized for schizophrenia between 1976 and 1995. Expected deaths were estimated from mortality rates in the general population. Across the twenty-year period of follow-up, standardized mortality ratios (rates of death among those with schizophrenia, divided by rates of death among those without) increased 1.7-fold in males and 1.3-fold in females. Similarly, in a study which compared mortality data among service utilizers in Northwest Wales in 1896 versus 1996, death as a direct consequence of mental illness was found to have increased in the so-called modern era.[307]

Specific causes of mortality among schizophrenics have been scrutinized by a number of research teams. In a study of more than 100 chronic patients in France, researchers found that neuroleptic dose was the most important variable accounting for premature death.[308]   In Ireland, an investigation of mortality among 88 chronically hospitalized schizophrenics (average age at study entry: 63) revealed that polypharmacy (more than one antipsychotic) and the absence of anticholinergic drugs were associated with a three-fold reduction in survival. Forty-four percent of these subjects died within ten years, usually from *respiratory disease.[309]   In a Dutch study performed between 1995 and 2001, over 550 cases of sudden cardiac death were compared against 4400 age- and gender-matched controls. Current use of antipsychotics (last prescription dispensed within 30 days of the time of death) was associated with a three-fold risk of sudden cardiac death. This risk increased significantly according to drug class (buytrophenones, such as haloperidol); dose (the higher the dose, the greater the risk of death); and duration of treatment (higher risk with use exceeding 90 days). Furthermore,

---

*respiratory disease – While smoking contributes to the high incidence of respiratory disease in patients with schizophrenia, an additional risk factor lies in dopamine blockade. Animal studies suggest how antipsychotic drugs might be harmful to pulmonary function. In rodents, dopamine has been shown to play a key role in the clearance of liquid from the epithelium of the lung. More specifically, D1 receptor stimulation has been linked to the clearance of fluid from the alveoli.[311-312] Medications which antagonize these activities may impair recovery from pulmonary edema – a potentially fatal condition in which the lung tissue fills with fluid, usually as a result of cardiac disease. Additional risks of medication include choking[313] and aspiration, due to the effects of dopamine antagonists upon the breathing centers of the brain (i.e., respiratory dyskinesia). Antipsychotics, such as clozapine, may also cause clots to form within the arteries of the lung, resulting in a frequently undiagnosed and rapidly fatal condition known as pulmonary embolism, or PE.

the risk of sudden cardiac death was elevated even at low doses, and even among patients who received antipsychotic drug therapy for non-schizophrenic conditions.[310]

Perhaps the most sobering aspect of antipsychotic toxicity is the fact that the patients exposed to it are already at risk for reduced longevity. According to a 2004 report of the New Zealand Mental Health Commission,[314] mental health patients in that country die approximately six to fourteen years sooner than the non-mentally ill. Excluding suicide, the mortality rates for mental health service users in New Zealand are 3-4 times higher than the general population. Leading causes of death are influenza, cancer, respiratory illnesses, diabetes, and heart disease. While the causes of these ailments are multifactorial (including poverty, poor access to health care, and smoking), the potential harmfulness of medication is a crucial variable which the New Zealand Mental Health Commission explicitly affirms:

> **"An individual must have the ability to improve their [sic] physical health. This ability [depends upon] ...access to appropriate services...physicians...who are aware of their role in improving and maintaining a person's good physical health [and] physicians who are aware of the dangers of iatrogenic illness."[315]**

Alternatives to Antipsychotic Drug Therapy

In a paper entitled "The Tragedy of Schizophrenia," Dr. Bert Karon challenges the prevailing notion that psychosis remains a largely incurable disease, best modified by pharmacological interventions.[316] Observing the historical fact that, within psychiatry, "there has never been a lack of treatments which do more harm than good,"[317] Karon explicitly contends that psychotherapy remains the treatment of choice for schizophrenia. He has good reasons for these assertions, explaining as he does both the problems of medications (limited effectiveness, the potential to induce tolerance, and the potential for irreversible and even lethal side effects); and the benefits of psychotherapy (e.g., insight into the motivations for behaviors and attitudes; the internalization of a corrective, healing relationship; the capacity to tolerate previously unbearable affect) when it is performed by motivated, competent practitioners. Increasingly since the 1950s, professionals and consumers have been led to believe that medications – though imperfect – represent the only effective treatment strategy for severe mental illness. Such a conviction ignores a substantial body of evidence from past and contemporary medical practice.

The Moral Treatment Movement refers to the work of practitioners who introduced humane approaches in the care of the insane during the late eighteenth century. Inspired by the ideals of the Enlightenment in France, and the Quakers in England, the proponents of Moral Treatment emphasized four essential elements in health care:[318]

> ➤ respect for the patient (no humiliation or cruelty)

> ➤ the encouragement of work and social relations

> ➤ the collection of accurate life histories

> ➤ the attempt to understand each person as an individual

In applying these imperatives in America and Europe, the rates of discharge from the first asylums reached 60-80% – far better than the 30% success rates of the 20th century. Although the Moral Treatment Movement was replaced in the late 1800s by biological psychiatry,[319] some of its elements were regenerated in the theory and practice of various psychosocial therapies (e.g., client-centered therapy, psychodynamic therapy, humanistic-existential therapy, peer counseling, vocational rehabilitation), the dismissal of which has led to the widespread *failure to understand* the unique experience of each person. It is this failure in understanding which Karon identifies as the real tragedy of schizophrenia (and, by implication, other conditions).

Pre-Neuroleptic Outcomes in Massachusetts

Writing in 1975, Bockoven and Harry Solomon evaluated the five-year outcomes of patients selected retrospectively from the rosters of two facilities in Massachusetts.[320] The study compared the prognoses of the first 100 patients committed for involuntary treatment at the Boston Psychopathic Hospital in 1947 (cohort 1947-1952) with the prognoses of the first 100 patients treated at the Solomon Mental Health Center in 1967 (cohort 1967-1972). Although the patients were similar in the severity of their symptoms, the interventions which they received were substantially different. Patients in the 1947 cohort received treatments that were limited to psychosocial therapies, while members of the 1967 cohort were exposed to psychotropic drugs throughout treatment. Results favored the non-neuroleptized. Relapse rates were lower among the patients treated before the advent of modern pharmacotherapies (40% of the Boston Psychopathic patients relapsed in five years vs. 70% of the patients from Solomon Center). Subjects treated in 1947 spent 50% more time in the hospital, due partly to stricter criteria for discharge (the average cumulative duration of inpatient care was two months shorter in 1967). Nevertheless, their long term outcomes appeared comparable in terms of community survival (76% vs. 87% of the two cohorts living in the community at five-year follow-up) and superior in terms of the need for rehospitalization (44% vs. 66% of the two cohorts requiring readmission, respectively). **While the use of medications reduced the cumulative duration of inpatient care during the first five years of treatment, medications were subsequently associated with higher numbers of patients relapsing, and a higher number of relapses per patient.**

Surprised by these research findings, the investigators drew the following conclusions:

> **"The finding of no substantial change in the outcome of schizophrenic patients was not expected in view of the absence of psychotropic drugs during the entire [five] years of the Boston Psychopathic Hospital follow-up period, compared with the extensive use of psychotropic drugs at Solomon Center for both initial treatment on admission and the entire period of aftercare. This finding suggests that the attitudes of personnel toward patients, the socioenvironmental setting, and community helpfulness guided by citizen organizations may be more important in tipping the balance in favor of social recovery than are psychotropic drugs...**

> **"The Solomon Center data also show that with today's community-based treatment more patients tend to relapse and the average number of relapses per patient during**

a 5-year period tends to be greater. The latter finding suggests that patients maintained in the community on psychotropic drugs may be less well established in their social recovery than were Boston Psychopathic patients, who did not receive psychotropic drugs."[321]

Vermont Longitudinal Study of Persons With Severe Mental Illness

In 1955, a multidisciplinary team of mental health care professionals developed a program of comprehensive rehabilitation and community placement for 269 severely disabled, back-wards patients at the Vermont State Hospital.[322-323] When none of these patients improved sufficiently following two or more years of chlorpromazine, they were offered a significantly revised plan of treatment. Conducted between January 1955 and December 1960, the rehabilitation program included the following components: drug treatment, open ward care in homelike conditions, group therapy, activity therapy, and vocational counseling. As patients became eligible for discharge, their treatment teams followed them into the community – in some cases, for 20 or more years. This provided an unrivalled degree of continuity in care. Previous therapists assisted patients with placement in outpatient clinics, living facilities (e.g., halfway houses), and jobs. At the time of their release to the community, the average age of each patient was 40 years, and the average duration of illness was sixteen years. Most patients had experienced multiple hospitalizations (median: two); persistent disability (ten years); and continuous residential confinement at the State facility for an average of six years.

Researchers were able to follow-up with 97% of the original cohort over a period which spanned three decades, making the Vermont State Hospital study one of the longest, most inclusive of its kind. Assessments were made with a variety of instruments in order to evaluate functioning in terms of employment, finances, relationships, basic self-care, and the use of the justice system. Outcome data were collected at several intervals, including ten-year and twenty-year follow-ups:

10-Year Follow-Up (1965)

70% of the original cohort were discharged from chronic, inpatient care

30% were discharged without any need for rehospitalization

20- to 25-Year Follow-Up (1980-1982)

50-66% were rated considerably improved or recovered

55% had slight or no impairment in terms of social functioning

50% were living independently

26% were employed (another 26% were retired)

Following the appearance of *DSM-III* in 1980, the research team re-examined the hospital records, classifying 118 patients according to the criteria for schizophrenia. Long term outcomes for this cohort were subsequently based upon direct interviews with the surviving subjects: 68% exhibited no signs of schizophrenia at the time of follow-up, and 45% displayed no psychiatric symptoms at all. Although the majority (84%) of patients had received psychotropic drugs at some point in their period of community treatment, 75% admitted that they had not consumed medication continuously. At the time of the 20-year follow-up, most had stopped receiving or using medication altogether (16% and 34% respectively), and another 25% had decided to use medication only intermittently.[324] Subsequent analyses revealed that all of the patients with full recoveries were among the 50% who had stopped medication.[325]

Michigan State Psychotherapy Project

Between 1966 and 1981, Drs. Bert Karon and Gary VandenBos supervised the Michigan State Psychotherapy Project in Lansing, Michigan.[326] Patients were randomly assigned to receive either 70 sessions of psychoanalytic therapy, medication, or both. Blinded assessments revealed that patients who received psychotherapy alone, or psychotherapy combined with time-limited drug treatment, achieved superior outcomes: earlier hospital discharge, fewer readmissions, and improvement in the quality of symptoms (e.g, thought disorder). The poorest outcomes occurred among the chronically medicated – even when drug treatment was combined with psychotherapy.

The Colorado Experiment: Humanizing a Psychiatric Ward

In 1970, Deikman and Whitaker presided over an innovative treatment ward at the University of Colorado.[327] Occurring just twenty years after the discovery of chlorpromazine, the Colorado "experiment" attached a priority to psychosocial interventions during the inpatient care of 51 subjects diagnosed with severe mental illness. As was true of the Moral Treatment Movement, the program emphasized collaboration, respect, and the understanding of behaviors as expressive of motive and meaning. Medications were used as interventions of last resort, in no small measure because the key investigators were keenly aware of the potential for neuroleptics to be administered punitively or in self-defense (to numb the patient in order to reduce the *therapist's* exposure to intensely unpleasant sensations). Individual and group psychotherapies were used with the goal of restoring pre-psychotic abilities and independent functioning, rather than the more limited goal of blunting symptoms in order to justify rapid discharge.

The study terminated after ten months, but not for a lack of success. Deikman and Whitaker had to move on to other professional responsibilities, while the hospital curtailed its budget for projects of this kind. Compared to the residents of the regular (phenothiazine) treatment wards, the recipients of the "experimental" therapies experienced lower recidivism (fewer readmissions after discharge) and lower mortality (one elopement with suicide in the initial summer months, compared to three suicides from the medication wards despite the fact that the latter quickly transferred the most difficult cases). These outcomes prompted the investigators to remark:

> "The question remains, 'Why are drugs the dominant treatment mode in most hospital settings?' In answering this question we would point to certain economic considerations on the one hand and to certain psychological factors on the other. In the short run, it would appear economic to hospitalize patients for less

than thirty days: many insurance plans will not pay for more than this length of stay. Thus, rapid reduction of symptoms becomes the main criterion for successful treatment outcome...Certain other goals of treatment, such as were established in our program, tend to be set aside in these efforts...The 'miracle' of drug treatment is then rather like the fable of the emperor's new clothes... In our opinion, the extreme reliance on drugs is wishful self-deception on the part of the psychiatric profession. In the long run, a practical approach to psychological treatment of severe emotional disturbance will have to be based on revised concepts of what constitutes good treatment and an implementation of these concepts in treatment plans."[328]

The Soteria Project

Between 1973 and 1981, Dr. Loren Mosher (then director of schizophrenia research at the National Institute of Mental Health) presided over an investigational treatment program in Northern California.[329] Over the course of nine years, the Soteria project involved the treatment of 179 young subjects, newly diagnosed with psychosis (schizophrenia or schizophrenia spectrum disorders). Consecutive patients arriving at a conventional medical facility in San Jose were assigned to receive care at a nearby psychiatric hospital or within the experimental component of the study. After excluding patients considered to be at imminent risk of harm to self or others, Soteria accepted psychotic patients into residential group homes within the community, where treatment was characterized by the following features:[330]

philosophy: a de-medicalized, de-biologized approach to dealing with psychotic experience; two laypersons provided the "formal" psychotherapy, with mental health professionals performing advisory or consultative roles

attitude: an attitude of *hopefulness* and an expectation of full recovery; staff members were selected for their attributes of intuition, introversion, flexibility, and tolerance

milieu: an atmosphere marked by involvement, support, and spontaneity

therapy: an emphasis upon the quality of staff-resident *relationships* as the key ingredient in therapy; a priority was placed upon the discovery of meaning within each subject's unique experience of psychosis

medication: a minimal use of neuroleptics and other drug therapies

This last feature was perhaps the most radical element of the Soteria project. Pharmacological treatments were not emphasized, due to the investigators' appreciation of their toxicities and limitations. This resulted in a striking contrast between the medication exposures of the Soteria subjects and the hospitalized controls:[331]

Neuroleptic Consumption - Soteria

76% of patients: no neuroleptics during initial six weeks of treatment

42% of patients: no neuroleptics during two-year follow-up

19% of patients: continuous neuroleptics throughout treatment

Neuroleptic Consumption - Community Hospital (controls)

94% of patients: continuous neuroleptic therapy, both during hospitalization and following discharge (average dose: 700 mg chlorpromazine)

After adjusting for differential rates of attrition (17% of Soteria, 37% of hospital controls), the Soteria cohort (all diagnoses) out-performed the hospital group by achieving significantly superior outcomes in terms of residual psychopathology and readmissions. For those diagnosed with schizophrenia, the advantages of Soteria were even greater, including reduced levels of psychopathology, a higher likelihood of psychopathology improvement, and a higher probability of returning to work.

Another California Experiment

In 1978, Rappoport et. al. summarized the findings of the clinical outcomes of 80 young males (aged 16-40), hospitalized in San Jose at the Agnews State Hospital for the treatment of early schizophrenia.[332]   Subjects were excluded for a history of ECT (electroshock therapy) within six months of admission; drug abuse immediately before admission; or multiple previous hospitalizations.   Following acceptance into the study, patients were randomly assigned to receive placebo or neuroleptic therapy (chlorpromazine).   Drug treatments were administered in a double-blinded fashion.   Treatment effectiveness was evaluated by comparing baseline assessment scores obtained at the time of entry (Brief Psychiatric Rating Scale, Global Assessment Rating Scale) with follow-up assessments conducted at multiple intervals for as long as 36 months after hospital discharge.

In order to control for the long-term behaviors of patients (many of whom changed treatments during follow-up), results were described by classifying participants according to the longitudinal course of their therapies:

placebo >> off >> placebo during hospitalization, no medication at follow-up

placebo >> on >> placebo during hospitalization, on antipsychotic drug at follow-up

chlorpromazine >> off >> chlorpromazine during hospitalization, no antipsychotic medication at follow-up

chlorpromazine >> on >> chlorpromazine during hospitalization, on antipsychotic medication at follow-up

At the time of last contact, 39 of the 80 subjects reported that they were receiving neuroleptic therapy (35% acknowledged current non-compliance, and 65% acknowledged intermittent non-compliance). The remainder of the patient group (41 of the original 80) stated that they were no longer consuming neuroleptics, and that they had been off medication for 70% of the post-hospital period.   The best outcomes – in terms of severity of illness – were found among the placebo/off treatment group. Furthermore, the patients who received placebo during hospitalization with little or no neuroleptic therapy afterwards manifested the greatest overall change in terms of symptomatic improvement; the lowest number of hospital readmissions (8% vs. 16-53% of the other treatment groups); and the fewest overall functional disturbances. Based upon their findings, the investigators observed:

> **"...for most patients, antipsychotic medication is the treatment of choice early in the course of schizophrenia, particularly if one is interested in symptom reduction. Our findings suggest, however, that antipsychotic medication is not the treatment of choice, at least for certain patients, if one is interested in long term clinical improvement."[333]**

Additionally, they offered speculations about why this might be so:

"A number of clinicians have suggested that the period immediately following an acute schizophrenic break is critical and that how a patient is treated during this time is quite important. The stormy phase.... can be looked upon as an attempt at reorientation, at solving problems of living...In order to solve these basic problems of living, the acute schizophrenic needs to retain his sensitivity and awareness and must have full access to all his psychological resources. Phenothiazines, by reducing neurological sensitivity, may interfere with these problem-solving, reintegrative responses."[334]

Finland: Acute Psychosis Integrated Treatment

In 1992, clinicians in Finland launched a multi-center research project using Acute Psychosis Integrated (API) Treatment.[335] Their goal was to investigate the role of neuroleptic therapy when psychosocial measures were applied maximally in first episode psychosis. Like their American predecessors who conceived and delivered Soteria, the API researchers were keenly aware of the problems associated with neuroleptic drug therapy, and highly enthusiastic about a model of care which would stress four central principles: family collaboration, teamwork, a basic therapeutic attitude, and adaptation to the specific needs of each patient.

The project enrolled 135 subjects with first episode psychosis (84 experimental, 51 controls) ranging in age from 25-34 (mean age: 29). All of them lacked previous exposure to neuroleptic drugs, and limited or no exposure to psychotherapy. Six different hospitals and their associated outpatient clinics agreed to apply the Finnish treatment model in terms of the central principles and orientation. However, three of the centers agreed to use antipsychotics sparingly:

Two Year Exposure to Antipsychotic Drug Therapy

	API Experimental Treatment	Control Group
no neuroleptics at any point in treatment (initial or follow-up)	43%	6%
mean total duration of neuroleptic treatment	43 weeks	57 weeks
percent of subjects receiving doses above 450 mg chlorpromazine equivalent at any point in treatment	3%	13%
percent of subjects receiving any form of psychotherapy	73%	54%

Despite the fact that the experimental group consisted of more patients with severe illness (schizophrenia), and longer durations of untreated psychosis (49 days vs. 23 days for the controls), their two year outcomes were superior:

257

Two Year Outcomes

	API Experimental Treatment	Controls
percent of subjects with fewer than two weeks in hospital	51%	26%
percent of subjects without psychosis in past year	58%	41%
percent of subjects with high functioning (Global Assessment Scale)	49%	25%

Among the experimental cohort, the patients who received neuroleptics did not differ from those who did not, in terms of premorbid adjustment, employment, diagnosis, or duration of untreated psychosis. Nevertheless, it was the neuroleptized subset of patients who manifested the poorest results – a finding which the investigators were inclined to attribute to the patient (underlying pathology) rather than pills. (Perhaps this reflected their unfamiliarity with the behavioral and cognitive toxicities of dopamine blockade.)

In summarizing the main findings of the API Treatment project, the researchers posed the following question:

> **"What do these results mean in practice? They clearly support the notion that psychosocial measures are useful and effective in the treatment of first-time psychotic patients. It also seems evident that ...neuroleptic treatment is not as essential as it has usually been considered, if intensive psychosocial treatment measures are provided."[336]**

Additional Examples of Effective Non-Medical Therapies

Before leaving the subject of non-pharmacological therapies and their role in the treatment of psychosis, it is important to underscore their value even among patients with chronic or severe symptoms. A little known French study was conducted for nine months in 1959, during which a psychiatrist and pharmacologist colluded in substituting placebo for neuroleptic therapy in the care of 68 chronic ward residents.[337] All of the subjects had received medication for six months to three years before the clandestine experiment. Throughout the placebo trial, neither staff members nor patients were aware of the project. Nevertheless, ward life continued without significant change. At the end of nine months, an endpoint analysis among treatment completers (39 subjects) showed surprising results: 56% of the subjects had improved, 39% had remained the same, and only 5% (two patients) had worsened. While this study had obvious problems in terms of the ethical nature of its design (i.e., none of the participants were informed that they might be exposed to placebo), its results were consistent with the high rates of placebo response (typically 20-40%) documented by other researchers. These findings should not be dismissed lightly by the advocates of drug therapy, since these efficacy rates rival those observed in even the most promising psychopharmacology trials.

The French study is not mentioned here as an endorsement of the surreptitious use of placebo (although, to be sure, some observers have suggested possible advantages if psychiatry were to return to this practice). Rather, the point here is to communicate the vital need for clinicians to consider a variety of therapeutic modalities (e.g., *pre-therapy, psychodrama, exercise, cognitive remediation) which have demonstrated their capacity to effect hopefulness and healing, and which appear to do so without the problems associated with drug-induced, allostatic load.

---

*pre-therapy – a type of therapy derived from client-centered theory and practice. As described and developed by Prouty, pre-therapy refers to a method of making contact with individuals who are not yet capable of engaging in expressive (particularly, verbal) forms of communication. It has been used successfully in hospital milieus in Europe and the U.K. in the treatment of psychosis and dementia.[338-340]

Chapter Nine
STIMULANTS AND
ATTENTION DEFICIT HYPERACTIVITY DISORDER (ADHD)

The History of Stimulant Medications

Stimulants, because of their existence in a variety of natural forms (the leaves of the coca plant, nicotine, caffeine, camphor, strychnine, arsenic, ma huang), have been used since ancient times to alter stamina and mood. It was not until the 20th century, however, that stimulants came to occupy a central role in Western medicine, when physicians discovered their utility in counteracting the symptoms of asthma and the respiratory effects of surgical anesthetics.[1-3]

In contrast to the rich literature which describes the development of antidepressant and antipsychotic drugs, the record on stimulants is nebulous. The story begins in Germany in 1887[4] with L. Edeleano's synthesis of the first amphetamine (phenylisopropylamine) as a part of his research in the fledgling field of organic chemistry. No medicinal applications were pursued, though, because the German efforts were interrupted by war.

In the 1920s, K.K. Chen and fellow chemists at Eli Lilly succeeded in isolating the active ingredient of the botanical stimulant, ma huang (Ephedra). Naming this substance ephedrine, the medication gained favor as a substitute for epinephrine in the treatment of asthma, because it was well absorbed from the stomach and bloodstream and worked effectively to open constricted airways. Around the same time period, a Californian team of researchers led by Gordon Alles revived the work of German chemists by producing several forms of amphetamines. The racemic mixture of amphetamine (named Benzedrine) became the key ingredient in over-the-counter inhalants, as it was useful in decreasing nasal secretions. The d-enantiomer of amphetamine (Dexedrine) became a treatment for narcolepsy and obesity.

Both amphetamines were quickly recognized by the consuming public for their euphoric and alerting effects. For example,

Benzedrine was consumed by many college students in the 1930s as a performance enhancer[5] when it was discovered that the paper strips inside the menthol inhalers could be removed and swallowed in order to relieve fatigue and enhance focus when cramming for final exams. Amphetamines were distributed in Europe and Japan to soldiers and industrial workers during World War II for much the same reason. Unfortunately, the post-war experience in Japan underscored the addictive potential of these drugs when an epidemic of amphetamine abuse emerged among 5% of the population (teenagers and young adults).[6] Partly in response to this development, the U.S. FDA banned Benzedrine inhalers in 1959 and restricted the availability of amphetamines to prescription use only.[7]

Within American psychiatry, the stimulants had a particularly fateful beginning. In 1937, a Rhode Island physician named Charles Bradley administered Benzedrine to children who had been hospitalized for a variety of neurological and behavioral disorders.[8] As a part of his comprehensive assessments, Bradley performed routine lumbar punctures (spinal taps) on his patients. Not surprisingly, this led him to seek a treatment for the severe or protracted headaches which often followed these invasive procedures. Speculating that the children's headaches were caused by the acute reduction of spinal fluid, Bradley hypothesized that Benzedrine (already famous for its respiratory uses) might be used to stimulate the choroid plexus of the brain to *speed up* the production of spinal fluid. Bradley believed that this would terminate the headache pain. In his first trials of Benzedrine, he discovered that the children's headaches persisted. Quite unexpectedly, though, fourteen of his patients reported an improvement in their learning capacity and subsequently referred to the Benzedrine tablets as "math pills." Bradley continued to use the stimulant in his patients, although his work was overlooked by neurologists and psychiatrists for more than a decade.

In 1944, Ciba (now Novartis) synthesized methylphenidate (Ritalin). It took ten years for scientists to determine its pharmacological mechanism of action, and almost ten more before researchers at Johns Hopkins University conducted the first Ritalin trial in children. Led by Leon Eisenberg in 1963, the landmark study evaluated the efficacy of Ritalin and Dexedrine in controlling the behaviors of institutionalized children. Four years later,[9] the same researchers expanded their studies to include schoolchildren (target symptoms included talking loudly, giggling for no reason, daydreaming, or using the bathroom too often).

In the 1960s, the support of NIMH (National Institute of Mental Health) and major universities propelled the use of stimulant medications for childhood behavioral disorders. This trend subsequently proliferated in the context of Congressional and special interest group support (e.g., the learning disability industry, the creators of *DSM-III* and its revisions, and pharmaceutical industry front groups like *CHADD and **NAMI).

Among adults, stimulants were historically regarded as effective treatments for fatigue and nervousness (non-melancholic depression). However, that role was gradually usurped by other drug therapies: first, by sedative-hypnotics (benzodiazepines); then, by chemicals which came to be defined by certain cultures as "specific remedies" for depression.[10] Today, stimulant medications are used in Western societies predominantly for the treatment of narcolepsy and ADHD, and less often for the treatment of obesity.

Due to the social costs of certain behavioral side effects (addiction, violence, joblessness), some observers express concern about the diversion of prescribed stimulants for recreational purposes. Others wonder about the implications and societal pressures associated with the growing use of stimulants for performance enhancement by students, laborers, and professionals who seek to alter their capacity to tolerate long periods of wakefulness or to sharpen their mental acuity for specific challenges (i.e., multi-tasking, tedium, or war).

---

*CHADD – Children and Adults with Attention Deficit/Hyperactivity Disorde, a national non-profit organization found in 1987 for the purposes of education, advocacy, and support.[11] CHADD has been criticized by the World Health Organization for serving as a conduit for pharmaceutical company advertising and lobbying, in violation of the 1971 Psychotropic Drugs Convention.[12]

**NAMI – National Alliance for the Mentally Ill, a nonprofit support and advocacy organization founded in the United States in 1979. NAMI now supports a number of "sister organizations" around the world.[13]

Examples of Stimulant Medications

d-amphetamine	(Dexedrine)	
methylphenidate	(Ritalin)	
pemoline	(Cylert)	removed from Canadian market in 1999 due to liver toxicity
atomoxetine	(Strattera)	On December 17, 2004, the FDA issued a safety alert to inform health care professionals about possible liver toxicity with Strattera, and to advise them about forthcoming changes in the product label to reflect this warning.

Mechanisms of Action

Based upon animal research, four major mechanisms have been advanced to describe the cellular effects of stimulant medications. The first of these processes involves the blockade of reuptake transporters on the neurons which make and release catecholamines (dopamine and norepinephrine). A second process involves the enhancement of catecholamine release from the nerve terminals where they are made and stored.

A third process involves the inhibition of a key enzyme (monoamine oxidase B) within the nerve terminal of these neurons, in order to prevent the breakdown of dopamine and norepinephrine. This presumably enhances the supply and availability of catecholamines for neurotransmission. A fourth process involves the direct effects of medications upon post-synaptic (alpha) adrenergic receptors in the brain.[14-16]

Dextro-amphetamine (Dexedrine) is thought to be unique among stimulants, as it not only blocks the reuptake of dopamine and norepinephrine through the respective transporters, but also enters nerve terminals to stimulate neurotransmitter release directly. Researchers believe that amphetamine exerts this latter effect by acting upon the newly synthesized pool of catecholamines within the cytoplasm of the neuron.[17]

Methylphenidate (Ritalin), like amphetamine, is a potent inhibitor of the dopamine transporter – in fact, two times more potent than cocaine.[18]   It also blocks the norepinephrine transporter. Some researchers believe that methylphenidate also dislodges catecholamines from the storage vesicles inside the cell (bouton).

Pemoline (Cylert) has an unknown mechanism of action.   Since its chemical and behavioral effects resemble amphetamine, researchers believe that pemoline acts through dopaminergic pathways. The cause of its heptaotoxicity remains unclear.

Atomoxetine (Strattera) was approved by the FDA in 2002. Like amphetamine, cocaine, and methylphenidate, atomoxetine binds to the norepinephrine transporter and blocks the reuptake of the neurotransmitter. This increases norepinephrine levels in diffuse regions of the brain and spinal cord. Levels of dopamine are also increased by atomoxetine in the frontal lobes.

How Stimulant Medications Are Defined

Historically, medicinal and non-medicinal compounds have been classified as stimulants with reference to their *chemical* effects (boosting the synthesis and release of catecholamines); *physiological* effects (stimulating the sympathetic nervous system: accelerating the heart rate, dilating the pupils, increasing the rate of breathing, diminishing secretions and gastric motility); and *neurobehavioral* effects (reducing fatigue, suppressing appetite, increasing motor activity, enhancing alertness).

This tradition is important to appreciate in the context of the marketing campaign of atomoxetine (Strattera), which has been boldly and inappropriately touted as the first "non-stimulant" drug treatment for ADHD. It is significant that neurologists in Europe have found that a pharmacologically identical drug (another selective norepinephrine reuptake inhibitor, known as reboxetine) produces alerting effects in patients with the sleep disorder narcolepsy. This finding has prompted these physicians to wonder why reboxetine has not yet been designated a neurostimulant.[19]

Even more striking is the fact that the World Health Organization has unambiguously identified atomoxetine (Strattera) as a *sympathomimetic agent according to the **ATC system of drug classification:

"Atomoxetine has been classified in the ATC group N06B Psychostimulants, agents used for ADHD, further in the ATC 4th level of N06BA centrally acting sympathomimetics - i.e., in the same 4th level as amphetamine. Drugs are classified in the ATC system according to the main therapeutic use, and according to the organ or system on which they act, and their chemical, pharmacological, and therapeutic properties."[20]

N **NERVOUS SYSTEM**

N06 **PSYCHOANALEPTICS**

N06B **PSYCHOSTIMULANTS, AGENTS USED FOR ADHD AND NOOTROPICS**

N06BA **Centrally acting sympathomimetics**

	DDD	Unit	Adm.route	Notes
N06BA01 **Amfetamine**	15	mg	O	
N06BA01 **Amfetamine**	15	mg	P	
N06BA02 **Dexamfetamine**	15	mg	O	
N06BA03 **Metamfetamine**	15	mg	O	
N06BA04 **Methylphenidate**	30	mg	O	
N06BA05 **Pemoline**	40	mg	O	
N06BA06 **Fencamfamin**				
N06BA07 **Modafinil**	0.3	g	O	
N06BA08 **Fenozolone**				
N06BA09 **Atomoxetine**				

Source: World Health Organization Collaborating Centre for Drug Statistics Methodology[21]

---

*sympathomimetic – mimicking the action of the sympathetic nervous system[22]

**ATC – Anatomical Therapeutic Chemical classification; a system of classifying medications, introduced by the Nordic Council of Medicines in 1975, and adopted by the World Health Organization in 1981 as a standardized system for international drug utilization studies[23]

How Do Stimulants Improve the Symptoms of ADHD ?

Despite the fact that stimulant medications have been prescribed by physicians for more than 60 years, the mechanisms through which they achieve beneficial effects remain speculative. Textbooks are frustratingly vague:

> **"Because of the multiple and widespread effects of amphetamines, it is difficult to demonstrate that a specific neurochemical change is responsible for ameliorating a particular symptom. A theoretically appealing possibility is that methylphenidate and amphetamine serve to boost dopamine transmission in the brain's attentional structures ...however, the complexity of attentional and motor control systems suggest that such a model is simplistic and incomplete."[24]**

Neuroscientists have been perplexed for years by the realization that drugs which boost dopamine in animals increase locomotor and stereotypical behaviors. This has been one of the facts which has led observers to refer to the calming effects of stimulants (when they occur in humans) as "paradoxical." To account for this discrepancy, researchers have suggested that the therapeutic value of dopamine boosting agents arises from their effects upon self-regulatory (executive) functions of the brain.

Consistent with this theme is the work of investigators who have suggested that stimulants change the homeostasis of dopamine transmission by diminishing the extent to which incoming nerve impulses are able to provoke the phasic release of dopamine.[25-27] According to this hypothesis, stimulants enhance task-related cell firing by improving the "signal to noise" ratio in the dopamine systems of the brain. For example, a stimulant might allow a fidgety or impulsive person to sit quietly while reading. In another context, however, the same stimulant would preserve the capacity of this individual to respond to novel or stressful stimuli. (On a cellular level, this model suggests that large enough afferent inputs to the dopamine neurons are able to override the tonic inhibition of neurotransmitter release which is mediated by autoreceptor processes. Presumably, this provides for task-dependent increases in motor activity and cognitive functions).

266

Long Term Effects

Animal research suggests that the chronic administration of stimulants leads to many adaptive changes in the brain,[28-31] including a **reduction in dopamine transporters** (with prepubertal or early administration of methylphenidate causing a persistent reduction of dopamine transporters in the striatum of the rat brain); a **decrease in dopamine D2 receptors; alterations in gene expression** (daily methylphenidate reducing the expression of *c-fos* in the striatum of prepubertal rats); and **morphological changes**. With regards to the latter, stimulants (amphetamine and cocaine) have been found to change the anatomy of the brain. These structural changes include dendritic lengthening and branching, and an increase in the spine density of cells in key brain regions (nucleus accumbens and frontal cortex) associated with learning and addiction. Since these anatomic changes persist long after drug-taking has ended, researchers speculate that they may be the basis of the behavioral sensitization (craving and addiction) and/or psychotic features which emerge in some individuals during periods of extended drug abstinence. In animal studies, researchers have also found that stimulant-induced changes in neuronal architecture interfere with the acquisition of new skills or behaviors.[32]

Human studies involving PET (positron emission tomography) scans of the brain have replicated many of these findings. For example, researchers in the Netherlands performed pre-treatment (Ritalin) and post-treatment imaging studies of six boys diagnosed with ADHD. Following three months of stimulant therapy, head scans revealed a 20% reduction in D2 receptors and a 75% reduction in dopamine transporters in the striatum.[33] One child underwent neuroimaging one month after stopping Ritalin. Although the D2 density in his brain returned to pre-treatment levels, the dopamine transporters in the left striatum increased *30-50% above the levels which had existed prior to stimulant therapy*. If, as some researchers surmise,[34] a high dopamine transporter level is one of the *causes* of ADHD, this finding suggests that the sequence of chronic Ritalin, followed by drug withdrawal, has the potential to induce a significant worsening of the original condition.

Although stimulants have been prescribed to children in the United States for more than six decades, it appears that no one has performed an epidemiological study which has followed subjects prospectively through adulthood in order to monitor specifically for the onset of dopamine-related neurological disease. Of particular concern are the tics[35] which arise in many children during active treatment, due to disruptions in dopamine transmission within the basal ganglia (the movement centers of the brain). If chronic stimulant therapy during childhood or adolescence begets changes in gene expression and neuronal connectivity within the nigrostriatal pathways, one must wonder about the potential for these drugs to contribute to Parkinson's disease or other dyskinetic disorders with advancing age.

Another potential long term effect of stimulant therapy is heart disease. While stimulants have been linked to sudden deaths in children, these events have presumably been rare. As a result, the cardiotoxicity of stimulants has generally been minimized by the medical profession. Nonetheless, since animal studies have documented structural changes in the heart tissue following treatment with stimulant drugs (e.g., lamellar membrane accumulations within the cells of the myocardium),[36] one must wonder about similar effects in humans. In other words, the cardiac effects of childhood medication might manifest themselves in adulthood (similar to the delayed effects of anabolic steroids) by contributing to the pathogenesis of cardiomyopathy, arrythmias, or other forms of heart disease.

Prescribing Trends

According to epidemiologists at the University of Maryland,[37] stimulant treatment for the condition of Attention Deficit Disorder in U.S. children doubled every four to seven years between 1971 and 1987. However, it was the congressional and presidential proclamations declaring the 1990s to be the "Decade of the Brain"[38] which appear to have stimulated the epidemic of ADHD, as the news media, pharmaceutical industry, professional organizations (American Psychiatric Association, American Psychological Association), and research institutions (National Institute of Mental Health) collaborated in a massive public awareness campaign which attributed variations in attention and impulse control to an underlying brain *pathology*. Thanks to that campaign, stimulant use by American youths *doubled*, continuation of stimulants through adolescence *tripled*, and the overall rate of juvenile ADHD *quadrupled*:[39-44]

Source #1: National Medical Expenditure Surveys

> ➤ 0.9 per 100 children treated for ADHD in 1987

> ➤ 3.4 per 100 children treated for ADHD in 1997

Source #2: Regional (Maryland) and National databases, DEA production quotas for methylphenidate (Ritalin)

> ➤ 3-4% (1.5 million) of U.S. youths aged 5-18 receiving Ritalin in mid-1995

> ➤ 6-fold rise in Ritalin production quotas between 1990 and mid-1995

> ➤ 1.8 to 2.5 fold increase in prevalence of Ritalin treatment of Maryland youths between 1990 and 1995. Baltimore County (school nurses' headcount) 2.5% of entire student body aged 5-14 receiving Ritalin in 1991; 3.2% of entire student body receiving Ritalin in 1993; 4.6% of entire student body receiving Ritalin in 1995

> ➤ more girls, more teens on medication than before

> ➤ longer duration of treatment: more youths continuing medication into teens; 11% of children continuing stimulants into high school in 1975; 31% of children continuing stimulants into high school in 1995

Source #3: Duke University study on ADHD and stimulants among children ages 9-16 in 11 counties of NC

> ➤ 3.4% of schoolchildren meeting criteria for ADHD

> ➤ 7.3% of the schoolchildren receiving stimulants

Source #4: Eastern Virginia Medical School study of in-school stimulant use among grade schoolers in 1995-1996

- ➢ 8-10% of the children in grades two through five receiving stimulants or other drugs from school nurse for diagnosed ADHD

- ➢ 18-20% of Caucasian males receiving ADHD medication by grade five

Source #5: Michigan State point prevalence rate of methylphenidate use in February and March 1992

- ➢ 11/1000 (0.1%) of residents aged 10-19 received a Ritalin prescription during study period

- ➢ 43/1000 (4.3%) of boys aged 10-11 received Ritalin 84% of the Ritalin prescriptions given by primary care physicians; 59% of the Ritalin prescriptions given by pediatricians; 50% of the Ritalin prescriptions given by 5% of the state's pediatricians

Source #6: Maryland Medicaid Youths 1991 data for methylphenidate use among children aged 5-14

- ➢ 2.2% of children receiving methylphenidate

- ➢ males four times more likely to receive methylphenidate than females

- ➢ whites 2.5 times more likely to receive methylphenidate than blacks

It is interesting to compare the reactions of physicians to these developments. In 1971, a concerned physician submitted the following letter to a major medical journal:

> "Like most pediatricians in private practice, I receive one or two calls a week about the first or second grade boy who is not sitting still in school, who is disturbing the other children, and whose parent or teacher or guidance counselor feels that my putting him on methylphenidate

hydrochloride (Ritalin) or dextroamphetamine (Dexedrine) would be of value.

"Recently a mother called me with this typical case history. I explained to her that during the child's recent complete physical examination I had detected no neurological abnormalities. I also pointed out that nothing in his prenatal or subsequent course had indicated neurological impairment... Further discussion centered around the fact that his hyperactivity would probably get better when he was around 9 or 10 years old, and it was worth waiting. It was also pointed out that, really, the long range effects of medication to make boys sit still are not well known.

"The boy's mother ended the conversation with a most heartwarming statement: 'In other words, Doctor, what you're telling me is that Ritalin wouldn't make my boy any better but would make the school better.'" [45]

Although such a letter would probably be censored by the same journal today, it remains true that many physicians express reservations about the use of medications for ADHD. A survey[46] conducted among 1000 physicians with a history of prescribing stimulant medications to children and adolescents revealed the following opinions (365 responding):

19% were worried about stimulant diversion (sharing of drugs among youths for euphoric or alerting effects)

22% were concerned about side effect of anxiety

32% were concerned about side effects of appetite or weight loss

38% stated that they would prefer to prescribe a non-stimulant

50% were concerned about side effect of sleep disruption

58% stated that they would prefer to prescribe a non-controlled substance instead of a medication which is ˙controlled because of abuse potential

There is a significant gap between the concerns which these physicians say they have, and the reality of their prescribing habits. While many physicians "talk the talk" of professional ambivalence, they "walk a walk" which has led to 4% to 10% of American youths swallowing stimulant medications to get through each school day. How has this been rationalized ?

Efficacy & Effectiveness

According to their advocates, nothing "works" as effectively for inattention or hyperactivity as stimulant medications. The overwhelming majority of articles appearing in medical textbooks and journals on the subject of ADHD present stimulants as the gold standard of treatment, with a reported efficacy rate of 70-90%. By efficacy (favorable short term response) it is suggested that children become less impulsive, less fidgety, and more focused. However, it is important to appreciate the quality of the studies which have been responsible for the construction of this opinion.

A ˙meta-analysis of sixty-two randomized controlled trials (RCTs) involving almost 3000 subjects with a primary diagnosis of ADHD demonstrated weak findings for short acting Ritalin.[47] Thirty-nine percent of published trials were of low quality; 26% of the trials reported results of Ritalin along with additional drugs or interventions; and at least eight trials suppressed teacher data which showed poorer Ritalin effects. Moreover, all trials noted significant adverse events:

˙controlled substances – In 1971, the U.S. Department of Health and Human Services implemented the Controlled Substance Act. This act classifies drugs into five categories, or schedules, according to their potential for abuse. Controlled substances have stringent record-keeping and storage requirements. Non-controlled substances are not subject to these restraints, due to a low potential for addiction. Of the stimulant medications, amphetamine and methylphenidate (DEA Schedule II) and pemoline (DEA Schedule IV) are controlled. Atomoxetine is a non-controlled stimulant. (continued on following page.)

number needed to harm for appetite suppression = 4

number needed to harm for insomnia = 7

number needed to harm for stomachache = 9

Note: number needed to harm is a statistical term which refers to the number of consecutive patients who need to be treated before a specific kind of adverse event is detected.

Based upon these findings, the authors concluded that "broad generalizations about the usefulness of Ritalin should probably be avoided,"[48] particularly due to the lack of long term trial evidence. However, long term studies *have* been conducted, and these investigations reinforce the opinion that stimulant utility is limited. Long term studies also raise questions about the very *process* of medicating children, in terms of the beliefs which the children themselves come to hold about the *causes* of their behavior.

The most important Randomized Controlled Trial (RCT) to date on the long term effectiveness of stimulants is the NIMH (National Institute of Mental Health) Multimodal Treatment Study of Children with Attention Deficit/Hyperactivity Disorder, otherwise known as the MTA study. Started in 1991, the MTA randomized 579 children diagnosed with ADHD into four groups for 14 months of treatment:[49, 50]

MTA Study

Group 1: medication management only

Stimulant medication was increased over a period of 28 days, then adjusted monthly to find the best dose. Patients were continued on medication indefinitely, receiving an average daily dose of 30.5

(continued from previous page)* meta-analysis – a method of combining the results of several independent studies of the same outcome so that an overall test of **statistical significance* can be determined

**statistical significance – generally interpreted as a result that would occur by chance less than 1 time in 20; it occurs when the null hypothesis is rejected or, in other words, when the findings of a particular study are thought to represent a "true" difference between two or more experimental groups

mg/day of Ritalin, divided into three portions (morning, noon, late afternoon).

Group 2: behavioral therapy

The behavioral therapy arm of the study consisted of parent training, child training, and teacher training. Parents received a maximum of twenty-seven group and eight individual sessions. Teachers received ten to sixteen biweekly consultations. In addition, a trained aide was provided to the classroom for twelve weeks of on-site assistance (coaching) with each ADHD child. The child-focused therapy consisted of an eight-week summer camp which included intensive behavioral interventions, academics, social skills, and recreation.

Group 3: medication combined with behavioral therapy

Individuals assigned to this treatment group received the same medication and behavioral elements described above. Behavioral therapy was gradually reduced over the course of six to nine months, while medication was continued indefinitely.

Group 4: community comparison

The community comparison arm of the study assigned children to treatment as usual in the community. This consisted of stimulant medication (generally at lower doses and twice a day instead of three times a day) in approximately two-thirds of the group. The remaining patients did not receive medication. Details of non-pharmacological interventions for these children were either unavailable or not reported.

Arguably the most important American study of ADHD children to date, the MTA featured significant methodological deficiencies which limit the applicability of its findings and the validity of its conclusions. Among the chief confounds were the following features:

1) study was not blinded

   Teachers, parents, evaluators, and patients all knew whether or not a child was receiving an active drug treatment. This may have led to exaggerated ratings of behavior, based upon the expectancies of adults and children alike.

2) over 1/3 of the children had received previous treatment with stimulants

This may have led to structural brain changes associated with sensitization in many children. When these same subjects were then randomized to the unmedicated, behavioral therapy arm of the study, they may have been psychologically or physiologically vulnerable to poorer outcomes.

3) drug treatment was continued throughout the 14 months of the study, whereas behavioral treatment interventions were gradually withdrawn over the course of 6-9 months

By the time of the 14 month endpoint, all of the children in the behavioral treatment arm had been off therapy for at least one month or more. This turned the MTA study into a comparison between treated versus untreated ADHD patients.

4) compliance within each intended treatment group was limited

in the medication group: 22% did not comply

in the behavioral therapy group: 37% did not comply

in the combined treatment group:

19% did not comply with the pharmacological component

36% did not comply with the behavioral component

5) behavioral therapy did not include any significant component of cognitive therapy[51]

To the extent that ADHD children experience deficits in skill sets (content), and not just in performance (process), the emphasis upon "contingency" therapy (operant conditioning) may have been inadequate to meet the needs of many children.

While it is true that the MTA 14-month outcomes favored subjects in the combined and medication treatment groups, it is also true that subjects in all treatment arms demonstrated significant improvements. Despite the significant methodological deficiencies, the behavioral treatment arm of the study still managed to demonstrate effectiveness which was equal to regular community treatment, where two-thirds of the children had been treated with stimulant drugs. More than 75% of the MTA behavioral treatment subjects were successfully maintained throughout the 14 months of the study without the use of medication. Furthermore, for the 34% of the subjects in the study who displayed anxiety disorders along with ADHD, behavioral treatment was associated with the most impressive responses of the four interventions. However, the MTA story does not end here.

As the MTA was devised as a long-term prospective study, the investigators continued evaluations at another assessment point.[52] At 24 months, 540 of 579 original subjects were re-examined on five domains of functioning:

ADHD symptoms rated by parent and teacher

ODD (Oppositional Defiant Disorder) symptoms rated by parent and teacher

Social skills rated by parent and teacher

Wechsler Individual Achievement test reading score

Negative parental discipline score

Evaluators compared the scores on these assessment instruments over time, to see how assigned treatment influenced each subject's progress. *Trajectories of recovery reversed between 14 and 24 months.* On three of the five outcome measures (ADD symptoms, socials skills, and negative parental discipline), *the groups receiving medication demonstrated a deterioration in their condition. In contrast, patients in the behavioral therapy or community comparison groups of the study remained stable.*

The long term findings of the NIMH Multimodal Treatment Study also suggest that stimulant therapies may have been poorly tolerated by many children:

	Children Remaining on Medications	
	at 14 months	at 24 months
combined therapy group (stimulants + behavioral therapy)	87%	68%
medication management group	93%	69%

Small increases in the use of drug therapy occurred among the subjects who were originally randomized to the behavioral therapy and community care arms of the study:

	Children on Medications	
	at 14 months	at 24 months
behavior therapy group	23 %	38%
community care group	55%	61%

The investigators maintained that the symptomatic deterioration patterns were partially dependent upon changing patterns of medication use during the follow-up period. However, subjects who *did not stop medication still manifested a slight deterioration* in their condition (mean increase of 0.15 points on the ADHD and ODD outcome measures).

This deterioration was *more pronounced* than that seen in patients who began the study in the unmedicated group and who remained drug free (mean increase of 0.10 points on ADHD and ODD outcome measures). Meanwhile, individuals who moved from a non-medicated to medicated status showed only a small improvement in their condition (mean decrease of 0.15 points on the ADHD and ODD outcome measures). In conclusion, the investigators conceded that their 24 month findings were consistent with *a decline in the effectiveness of medication therapy (when it was continued), and a significant worsening of symptoms when it was stopped:*

"deterioration was largest in groups that had initially shown the greatest benefits."

Of the children who started the investigation in the behavioral therapy group, 58% remained drug free. Most of these subjects maintained their response over the two year period of follow-up, despite the fact that they received no ongoing active therapy. Of the children who started the investigation in a medication group, only 23% became drug-free. Unlike behavioral therapy, the termination of drug therapy was associated with limited carryover effects. When queried specifically about *satisfaction* with treatment, both parents and teachers rated behavioral therapy as superior to medication.

Additional evidence about long term outcomes of stimulant therapy for ADHD may be inferred from the observational, case-controlled studies of two cohorts of children, followed by a group of researchers in New York.[53-54] The first study involved the identification 101 Caucasian males (age range 16-23) who had been diagnosed with hyperactivity in childhood between 1970-1975 (ages 6-12, mean age: 9). Most of these individuals had received treatment restricted to pharmacotherapy. When 98% of the original cohort were re-evaluated as young adults (mean age: 18), the investigators found evidence of the following psychiatric conditions :

16% with a non-alcohol substance use disorder

27% with conduct disorder or antisocial personality disorder

40% with continuing full or partial ADD or ADHD

A second cohort, selected in order to check the accuracy of findings from the first group, identified 111 patients at a behavioral disorders clinic between 1970-1977. Subjects included children who were diagnosed with hyperactivity syndrome (*DSM-III*) between the ages of 5-11 (mean age: 7.3), with treatment that included medication and/or behavioral therapy. A ten year follow-up (mean age: 18.5) of 90% of the subjects revealed the following diagnoses:

10% with a non-alcohol substance use disorder

32% with conduct disorder or antisocial personality disorder

43% with continuing full or partial ADD or ADHD

Based upon the findings in both cohorts, children first treated for ADHD between ages of five and twelve were *four to five times more likely to develop conduct disorder* or *antisocial personality disorder* by age 18; and they were *five to eight times more likely to develop a non-alcohol substance use disorder,* relative to age matched controls.

Although the investigators noted in passing that subjects in both cohorts had received medication, they offered no analysis of the duration of treatment with stimulant therapies, the age at which stimulant medication was initiated, or the doses that were consumed *relative to the development or continuation of behavioral difficulties.* Yet, despite this omission, the researchers did not hesitate to make the following claim:

> "...there is no direct link between childhood hyperactivity and later substance abuse. In both studies, the development of an antisocial syndrome regularly preceded dysfunction associated with drug use. Therefore, the public health concern that medication to control hyperactivity in childhood leads to later drug abuse was unsubstantiated. There was no evidence to support the notion that these children adopt a psychology of 'pill taking' that, in turn, leads them to drugs of abuse."[55]

However, this conclusion was not supported by the study design. The investigators did not perform sufficiently detailed analyses of the case histories to evaluate the correlation between stimulant exposure and eventual substance abuse. Similarly, the investigators ignored the question of whether or not stimulants were connected to the emergence of antisocial activity. In other words, they did not consider the possibility that stimulant use might have been an *indirect* cause of substance abuse problems, either by failing to contribute to the motivation for complying with society's rules; or by failing to contribute to the development of the self-regulatory capacities needed for complying with those rules.

Some researchers have suggested that ADHD itself is a cause of conduct disorder, particularly when it is not adequately treated. However, a further follow-up study[56] conducted by the same New York group of researchers revealed the following results, when they interviewed 82% of their second cohort in early adulthood (mean age 24):

12% with antisocial personality disorder

12% with a non-alcohol substance abuse

4% with ADHD continuing in adulthood

These findings suggest that it is unlikely that active attentional decrements (or the same underlying "neuronal pathways") are the cause of continuing problems with antisocial conduct or substance abuse. Although many researchers consistently deny it, the common thread in a number of naturalistic studies appears to be the consistent link between ADHD in childhood, treatment with stimulants, and eventual substance abuse or sociopathy. The question remains: why do so many children who receive the diagnosis of ADHD develop serious misconduct and addictions?

ADHD, Stimulants, and Psychological Effects

A prominent concern of many researchers has been the effect of stimulant therapy upon academic achievement, social development, and cognition. The summer treatment programs (1991-1995) which were conducted as a part of the MTA study (described above) included several self-contained investigations. In one of these studies,[57] researchers compared the academic performance of 120 boys with ADHD (aged 7.4 – 12.7, mean age: 9.6) against 67 age-matched controls. Several cognitive dimensions were assessed, including pre-task expectancies, post-task self-evaluations, and causal attributions. Relative to controls, ADHD children solved fewer puzzles correctly, quit more often before the time limit had expired, and were less persistent at the task. In terms of pre-task expectancy, the ADHD subjects made predictions about their anticipated performance which were significantly inflated. In terms of attributions, both the ADHD subjects and the controls showed evidence of a self-serving, or "positive illusory bias," whereby they attributed success to their own effort (more than to ability, ease of task, or luck). When it came to failure, however, the ADHD subjects were less likely to give lack of effort as the primary cause of problems.

In a similar investigation[58] involving participants at the Summer Training Program (120 ADHD subjects versus 65 age matched controls), experimenters compared the performance of children on a social skills, "get acquainted" task. This time, ADHD subjects again displayed evidence of a "positive illusory bias" in terms of unrealistic, inflated opinions about predicted performance. Following the completion of the experiment, ADHD children were more likely than controls to attribute successful outcomes to "ease of task" or "luck," and they were more likely than controls to deny "lack of effort" as a possible cause of failure. The overall pattern was consistent with a denial of personal responsibility for both positive and negative outcomes on a task of social effectiveness.

These findings resonate with earlier studies, such as a 1977 investigation[59] involving 23 hyperactive children and 39 age-matched controls, ranging in age from 7 ½ to 11 (mean age: 9 years 7 months). The investigation was a double-blind study which compared the performance of ADHD children with and without their regular stimulant medication. The experiment involved dyads (one ADHD subject, one normal control) participating in a test of communication content and style. Each child took turns performing an astronaut role (receiving messages from a concealed mission controller about how to manipulate blocks into a particular array) and a mission control role (giving directions to the astronaut about how to manipulate the blocks correctly) on two separate occasions. The study found that stimulants had a far greater impact upon behavioral style than upon task competence. When medicated, ADHD children were less emotionally expressive, sadder in affect, and less positive with their peers. Regardless of medication status, ADHD subjects demonstrated more disagreement with their peers; more role inappropriate behaviors; and less vicarious learning (generalizing from astronaut role to future performance in the mission control position) than normal controls. The investigation corroborated the difficulties of ADHD children in responding to environmental cues for appropriate behavior, and it underscored the inability of medication to improve this function.

Perhaps one explanation for the failure of stimulants to improve academic achievement, social adaptability, and communication skills is the impact they can have upon children's self-perceptions. As one group of researchers has observed:

> **"...The use of external agents such as psychoactive medication to achieve normative performance levels is a pronounced departure from the typical socialization processes...one that may affect a child's emerging sense of personal control and mastery."[60]**

In a five-week study[61] which compared the expectancies and self-evaluations of 15 ADHD children on computer games rigged for success or failure, investigators assessed the impact of placebo or regular stimulant therapy when given in a blinded fashion. Investigators made the following discoveries:

1) ADHD subjects predicted that they would perform better when they believed they had been given their regular medication prior to the test situation

2) ADHD subjects receiving placebo, but informed that they had been given the stimulant, felt that they had performed better and tried harder than they did when the researchers told them that a placebo had been given

3) ADHD subjects were more likely to attribute poor performance to the difficulty of the task when they *thought* they had been given a placebo; however, ADHD subjects who had actually received placebo were more likely than medicated subjects to include effort (not trying) as an important reason for poor performance

4) ADHD subjects evaluated their own performance more positively after success, and judged the task to be more difficult after failure

5) ADHD subjects predicted a poorer performance when asked what would happen if they were shifted from medication to placebo.

The investigators concluded that stimulant therapy has unintended but detectable effects on self-cognition. Children who were given placebo were the most susceptible to the effects of "medication information" (expectancy bias), believing that their performance would be suboptimal whenever they did not get their usual drug.

The cognitive and psychological effects of stimulant drugs are concerning for several reasons. First, stimulant medications appear to induce psychological dependence in many patients, who come to believe that they cannot handle life situations in an unmedicated state. Because ADHD symptoms are generally time-limited[62] and situationally defined, the use of stimulants may be creating an unnecessary set of expectancies or fears – in other words, a phobia of drug-free living. Second, the use of stimulant medications may be depriving many children of the kinds of self-belief which they need in order to capitalize upon their talents. Most of the medicated children interviewed in the aforementioned studies on attributions believed that effort was irrelevant to their academic and social performance. Such a belief system could lead to a negative, self-fulfilling prophecy (lack of belief that situations can change through effort >> lack of effort to change situations >> stronger belief that situations cannot change, etc.). Third, and perhaps most serious, the use of stimulants for some children may lead to a chronic denial of responsibility (enhanced self-serving bias) which is consistent with the kind of narcissism that may fuel oppositional, aggressive, or destructive behaviors.

To the extent that stimulants and the ADHD label contribute to an unrealistic and inflated view of the self, they may reinforce hostility and misconduct. The "positive illusory bias" documented in many studies of ADHD children may be consistent with attitudes of superiority which – *when challenged* – lead to acts of aggression or defiance. While this does not suggest that stimulants must or necessarily do provoke sociopathy, it does suggest that the process of medicating children with stimulants may contribute to hostile or antisocial behaviors by setting up the kinds of cognitive belief systems which make children particularly vulnerable to perceived attacks upon their ego (i.e., less able to deal with their own imperfections):

> "...**High self esteem involves thinking well of oneself. Narcissism involves passionately *wanting* to think well of**

oneself...with a proneness to feeling angry and hostile in response to criticism."[63]

Unless adults do more to protect children equally against the ego-inflating, as well as the ego-degrading, effects of the ADHD label and its treatments, it is highly unlikely that the rates of disruptive behavior disorders (the 30-40% rate of co-morbid antisocial personality disorder and conduct disorder) will change appreciably. Also missing from the ADHD literature is an emphasis upon the inherent wellness of each child, rather than checklists of personal defects, so that narcissistic defenses are not mounted as *understandable responses* to the labels and drugs of psychiatry.

Safety

Despite the precipitous increase in the use of stimulant medications to control childhood behaviors, particularly within the United States, scant attention has been paid to the deleterious effects of these drugs. It is typical of the psychiatric literature to refer to stimulant side effects as "mild, time-limited, and well tolerated." For some children, this may indeed be true. For other children, however, the drugs have been quite harmful and even lethal.

The most common short-term effects of stimulant therapy include insomnia, appetite suppression, gastrointestinal distress, and dizziness. In the MTA study, for example, 245 families provided information about side effects:

36% reported no side effects

50% reported mild side effects

11% reported moderately severe side effects

3% reported severe side effects

Obviously, there is a great deal of missing data (579 families participated in the study) and the overall rate or severity of side effects may have been greater than these statistics reveal. For example, the latest published data from the MTA study show that approximately one-third of all the medicated subjects stopped their drugs by the time the evaluators conducted their two-year follow-up.

In a double blind, placebo-controlled crossover study,[64] researchers compared the reactions of 206 children between the ages of five and fifteen to Ritalin and placebo. Treatments were rotated on a weekly basis, and side effects were evaluated using the Barkley Side Effect Rating Scale. Overall response to Ritalin was quite poor, with just 62% of children demonstrating an improvement in their behaviors. Five side effects increased significantly with Ritalin therapy: appetite disturbance (19 times more likely than placebo); dizziness (8 times more likely than placebo); stomachache (7 times more likely than placebo); headache (5 times more likely than placebo); insomnia (3 times more likely than placebo).

A study of ambulatory patients seen at the Melbourne Royal Children's Hospital[65] between 1995 and 1996 compared side effects experienced by ADHD children (aged 5 to 15) in a double-blind crossover trial. Subjects were randomized to Dexedrine (d-amphetamine) or Ritalin (methylphenidate) treatments for two weeks at a time; then, after a 24 hour drug washout period, they were continued for another two weeks on the other medication. Favorable response rates, as assessed by parents, were 69% and 72% for Dexedrine and Ritalin, respectively. Appetite reduction was a prominent side effect of both drugs. Insomnia was worsened by Dexedrine, but not by Ritalin. The investigators concluded that their results were fairly consistent with the side effects studies conducted by other researchers:

Barkley (1990) **83 children on Ritalin for 7-10 day study side effects included insomnia, decreased appetite, headache, stomachache on both low and high doses of the drug**

Borcherding (1991) **48 children on Ritalin and Dexedrine in crossover study**
83% experienced significant (mild to moderately severe)
side effects, including decreased appetite, sleep disturbance, unhappiness

Millichap (1967)	reviewed 15 different RCTs of stimulants
	15-70% of Ritalin patients experienced adverse effects
	5-100% of Dexedrine patients experienced adverse effects

For many patients, it appears to be true that the somatic effects of stimulant therapy – such as appetite disturbance, headaches, and dizziness – may be mild and short-lived. However, the same cannot be said about endocrine, cognitive, and behavioral effects.

Endocrine Effects of Stimulants

The negative effects of stimulant drugs upon growth rates have been recognized for years. However, many researchers have inappropriately "blamed the patient" (a common theme in psychopharmacology) suggesting that ADHD itself is the cause of growth retardation in stimulant-treated children. The evidence against this argument is abundant. In a recent study conducted by physicians in Australia,[66] none of the 52 ADHD children treated in their practice were growth deficient *until* stimulant therapy was initiated. Animal studies have confirmed the growth-impairing effects of methylphenidate (Ritalin) in behaviorally normal rats.[67]

If anything, the most recent research has confirmed a disturbingly cavalier attitude among physicians with regards to the growth suppressing effects of psychotropic drugs. Returning to the aforementioned study in Australia, researchers found that stimulants were associated with progressive declines in both height and weight in 86% of their subjects. The decreases were especially prominent in the first 6 to 18 months of treatment, but they did not stop throughout the course of treatment. (One patient, who stopped taking dexamphetamine for six months to see if it was still needed for behavioral reasons, experienced a fairly immediate weight gain of 16 pounds, but no catch-up in height for another twelve months.)

Researchers at Yale University[68] have detected similar findings. In a study involving 84 ADHD children (ages 5-17) treated at two large pediatric practices, investigators compared the growth rates of Ritalin patients against their own unmedicated siblings. Subjects had to have taken Ritalin for at least two years without interruption. Siblings had to be healthy, born within three years of the patient, and living within the same household. Using height standard deviation scores to compare subjects, the researchers detected notable effects of Ritalin upon mean height and growth velocity: 76% of the males and 90% of the females experienced significant height suppression after three years of therapy. These effects did not reverse or stabilize at any point during treatment. Growth suppression occurred over a broad range of doses, with boys and girls experiencing an overall height deficit of approximately 3-4 cm (1.2 – 1.6 inches).

In the MTA study,[69] significant growth suppression was noted in children who took Ritalin or other stimulants continuously. Investigators were surprised to discover that growth effects were not only apparent in the first 14 months of the study, but persistent throughout the 24 months of follow-up. Findings included an average growth deficit of 1 cm (0.39 inches) per year, and an average weight loss of 1.25 kg (2.75 pounds) per year. Children who experienced an interruption in stimulant therapy underwent smaller overall growth suppression. Unmedicated subjects demonstrated *above average* growth rates, consistent with the height rebound phenomenon of children who discontinue stimulant therapy after many years of treatment (and consistent with the fact that ADHD itself was not the cause of their growth retardation).

In an attempt to downplay the significance of these findings, the research team concluded that "most of these children had not yet hit adolescence" – a time when the sex hormones of puberty may be strong enough to overcome the deleterious effects of stimulant medications upon bone development. The investigators acknowledged that stimulants may reduce *growth rates*, but they were optimistic that the drugs might lengthen the duration of each child's growth period (postponing puberty or delaying the closure of the epiphyseal growth plates). This latter theory, while hopeful, has not been adequately studied or confirmed.

What is most concerning about these findings is not only the growth suppression, but the fact that neuroscientists and physicians do not yet understand the mechanism which causes it. Many hypotheses have been advanced, but all of them have weaknesses due to inconsistent evidence from clinical and physiological investigations:[70-71]

Possible Causes of Stimulant Induced Growth Suppression

Hypothesis	Weakness
malnutrition [protein, carbohydrate, fat deficiency]	height suppression has occurred in many children despite normal weight and normal appetite
growth hormone deficiency	inconsistent findings most studies have shown acute increases in growth hormone in response to stimulants, but normalization of GH over time
somatomedin deficiency	inconsistent findings
deficiency in growth hormone receptor function	not yet studied
prolactin decrease	stimulants have been found to retard prolactin secretion acutely; however, it is not clear that prolactin levels play a significant role in childhood growth [also, *high* prolactin levels have been associated with osteoporosis or thinning of the bones, which argues against low prolactin as a cause of growth suppression in children]
cortisol excess (too much glucocorticoid)	unclear to what extent cortisol levels remain elevated with stimulant therapy; unclear to what extent this would impair growth in childhood
sleep disturbance	growth hormone is released in pulsatile bursts during slow wave sleep; the overall reduction in total sleep time caused by stimulants may reduce growth hormone secretion at critical times during the sleep cycle

At least one research group[72] has detected a possible explanation for stimulant-induced height suppression in the *target* of growth hormone, rather than in the complex endocrine systems (hypothalamus/pituitary/adrenal axis) which control its synthesis and release. Investigators examining the effects of several stimulants (pemoline, methylphenidate, and methamphetamine) upon cartilage discovered that all three drugs inhibited the uptake of sulfate and impaired the formation of glycosaminoglycans. Although these findings have not yet been verified *in vivo* (live humans), they offer an important mechanism through which stimulants may impede the linear growth rates of children.

Nevertheless, the possibility still remains that stimulants are disruptive to the regulation of *growth hormone homeostasis*. This has not been consistently disproven, and several studies[73] *have* detected associations between stimulants and deficiencies in growth hormone and other growth-related proteins (such as IGF-1 and growth hormone binding protein). To the extent that they disrupt the body's formation of trophic factors, and/or the cellular responses to them, it remains possible that stimulant medications exert an equally disruptive effect upon the *development of the human brain*, as they do upon the developing skeleton.

Cognitive Effects

Most discussions of stimulant drugs emphasize their short-term effects upon cognitive functioning. Among the favorable effects noted by researchers and patients have been improvements in sustained attention, reaction times, time on task, ability to switch mental sets, academic productivity, impulse control, and certain aspects of learning. However, most long term studies have documented a waning of drug benefits over time, either because of tolerance to the effects of the drug; changes in the underlying condition (e.g., natural maturation of the brain, decrease in situational demands, or a modification of life stressors); or the toxic effects of stimulants upon specific aspects of brain physiology and human performance, particularly as drug use becomes chronic.

Given that fact that CHADD and other groups regularly advocate for ADHD as a proven brain disease, for which stimulants are the best treatment, it is important to appreciate the opinions of neurologists who work with clear cases of neuropathology. Since the late 1980s, the traumatic brain injury (TBI) field has investigated the use of neurostimulants as adjunctive therapies in the rehabilitation of head injuries. A number of investigators have published the results of double-blind, placebo controlled crossover studies, in which TBI patients have been evaluated on cognitive and social tests following short trials of placebo and stimulant therapies (varying doses). These studies[74-75] have generally revealed mixed findings: some patients responding well, others displaying equal responses to placebo, and few responders experiencing protracted benefits beyond six to twelve months of stimulant therapy. These observations have led investigators to conclude that stimulants are either ineffective for head injury patients; or that there is a short "window of opportunity" during which stimulants may jump start a recovery process before they become superfluous or toxic.

The results of neuroimaging studies may provide an important explanation for these impressions. In the 1980s,[76] a team of researchers performed C.T. (computed tomography) scans on 22 young males (mean age: 23.2 years) who had been diagnosed with ADHD and treated with stimulants in childhood (mean age at diagnosis: 8.7 years). The results of their head scans were compared to findings from 27 slightly older males (mean age 28.7 years). Even when compared to older healthy controls, the stimulant-exposed subjects demonstrated significant *sulcal widening (58% of the ADHD group vs. 3.8% of the controls) and **cerebellar atrophy (25% of the ADHD group vs. 3.8% of the controls). The investigators concluded that "more research was needed" to determine if the cortical atrophy detected in these ADHD subjects was the result of stimulant therapy or an underlying neurological condition.

In the early 1990s, a different team of investigators performed a neuroimaging study[77] involving five healthy males between the ages of 21 and 40. In that study, subjects were injected with intravenous doses (0.5mg/kg) of methylphenidate (Ritalin) followed by PET (positron emission tomography) scans 5-10 minutes and 30 minutes after injection.

The goal of the study was to identify the effects of Ritalin upon cerebral blood flow. Findings were significant for consistent, global reductions in blood flow compared to baseline: 14-36% reduction at 5-10 minutes, 10-30% reduction at 30 minutes. Because these

---

*sulcal – pertaining to sulci, or invaginations of the brain surface; these furrows appear to widen as the underlying brain tissue shrinks or recedes

**cerebellar atrophy – shrinking of the cerebellum, a posterior brain structure involved in balance, coordination, and cognitive functions

changes were seen throughout the brain (unlike the regional effects detected by neuroimaging techniques which focus upon glucose metabolism), the researchers concluded that the findings were reflective of direct effects upon the cerebral vasculature rather than neurons. The investigators concluded:

> **"Though CBF [cerebral blood flow] changes after oral MP [methylphenidate] are probably smaller than with intravenous MP, its pharmacokinetics may be slower, and CBF decrements may last longer. The extent to which prolonged decrements in CBF with chronic MP occur needs to be evaluated."[78]**

As of 2004, no such follow-up investigations had been performed. However, the lead author of the study has reported that he has received funding from the National Institutes of Health for a project to address the "long term" (one year) effects of oral methylphenidate upon the dopamine system of drug naïve ADHD subjects.[79]

Questions have been raised by numerous investigators about the qualitative effects of stimulant drugs upon cognition. A number of studies[80-81] have confirmed the phenomenon of state dependent learning in ADHD children, whereby material learned in the medicated condition by *stimulant responders* (children whose learning has been facilitated by stimulant therapy) has been more successfully retrieved (recalled) in the medicated rather than unmedicated state. While the findings have been restricted to lab tests (such as tasks of paired-associates learning), the implications are worrisome if they generalize to the classroom environment. There is a suggestion that material acquired in the context of stimulant therapy – particularly, material of low salience-may not be as accurately or consistently recalled by subjects, should they undergo an interruption or termination of their usual medicated condition.

Other investigators[82-83] have expressed concern about *dose effects* upon cognitive functioning. In one study of 19 children exposed to varying amounts of Ritalin (0.15, 0.3, and 0.6 mg/kg), researchers documented a decrease in academic performance at higher doses. This was consistent with earlier research documenting a decrement in learning among children who received doses of Ritalin exceeding 0.3mg/kg.

Sophisticated experiments have been developed to evaluate the functioning of different hemispheres of the brain. In one such experiment,[84] the responses of 26 ADHD children (ages 8-15) to tachistopic tasks were compared under Ritalin and placebo conditions. [Tachistopy is a test of visual field dominance which evaluates the speed of processing based upon the appearance of stimuli – dots or digits – to the left or right of a central fixation point.] Reaction times to stimuli producing left visual field advantages (right hemisphere processing) were slower than stimuli producing advantages in the right visual field.

The concern here is that the ADHD literature has been so focused upon the left hemisphere effects of stimulants (such as verbal tasks and sustained attention) that it has forgotten about the other half of the brain. Right hemisphere deficits have been linked to reductions in diffuse attentional mechanisms, emotional intensity, social responsiveness, and mood (depression and anxiety). Following right hemisphere lesions (such as strokes), patients may develop a "semantic pragmatic disorder"[85] which is characterized by an impaired capacity to express themselves in language; flattened intonation; and an inability to perceive emotion, metaphor, humor, and subtleties in the world around them. If stimulants induce a similar lateralized disorder in children, it is understandable that ADHD subjects could demonstrate the onset or worsening of deficits in eye contact, playfulness, spatial awareness, the perception of social cues, the use of imagery, the control of impulsive responding, and the holistic integration of feelings, context, and interpersonal relationships – all of which are predominantly right hemisphere functions.

The effects of stimulants upon driving and flying performance have raised additional concerns about their safety. While stimulants have long been used by pilots in the U.S. military for their alerting properties during extended missions, the self-administration of "combat amphetamines" has provoked criticism in the aftermath of serious accidents involving medicated pilots. In the summer of 2002, two Air National Guard pilots mistakenly bombed and killed Canadian troops over Afghanistan, claiming that "go pills" consumed before the mission had impaired their judgment.[86] According to a retired Navy admiral,[87] "the better warrior through chemistry field" is now the focus of aggressive research. While Pentagon officials believe that the "capability to operate effectively, without sleep" will "fundamentally change current military concepts of operational tempo,"[88] critics believe that it is hazardous to manipulate human sleep schedules artificially. Of particular concern in jet and bomber pilots is the induction of stimulant psychosis (hallucinations or delusions), as well as side effects including tremor, blurred vision, and dizziness.[89]

The topic is pertinent for children and adults with ADHD, almost all of whom receive treatment with stimulants. Several investigations conducted in the U.S. and Canada have documented higher rates of motor vehicle accidents among ADHD drivers, relative to non-ADHD controls. In a study which evaluated the driving records and knowledge of 25 young adults with ADHD,[90] investigators found that ADHD subjects had no deficit in their understanding of road rules. However, ADHD drivers were more likely to have had their licenses suspended or revoked; more likely to have received repeated traffic citations (mostly for speeding); and more likely to have experienced car crashes while driving (four times more accidents than controls). Although the researchers attributed the accidents and reckless driving styles to the underlying condition of ADHD, rather than to its treatment, the experience of the U.S. military should be instructive for more critical observers. Whatever else one concludes about ADHD drivers, it is apparent that stimulant medications often fail to control impulsive habits, and possibly exacerbate errors in judgment in the same way that amphetamines have been found to impair the performance of combat pilots.

Psychiatric and Behavioral Effects

While the psychiatric literature focuses almost exclusively on the effects of stimulants upon attention and hyperactivity, it commonly disregards the severity and frequency of unwanted psychological and behavioral effects. It should concern physicians that as many as 7% of the stimulant-treated, ADHD children in one Canadian practice[91] developed clear symptoms of psychosis after the initiation of drug therapy. In most of these cases, the psychosis resolved completely upon the termination of pharmacotherapy, dispelling the notion that "the underlying ADHD" was the cause of psychosis in these children. Other researchers have commented upon the high overlap between ADHD and bipolar diagnoses in children, noting the difficulty of delineating the two conditions because of their common features: high activity levels, distractability, poor impulse control, and emotional lability.

In this context, the use of stimulant medications is concerning for several reasons. First, many children on stimulants experience "rebound" effects as their drug levels drop between doses. Many of these stimulant withdrawal symptoms – which include moodiness, excessive talk, insomnia, and excitability – can be misidentified as features of hypomania or mania. This leads to an inappropriate labeling of children as bipolar[92] when, in fact, the symptoms should be recognized as iatrogenic. Second, the dopaminergic action of stimulants[93] may be direct causes of mood disorders (depression and/or mania, with or without psychotic features) in many children. (Unfortunately, there have been no epidemiological studies which identify a cohort of drug naïve ADHD subjects, and then follow them longitudinally to monitor the emergence of new or worsening symptoms in relation to the use of psychotropic drugs.) Third, the use of stimulant therapies appears to worsen the prognosis of children who are eventually diagnosed[94] or hospitalized[95] with bipolar conditions, with stimulant-exposed subjects experiencing an earlier age at onset of bipolar features, a younger age at the time of first hospitalization (13.7 years vs. 15.1 years), and a more severe hospital course relative to non-stimulant exposed peers.

Stimulants and Addiction

Beginning in the 1960s, central nervous system stimulants came under increasing regulatory control due to concerns about illicit manufacture and distribution. In 1971, the World Health Organization classified methylphenidate (Ritalin) as a Schedule II drug, due to its "high abuse potential." Concerns about Ritalin abuse were relatively moderate for two decades. Curiously, production of the stimulant soared from less then three tons in 1990, to more than thirteen tons by 1997.[96] These developments were alarming to the international community. In 1996 and 1997, the World Health Organization issued press releases (and several letters to the U.S. Drug Enforcement Agency) about the exponential rise in Ritalin, noting that the United States was responsible for 90% of the drug's production and consumption. The International Narcotics Control Board (the World Health Organization agency responsible for monitoring the production and use of controlled substances) explicitly identified a number of concerns about these American developments, including the dangers of inappropriate diagnosis of ADHD; widely divergent prescribing patterns; off-label prescribing to children under six; and excessive duration of treatment (many countries continue to restrict Ritalin use to three years). The INCB was especially worried about the expanding black market for Ritalin, based upon increasing evidence of abuse by individuals who confiscate pills prescribed to others.

Despite the real-world concerns of regulatory authorities, the psychiatric literature has consistently minimized or ignored the addictive potential of psychostimulants. More alarmingly, the recent publications of several research teams have suggested that ADHD children should be *encouraged* to use stimulants, in order to *prevent* the emergence of cocaine or other substance dependencies.[97-98]

There are several critical points to be made about psychostimulants and addiction. First, although it is uncommon, it is possible for ADHD children to become directly dependent upon their prescribed therapies. In an informative review of the subject,[99] Volkow and Swanson outline five critical factors which appear to mediate stimulant addiction:

1) drug dose

   For cocaine and Ritalin, a dose that leads to the blockade of at least 50% of the dopamine transporters appears to be a pre-requisite for subjects to experience sensations of euphoria (feeling high) or drug-liking.

2) route of administration

   Intranasal stimulants produce the fastest drug high. A dose of 50-100 mg of intranasal cocaine is equivalent to 25-50 mg of intranasal Ritalin. The second quickest route for stimulant intoxication is intravenous (injected). The reinforcing effects

295

of intravenous Ritalin are *identical* to intravenous cocaine. In fact,

Ritalin is about twice as potent as cocaine (0.075mg/kg IV Ritalin = 0.13 mg/kg IV cocaine – doses which block 50% of the dopamine transporters in the striatum and nucleus accumbens). The usual clinical doses of oral Ritalin require two hours to reach the 50% level of dopamine transporter blockade, and do not reliably induce a state of euphoria. However, it is possible that sufficient quantities of oral Ritalin (80 mg or more) might produce levels of dopamine transporter blockade as quickly as intravenous doses.

3) pharmacokinetics (how the human body metabolizes the drug)

Two features of pharmacokinetics determine drug levels in the body. T_{max} refers to the time it takes for a drug to reach its maximum concentration. $T^{\frac{1}{2}}$ refers to the time it takes for the maximum drug concentration to fall by 50%. Intravenous cocaine and Ritalin have almost identical T_{max} values, with cocaine reaching a peak level in the striatum in 4-6 minutes, and Ritalin reaching a peak level in 6-10 minutes. (By contrast, oral Ritalin reaches peak levels in 1.5 hours.) Where the two drugs differ, however, is in their *rates of clearance* from the brain. Cocaine clears the striatum in 20 minutes, but Ritalin clears the striatum in 90 minutes. Researchers speculate that the initial fast rate of dopamine transporter blockade determines the onset of the drug high, while the rate of clearance from the brain determines the frequency of repeated self-administration.

4) individual differences

There is a large variability between subjects in the magnitude of dopamine changes produced by stimulant drugs. In some cases, a high level of dopamine transporter blockade (> 50%) may lead to little or no significant change in extracellular dopamine levels. This may be due to low background rates of cell activity and transmitter synthesis in some individuals. Another difference which might account for variable drug response is the availability of striatal D2 receptors, with low levels associated with more "drug liking" and addiction.

5) context of administration

A diverse literature documents the role of context in the quality and quantity of drug effects. For example, children who receive Ritalin in the classroom situation demonstrate a greater drug response than they do in the setting of the playground. This observation appears to resonate with neuroimaging studies which reveal larger increases in striatal dopamine levels when Ritalin subjects are exposed to salient rather than neutral stimuli. Another important aspect of context pertains to personal expectations (expectations of drug-induced euphoria) and attributions of salience. When drug use within a particular environment leads to significant elevations in dopamine transmission, the behavioral context enhances the psychological and physiological effects. This may explain why the illicit use of Ritalin, or the use of Ritalin in novel settings, produces euphoria while the medical use of the drug typically does not.

Although Volkow and Swanson do not mention it, a sixth variable must be considered in the emergence of stimulant dependence. This is the process of neuronal development and synaptogenesis. Given the fact that the human brain develops a maximum number of neurons between the ages of six and seven, and then devotes the remainder of childhood and adolescence to pruning the connections between them, it stands to reason that the addictive potential of stimulants might depend upon the maturation of key regions of the brain (such as the striatum and the nucleus accumbens, and their connections to the frontal cortex). Thus, it is possible that the addiction to stimulants cannot appear until pertinent brain circuits have emerged.

The addictive liability of stimulants appears to be rare *during childhood*, as long as the drugs are consumed orally (rather than intravenously or intranasally) and in the amounts prescribed. In contrast, it is quite possible for Ritalin and other stimulants to change the human brain – even in childhood – in ways that accelerate an individual's vulnerability to chemical dependencies as a teenager or adult. A number of animal studies have documented precisely this phenomenon, with stimulant medications *sensitizing* the brain to cocaine.[100-01] Although the precise neurophysiological mechanisms have not been identified, hypotheses include the down-regulation of the dopamine transporter (a posited cause of "craving"), changes in post-synaptic dopamine receptor function or density, the induction of intranuclear proteins (such as delta c-fos), and alterations in neural plasticity (synaptic connections).

If it were true that stimulant medications *prevent*, rather than induce, future chemical addictions, one should find evidence of that link in epidemiological studies. A large-scale, prospective study of 492 ADHD children in Northern California[102] was begun in 1974. Stimulant-treated subjects developed higher rates of cocaine and nicotine dependence than unmedicated peers diagnosed with either ADHD or behavioral (conduct) disorders:

Percent of Subjects Developing Addiction

	ADHD No stimulant exposure	ADHD Up to 1 year of stimulant drug	ADHD 1 year or more of stimulant drug	Behavior Disorder no stimulant
	n = 81	n = 9	n = 84	n = 41
Tobacco	**32.1%**	**38.5%**	**48.8%**	**32%**
Alcohol	32.1%	33.3%	45.2%	39%
Marijuana	22.5%	23.1%	32.1%	34%
Cocaine	**15.0%**	**17.9%**	**27.4%**	**12%**

A second investigation,[103] conducted by a different research team, followed 147 hyperactive children (diagnosed between ages 5-12) prospectively for approximately thirteen years. The subjects were interviewed at age fifteen (78% follow-up) and again in early adulthood (mean age 21, range: 19-25) to explore the use of various substances in relation to ADHD and its treatment. *Childhood exposure to stimulant therapy* was significantly associated with higher experimentation with cocaine (26% stimulant treated vs. 5% of unmedicated) by early adulthood. *Adolescent exposure to stimulant therapy* was significantly associated with greater frequency of cocaine use as adults. Even after controlling for the severity of ADHD symptoms and the lifetime prevalence of conduct disorder features, the researchers detected a statistically significant relationship between prescribed stimulants during high school and a higher rate of cocaine experimentation ("ever use") of cocaine as young adults. Despite the limitations of this study (probably underpowered; insufficient attention paid to the possible link between stimulant medication and conduct disorder; and questionable validity with regards to perplexing assessment tools and data analysis), several findings were consistent with the hypothesis of stimulant-induced sensitization and drug abuse.

There is, of course, a simpler way to test the theory that stimulants in ADHD children prevent cocaine dependence. Researchers need only spend time in prisons or rehabilitation programs to identify the rate of childhood stimulant exposure among adults who have ultimately developed stimulant addiction. A cross-sectional analysis of 201 participants at two chemical dependency treatment centers demonstrated that 24% of the subjects met criteria for ADHD.[104] Another study,[105] involving 298 adults seeking treatment for cocaine abuse, found that 35% of the subjects met criteria for childhood ADHD. These subjects reported more severe substance use (including earlier onset, more frequent, and more intense use of cocaine) relative to non-ADHD subjects. Yet another study[106] involving 30 teenagers (ages 14-19) in treatment for substance abuse, revealed that 50% of the participants met criteria for ADHD. These subjects began drug use at an earlier age and progressed to more severe habits than their non-ADHD peers.

Although none of the researchers in these investigations commented on the relationship between stimulant exposure and chemical dependency, it is quite likely that many of these patients had received stimulants when their ADHD conditions were first diagnosed. In light of the fact that these same individuals progressed to cocaine and other chemical dependencies, it is apparent that ADHD medications were not successful in preventing drug abuse in these cases.

It has now become popular for mental health researchers to suggest that cocaine and other substance abusers resort to street drugs as a method of 'self-medicating' their underlying psychiatric conditions. These professionals contend that a properly medicated ADHD patient will not develop any dependence upon street drugs, as long as the symptoms of ADHD are effectively controlled. The evidence from substance abuse programs contradicts this line of reasoning in several ways. First, the prescribed use of Ritalin among non-ADHD subjects in rehabilitation programs has been inconsistent in reducing cocaine cravings and drug-seeking behaviors.[107-108] This observation suggests that Ritalin may reinforce, rather than diminish, the behavioral sensitization associated with illicit stimulants. Second, the use of Ritalin as a cocaine substitute among ADHD substance abusers has not contributed to abstinence, even when the same subjects have reported an improvement in their ADHD symptoms.[109] All of these findings are consistent with the demonstrated abuse potential and sensitizing effects of Ritalin in over sixty studies of nonhuman and human subjects.[110]

Alternatives to Stimulants

The summer treatment programs, conducted as part of the MTA study, evaluated children throughout a comprehensive, eight week therapeutic camp. One treatment cycle[111] compared the progress of 57 children in the combined treatment group (medication + behavioral therapies) against 60 children who remained unmedicated for the duration of the summer. Behavioral therapy included a variety of interventions, including classroom instruction; sports and social skills training; daily group sessions and tasks to promote cooperation; parent training with reinforcement systems; and regular feedback to children in the form of daily report cards. By the last day of the program, the two groups (medicated and unmedicated) did not differ significantly on any of the overall ratings of improvement. Medication did not facilitate the rate at which children improved, and by the end of the summer, the two groups of children were essentially indistinguishable on counselor, parental, and teacher ratings of change. This led the investigators to draw the following conclusion:

"...The results therefore demonstrate that the MTA results at 14-month outcome showing large incremental effects of medication beyond a faded [discontinued] clinical behavioral intervention were not apparent when the behavioral condition in the study was active and intensive."...Somewhat to our surprise, the children who received behavioral treatment alone performed as well as those who received concurrent medication throughout the summer...The Summer Treatment Program context, with its daily objective measures, provided a unique opportunity to answer this question...The answer appears to be that medication does not facilitate the rate at which children improve in a concurrent, intensive behavioral treatment."[112]

Other researchers have documented similar benefits with a variety of non-pharmacological approaches, including exercise (martial arts); massage therapy;[113] music therapy;[114] cognitive therapy;[115-117] and neurofeedback.[118] One particularly innovative team has documented favorable results with the use of weighted vests as an intervention to calm hyperactive children without the use of pharmaceuticals.[119] More recently, researchers in California have coordinated a two-month research intervention for children and adults diagnosed with ADHD, emphasizing mindfulness attention (meditation) as a way to facilitate the capacity for self-regulation.   Presumably, these investigators have been encouraged by the positive neurocognitive effects of meditation upon other conditions, such as depression and anxiety.[120-121]   Finally, it is worth re-emphasizing the findings of the MTA study, in which 75% of the children in the behavioral therapy group experienced sustained improvements without the addition of medication.

Epilogue
The Need for An Adequately Informed Consent to Care

"The manipulation of the brain by any of the biological techniques which can be developed in the foreseeable future would involve such drastic invasions of privacy, integrity, and the unalienable rights of the individual that in their application behavioral control would already have been achieved even if the electrodes carried no current and the pill were placebo."[1]

While different countries and commentators have attached qualifications that remain the subject of pointed debate, the *doctrine of informed consent* has become the basis of shared decision making according to bioethics and health law.[2-4] *Referring specifically to the right of a competent patient to receive or refuse treatment,* **informed consent** *depends upon the exchange of* **adequate information** *so that consumers can make knowledgeable decisions about the utility of proposed care.*

Increasingly, however, informed consent has been jeopardized by the subjugation of medicine to the motives and methods of industry.[5] Profits rather than patients have become the focus of many training programs, professional associations, research institutions, insurance companies, pharmaceutical corporations, the government, and the media. To use the language of *Baudrillard, a Simulacrum of medicine has been forged, based upon illusion. By medicalizing all aspects of the *human* condition, new diseases have been invented in order to create markets for new drug therapies, as well as patent extensions for the old.[8-10] By manipulating all

---

*Jean Baudrillard[6-7] – a French social theorist who has provided creative insights into American culture, akin to de Tocqueville. Baudrillard's concept of Simulacra refers to the historical phenomenon through which various images or signs have come to replace their authentic referents. Modern examples include large screen TVs at a ball park, which allow fans to watch the "real" game while dismissing the events on the field in front of them; cloning; Disneyland; opinion polls – all of which represent the collapse of the real with the imaginery, or the birth of the "hyperreal" – a phenomenon through which the reproduction becomes more real than the object which is reproduced.

302

aspects of the *physician* condition, unnecessary and dangerous interventions have been sold.

With the philosophical bankruptcy of Evidence Based Medicine, the scientific bankruptcy of methodologically deficient RCTs, and the moral bankruptcy of those who place earnings ahead of truth, it is the adequacy of medical information which hangs in doubt:

> **"Where once the psychopharmacology literature was invested with the authority of clinicians who knew at first hand what they were describing, by the end of the century an increasingly large amount of the literature had become the psychiatric equivalent of a *Big Mac."**[11]

Maintained on a steady diet of empty but convenient evidence, many physicians remain oblivious to the signs of their professional malnourishment. One sign appeared in 2002 when the *New England Journal of Medicine* announced the relaxation of its code of ethics regarding conflicts of interest. Citing the fact that growing "relationships between authors and biomedical companies" had made it too difficult to locate independent authorities, the editors announced the following policy:

> **"More than a decade ago, the editors became concerned about the possible influence of commercial associations on viewpoints and opinions expressed in the *Journal*... Because the essence of reviews and editorials is selection and interpretation of the literature, the *Journal* expects that authors of such articles will not have any financial interest in a company (or its competitor) that makes a product discussed in the article...Therefore, beginning with this issue... we have modified the statement on Information for Authors to read as follows: ...the *Journal* expects that authors of such articles will not have any *significant* financial interest in a company (or its competitor) that makes a product discussed in the article."[12] (emphasis added)**

---

*Big Mac – a lighthearted reference to the nutritional value of fast food; in this case, the McDonald's sandwich consisting of two all beef patties, special sauce, extra cheese, pickles, onions, and a sesame seed bun; 560 calories, 30 grams of fat.

The word significant referred to the ownership of at least $10,000 of stock or patents, and no major funding from the relevant companies within two years of the publication date. However, the revised policy exempted fees received as honoraria for "occasional" educational lectures sponsored by biomedical companies, as these were deemed by the new editors to be "minor and unlikely to influence an author's judgment."

A second sign appeared in a 2004 editorial, this time in the pages of *JAMA*.[13] Motivated by a rapid sequence of public health scandals in the drug safety domain (e.g., SSRIs and suicide, cox-2 inhibitors and cardiovascular disease, cerivastatin and rhabdomyolysis), the authors conveyed an open acknowledgement of pharmaceutical industry malfeasance and regulatory incompetence:

> "Yet, the major problem with the current system for ensuring the safety of medications is that drug manufacturers are largely responsible for collecting, evaluating, and reporting data from postmarketing studies of their own products...it appears that fewer than half of the postmarketing studies that manufacturers have made commitments to undertake as a condition of approval have been completed and many have not even been initiated...moreover...drug manufacturers may be tempted to conceal valuable data that may signal the possibility of major risks. In some cases, the FDA and drug manufacturers may fail to act on that information and fail to conduct appropriate studies to examine a potential risk rigorously and promptly."[14]

The repercussions of a broken drug evaluation system are reflected in news items and press releases which appear faster than most physicians can keep up. During the writing of this book, for example, the following actions and announcements occurred:

December 17, 2004 - Strattera
FDA released an advisory announcing new warnings on the label of the ADHD drug atomoxetine (Strattera) relative to the potential side effect of severe liver disease

February 9, 2005 - Adderall XR
FDA released an alert about Health Canada's decision to remove the ADHD drug Adderall XR (extended release mixed amphetamines) from the Canadian market due to concern about reports of sudden deaths in children (not always associated with structural heart defects). The FDA denied that recommended doses of Adderall could cause sudden unexplained death but stated that it would continue to evaluate "the data."

February 15, 2005 - SSRIs
The semi-monthly newspaper, *Family Practice News*, published an article about bone loss associated with the use of SSRIs (selective serotonin reuptake inhibitors). Briefly summarizing research conducted by investigators in Oregon and Minnesota, the article noted reductions in bone density among female *and* male adult users of SSRIs.

February 16, 2005 - Ritalin
Researchers in Texas published an on-line paper in the journal *Cancer Letters* announcing the discovery of a three- to four-fold increase in chromosomal abnormalities among 12 children treated for three months with the ADHD drug methylphenidate (Ritalin). Results were discussed with caution, due to the small size of the treatment group and the need for replication. Nevertheless, the investigators expressed concern about their findings in terms of the well-documented relationship between chromosomal aberrations and the increased risk of cancer.

February 18, 2005 - Gabitril
FDA released an advisory announcing a new bold print warning strongly discouraging the off-label use of the anti-convulsant drug tiagabine (Gabitril) due to the potential for drug-induced seizures

March 24, 2005 - Cylert
Abbott laboratories announced plans to withdraw its ADHD drug pemoline (Cylert) from the US market, due to declining sales related to the product's hepatotoxicity (liver disease).

April 11, 2005 - Atypical Antipsychotics
FDA released an advisory alerting the public about the risk of higher death rates in elderly patients with dementia who have received atypical antipsychotics for behavioral control. The agency requested that manufacturers add a boxed warning about the risk of increased mortality in older patients, particularly with regards to death from cardiac or respiratory disease. The FDA stated that it was still reviewing data on the safety of neuroleptics within this population of patients.

By surface appearances, one might believe that these announcements herald a new age of integrity in the conduct of medical research and post-marketing surveillance. Other developments, however, suggest a persistent need for improvements in oversight and accountability.

The FDA Retreat on Antidepressant Suicide Warnings

Following the tightening of antidepressant warnings on October 28, 2004 the FDA came under pressure from the American Psychiatric Association to soften the label changes it had proposed regarding the problem of drug-induced suicide. In response to a marked reduction in antidepressant sales over the last quarter of 2004 (as well as physician complaints about increased malpractice insurance fees related to antidepressant prescribing), the FDA backed off on its October recommendations.[15-18] When a new Labeling Change Request Letter was issued on January 26, 2005, the following words had been *deleted*: "a causal role for antidepressants in inducing suicidality has been established in pediatric patients." The FDA's political retreat was indefensible in the face of the evidence presented at three intensive hearings (9/91, 2/04, 9/04), in addition to the findings of two large epidemiological investigations (Mosholder, Columbia University) which independently affirmed the drug-related induction or enhancement of suicidality in young users of SSRIs.

Conflicts of Interest at the NIH[19-21]

On February 1, 2005, the National Institutes of Health announced sweeping ethics reforms in response to media and Congressional attention to conflicts of interest among its employees. Arising partly from changes in federal legislation during the 1980s and partly from changes in internal policy which occurred a decade later, the conflicts of interest had grown to include more than one hundred high paid employees. According to concerned observers, researchers and administrators had maintained and concealed consultative and financial relationships (in some cases, worth hundreds of thousands of dollars) with pharmaceutical and biotech companies, in violation of government ethics rules. Investigations of impropriety have continued. Among the officials under scrutiny has been the NIMH Chief of Geriatric Psychiatry, who allegedly received (but failed to disclose) more than a half million dollars from pharmaceutical corporations in payment for consultations, honoraria (speaker's fees), and travel claims.

Climates of Intimidation

In 2002, the inspector general of the Department of Health and Human Services conducted a survey among scientists employed by the FDA.[22] With 360 individuals responding, the survey revealed prominent concerns about the content and process of agency deliberations: 36% of the scientists expressed only some confidence or no confidence about FDA decisions on drug safety; 22% of the scientists expressed only some confidence or no confidence about agency decisions on drug effectiveness; and 18% expressed that they had felt pressured to approve or recommend approval for a new product despite reservations about its efficacy, safety, or quality. Furthermore, a full 21% of the respondents affirmed that the work environment within the CDER (Center for Drug Evaluation and Research) allowed little dissent or stifled scientific disagreement completely.

Although these results did not appear publicly for more than two years (due to a Freedom of Information Act request filed by public interest groups), they clearly presaged the revelations of Dr. David Graham. A career epidemiologist who has acknowledged the climate of intimidation within the FDA, it was Graham's testimony before Congress in November 2004 which unleashed a firestorm of government and media attention to America's broken system of drug research, approval, and oversight. Unfortunately, the tentacles of that system are widespread. On April 10, 2005, newspapers exposed a similar environment of intimidation inside the National Institutes of Health. Referring to misconduct occurring within the AIDS research division, senior NIH medical officers have testified under oath:[23]

> **"There are a number of things that you really don't talk about...You don't hold up any projects even if you feel there are safety issues for certain projects...."**

Speaking directly about the plight of *Dr. Jonathan Fishbein, the AIDS division's compliance officer for human research protection has explained that Fishbein was a strong advocate for improving the safety of research participants. The Institute's reprisals against him have been interpreted by at least one employee as a clear warning to others, comparable to an act of scientific terrorism.[24]

In the face of these ethical and informational exigencies, one may wonder if there are any bright spots or solutions. Recommendations have been made, such as the creation of an outside (non-FDA) drug safety evaluation board; the implementation of a mandatory, publicly accessible clinical trial database (containing raw data from all trials, completed or in progress); and the repeal of PDUFA (the 1992 Prescription Drug User Fee Act), the law which transferred a large portion of the FDA's purse strings from the taxpayers to the very industry which that agency is entrusted to oversee. Of course, none of these changes – as favorable as they might be – will *necessarily* result in the supply of adequate information, upon which the institution of informed consent must logically depend.

> ➢ Not until researchers and regulators acknowledge and correct the methodological deficiencies of the psychotropic RCT...

---

*Fishbein - an NIH researcher who was removed from his position after exposing research misconduct and safety problems related to the AIDS drug, nevirapine[25-26]

➢ Not until clinicians recognize the philosophical limitations of an Evidence Based (rather than Reality Based) Medicine...

➢ Not until physicians are *allowed and unafraid* to reject the conflict-ridden, profit driven guidelines, consensus statements, and review processes which are now imposed upon them...

... not until then, will clincians and patients be free to participate in the exchange of an authentically informed consent to care.

Endnotes

Prologue

1 Thomas Kramer, "All the Things They Taught Us That Were Wrong," *Medscape* 6 (2004) accessed 09 MAR 2005 on-line at: http://64.233.161.104/search?q=cache:p2lsyPcufg8J:www. medscape.com/viewarticle/472673_print+all+the+things+they+tau ght+us+that+were+wrong+kramer&hl=en

2 Carolyn Faulder, *Whose Body Is It?* (London: Virgo, 1985), pg. 2, as quoted in anonymous, untitled essay accessed 09 APR 2005 online at: http://studentmidwives.co.uk/pages/essays.htm

Chapter One

Public Opinion About Psychiatric Drugs

1 T.W. Croghan, M. Tomlin, B.A, Pescosolido, J. Schnittker, and J. Martin, "American Attitudes Toward and Willingness to Use Psychiatric Medications," *The Journal of Nervous and Mental Disease* 191 (2003): 166-174.

2 *Ibid.*, p. 173.

3 R.G. Priest, C. Vize, A. Roberts, M. Roberts, and A. Tylee, "Lay people's attitudes to treatment of depression: results of opinion poll for Defeat Depression Campaign just before its launch," *British Medical Journal* 313 (1996): 858-859.

4 E.S. Paykel, A. Tylee, A. Wright, R.G. Priest, S. Rix, and D. Hart, "The Defeat Depression Campaign: Psychiatry in the Public Arena," *American Journal of Psychiatry* 154 (1997): 59-65.

5 R.G. Priest, C. Vize, A. Roberts, M. Roberts, and A. Tylee, "Lay people's attitudes to treatment of depression: results of opinion poll for Defeat Depression Campaign just before its launch," pp. 858-859.

6 E.S. Paykel, A. Tylee, A. Wright, R.G. Priest, S. Rix, and D. Hart, "The Defeat Depression Campaign: Psychiatry in the Public Arena," p. 60.

7 S. Rix, R.S. Paykel, P. Lelliott, A. Tylee, P. Freeling, L. Gask, and D. Hart, "Impact of a national campaign on GP education: an evaluaton of the Defeat Depression Campaign [Abstract]," *British Journal of General Practice* 49 (1999): 99-102.

8 E.S. Paykel, A. Tylee, A. Wright, R.G. Priest, S. Rix, and D. Hart, "The Defeat Depression Campaign: Psychiatry in the Public Arena," p. 64.

9 E.S. Paykel, D. Hart, and R.G. Priest, "Changes in public attitudes to depression during the Defeat Depression Campaign," *British Journal of Psychiatry* 173 (1998): 519-522.

10 M.C. Angermeyer and H. Matschinger, "Public attitude towards psychiatric treatment," *Acta Psychiatrica Scandinavica* 94 (1996): 326-336.

11 *Ibid.*, p. 334.

12 M.C. Angermeyer and H. Matschinger, "Public Attitudes Towards Psychotropic Drugs: Have there been any Changes in Recent Years [Abstract]?" *Pharmacopsychiatry* 37 (2004): 152-156.

Chapter Two

How A Psychiatric Drug Comes to Market

1 "The New Drug Development Process," CDER Handbook, accessed 08 MAR 03 on-line at: http://www.fda.gov/cder/handbook/develop.htm.

2 Z.Ashton, "Clinical Trials and the FDA," accessed 27 JAN 04 on-line at: http://www.fool.com/specials/2000/sp000405fda.htm.

3 T. Kramer, "Drug Development," Medscape General Medicine (2002), accessed 08 MAR 03 on-line at: http://216.239.39.100/search?q=cache:NRbhPem1CpsC:www.medscape.com/viewarticle/4391.

4 E.D. Hall, "Drug development in spinal cord injury: What is the FDA looking for?" Journal of Rehabilitation Research and Development 40 (2003): 1-3.

5 R.S. Sobel, "Public Health and the Placebo: The Legacy of the 1906 Pure Food and Drugs Act," Independent Institute Working Paper No. 28 (2001), accessed 23 SEP 04 on-line at: http://216.239.39.104/search?q=cache:FgnAdSn43H8J:www.independent.org/pdf/working_papers/28_public_health.pdf.

6 E.D. Hall, "Drug development in spinal cord injury: What is the FDA looking for?" p. 3.

7 *Ibid.*

8 *Ibid.*

9 NDA 20-592, Memo from Paul Leber to File and Robert Temple Re: endorsement of approvable action, August 18, 1996, p. 2. Department of Health and Human Services, Public Health Service, Food and Drug Administration, Rockville, Maryland. Obtained through the Freedom of Information Act.

10 *Ibid.*, p. 7.

11 Z.Ashton, "Clinical Trials and the FDA."

12 M. Angell, *The Truth About the Drug Companies*, (NY: Random House, 2004), pp. 27-30.

13 *Ibid.*, pp.161-166.

14 "Drug Experience/Epidemiologic Sources Available to FDA," CDER Handbook,accessed 08 MAR 03 on-line at: http://www.fda.gov/cder/handbook/pmsinfo.htm.

15 T.J. Moore, B.M. Psaty, and C.D. Furberg, "Time to Act on Drug Safety," *JAMA* 279 (1998): 1571-1573.

16 D.A. Kessler, "Introducing MedWatch: a new approach to reporting medication and device adverse effects and product problems [Abstract]," *JAMA* 269 (1993): 2765-2786.

Chapter Three

Evidence Based Medicine

1 M. Dongier, "Evidence-Based Psychiatry: The Pros and Cons," *Canadian Journal of Psychiatry* 46 (2001): 394-395.

2 A.S. Lyons and R.J. Petrucelli, *Medicine: An Illustrated History*, (New York: Harry N. Abrams, Inc., 1987), pp. 219-222

3 H.R. Wulff, S.A. Pedersen, and R. Rosenberg, *Philosophy of Medicine: an introduction*, 2nd ed. (Boston: Blackwell Scientific Publications, 1990), pp. 203-217.

4 M. Dongier, "Evidence-Based Psychiatry: The Pros and Cons," p. 394.

5 J.C. Eccles, *Evolution of the Brain: Creation of the Self*, (New York: Routledge, 2001), pp. 172-243.

6 Evidence Based Medicine Working Group, "Evidence-Based Medicine: A New Approach to Teaching the Practice of Medicine," *JAMA* 268 (1992): 2420-2425.

7 *Ibid.*, p. 2420.

8 G.D. Rubenfeld, "Understanding Why We Agree on the Evidence but Disagree on the Medicine," *Respiratory Care* 46 (2001): 1442-1449.

9 L. Crawley, "Evidence-Based Medicine: A New Paradigm for the Patient," *JAMA* 269 (1993): 1253.

10 A. Leighton, "Evidence Based Psychiatry," *Canadian Journal of Psychiatry* 47 (2002): 384.

11 G.N. Fox, "Evidence-Based Medicine: A New Paradigm for the Patient," *JAMA* 269 (1993): 1253.

12 M.R. Tonelli, "The limits of evidence based medicine," *Respiratory Care* 46 (2001): 1435-1441.

13 T.J. Kaptchuk, "Intentional Ignorance: A History of Blind Assessment and Placebo Controls in Medicine," *Bulletin of the History of Medicine* 72 (1998): 389-433.

14 *Ibid.*

15 A.J.M. de Craen, T.J. Kaptchuk, J.G.P. Tijssen, and J. Kleijnen, "Placebos and placebo effects in medicine: a historical overview," *Journal of the Royal Society of Medicine* 92 (1999): 511-515.

16 G. E. Jackson, "A Plea for Psyche," Review of Existential Psychology & Psychiatry 26 (2003): 97-110.

17 M.R. Tonelli and T.C. Callahan, "Why Alternative Medicine Cannot Be Evidence-based," *Academic Medicine* 76 (2001): 1217.

18 *Ibid.*

19 G.D. Rubenfeld, "Understanding Why We Agree on the Evidence but Disagree on the Medicine," pp. 1442-1449.

20 S. Gottlieb, "New England Journal loosens its rules on conflict of interest," *BMJ* 324 (2002): 1474.

21 A.S. Relman and M. Angell, "How the drug industry distorts medicine and politics. America's Other Drug Problem," *The New Republic* (December 16, 2002): 27-41.

22 N.K. Choudry, H.T. Stelfox, A.S. Detsky, "Relationships Between Authors of Clinical Practice Guidelines and the Pharmaceutical Industry," *JAMA* 287 (2002): 612-617.

23 D.J. Safer, "Design and Reporting Modifications in Industry Sponsored Comparative Psychopharmacology Trials," *The Journal of Nervous and Mental Disease* 190 (2002): 583-592.

24 D.A. Antonuccio, W.G. Danton, and T.M. McClanahan, "Psychology in the Prescription Era: Building a Firewall Between Marketing and Science," *American Psychologist* 58 (2003): 1028-1043.

Chapter Four

The Randomized Controlled Trial:
Origins, Assumptions, Deficiencies

1 Val J. Gebski, Elaine M. Beller, Anthony C. Keech, "Randomised controlled trials: elements of a good study," *Medical Journal of Australia* 175 (2001): 272.

2 Ted J. Kaptchuk, "Intentional Ignorance: A History of Blind Assessment and Placebo Controls in Medicine," *Bulletin of the History of Medicine* 72 (1998): 389-433.

3 *Ibid.*, p. 407.

4 Ted J. Kaptchuk, "The double-blind, randomized, placebo-controlled trial: Gold standard or golden calf?" *Journal of Clinical Epidemiology* 54 (2001): 541-549.

5 Martin Enserink, "Can the Placebo Be the Cure?" *Science* 284 (1999): 238-240.

6 Russell S. Sobel, "Public Health and the Placebo: The Legacy of the 1906 Pure Food and Drugs Act," Independent Institute Working Paper No. 28 (2001), accessed 23 SEP 04 on-line at: http://www.independent.org/pdf/working_papers/28_public_health.pdf.

7 Helen S. Mayberg, J. Arturo Silva, Steven K. Brannan, Janet L. Tekell, Roderick K. Mahurin, Scott McGinnis, Paul A. Jerabek, "The functional neuroanatomy of the placebo effect," *American Journal of Psychiatry* 159 (2002): 728-737.

8 Andrew .F. Leuchter, Ian A. Cook, Elise A. Witte, Melinda Morgan, Michelle Abrams, "Changes in brain function of depressed subjects during treatment with placebo," *American Journal of Psychiatry* 159 (2002): 122-129.

9 Kaptchuk, "The double-blind, randomized, placebo-controlled trial: Gold standard or golden calf?" p. 543.

10 Gebski, Beller, and Keech, "Randomised controlled trials: elements of a good study," pp. 272-274.

11 Douglas G. Altman, Kenneth F. Schulz, Daniel Moher, Matthias Egger, Frank Davidoff, Diana Elbourne, Peter C. Gotzsche, Thomas Lang, "The Revised CONSORT Statement for Reporting Randomized Trials: Explanation and Elaboration," *Annals of Internal Medicine* 134 (2001): 663-694.

12 David Moher, Kenneth F. Schulz, Douglas G. Altman, "The CONSORT statement: revised recommendations for improving the quality of reports of parallel group randomized trials," *BMC Medical Research Methodology* 1 (2001), accessed 17 SEP 04 on-line at: http://www.biomedcentral.com/1471-2288/1/2.

13 David Moher, Alison Jones, Leah Lepage, "Use of the CONSORT Statement and Quality of Reports of Randomized Trials: A Comparative Before and After Evaluation," *JAMA* 285 (2001): 1992-1995.

14 David Moher, Kenneth F. Schulz, Douglas G. Altman, "The CONSORT Statement: Revised Recommendations for Improving the Quality of Reports of Parallel-Group Randomized Trials," *JAMA* 285 (2001): 1987-1991.

15 *Ibid.*, p. 1987.

16 Arif Khan, Shirin R. Khan, Robyn M. Leventhal, K. Ranga, R. Krishnan, Jack M. Gorman, "An Application of the Revised CONSORT Standards to FDA Summary Reports of Recently Approved Antidepressants and Antipsychotics," *Biological Psychiatry* 52 (2002): 62-67.

17 David S. Celermajer, "Evidence-based medicine: how good is the evidence?" *Medical Journal of Australia* 174 (2001): 293-295.

18 Marcia Angell, *The Truth About the Drug Companies: How They Deceive Us and What To Do About It*, (New York: Random House, 2004), pp. 37-51.

19 Perry Glasser, "Case Study: Eli Lilly and Using IT to Accelerate Research," *Ziff Davis CIO Insight: Strategies for IT Business Leaders* (October 10, 2002) accessed 29 SEP 04 on-line at: http://www. cioinsight.com/print_article/0,1406,a=32514,00.asp

20 Marshal Mandelkern, "Manufacturer support and outcome," *Journal of Clinical Psychiatry* 60 (1999): 122.

21 Paula A. Rochon, Jerry H. Gurwitz, Robert W. Simms, Paul R. Fortin, David T. Felson, Kenneth L. Minaker, and Thomas C. Chalmers, "A study of manufacturer-supported trials of nonsteroidal anti-inflammatory drugs in the treatment of arthritis," *Archives of Internal Medicine* 154 (1994): 157-163.

22 Thomas Bodenheimer, "Uneasy alliance: clinical investigators and the pharmaceutical industry," *The New England Journal of Medicine* 342 (2000): 1539-1544.

23 Mildred K. Cho and Lisa A. Bero, "The quality of drug studies in symposium proceedings,"*Annals of Internal Medicine* 124 (1996): 485-489.

24 R. Moynihan, "Drug firms hype disease as sales ploy, industry chief claims," *BMJ* 324 (2002): 867.

25 Robert Steinbrook, "Public Registration of Clinical Trials," *The New England Journal of Medicine* 351 (2004): 315-317.

26 Drummond Rennie, "Trial Registration: A Great Idea Switches From Ignored to Irresistable," *JAMA* 292 (2004): 1359-1362.

27 Daniel J. Safer, "Design and Reporting Modifications in Industry Sponsored Comparative Psychopharmacology Trials," *The Journal of Nervous and Mental Disease* 190 (2002): 583-592.

28 Joanna Moncrieff, "Are Antidepresants Overrated? A Review of Methodological Problems in Antidepressant Trials," *The Journal of Nervous and Mental Disease* 189 (2001): 288-295.

29 Robert Whitaker, *Mad in America*, (Cambridge, MA: Perseus Publishing, 2002).

30 Peter R. Breggin, *Talking Back to Prozac*, (NY: St. Martin's Press, 1994).

31 David O. Antonuccio, William G. Danton, and Terry M. McClanahan, "Psychology in the Prescription Era: Building a Firewall Between Marketing and Science," *American Psychologist* 58 (2003): 1028-1043.

32 Hershel Jick, James A. Kaye, Susan S. Jick, "Antidepressants and the Risk of Suicidal Behavior," *JAMA* 292 (2004): 338-343.

33 *Ibid.*, p. 340.

34 John March, Susan Silva, Stephen Petrycki, John Curry, Karen Wells, et. al., "Fluoxetine, Cognitive-Behavioral Therapy, and Their Combination for Adolescents With Depression: Treatment for Adolescents With Depression Study (TADS) Randomized Controlled Trial," *JAMA* 292 (2004): 807-820.

35 NDA 20-592, Review and Evaluation of Clinical Data, July 29, 1996, Department of Health and Human Services, Public Health Service, Food and Drug Administration, Rockville, Maryland. Obtained through the Freedom of Information Act.

36 Kalyna Z. Bezchlibynk-Butler, and J. Joel Jeffries, *Clinical Handbook of Psychotropic Drugs*, (Seattle: Hogrefe & Huber, Publishers, 2002), pp. 90-91.

37 R. Rosenheck, D. Perlick, S. Bingham, W. Liu-Mares, J. Collins, et. al., "Effectiveness and cost of olanzapine and haloperidol in the treatment of schizophrenia: a randomized controlled trial," *JAMA* 290 (2003): 2693-2702.

38 Breggin, *Talking Back to Prozac.*

39 D.E. Faries, J.H. Heiligenstein, G.D. Tollefson, and W.Z. Potter, "The double-blind variable placebo lead-in period: results from two antidepressant clinical trials [Abstract]," *Journal of Clinical Psychopharmacology* 21 (2001): 561-568.

40 Metin Basoglu, Isaac Marks, Maria Livanou, and Richard Swinson, "Double-blindness procedures, rater blindness, and ratings of outcome. Observations from a controlled trial [Abstract]," *Archives of General Psychiatry* 54 (1997): 744-748.

41 Charles M. Morin, Cheryl Colecchi, Doug Brink, Manual Astruc, James Mercer, and Stephanie Remsberg, "How 'blind' are double-blind placebo-controlled trials of benzodiazepine hypnotics [Abstract]?" *Sleep* 18 (1995): 240-245.

42 Kathleen M. Carroll, Bruce J. Rounsaville, and Charla Nich, "Blind man's bluff: effectiveness and significance of psychotherapy and pharmacotherapy blinding procedures in a clinical trial," *Journal of Consulting and Clinical Psychology* 62 (1994): 276-280.

43 Jurgen Margraf, Anke Ehlers, Walton T. Roth, Duncan B. Clark, Javaid Sheikh, W. Stewart Agras, and C. Barr Taylor, "How 'blind' are double-blind studies?" *Journal of Consulting and Clinical Psychology* 59 (1991): 184-187.

44 Mauro Moscucci, Louise Byrne, Michael Weintraub, and Christopher Cox, "Blinding, unblinding, and the placebo effect: an analysis of patients' guesses of treatment assignment in a double-blind clinical trial," *Clinical Pharmacology and Therapeutics* 41 (1987): 259-265.

45 Arif Khan, Heather A. Warner, and Walter A. Brown, "Symptom Reduction and Suicide Risk in Patients Treated With Placebo in Antidepressant Clinical Trials," *Archives of General Psychiatry* 57 (2000): 311-317.

46 Arif Khan, Shirin R. Khan, Robyn M. Leventhal, and Walter A. Brown, "Symptom Reduction and Suicide Risk Among Patients Treated With Placebo in Antipsychotic Clinical Trials: An Analysis of the Food and Drug Administration Database," *American Journal of Psychiatry* 158 (2001): 1449-1454.

47 NDA 20-592, Review and Evaluation of Clinical Data, July 29, 1996, Department of Health and Human Services, Public Health Service, Food and Drug Administration, Rockville, Maryland. Obtained through the Freedom of Information Act, p. 41.

48 Safer, "Design and Reporting Modifications in Industry Sponsored Comparative Psychopharmacology Trials," pp. 584-585.

49 Esther Cherland and Renee Fitzpatrick, "Psychotic Side Effects of Psychostimulants: A 5-Year Review," *Canadian Journal of Psychiatry* 44 (1999): 811-813.

50 Joseph Glenmullen, *Prozac Backlash*, (NY: Simon & Schuster, 2000), p. 353.

51 NDA 20-592, Review and Evaluation of Clinical Data, July 29, 1996, Department of Health and Human Services, Public Health Service, Food and Drug Administration, Rockville, Maryland. Obtained through the Freedom of Information Act. p. 124.

52 Michael Doherty, "Redundant Publication," *bmj.com* (undated), accessed 30 SEP 04 on-line at: http://bmj.bmjjournals.com/misc/cope/tex5.shtml

53 Safer, "Design and Reporting Modifications in Industry Sponsored Comparative Psychopharmacology Trials," 585-586.

54 Hypericum Depression Trial Study Group, "Effect of Hypericum perforatum (St. John's wort) in major depressive disorder: a randomized controlled trial," *JAMA* 287 (2002): 1807-1814.

55 David O. Antonuccio, William G. Danton, and Terry M. McClanahan, "Psychology in the Prescription Era: Building a Firewall Between Marketing and Science," pp. 1033-1034.

56 Joanna Moncrieff, "Is Psychiatry For Sale? An Examination of the Influence of the Pharmaceutical Industry on Academic and Practical Psychiatry," *Healthy Skepticism International News* 22 (2003), accessed 05 APR 04 on-line at: www.healthyskepticism.org

57 Scott Gottlieb, *"New England Journal* loosens its rules on conflict of interest," *BMJ* 324 (2002): 1474.

58 Jeffrey M. Drazen and Gregory D. Curfman, "Financial Associations of Authors," *The New England Journal of Medicine*," 346 (2002): 1901-1902.

59 Thomas Bodenheimer, "Uneasy alliance: clinical investigators and the pharmaceutical industry."

60 Joanna Moncrieff, "Is Psychiatry For Sale? An Examination of the Influence of the Pharmaceutical Industry on Academic and Practical Psychiatry," *Healthy Skepticism International News* 22 (2003), accessed 05 APR 04 on-line at: www.healthyskepticism.org

61 Marilynn Larkin, "Whose article is it anyway," *The Lancet* 354 (1999): 136.

62 Joanna Moncrieff, "Is Psychiatry For Sale? An Examination of the Influence of the Pharmaceutical Industry on Academic and Practical Psychiatry," *Healthy Skepticism International News* 22 (2003), accessed 05 APR 04 on-line at: www.healthyskepticism. org

63 David O. Antonuccio, William G. Danton, and Terry M. McClanahan, "Psychology in the Prescription Era: Building a Firewall Between Marketing and Science," p. 1031.

64 Kay Dickersin and Drummond Rennie, "Registering Clinical Trials," *JAMA* 290 (2003): 516-523.

Chapter Five

Psychiatric Drugs and the Human Brain

1 Jack Gorman, *The Essential Guide to Psychiatric Drugs*, (New York: St. Martin's Paperbacks, 1995), p. 365.

2 Paul D. MacLean, The Triune Brain in Evolution, (N.Y.: Plenum Press, 1990).

3 Richard S. Snell, *Clinical Neuroanatomy for Medical Students*, 4th Ed. (Philadelphia: Lippincott-Raven, 1997), p. 77.

4 Duane E. Haines, Ed., *Fundamental Neuroscience*, 2nd Ed. (New York: Churchill Livingstone, 2002), p. 59.

5 George J. Siegel, Bernard W. Agranoff, R. Wayne Albers, Stephen K. Fisher, and Michael D. Uhler, *Basic Neurochemistry: Molecular, Cellular, and Medical Aspects*, 6th Ed., (Philadelphia: Lippincott Williams & Wilkins, 1999), p. 365.

6 Jack R. Cooper, Floyd E. Bloom, and Robert H. Roth, *The Biochemical Basis of Neuropharmacology*, 8th Ed., (New York: Oxford University Press, 2003), p. 66.

7 "Ligand." *Dorland's Pocket Medical Dictionary*, 24th Ed., (Philadelphia: W.B. Saunders Company, 1989).

Chapter Six

Allostasis and the Problem of Allostatic Load

1 Bruce S. McEwen, "Protective and Damaging Effects of Stress Mediators," *The New England Journal of Medicine* 338 (1998): 171-179.

2 Bruce S. McEwen and Eliot Stellar, "Stress and the Individual: Mechanisms Leading to Disease," *Archives of Internal Medicine* 153 (1993): 2093-2101.

3 Bruce S. McEwen, "Mood Disorders and Allostatic Load," *Biological Psychiatry* 54 (2003): 200-207.

4 Nancy Krieger, "Theories for social epidemiology in the 21st century: an ecosocial perspective," *International Journal of Epidemiology* 30 (2001): 668-677.

5 Darryl W. Eyles, Kathryn M. Avent, Terry J. Stedman, and Susan M. Pond, "Two pyridinium metabolites of haloperidol are present in the brain of patients at post-mortem [Abstract]," *Life Sciences* 60 (1997): 529-534.

6 Serge Przedborski, Vernice Jackson-Lewis, Ali B. Naini, Michael Jakowec, Giselle Petzinger, Reginald Miller, and Muhammad Akram, "The parkinsonian toxin 1-methyl-4-phenyl-1,2,3,6-tetrahydropyridine (MPTP): a technical review of its utility and safety," *Journal of Neurochemistry* 76 (2001): 1265-1274.

7 J. Fang, D. Zuo, and P.H. Yu, "Comparison of cytotoxicity of a quaternary pyridinium metabolite of haloperidol (HP+) with neurotoxin N-methyl-4-phenylpyridinium (MPP+) towards culture dopaminergic neuroblastoma cells [Abstract]," *Psychopharmacology* 121 (1995): 373-378.

8 H. Rollema, M. Skolnik, J. D'Engelbronner, K. Igarashi, E. Usuki, and N. Castagnoli, Jr., "MPP(+)-like neurotoxicity of a pyridinium metabolite derived from haloperidol: in vivo microdialysis and in vitro mitochondrial studies [Abstract]," *Journal of Pharmacology and Experimental Therapeutics* 268 (1994): 380-387.

9 Madhu Kalia, James P. O'Callaghan, Diane B. Miller, and Michael Kramer, "Comparative study of fluoxetine, sibutramine, sertraline and dexfenfluramine on the morphology of serotonergic nerve terminals using serotonin immunohistochemistry," *Brain Research* 858 (2000): 92-105.

10 World Health Organization, "Lexicon of alcohol and drug terms published by the World Health Organization," accessed 30 October 2004 on-line at: http://www.who.int/substance_abuse/terminology/who_lexicon/en/

11 *Ibid.*

12 American Psychiatric Association, *Diagnostic and Statitstical Manual of Mental Disorders*, 4th Ed., (Washington, D.C.: American Psychiatric Assocation, 1994), pp. 181-183,

13 Terry E. Robinson and Kent C. Berridge, "The psychology and neurobiology of addiction: an incentive-sensitization view," *Addiction* 95 suppl 2 (2000): S91-S117.

14 C. Schindler, "Cocaine and cardiovascular toxicity," *Addiction Biology* 1 (1996): 31-47.

15 Terry E. Robinson and Kent C. Berridge, "The psychology and neurobiology of addiction: an incentive-sensitization view,"

16 Nadine Lambert, Marsha McLeod, and Susan Schenk, "Subjective responses to initial experience with cocaine as measures of cocaine abuse liability: An exploration of the incentive-sensitization theory of drug abuse," unpublished (personal communication with lead author, 28 October 2004).

17 Alice M. Young and Andrew J. Goudie, "Adaptive Processes Regulating Tolerance to Behavioral Effects of Drugs," in *Psychopharmacology: The Fourth Generation of Progress*, Floyd E. Bloom and David J. Kupfer, Ed. (New York: Raven Press, 1995), pp. 733-741.

18 Nicoletta Sonino, Giovanni A. Fava, Francesco Fallo, Antonella Franceschetto, Pierra Belluardo, and Marco Boscaro, "Effect of the Serotonin Antagonists Ritanserin and Ketanserin in Cushing's Disease," *Pituitary* 3 (2000): 55-59.

Chapter Seven

Antidepressants

1 Kathryn Schulz, "Did Antidepressants Depress Japan," *The New York Times* (August 22, 2004), accessed 03 SEP 2004 on-line at: http://www.pewfellowships.org/stories/japan/pf_japan_depressed.htm

2 David Healy, *Let Them Eat Prozac*, (Toronto: James Lorimer & Company Ltd., Publishers, 2003), pp. 1-57.

3 Joanna Moncrieff, "An investigation into the precedents of modern drug treatment in psychiatry," *History of Psychiatry* 10 (1999): 475-490.

4 Healy, *Let Them Eat Prozac*, pp.53-57.

5 *Ibid.*

6 Joseph J. Schildkraut, "The catecholamine hypothesis of affective disorders: a review of supporting evidence," *American Journal of Psychiatry* 122 (1965): 509-522.

7 Stephen M. Stahl, *Essential Psychopharmacology: Neuroscientific Basis and Practical Applications*, 2nd Ed. (Cambridge: Cambridge University Press, 2000).

8 Kalnya Z. Bezchlibynk-Butler and J. Joel Jeffries, Ed. *Clinical Handbook of Psychotropic Drugs*, 13th Ed. (Cambridge, MA: Hogrefe & Huber, 2003).

9 Y.G. Ni and R. Miledi, "Blockage of 5HT2C serotonin receptors by fluoxetine (Prozac)," *Proceedings of the National Academy of Sciences of the United States of America* 94 (1997): 2036-2040.

10 J. Garcia-Colunga, J.N. Awad, and R. Miledi, "Blockage of muscle and neuronal acetylcholine receptors by fluoxetine (Prozac)," *Proceedings of the National Academy of Sciences of the United States of America* 94 (1997): 2041-2044.

11 Ron Pies, "Must We Now Consider SRIs Neuroleptics?" *Journal of Clinical Psychopharmacology* 17 (1997): 443-445.

12 Ni and Miledi, "Blockage of 5HT2C serotonin receptors by fluoxetine (Prozac)."

13 E.P. Palvimaki, B.L. Roth, H. Majasuo, A. Laakso, M. Kuoppamaki, E. Syvlahti, and J. Hietala, "Interactions of selective serotonin reuptake inhibitors with the serotonin 5HT2C receptor [Abstract]," *Psychopharmacology* 126 (1996): 234-240.

14 David J. Nutt, "The neuropharmacology of serotonin and noradrenaline in depression," *International Clinical Psychopharmacology* 17 (2002): S1-S12.

15 Eric J. Nestler, Steven E. Hyman, and Robert C. Malenka, *Molecular Neuropharmacology: A Foundation for Clinical Neuroscience*, (New York: The McGraw-Hill Companies, Inc., 2001), p. 192.

16 Jack R. Cooper, Floyd E. Bloom, and Robert H. Roth, *The Biochemical Basis of Neuropharmacology*, Eighth Ed., (New York: Oxford University Press, 2003), pp. 271-304.

17 Nestler, Hyman, and Malenka, p. 195.

18 Alan Frazer and Julie G. Hensler, "Serotonin," in George J. Siegel, Bernard W. Agranoff, R. Wayne Albers, Stephen K. Fisher, and Michael D. Uhler, Ed., Sixth Edition, *Basic Neurochemistry: Molecular, Cellular, and Medical Aspects*, (New York: Lippincott Williams & Wilkins, 1999), pp. 276-284.

19 J. Longmore, D. Shaw, D. Smith, R. Hopkins, G. McAllister, J.D. Pickard, D.J. Sirinathsinghji, A.J. Butler, and R.G. Hill, "Differential distribution of 5HT1D- and 5HT1B-immunoreactivity within the human trigemino-cerebrovascular system: implications for the discovery of new antimigraine drugs [Abstract]," *Cephalagia* 17 (1997): 833-842.

20 Janet F. Czachura and Kurt Rasmussen, "Effects of acute and chronic administration of fluoxetine on the activity of serotonergic neurons in the dorsal raphe nucleus of the rat," *Naunyn Schmiedeberg's Archives of Pharmacology* 362 (2000): 266-275.

21 P. Blier and C. de Montigny, "Serotonergic but not noradrenergic neurons in rat central nervous system adapt to long-term treatment with monoamine oxidase inhibitors [Abstract]," *Neuroscience* 16 (1985): 949-955.

22 E. Le Poul, N. Laaris, E. Doucet, A.M. Laporte, M. Hamon, and L. Lanfumey, "Early desensitization of somato-dendritic 5HT1A autoreceptors in rats treated with fluoxetine or paroxetine [Abstract]," *Naunyn Schmiedeberg's Archives of Pharmacology* 352 (1995): 141-148.

23 P. Blier, C. de Montigny, and Y. Chaput, "A role for the serotonin system in the mechanism of action of antidepressant treatments: preclinical evidence [Abstract]," *Journal of Clinical Psychiatry* 51 (1990): 4-8.

24 P.A. Sargent, K.H. Kjaer, C.J. Bench, E.A. Rabiner, C. Messa, and J. Meyer, "Brain serotonin 1A receptor binding measured by positron emission tomography with [11c] WAY-100635: effects of depression and antidepressant treatment [Abstract]," *Archives of General Psychiatry* 57 (2000): 174-180.

25 G. Pineyro, P. Blier, T. Dennis, and C. de Montigny, "Desensitization of the neuronal 5-HT carrier following its long-term blockade [Abstract]," *Journal of Neuroscience* 14 (1994): 3036-3047.

26 S. Horschitz, R. Hummerich, and P. Schloss, "Downregulation of the rat serotonin transporter upon exposure to a selective serotonin reuptake inhibitor [Abstract]," *Neuroreport* 20 (2001): 2181-2184.

27 N. Bal, G. Figueras, M.T. Vilaro, C. Sunol, and F. Artigas, "Antidepressant drugs inhibit a glial 5-hydroxytryptamine transporter in rat brain [Abstract]," *European Journal of Neuroscience* 9 (1997): 1728-1738

28 J. Sprouse, J. Braselton, L. Reynolds, T. Clarke, and H. Rollema, "Activation of postsynaptic 5HT1A receptors by fluoxetine despite the loss of firing-dependent serotonergic input: electrophysiological and neurochemical studies [Abstract]," *Synapse* 41 (2001): 49-57.

29 Saloua Benmansour, William A. Owens, Marco Cecchi, David A. Morilak, and Alan Frazer, "Serotonin Clearance *In Vivo* Is Altered to a Greater Extent by Antidepressant-Induced Downregulation of the Serotonin Transporter than by Acute Blockade of this Transporter," *Journal of Neuroscience* 22 (2002): 6766-6772.

30 A. Kugaya, N.M. Seneca, P.J. Snyder, S.A. Williams, R.T. Malison, R.M. Baldwin, J.P. Seibyl, and R.B. Innis, "Changes in human in vivo serotonin and dopamine transporter availabilities during chronic antidepressant administration [Abstract]," *Neuropsychopharmacology* 28 (2003): 413-420.

31 M.L. Filipenko, A.G. Beilina, O.V. Alekseyenko, V.V. Dolgov, and N.N. Kudryavtseva, "Repeated experience of social defeats increases serotonin transporter and monoamine oxidase A mRNA levels in raphe nuclei of male mice [Abstract]," *Neuroscience Letter* 321 (2002): 25-28.

32 M. Willeit, N. Praschak-Rieder, A. Neumeister, W. Pirker, S. Asenbaum, O. Vitouch, J. Tauscher, E. Hilger, J. Stastny, T. Brucke, and S. Kasper, "[123I]-beta-CIT SPECT imaging shows reduced brain serotonin transporter availability in drug-free depressed patients with seasonal affective disorder [Abstract]," *Biological Psychiatry* 47 (2000): 482-489.

33 Marie Asberg, Lil Traskman, and Peter Thoren, "5-HIAA in the Cerebrospinal Fluid: A Biochemical Suicide Predictor?" *Archives of General Psychiatry* 33 (1976): 1193-1197.

34 D. Lester, "The Concentration of Neurotransmitter Metabolites in the Cerebrospinal Fluid of Suicidal Individuals: a Meta-Analysis," *Pharmacopsychiatry* 28 (1995): 45-50.

35 H. Nagayama, J. Akiyoshi, and M. Tobo, "Action of Chronically Administered Antidepressants on the Serotonergic Postsynapse in a Model of Depression," *Pharmacology Biochemistry & Behavior* 25 (1986): 805-811.

36 H. Nagayama, J.N. Hingtgen, and M.H. Aprison, "Postsynaptic action by four antidepresssive drugs in an animal model of depression [Abstract]," *Pharmacology Biochemistry & Behavior* 15 (1981): 125-130.

37 R. Takahashi, K.H. Tachiki, K. Nishiwaki, E. Nakamura, and T. Tateishi, "Biochemical basis of an animal model of depressive illness - a preliminary report [Abstract]," *Folia Psychiatrica et Neurologica Japonica* 30 (1976): 208-218.

38 Saloua Benmansour, William A. Owens, Marco Cecchi, David A. Morilak, and Alan Frazer, "Serotonin Clearance *In Vivo* Is Altered to a Greater Extent by Antidepressant-Induced Downregulation of the Serotonin Transporter than by Acute Blockade of this Transporter."

39 Saloua Benmansour, Marco Cecchi, David A. Morilak, Greg A. Gerhardt, Martin A. Javors, Georgianna G. Gould, and Alan Frazer, "Effects of Chronic Antidepressant Treatment on Serotonin Transporter Function, Density, and mRNA Level," *Journal of Neuroscience* 19 (1999): 10494-10501.

40 K.P. Lesch, C.S. Aulakh, B.L. Wolozin, T.J. Tolliver, J.L. Hill, and D.L. Murphy, "Regional brain expression of serotonin transporter mRNA and its regulation by reuptake inhibiting antidepressants [Abstract]," *Molecular Brain Research* 17 (1993): 31-35

41 J.F. Neumaier, D.C. Root, and M.W. Hamblin, "Chronic fluoxetine reduces serotonin transporter mRNA and 5HT1B mRNA in a sequential manner in the rat dorsal raphe nucleus [Abstract]," *Neuropsychopharmacology* 15 (1996): 515-522

42 Theresa M. Cabrera-Vera, Francisca Garcia, Wilfred Pinto, and George Battaglia, "Effect of Prenatal Fluoxetine (Prozac) Exposure on Brain Serotonin Neurons in Prepubescent and Adult Male Rat Offspring," *Journal of Pharmacology and Experimental Therapeutics* 280 (1997): 138-145.

43 Theresa M. Cabrera-Vera and George Battaglia, "Delayed decreases in brain 5-hydroxytryptamine 2A/2C receptor density and function in male rat progeny following prenatal fluoxetine [Abstract]," *Journal of Pharmacology and Experimental Therapeutics* 269 (1994): 637-645.

44 Theresa M. Cabrera-Vera and George Battaglia, "Prenatal exposure to fluoxetine (Prozac) produces site-specific and age-dependent alterations in brain serotonin transporters in rat progeny: evidence from autoradiographic studies [Abstract]," *Journal of Pharmacology and Experimental Therapeutics* 286 (1998): 1474-1481.

45 D. Montero, M.L. de Ceballos, and J. Del Rio, "Down-regulation of 3H-imipramine binding sites in rat cerebral cortex after prenatal exposure to antidepressants [Abstract]," *Life Sciences* 46 (1990): 1619-1626.

46 C. Maudhuit, M. Hamon, and J. Adrien, "Electrophysiological activity of raphe dorsalis serotonergic neurones in a possible model of endogenous depression [Abstract]," *Neuroreport* 7 (1995): 681-684.

47 H.H. Hansen, C. Sanchez, and E. Meier, "Neonatal Administration of the Selective Serotonin Reuptake Inhibitor Lu 10-134-C Increases Forced Swimming-Induced Immobility in Adult Rats: A Putative Animal Model of Depression?" *Journal of Pharmacology and Experimental Therapeutics* 283 (1997): 1333-1341.

48 *Ibid.*, p. 1333.

49 D.K. Raap, F. Garcia, N.A. Muma, W.A. Wolf, G. Battaglia, and L.D. van de Kar, "Sustained Desensitization of Hypothalamic 5-Hydroxytryptamine 1A Receptors after Discontinuation of Fluoxetine: Inhibited Neuroendocrine Responses to 8-Hydroxy-2-(Dipropylamino)Tetralin in the Absence of Changes in $G_{i/o/z}$ Proteins," *Journal of Pharmacology and Experimental Therapeutics* 288 (1999): 561-567.

50 Z. Bhagawagar, E.A. Rabiner, P.A. Sargent, P.M. Grasby, and P.J. Cowen, "Persistent reduction in brain serotonin 1A receptor binding in recovered depressed men measured by positron emission tomography with [11C]WAY-100635 [Abstract]," *Molecular Psychiatry* 9 (2004): 386-392.

51 G.R. Heninger, P.L. Delgado, and D.S. Charney, "The Revised Monoamine Theory of Depression: A Modulatory Role for Monoamines, Based on New Findings From Monoamine Depletion Experiments in Humans," *Pharmacopsychiatry* 29 (1996): 2-11.

52 *Ibid.*, p. 8.

53 Dani K. Raap and Louis D. Van de Kar, "Minireview: Selective Serotonin Reuptake Inhibitors and Neuroendocrine Function," *Life Sciences* 65 (1999): 1217-1235.

54 U. Von Bardeleben, A. Steiger, A. Gerken, and F. Holsboer, "Effects of fluoxetine upon pharmacoendocrine and sleep-EEG parameters in normal controls [Abstract]," *International Clinical Psychopharmacology* 4 (1989): 1-5.

55 C. Reist, D. Helmeste, L. Albers, H. Chhay, S.W. Tang, "Serotonin indices and impulsivity in normal volunteers [Abstract]," *Psychiatry Research* 60 (1996): 177-184.

56 E. Seifritz, P. Baumann, M.J. Muller, O. Annen, M. Amey, U. Hemmeter, M. Hatzinger, F. Chardon, and E. Holsboer-Trachsler, "Neuroendocrine effects of a 20-mg citalopram infusion in healthy males. A placebo-controlled evaluation of citalopram as 5HT function probe [Abstract]," *Neuropsychopharmacology* 14 (1996): 253-263.

57 R.W. Fuller, H.D. Snoddy, B.B. Molloy, "Pharmacologic evidence for a serotonin neural pathway involved in hypothalamus-pituitary-adrenal function in rats [Abstract]," *Life Sciences* 19 (1976): 337-345.

58 L. Krulich, "The effect of a serotonin reuptake inhibitor (Lilly 110140) on the secretion of prolactin in the rat [Abstract]," *Life Sciences* 17 (1975): 1141-1144.

59 J.A. Clemens, M.E. Roush, and R.W. Fuller, "Evidence that serotonin neurons stimulate secretion of prolactin releasing factor [Abstract]," *Life Sciences* 22 (1978): 2209-2213.

60 J. M. Massou, C. Trichard, D. Attar-Levy, A. Feline, E. Corruble, B. Beaufils, J.L. Martinot, "Frontal 5HT2A receptors studied in depressive patients during chronic treatment by selective serotonin reuptake inhibitors [Abstract]," *Psychopharmacology* 133 (1997): 99-101.

61 A. K. Cadogan, C.A. Marsden, I. Tulloch, and D.A. Kendall, "Evidence that chronic administration of paroxetine or fluoxetine enhances 5HT2 receptor function in the brain of the guinea pig [Abstract]," *Neuropharmacology* 32 (1993): 249-256.

62 P.D. Hrdina and T.B. Vu, "Chronic fluoxetine treatment upregulates 5HT uptake sites and 5HT2 receptors in rat brain: an autoradiographic study [Abstract]," *Synapse* 14 (1993): 324-331.

63 Nicoletta Sonino and Giovanni A. Fava, "Erratum to 'CNS drugs in Cushing's disease: pathophysiological and therapeutic implications for mood disorders,'" *Progress in Neuro-Psychopharmacology & Biological Psychiatry* 26 (2002): 1011-1018.

64 Ana B.F. Emiliano and Julie L. Fudge, "From Galactorrhea to Osteopenia: Rethinking Serotonin-Prolactin Interactions," *Neuropsychopharmacology* 29 (2004): 833-846.

65 P.J. Cowen and P.A. Sargent, "Changes in plasma prolactin during SSRI treatment: evidence for a delayed increase in 5HT neurotransmission [Abstract]," *Journal of Psychopharmacology* 11 (1997): 345-348.

66 Emiliano and Fudge, "From Galactorrhea to Osteopenia: Rethinking Serotonin-Prolactin Interactions."

67 H.G. Kwa, F. Cleton, D.Y. Wang, R.D. Bulbrook, J.C. Bulstrode, J.L. Hayward, R.R. Millis, and J. Cuzick, "A prospective study of plasma prolactin levels and subsequent risk of breast cancer [Abstract]," *International Journal of Cancer* 28 (1981): 673-676.

68 Susan E. Hankinson, Walter C. Willett, Dominique S. Michaud, JoAnn E. Manson, Graham A. Colditz, Christopher Longcope, Bernard Rosner, and Frank E. Speizer, "Plasma Prolactin Levels and Subsequent Risk of Breast Cancer in Postmenopausal Women," *Journal of the National Cancer Institute* 91 (1999): 629-634.

69 C.W. Welsch and H. Nagasawa, "Prolactin and murine mammary tumorigenesis: a review [Abstract]," *Cancer Research* 37 (1977): 951-963.

70 C.J. Limas, C. Kroupis, A. Haidaroglou, and D.V. Cokkinos, "Hyperprolactinemia in patients with heart failure: clinical and immunogenetic correlations [Abstract]," *European Journal of Clinical Investigation* 32 (2002): 74-78.

71 G. Curtarelli and C. Ferrari, "Cardiomegaly and heart failure in a patient with prolactin-secreting pituitary tumour [Abstract]," *Thorax* 34 (1979): 328-331.

72 Fabien Van Coppenolle, Christian Slomianny, Francoise Carpentier, Xuefen Le Bourhis, Ahmed Ahidouch, Dominique Croix, Guillaume Legrand, Etienne Dewailly, Sarah Fournier, Henri Cousse, Dominique Authie, Jean-Pierre Raynaud, Jean-Claude Beauvillain, Jean-Paul Dupouy, and Natalia Prevarskaya, "Effects of hyperprolactinemia on rat prostrate growth: evidence of androgeno-dependence," *American Journal of Physiology – Endocrinology and Metabolism* 280 (2001): E120-E129.

73 R. Coelho, C. Silva, A. Maia, J. Prata, and H. Barros, "Bone mineral density: a community study in women [Abstract]," *Journal of Psychosomatic Research* 46 (1999): 29-35.

74 Jean-Philippe Bonjour, "Delayed puberty and peak bone mass," *European Journal of Endocrinology* 139 (1998): 257-259.

75 Carolina Di Somma, Aannamaria Colao, Antonella Di Sarno, Michele Klain, Maria Luisa Landi, Giuseppina Facciolli, Rosario Pivonello, Nicola Panza, Marco Salvatore, and Gaetano Lombardi, "Bone marker and bone density reponses to dopamine agonist therapy in hyperprolactinemic males," *Journal of Clinical Endocrinology & Metabolism* 83 (1998): 807-813.

76 M.G. Subramanian, C.L. Kowalczyk, R.E. Leach, D.M. Lawson, C.M. Blacker, K.A. Ginsburg, J.F. Randolph, Jr., M.P. Diamond, and K.S. Moghissi, "Midcycle increase of prolactin seen in normal women is absent in subjects with unexplained infertility [Abstract]," *Fertility and Sterility* 67 (1997): 644-647.

77 Madhu Kalia, James P. O'Callaghan, Diane B. Miller, and Michael Kramer, "Comparative study of fluoxetine, sibutramine, sertraline and dexfenfluramine on the morphology of serotonergic nerve terminals using serotonin immunohistochemistry," *Brain Research* 858 (2000): 92-105.

78 S.D. Norrholm and C.C. Ouimet, "Chronic fluoxetine administration to juvenile rats prevents age-associated dendritic spine proliferation in hippocampus [Abstract]," *Brain Research* 883 (2000): 205-215.

79 B.L. Jacobs, H. Praag, and F.H. Gage, "Adult brain neurogenesis and psychiatry: a novel theory of depression [Abstract]," *Molecular Psychiatry* 5 (2000): 262-269.

80 J.E. Malberg, A.J. Eisch, E.J. Nestler, and R.S. Duman, "Chronic antidepressant treatment increases neurogenesis in adult rat hippocampus,"*Journal of Neuroscience* 20 (2000): 9104-9110.

81 Elizabeth Gould and Charles G. Gross, "Neurogenesis in Adult Mammals: Some Progress and Problems," *Journal of Neuroscience* 22 (2002): 619-623.

82 Fred H. Gage, "Neurogenesis in the Adult Brain," *Journal of Neuroscience* 22 (2022): 612-613.

83 Y. Kozorovitskiy and E. Gould, "Adult neurogenesis: a mechanism for brain repair [Abstract]?" *Journal of Experimental Neuropsychology* 25 (2003): 721-732.

84 Z. Kokaia and O. Lindvall, "Neurogenesis after ischaemic brain insults [Abstract]," *Current Opinions in Neurobiology* 13 (2003): 127-132.

85 S. Goldman and F. Plum, "Compensatory regeneration of the damaged adult human brain: neuroplasticity in a clinical perspective [Abstract]," *Advances in Neurology* 73 (1997): 99-107.

86 Jack M. Parent, "The role of seizure-induced neurogenesis in epileptogenesis and brain repair [Abstract]," *Epilepsy Research* 50 (2002): 179-189.

87 Jack M. Parent, "Injury-induced neurogenesis in the adult mammalian brain [Abstract]," *The Neuroscientist* 9 (2003): 261-272.

88 H.G. Kuhn, T.D. Palmer, and E. Fuchs, "Adult neurogenesis: a compensatory mechanism for neuronal damage [Abstract]," *European Archives of Psychiatry and Clinical Neuroscience* 251 (2001): 152-158.

89 Nicolas R. Bolo, Yann Hode, Jean-Francois Nedelec, Eric Laine, Gabrielle Wagner, and Jean-Paul Macher, "Brain Pharmacokinetics and Tissue Distribution *In Vivo* of Fluvoxamine and Fluoxetine by Fluorine Magnetic Resonance Spectroscopy," *Neuropsychopharmacology* 23 (2000): 428-438.

90 W.L. Strauss and S.R. Dager, "Magnetization transfer of fluoxetine in the human brain using fluorine magnetic resonance spectroscopy [Abstract]," *Biological Psychiatry* 49 (2001): 798-802.

91 N.R. Bolo, Y. Hode, J.-P. Macher, "Long-term sequestration of fluorinated compounds in tissues after fluvoxamine or fluoxetine treatment: a fluorine magnetic resonance spectroscopy study in vivo," *Magma* 16 (2004): 268-276.

92 Healy, *Let Them Eat Prozac*.

93 David O. Antonuccio, David D. Burns, and William G. Danton, "Antidepressants: A Triumph of Marketing Over Science?" Prevention & Treatment 5 (2002) accessed 12 JUL 2002 on-line at: http://journals.apa.org/prevention/volume5/pre0050025c.html

94 Jitschak G. Storosum, Barbara J. van Zwieten, Wim van den Brink, Berhold P.R. Gersons, and Andre W. Broekmans, "Suicide Risk in Placebo-Controlled Studies of Major Depression," *American Journal of Psychiatry* 158 (2001): 1271-1275.

95 Helen S. Mayberg, J. Arturo Silva, Steven K. Brannan, Janet L. Tekell, Roderick K. Mahurin, Scott McGinnis, and Paul A. Jerabek, "The Functional Neuroanatomy of the Placebo Effect," *American Journal of Psychiatry* 159 (2002): 728-737.

96 Andrew F. Leuchter, Ian A. Cook, Elise A. Witte, Melinda Morgan, and Michelle Abrams, "Changes in Brain Function of Depressed Subjects During Treatment With Placebo," *American Journal of Psychiatry* 159 (2002): 122-129.

97 Healy, *Let Them Eat Prozac*, pp. 58-90.

98 Comments of Robert A. Temple, Director, FDA Office of Drug Evaluation / Center for Drug Evaluation and Research, "Joint Meeting of the CDER Psychopharmacologic Drugs Advisory Committee and the FDA Pediatric Advisory Committee – re: antidepressant drugs in pediatric patients and suicidality," Holiday Inn, Bethesda, MD, 14 SEP 2004.

99 Graham J. Emslie, John H. Heilgenstein, Karen Dineen Wagner, Sharon L. Hoog, Daniel E. Ernest, Eileen Brown, Mary Nilsson, and Jennie G. Jacobson, "Fluoxetine for Acute Treatment of Depression in Children and Adolescents: A Placebo-Controlled Randomized Clinical Trial," *Journal of the American Academy of Child and Adolescent Psychiatry* 41 (2002): 1205-1215.

100 Irving Kirsch, Thomas J. Moore, Alan Scoboria, and Sarah S. Nicholls, "The Emperor's New Drugs: An Analysis of Antidepressant Medication Data Submitted to the U.S. Food and Drug Administration," Prevention & Treatment 5 (2002) accessed 12 JUL 2002 on-line at: http://journals.apa.org/prevention/volume5/pre0050023a.html

101 Irving Kirsch, Alan Scoboria, and Thomas J. Moore, "Response to the commentaries – Antidepressants and Placebos: Secrets, Revelations, and Unanswered Questions," Prevention & Treatment 5 (2002) accessed 17 JUL 2002 on-line at: http://journals.apa.org/prevention/volume5/pre0050033r.html

102 Joanna Moncrieff, "The antidepressant debate," British Journal of Psychiatry 180 (2002): 193-194.

103 Joanna Moncrieff, Simon Wessely, and Rebecca Hardy, "Meta-analysis of trials comparing antidepressants with active placebos," *British Journal of Psychiatry* 172 (1998): 227-231.

104 S.D. Hollon, R.J. De Rubeis, R.C. Shelton, and B. Weiss, "The emperor's new drugs: Effect size and moderation effects," Prevention & Treatment 5 (2002), accessed 12 JUL 2002 on-line at: http://journals.apa.org/prevention/volume5/pre0050028c.html

105 Healy, *Let Them Eat Prozac*, p. 86.

106 Carl O'Brien, "Drug firm to drop non-addiction claim," *The Irish Times* 10 May 2003.

107 Antonuccio, Burns, and Danton, "Antidepressants: A Triumph of Marketing Over Science?"

108 Jan Spijker, Ron de Graaf, Rob V. Bijl, Aartjan T.F. Beekman, Johan Ormel, and Willem A. Nolen, "Duration of major depressive episodes in the general population: results from the Netherlands Mental Health Survey and Incidence Study (NEMESIS)," *British Journal of Psychiatry* 181 (2002): 208-213.

109 L.L. Judd, M.J. Paulus, P.J. Schettle, H.S. Akiskal, J. Endicott, A.C. Leon, J.D. Maser, T. Mueller, D.A. Solomon, and M.B. Keller, "Does incomplete recovery from first lifetime major depressive episode herald a chronic course of illness?" *American Journal of Psychiatry* 157 (2000): 1501-1504.

110 T.S. Brugha, P.E. Bebbington, B. MacCarthy, E. Sturt, and T. Wykes, "Antidepressants may not assist recovery in practice: a naturalistic prospective survey," *Acta Psychiatrica Scandinavica* 86 (1992): 5-11.

111 E.M. van Weel-Baumgarten, W.J. van den Bosch, Y.A. Hekster, H.J. van den Hoogen, and F.G. Zitman, "Treatment of depression related to recurrence: 10-year follow-up in general practice," *Journal of Clinical Pharmacology and Therapeutics* 25 (2000): 61-66.

112 Tomas Helgason, Helgi Tomasson, and Tomas Zoega, "Antidepressants and public health in Iceland," *British Journal of Psychiatry* 184 (2004): 157-162.

113 Healy, *Let Them Eat Prozac*, pp. 54-57.

114 David Healy, Letter to Peter J. Pitts, Associate Commissioner for External Relations, Food and Drug Administration (February 19, 200), accessed 01 APR 2004 on-line at: http://www.researchprotection.org/risks/healy/FDA0204.htm.

115 Glenmullen, *Prozac Backlash*, p. 161.

116 Healy, *Let Them Eat Prozac*, pp. 119-121, 211, 295-296.

117 Glenmullen, *Prozac Backlash*, pp. 159-165

118 Mitchell Zuckoff, "Science, money drive a makeover," *Boston Globe* (June 11, 2000).

119 Robert Temple, MD, Statement before Subcommittee on Oversight and Investigations, Committee on Energy and Commerce, House of Representatives (September 23, 2004) accessed 23 September 2004 on-line at: http://www.fda/gov/ola/2004/antidepressant0923.html

120 Healy, Letter to Peter J. Pitts.

121 David Healy, Antidepressants and Suicide Briefing Paper (June 20, 2003), accessed 11 APR 2004 on-line at: http://www.socialaudit.org.uk/58090-DH.htm

122 Alison Langley, Department of Health Press Release (10 June 2003), accessed 11 APR 2004 on-line at: http://www.mhra.gov.uk/news/2003/seroxat10603.pdf

123 Norman T. Begg, Letter to Healthcare Professionals (18 June 2003), accessed 18 DEC 2004 on-line at: http://www.ahrp.org/risks/PaxilRisks0603.php

124 Victoria Kusiak, Wyeth Dear Health Care Professional Letter (22 AUG 2003).

125 MHRA Press Release, Safety review of antidepressants used by children completed (11 DEC 2003), accessed 16 DEC 2004 on-line at: http://www.mhra.gov.uk/news/ssri_101203.htm

126 Eli Lilly, Prozac Abbreviated Prescribing Information (December 2003), accessed 16 DEC 2004 on-line at: http://www.ahrp.org/risks/ProzacsKids1203.php

127 Andrew D. Mosholder, Memorandum to Russell Katz, MD, Director - Division of Neuropharmacological Drug Products, FDA (February 18, 2004) accessed 18 DEC 2004 on-line at: http://psychrights.org/Research/Digest/AntiDepressants/Mosholder/MosholderReport.pdf

128 Healy, Letter to Peter J. Pitts.

129 Gardiner Harris, "FDA Links Drugs to Being Suicidal," *New York Times* (September 14, 2004).

130 Alliance for Human Research Protection Press Conference, presentation of Dr. David Healy re: antidepressant drugs in pediatric patients and suicidality, Holiday Inn, Bethesda, MD, 14 SEP 2004.

131 Healy, Letter to Peter J. Pitts

132 David Healy and Graham Aldred, "Antidepressant drug use & the risk of suicide," *International Review of Psychiatry* 17 (2005): 163-172.

133 Anna Wilde Mathews, "Congress Will Discuss Drug Trial Issues," *Wall Street Journal*, September 8, 2004, B1.

134 Maggie McKee, "Unpublished data reverses risk-benefit of drugs," *New Scientist* 23 April 2004 accessed on-line at: http://www.biopsychiatry.com/bigpharma/childsuicides.html

135 Alliance for Human Research Protection Press Conference, presentation of Dr. David Healy re: antidepressant drugs in pediatric patients and suicidality, Holiday Inn, Bethesda, MD, 14 SEP 2004.

136 Thomas P. Detre and Henry G. Jarecki, *Modern Psychiatric Treatment* (Philadelphia: J.B. Lippincott Company, 1971), p. 54.

137 *Ibid.*, p. 59.

138 Robert E. Hales, Stuart C. Yudofsky, and John A. Talbott, Ed., *Textbook of Psychiatry*, 3rd Ed. (Washington, D.C.: The American Psychiatric Press, 1999).

139 Armand M. Nicholi, Ed., *The Harvard Guide to Psychiatry*, 3rd Ed. (Cambridge, Massachusetts: The Belknap Press of Harvard University Press, 1999).

140 *Diagnostic and Statistical Manual of Mental Disorders*, Fourth Edition, (Washington, D.C.: American Psychiatric Association, 1994), p. 745.

141 Source: Margaret S. Hamilton and Lewis A. Opler, "Akathisia, Suicidality, and Fluoxetine," *Journal of Clinical Psychiatry* 53 (1992): 401-406.

142 J. John Mann and Shitij Kapur, "The Emergence of Suicidal Ideation and Behavior During Antidepressant Pharmacotherapy," *Archives of General Psychiatry* 48 (1991): 1027-1033.

143 Ronald Pies, "Must We Now Consider SRIs Neuroleptics?" *Journal of Clinical Psychopharmcology* 17 (1997): 443-445.

144 E. Jane Garland and Elizabeth A. Baerg, "Amotivational Syndrome Associated with Selective Serotonin Reuptake Inhibitors in Children and Adolescents," *Journal of Child and Adolescent Psychopharmacology* 11 (2001): 181-186.

145 M.S. George and M.R. Trimble, "A fluvoxamine-induced frontal lobe syndrome in a patient with co-morbid Gilles de la Tourette syndrome and obsessive compulsive disorder [Abstract]," *Journal of Clinical Psychiatry* 53 (1992): 379-380.

146 W.J. Barnhart, E.H. Makela, and M.J. Latocha, "SSRI-induced apathy syndrome: a clinical review [Abstract]," *Journal of Psychiatric Practice* 10 (2004): 196-199.

147 Rudolf Hoehn-Saric, Gordon J. Harris, Godfrey D. Pearlson, Christiane S. Cox, Steven R. Machlin, and Edwaldo E. Camargo, "A Fluoxetine-Induced Frontal Lobe Syndrome in an Obsessive Compulsive Patient," *Journal of Clinical Psychiatry* 52 (1991): 131-133.

148 Jules Angst, "Switch from Depression to Mania – A Record Study over Decades between 1920 and 1982," *Psychopathology* 18 (1985): 140-154.

149 *Ibid.*

150 Angst, "Switch from Depression to Mania – A Record Study over Decades between 1920 and 1982," p. 145.

151 Joanna Moncrieff, "An investigation into the precedents of modern drug treatment in psychiatry," *History of Psychiatry* 10 (1999): 475-490.

152 Angst, "Switch from Depression to Mania – A Record Study over Decades between 1920 and 1982," p. 146.

153 Joseph F. Goldberg, Martin Harrow, and Joyce E. Whiteside, "Risk for Bipolar Illness in Patients Initially Hospitalized for Unipolar Depression," *American Journal of Psychiatry* 158 (2001): 1265-1270.

154 A. Martin, C. Young, J.F. Leckman, C. Mukonoweshuro, R. Rosenheck, and D. Leslie, "Age effects on antidepressant-induced manic conversion," *Archives of Pediatric and Adolescent Medicine* 158 (2004): 773-780.

155 D. Cicero, R.S. El-Mallakh, J. Holman, and J. Robertson, "Antidepressant exposure in bipolar children [Abstract]," *Psychiatry 66 (2003): 317-322.*

156 L.L. Altshuler, R.M. Post, G.S. Leverich, K. Mikalauskas, A. Rosoff, and L. Ackerman, "Antidepressant-induced mania and cycle acceleration: a controversy revisited [Abstract]," *American Journal of Psychiatry* 152 (1995): 1130-1138.

157 Timothy E. Wilens, Joseph Biederman, Anne Kwon, Rhea Chase, Laura Greenberg, Eric Mick, and Thomas J. Spencer, "A Systematic Chart Review of the Nature of Psychiatric Adverse Events in Children and Adolescents Treated with Selective Serotonin Reuptake Inhibitors," Journal of Child and Adolescent Psychopharmacology 13 (2003): 143-152.

158 J. Allan Hobson, *The Dreaming Brain*, (Basic Books, 1988), p. 134-154.

159 J. Allan Hobson, *Sleep,* (New York: Scientific American Library, 1995), pp. 140-141.

160 *Ibid.*

161 Carlos H. Schenck and Mark W. Mahowald, "Motor Dyscontrol in Narcolepsy: Rapid-Eye-Movement (REM) Sleep without Atonia and REM Sleep Behavior Disorder," *Annals of Neurology* 32 (1992): 3-10.

162 H.P. Attarian, C.H. Schenck, and M.W. Mahowald, "Presumed REM sleep behavior disorder arising from cataplexy and wakeful dreaming," *Sleep Medicine* 1 (2000): 131-133.

163 John W. Winkelman and Lynette James, "Serotonergic antidepressants are associated with REM sleep without atonia," *Sleep* 27 (2004): 317-321.

164 C.H. Schenck, M.W. Mahowald, S.W. Kim, K.A. O'Connor, and T.D. Hurwitz, "Prominent eye movements during NREM sleep and REM sleep behavior disorder associated with fluoxetine treatment of depression and obsessive-compulsive disorder [Abstract]," *Sleep* 15 (1992): 226-235.

165 D.J. Kupfer, C.L. Ehlers, E. Frank, V.J. Grochocinski, A.B. McEachran, and A. Buhari, "Persistent effects of antidepressants: EEG sleep studies in depressed patients during maintenance treatment," *Biological Psychiatry* 35 (1994): 781-793.

166 G.E. Ott, U. Rao, K.M. Lin, L. Gertsik, and R.E. Poland, "Effect of treatment with bupropion on EEG sleep: relationship to antidepressant response [Abstract]," *International Journal of Neuropsychopharmacology* 7 (2004): 275-281.

167 E.A. Nofzinger, C.F. Reynolds 3rd, M.E. Thase, E. Frank, J.R. Jennings, A.L. Fasicka, L.R. Sullivan, D.J. Kupfer, "REM sleep enhancement by bupropion in depressed men [Abstract]," *American Journal of Psychiatry* 152 (1995): 274-276.

168 L.I. Mason, C.N. Alexander, F.T. Travis, G.Marsh, D.W. Orme-Johnson, J. Gackenbach, D.C. Mason, M. Rainforth, K.G. Walton, "Electrophysiological correlates of higher states of consciousness during sleep in long-term practitioners of the Transcendental Meditation program [Abstract]," Sleep 20 (1997): 102-110.

169 Harold Sampson, "Psychological Effects of Deprivation of Dreaming Sleep," *Journal of Nervous and Mental Disease* 143 (1966): 305-317.

170 A. Kales, F.S. Hoedemaker, A. Jacobson, and E.L. Lichtenstein, "Dream deprivation: An experimental reappraisal [Abstract]," *Nature* 204 (1964): 1337-1338.

171 Stanley R. Clemes and William C. Dement, "Effect of REM Sleep Deprivation on Psychological Functioning," *Journal of Nervous and Mental Disease* 144 (1967): 485-491.

172 Hobson, *Sleep*, pp. 189-203.

173 G.A. Christos, "Is Alzheimer's Disease Related to a Deficit or Malfunction of Rapid Eye Movement (REM) Sleep?" *Medical Hypotheses* 41 (1993): 435-439.

174 Michelle Cotterchio, Nancy Kreiger, Gerarda Darlington, and Allan Steingart, "Antidepressant Medication Use and Breast Cancer Risk," *American Journal of Epidemiology* 151 (2000): 951-957.

175 W.A.H. Wallace, M. Balsitis, and B.J. Harrison, "Male breast neoplasia in association with selective serotonin re-uptake inhibitor therapy: a report of three cases," *European Journal of Surgical Oncology* 27 (2001): 429-431.

176 Naomi Weintrob, Daniela Cohen, Yaffa Klipper-Aurbach, Zvi Zadik, and Zvi Dickerman, "Decreased Growth During Therapy With Selective Serotonin Reuptake Inhibitors," *Archives of Pediatric and Adolescent Medicine* 156 (2002): 696-701.

177 Mary Nilsson, Melissa J. Joliat, Cherri M. Miner, Elieen B. Brown, and John H. Heiligenstein, "Safety of Subchronic Treatment with Fluoxetine for Major Depressive Disorder in Children and Adolescents," *Journal of Child and Adolescent Psychopharmacology* 14 (2004): 412-417.

178 *Ibid.*, p. 417.

179 Barbara A. Liu, Nicole Mittmann, Sandra R. Knowles, and Neil H. Shear, "Hyponatremia and the Syndrome of Inappropriate Secretion of Antidiuretic Hormone Associated with the Use of Selective Serotonin Reuptake Inhibitors: A Review of Spontaneous Reports," *Canadian Medical Association Journal* 155 (1996): 519-527.

180 Philippe Birmes, Dominique Coppin, Laurent Schmitt, and Dominique Lauque, "Serotonin Syndrome: A Brief Review," *Canadian Medical Association Journal* 180 (2003): 1439-1442.

181 Joseph R. Carbone, "The Neuroleptic Malignant and Serotonin Syndromes," *Emergency Medicine Clinics of North America* 18 (2000): 317-325.

182 Thomas G. Martin, "Serotonin Syndrome," *Annals of Emergency Medicine* 28 (1996): 520-526.

183 Michel Lejoyeux and Jean Ades, "Antidepressant Discontinuation: A Review of the Literature," *Journal of Clinical Psychiatry* 58 (suppl 7): 11-16.

184 Peter Haddad, "Newer Antidepressants and the Discontinuation Syndrome," Journal of Clinical Psychiatry 58 (suppl 7): 17-22.

185 A.H. Young and Alan Currie, "Physicians' Knowledge of Antidepressant Withdrawal Effects: A Survey," *Journal of Clinical Psychiatry* 58 (suppl 7): 28-30.

186 Carl O'Brien, "Drug firm to drop non-addiction claim," *The Irish Times*, (May 10, 2003).

187 David Healy, "SSRIs & Withdrawal//Dependence," (June 20, 2003), accessed 21 April 2004 on-line at: http://www.socialaudit.org.uk/58092-DH.htm

188 S.C. Dilsaver, J.F. Greden, and R.M. Snider, "Antidepressant withdrawal syndromes: phenomenology and pathophysiology [Abstract]," *International Clinical Psychopharmacology* 2 (1987): 1-19.

189 M.T. Halle, S.C. Dilsaver, "Tranylcypromine withdrawal phenomena [Abstract]," *Journal of Psychiatry and Neuroscience* 18 (1993): 49-50.

190 Peter Haddad, "Newer Antidepressants and the Discontinuation Syndrome."

191 Alan F. Schatzberg, Peter Haddad, Eric M. Kaplan, Michel Lejoyeux, Jerrold F. Rosenbaum, A.H. Young, and John Zajecka, "Serotonin Reuptake Inhibitor Discontinuation Syndrome: A Hypothetical Definition," *Journal of Clinical Psychiatry* 58 (suppl 7): 5-10.

192 N.J. Coupland, C.J. Bell, and J.P. Potokar, "Serotonin reuptake inhibitor withdrawal," *Journal of Clinical Psychopharmacology* 16 (1996): 356-362.

193 W. Law, T.A. Petti, and A. Kazdin, "Withdrawal symptoms after graduated cessation of imipramine in children [Abstract]," *American Journal of Psychiatry* 118 (1981): 647-650.

194 Jerrold F. Rosenbaum, Maurizio Fava, Sharon L. Hoog, Richard C. Ascroft, and William B. Krebs, "Selective Serotonin Reuptake Inhibitor Discontinuation Syndrome: A Randomized Clinical Trial," *Biological Psychiatry* 44 (1998): 77-87.

195 David Michelson, Maurizio Fava, Jay Amsterdam, Jeffrey Apter, Peter Longborg, Roy Tamura, and Rosalinda G. Tepner, "Interruption of selective serotonin reuptake inhibitor treatment," British Journal of Psychiatry 176 (2000: 363-368.

196 Alan F. Schatzberg, Jonathan O. Cole, and Charles DeBattista, *Manual of Clinical Psychopharmacology*, 4th Edition, (Washington, D.C.: American Psychiatric Publishing, Inc., 2003), p. 46.

197 Irene Elkin, Tracie Shea, John T. Watkins, Stanley Imber, Stuart M. Sotsky, Joseph F. Collins, David R. Glass, Paul A. Pilkonis, William R. Leber, John P. Docherty, Susan J. Fiester, and Morris B. Parloff, "National Institute of Mental Health Treatment of Depression Collaborative Research Program," *Archives of General Psychiatry* 46 (1989): 971-982.

198 M. Tracie Shea, Irene Elkin, Stanley D. Imber, Stuart M. Sotsky, John T. Watkins, Joseph F. Collins, Paul A. Pilkonis, Edward Beckham, David R. Glass, Regina T. Dolan, and Morris B. Parloff, "Course of Depressive Symptoms Over Follow-Up: Findings From the National Institute of Mental Health Treatment of Depression Collaborative Research Program," *Archives of General Psychiatry* 49 (1992): 782-787.

199 G.E. Murphy, A.D. Simons, R.D. Wetzel, and P.J. Lustman, "Cognitive therapy and pharmacotherapy: Singly and together in the treatment of depression [Abstract]," *Archives of General Psychiatry* 41 (1984): 33-41.

200 P.D. McLean and A.R. Hakstian, "Relative endurance of unipolar depression treatment effects: Longitudinal follow-up [Abstract]," *Journal of Consulting and Clinical Psychology* 58 (1990): 482-488.

201 S.M. Steinbrueck, S.E. Maxwell, and G.S. Howard, "A meta-analysis of psychotherapy and drug therapy in the treatment of unipolar depression with adults [Abstract]," *Journal of Consulting and Clinical Psychology* 51 (1983): 856-863.

202 I.M. Blackburn, S. Bishop, A.I.M. Glen, L.J. Whalley, and J.E. Christie, "The efficacy of cognitive therapy in depression: A treatment trial using cognitive therapy and pharmacotherapy, each alone and in combination [Abstract]," *British Journal of Psychiatry* 139 (1981): 181-189.

203 M.D. Evans, S.D. Hollon, R.J. DeRubeis, J.M. Piasecki, W.M. Grove, M.J. Garvey, and V.B. Tuason, "Differential relapse following cognitive therapy and pharmacology for depression [Abstract]," *Archives of General Psychiatry* 49 (1992): 802-808.

204 L. Mufson, K.P. Dorta, P. Wickramaratne, Y. Nomura, M. Olfson, and M.M. Weissman, "A randomized effectiveness trial of interpersonal psychotherapy for depressed adolescents [Abstract]," *Archives of General Psychiatry* 61 (2004): 577-584.

205 D.A. Santor and V. Kusumakar, "Open trial of interpersonal therapy in adolescents with moderate to severe major depression: effectiveness of novice IPT therapists [Abstract]," *Journal of the American Academy of Child and Adolescent Psychiatry* 40 (2001): 236-240.

206 B.E. Wexler and D.V. Cicchetti, "The outpatient treatment of depression: Implications of outcome research for clinical practice," *Journal of Nervous and Mental Disease* 180 (1992): 277-286.

207 James A. Blumenthal, Michael A. Babyak, Kathleen A. Moore, Edward Craighead, Steve Herman, Parinda Khatri, Robert Waugh, Melissa A. Napolitano, Leslie M. Forman, Mark Appelbaum, Murali Doraiswamy, and K. Ranga Krishnan, "Effects of Exercise Training on Older Patients With Major Depression," *Archives of Internal Medicine* 159 (1999): 2349-2356.

208 Michael Babyak, James A. Blumenthal, Steve Herman, Parinda Khatri, Murali Doraiswamy, Kathleen Moore, W. Edward Craighead, Teri T. Baldewicz, and K. Ranga Krishnan, "Exercise Treatment for Major Depression: Maintenance of Therapeutic Benefit at 10 Months," *Psychosomatic Medicine* 62 (2000): 633-638.

209 G.A. Fava, C. Rafanelli, S. Grandi, S. Conti, and P. Belluardo, "Prevention of recurrent depression with cognitive behavioral therapy: preliminary findings [Abstract]," *Archives of General Psychiatry* 55 (1998): 816-820.

210 I.M. Blackburn and R.G. Moore, "Controlled acute and follow-up trial of cognitive therapy and pharmacotherapy in out-patients with recurrent depression [Abstract]," *British Journal of Psychiatry* 171 (1997): 328-334.

211 E.S. Paykel, J. Scott, J.D. Teasdale, A.L. Johnson, A. Garland, R. Moore, A. Jenaway, P.L. Cornwall, H. Hayhurst, R. Abbott, and M. Pope, "Prevention of relapse in residual depression by cognitive therapy: a controlled trial [Abstract]," *Archives of General Psychiatry* 56 (1999): 829-835.

212 P.D. McLean and S. Taylor, "Severity of unipolar depression and choice of treatment [Abstract]," *Behaviour Research and Therapy* 30 (1992): 443-451.

213 Robert J. DeRubeis, Lois A. Gelfand, Tony Z. Tang, and Anne D. Simons, "Medications Versus Cognitive Behavior Therapy for Severely Depressed Outpatients: Mega-Analysis of Four Randomized Comparisons," *American Journal of Psychiatry* 156 (1999): 1007-1013.

214 Jitschak G. Storosum, Barbara J. van Zwieten, Wim van den Brink, Berthold P.R. Gersons, and Andre W. Broekmans, "Suicide Risk in Placebo-Controlled Studies of Major Depression," *American Journal of Psychiatry* 158 (2001): 1271-1275.

215 S.D. Hollon, R.C. Shelton, and P.T. Loosen, "Cognitive therapy and pharmacotherapy for depression," *Journal of Consulting and Clinical Psychology* 59 (1991): 88-90.

216 A.D. Simons, G.E. Murphy, J.L. Levine, and R.D. Wetzel, "Cognitive therapy and pharmacotherapy for depression: Sustained improvement over one year," *Archives of General Psychiatry* 43 (1986): 43-48.

217 David O. Antonuccio, William G. Danton, and Garland Y. DeNelsky, "Psychotherapy Versus Medication for Depression: Challenging the Conventional Wisdom With Data," *Professional Psychology: Research and Practice* 26 (1995): 574-585.

Chapter Eight

Antipsychotics

1 David Healy, *The Creation of Psychopharmacology*, (Cambridge, Massachusetts: Harvard University Press, 2002).

2 Elliot S. Valenstein, *Blaming the Brain: The Truth About Drugs and Mental Health*, (New York: The Free Press, 1998), pp. 19-35.

3 David S. Cohen, "A Critique of the Use of Neuroleptic Drugs," in Seymour Fisher and Roger P. Greenberg, Ed., *From Placebo to Panacea: Putting Psychiatric Drugs to the Test*, (New York: John Wiley & Sons, Inc., 1997), pp. 173-228.

4 Healy, *The Creation of Psychopharmacology*.

5 Valenstein, *Blaming the Brain*, pg. 34.

6 Cohen, "A Critique of the Use of Neuroleptic Drugs," p. 180.

7 Healy, *The Creation of Psychopharmacology*, pg. 80.

8 Cohen, "A Critique of the Use of Neuroleptic Drugs," p. 180.

9 *Dorland's Pocket Medical Dictionary*, 24th Ed., (Philadelphia: W.B. Saunders Company, 1989), p. 582.

10 Healy, *The Creation of Psychopharmacology*, pg. 117.

11 Sheldon Gelman, Medicating Schizophrenia: A History, (New Brunswick, N.J.: Rutgers University Press, 1999).

12 R.J. Baldessarini, B.M. Cohen, and M.H. Teicher, "Significance of neuroleptic dose and plasma level in the pharmacological treatment of psychoses," *Archives of General Psychiatry* 45 (1988): 79-91.

13 *Dorland's Pocket Medical Dictionary*, 24th Ed., (Philadelphia: W.B. Saunders Company, 1989), p. 193.

14 Cohen, "A Critique of the Use of Neuroleptic Drugs," pp. 190-191.

15 Healy, *The Creation of Psychopharmacology*, p. 239.

16 *Ibid.*, p. 241.

17 J. Idanpaan-Keikkila, E. Alhava, M. Olkinuora, and I.P. Palva, "Agranulocytosis during treatment with chlozapine [Abstract]," *European Journal of Clinical Pharmacology* 11 (1977): 193-198.

18 Kalnya Z. Bezchlibnyk-Butler and J. Joel Jeffries, *Clinical Handbook of Psychotropic Drugs*, 13th Revised Edition, (Cambridge, Massachusetts: Hogrefe & Huber, 2003), pp. 71-104.

19 Healy, *The Creation of Psychopharmacology.*

20 Solomon H. Snyder, *Drugs and the Brain*, (New York: Scientific American Library, 1996), pp. 71-83.

21 S.H. Snyder, "Schizophrenia," *Lancet* 30 (1982): 970-974.

22 A. Carlsson, "The current status of the dopamine hypothesis[Abstract]," *Neuropsychopharmacology* 1 (1988): 179-186.

23 Eva Edelman, *Natural Healing for Schizophrenia*, 3rd Edition (Eugene, Oregon: Borage Books, 2001), p. 148.

24 Healy, *The Creation of Psychopharmacology*, pp. 254-259.

25 Jack R. Cooper, Floyd E. Bloom, and Robert H. Roth, *The Biochemical Basis of Neuropharmacology*, Eighth Edition, (New York: Oxford University Press, 2003), pp. 225-270.

26 Eric J. Nestler, Steven E. Hyman, and Robert C. Malenka, *Molecular Neuropharmacology: A Foundation for Clinical Neuroscience*, (New York: The McGraw-Hill Companies, Inc., 2001), pp. 167-190.

27 Michael J. Kuhar, Pastor R. Couceyro, and Philip D. Lambert, "Catecholamines," in George J. Siegel, Bernard W. Agranoff, R. Wayne Albers, Stephen K. Fisher, and Michael D. Uhler, Ed., Sixth Edition, *Basic Neurochemistry: Molecular, Cellular, and Medical Aspects*, (New York: Lippincott Williams & Wilkins, 1999), pp. 243-260.

28 Robert H. Roth and John D. Elsworth, "Biochemical Pharmacology of Midbrain Dopamine Neurons," accessed 26 JAN 2005 on-line at: http://www.acnp.org/g4/GN40100021/CH021.html.

29 Michael J. Kuhar, Pastor R. Couceyro, and Philip D. Lambert, "Catecholamines," pp. 252-255.

30 Jack R. Cooper, Floyd E. Bloom, and Robert H. Roth, *The Biochemical Basis of Neuropharmacology*, pp, 242, 251-253.

31 C. Cavallotti, F. Nuti, P. Bruzzone, and M. Mancone, "Age-related changes in dopamine D2 receptors in rat heart and coronary vessels [Abstract]," *Clinical and Experimental Pharmacology and Physiology* 29 (2002): 412-418.

32 T. Hussain and M.F. Lokhandwala, "Renal dopamine receptors and hypertension," *Experimental Biology and Medicine* 228 (2003): 134-142.

33 Robert H. Roth and John D. Elsworth, "Biochemical Pharmacology of Midbrain Dopamine Neurons."

34 Shitij Kapur, "Psychosis as a State of Aberrant Salience: A Framework Linking Biology, Phenomenology, and Pharmacology in Schizophrenia," *American Journal of Psychiatry* 160 (2003): 13-23.

35 *Ibid.*

36 C.F. Shakespeare, D. Katritsis, A. Crowther, I.C. Cooper, J.D. Coltart, M.W. Webb-Peploe, "Differences in autonomic nerve function in patients with silent and symptomatic myocardial ischaemia [Abstract]," *British Heart Journal* 71 (1994): 22-29.

37 E. Sigurdsson, N. Sigfusson, H. Sigvaldson, and G. Thorgeirsson, "Silent ST-T changes in an epidemiologic cohort study – a marker of hypertension or coronary heart disease, or both: the Reykjavik study [Abstract]," *Journal of the American College of Cardiology* 27 (1996): 1140-1147.

38 N. Hagelberg, I.K. Martikainen, H. Mansikka, S. Hinkka, K. Nagren, J. Hietala, H. Scheinin, and A. Pertovaara, "Dopamine D2 receptor binding in the human brain is associated with the response to painful stimulation and pain modulatory capacity [Abstract]," *Pain* 99 (2002): 273-279.

39 D.C. Main, A.E. Waterman, and I.C. Kilpatrick, "Behavioural analysis of changes in nociceptive thresholds produced by remoxipride in sheep and rats [Abstract]," *European Journal of Pharmacology* 287 (1995): 221-231.

40 Robert H. Roth and John D. Elsworth, "Biochemical Pharmacology of Midbrain Dopamine Neurons."

41 Paul J. Harrison, "The neuropathological effects of antipsychotic drugs," *Schizophrenia Research* 40 (1999): 87-99.

42 L.J. Seidman, S.V. Faraone, J.M. Goldstein, J.M. Goodman, W.S. Kremen, R. Toomey, J. Tourville, D. Kennedy, N. Makris, V.S. Caviness, and M.T. Tsuang, "Thalamic and amygdala-hippocampal volume reductions in first-degree relatives of patients with schizophrenia: an MRI-based morphometric analysis [Abstract]," *Biological Psychiatry* 46 (1999): 941-954.

43 W. Cahn, H.E. Hulshoff Pol, M.S. Bongers, H.G. Schnack, R.C.W. Mandl, N.E.M. Van Haren, S. Durston, H. Koning, J.A. Van Der Linden, and R.S. Kahn, "Brain morphology in antipsychotic-naïve schizophrenia: a study of multiple brain structures," *British Journal of Psychiatry* 181 (2002): s66-s72.

44 K. Jellinger, "Neuropathologic findings after neuroleptic long-term therapy," in L. Roizin, H. Shiraki, N. Grcevic, Editors, *Neurotoxicology* (New York: Raven Press, 1977), pp. 25-42.

45 Raquel Gur, Patricia Cowell, Bruce I. Turetsky, Fiona Gallacher, Tyrone Cannon, Warren Bilker, and Ruben C. Gur, "A Follow-Up Magnetic Resonance Imaging Study of Schizophrenia," *Archives of General Psychiatry* 55 (1998): 145-152.

46 Beng-Choon Ho, Nancy C. Andreasen, Peg Nopoulos, Stephan Arndt, Vincent Magnotta, and Michael Flaum, "Progressive Structural Brain Abnormalities and Their Relationship to Clinical Outcome," *Archives of General Psychiatry* 60 (2003): 585-594.

47 A.L. Madsen, A. Karle, P. Rubin, M. Cortsen, H.S. Andersen, and R. Hemmingsen, "Progressive atrophy of the frontal lobes in first-episode schizophrenia: interaction with clinical course and neuroleptic treatment," *Acta Psychiatrica Scandinavica* 100 (1999): 367-374.

48 A.L. Madsen, N. Keiding, A. Karle, S. Esbjerg, R. Hemmingsen, "Neuroleptics in progressive brain abnormalities in psychiatric illness," *Lancet* 352 (1998): 784-785.

49 Miranda H. Chakos, Jeffrey A. Lieberman, Robert M. Bilder, Michael Borenstein, Gail Lerner, Bernhard Bogerts, Houwei Wu, Bruce Kinon, and Manzar Ashtari, "Increase in Caudate Nuclei Volumes of First-Episode Schizophrenic Patients Taking Antipsychotic Drugs," *American Journal of Psychiatry* 151 (1994): 1430-1436.

50 Patricia W. Corson, Peg Nopoulos, Del D. Miller, Stephan Arndt, and Nancy C. Andreasen, "Change in Basal Ganglia Volume Over 2 Years in Patients With Schizophrenia: Typical Versus Atypical Neuroleptics," *American Journal of Psychiatry* 156 (1999): 1200-1204.

51 Donna J. Lang, Lili C. Kopala, Robert A. Vandorpe, Qing Rui, Geoffrey N. Smith, Vina M. Goghari, Jocelyne S. Lapointe, and William G. Honer, "Reduced Basal Ganglia Volumes After Switching to Olanzapine in Chronically Treated Patients With Schizophrenia [Abstract]," *American Journal of Psychiatry* 161 (2004): 1829-1836.

52 Floortje E. Scheepers, Christine C. Gispen de Wied, Hilleke E. Hulshoff Pol, and Rene S. Kahn, "Effect of Clozapine in Caudate Nucleus Volume in Relation to Symptoms of Schizophrenia," *American Journal of Psychiatry* 158 (2001): 644-646.

53 Beng-Choon Ho, Nancy C. Andreasen, Peg Nopoulos, Stephan Arndt, Vincent Magnotta, and Michael Flaum, "Progressive Structural Brain Abnormalities and Their Relationship to Clinical Outcome," pp. 591-592.

54 Michael S. Gazzaniga, Richard B. Ivry, and George R. Mangun, *Cognitive Neuroscience: The Biology of the Mind,* (New York: W.W. Norton & Company, 1998), pp. 371-373

55 Hong S. Chun, Gary E. Gibson, Lorraine A. DeGiorgio, H. Zhang, Vincent J. Kidd, and Jin H. Son, "Dopaminergic cell death induced by MPP+, oxidant and specific neurotoxicants shares the common molecular mechanism," *Journal of Neurochemistry* 76 (2001): 1010-1021.

56 K. Iwahashi, K. Anemo, K. Nakamura, I. Fukunishi, and K. Igarashi, "Analysis of the metabolism of haloperidol and its neurotoxic pyridinium metabolite in patients with drug-induced parkinsonism [Abstract]," *Neuropsychobiology* 44 (2001): 126-128.

57 Jian Fang and Peter H. Yu, "Effects of a quaternary pyridinium metabolite of haloperidol (HP+) on the viability and catecholamine levels of cultured PC12 cells," *Canadian Journal of Physiology and Pharmacology* 75 (1997): 996-1000.

58 D.W. Eyles, K.M. Avent, T.J. Stedman, and S.M. Pond, "Two pyridinium metabolites of haloperidol are present in the brain of patients at post-mortem [Abstract]," *Life Sciences* 60 (1997): 529-534.

59 D.W. Eyles, H.R. McLennan, A. Jones, J.J. McGrath, T.J. Stedman, and S.M. Pond, "Quantitative analysis of two pyridinium metabolites of haloperidol in patients with schizophrenia [Abstract]," *Clinical Pharmacology and Therapeutics* 56 (1994): 512-520.

60 G.M. Halliday, S.M. Pond, H. Cartwright, D.A. McRitchie, N. Castagonoli, Jr., and C.J. Van der Schyf, "Clinical and neuropathological abnormalities in baboons treated with HPTP, the tetrahydropyridine analog of haloperidol [Abstract]," *Experimental Neurology* 158 (1999): 155-163.

61 R. Galili, Gil-Ad Mosberg, A. Weizman, E. Melamed, and D. Offen, "Halperidol-induced neutotoxicity – possible implications for tardive dyskinesia [Abstract]," *Journal of Neural Transmission* 107 (2000): 479-490.

62 S. Muraoka and T. Miura, "Inactivation of cholinesterase induced by chlorpromazine cation radicals [Abstract]," *Pharmacology and Toxicology* 92 (2003): 100-104.

63 Y. Sagara, "Induction of reactive oxygen species in neurons by haloperidol [Abstract]," *Journal of Neurochemistry* 71 (1998): 1002-1012.

64 Guochuan Tsai, Donald C. Goff, Robert W. Chang, James Flood, Lee Baer, and Joseph T. Coyle, "Markers of Glutamatergic Neurotransmission and Oxidative Stress Associated With Tardive Dyskinesia [Abstract]," *American Journal of Psychiatry* 155 (1998): 1207-1213.

65 N. Nishioka and S.E. Arnold, "Evidence for oxidative DNA damage in the hippocampus of elderly patients with chronic schizophrenia [Abstract]," *American Journal of Geriatric Psychiatry* 12 (2004): 167-175.

66 M. Polydoro, N. Schroder, M.N. Lima, F. Caldana, D.C. Laranja, E. Bromberg, R. Roesler, J. Quevedo, J.C. Moreira, F. Dal-Pizzol, "Haloperidol- and clozapine-induced oxidative stress in the rat brain [Abstract]," *Pharmacology of Biochemical Behavior* 78 (2004): 751-756.

67 C. Burkhardt, J.P. Kelly, Y.H. Lim, C.M. Filley, and W.D. Parker, Jr., "Neuroleptic medications inhibit complex I of the electron transport chain [Abstract]," *Annals of Neurology* 33 (1993): 512-517.

68 R.S. Sohal, B.H. Sohal, and U.T. Brunk, "Relationship between antioxidant defenses and longevity in different mammalian species," *Mechanisms of Ageing and Development* 53 (1990): 217-227.

69 Lauren B. Marangell, Jonathan M. Silver, and Stuart C. Yudofsky, "Psychopharmacology and ECT," in Robert E. Hales, Stuart C. Yudofsky, and John A. Talbott, Ed., *Textbook of Psychiatry*, 3rd Edition, (Washington, DC: American Psychiatric Press, Inc., 1999), pp. 1063-1065.

70 Ned H. Cassem, Theodore A. Stern, Jerrold F. Rosenbaum, and Michael S. Jellinek, 4th Ed. *Massachusetts General Hospital Handbook of General Psychiatry*, (Boston: Mosby, 1997), pp. 160-161.

71 Philip G. Janicak, John M. Davis, Sheldon H. Preskorn, Frank J. Ayd, Jr., *Principles and Practice of Psychopharmacology* (Baltimore: Williams and Wilkins, 1993), p. 98.

72 *Ibid.*

73 Beng-Choon Ho, Daniel Alicata, Julianna Ward, David J. Moser, Daniel S. O'Leary, Stephan Arndt, and Nancy C. Andreasen, "Untreated Initial Psychosis: Relation to Cognitive Deficits and Brain Morphology in First-Episode Schizophrenia," *American Journal of Psychiatry* 160 (2003): 142-148.

74 Robert K. Heaton, Julie Akiko Gladsjo, Barton W. Palmer, Julia Kuck, Thomas D. Marcotte, and Dilip V. Jeste, "Stability and Course of Neuropsychological Deficits in Schizophrenia [Abstract]," *Archives of General Psychiatry* 58 (2001): 24-32.

75 T.J. Craig, E.J. Bromet, S. Fennig, M. Tanenberg-Karant, J. Lavelle, and N. Galambos, "Is there an association between duration of untreated psychosis and 24-month clinical outcome in a first-admission series?" *American Journal of Psychiatry* 157 (2000): 60-66.

76 L. de Haan, M. van Der Gaag, and J. Wolthaus, "Duration of untreated psychosis and the long-term course of schizophrenia [Abstract]," *European Psychiatry* 15 (2000): 264-267.

77 John R. Bola and Loren R. Mosher, "Treatment of Acute Psychosis Without Neuroleptics: Two-Year Outcomes From the Soteria Project," *Journal of Nervous and Mental Disease* 191 (2003): 219-229.

78 V. Lehtinen, J. Aaltonen, T. Koffert, V. Rakkolainen, and E. Syvalahti, "Two-year outcome in first-episode psychosis treated according to an integrated model. Is immediate neuroleptisation always needed?" *European Psychiatry* 15 (2000): 312-320.

79 Courtenay M. Harding, George W. Brooks, Takamaru Ashikaga, John S. Strauss, and Alan Breier, "The Vermont Longitudinal Study of Persons With Severe Mental Illness, II: Long-Term Outcome of Subjects Who Retrospectively Met DSM-III Criteria for Schizophrenia," *American Journal of Psychiatry* 144 (1987): 727-735.

80 C.M. Harding and J.M. Zahniser, "Empirical correction of seven myths about schizophrenia with implications for treatment," *Acta Psychiatrica Scandinavica* 90, suppl. 384 (1994): 140-146

81 Luc Ciompi, "Catamnestic Long-term Study on the Course of Life and Aging of Schizophrenics," *Schizophrenia Bulletin* 6 (1980): 606-617.

82 A. Jablensky, N. Sartorius, G. Ernberg, M. Ansker, A. Korten, and J. Cooper, et. al. "Schizophrenia: manifestations, incidence, and course in different cultures – A World Health Organization ten-country study [Abstract]," *Psychological Medicine* 20 monograph suppl. (1992): 1-95.

83 J. Leff, N. Sartorius, a. Korten, and G. Ernberg, "The International Pilot Study of Schizophrenia: five-year follow-up findings [Abstract]," *Psychological Medicine* 22 (1992): 131-145.

84 Robert Whitaker, *Mad in America: Bad Science, Bad Medicine, and the Enduring Mistreatment of the Mentally Ill*, (Cambridge, Massachusetts: Perseus Publishing, 2001).

85 Colin Ross and John Read, "Antipsychotic Medications: myths and facts," in John Read, Loren R. Mosher, and Richard P. Bentall, Ed., *Models of Madness* (New York: Brunner-Routledge, 2004), pp. 101-113.

86 *Ibid.*

87 Joel S. Kanter, "Integrating Case Management and Psychiatric Hospitalization," Health and Social Work 16 (1991): 34-42.

88 Robert Whitaker, "The case against antipsychotic drugs: a 50-year record of doing more harm than good," *Medical Hypotheses* 62 (2004): 5-13.

89 *Ibid.*

90 David Healy, *The Creation of Psychopharmacology.*

91 Ben Thornley and Clive Adams, "Content and quality of 2000 controlled trials in schizophrenia over 50 years," *British Medical Journal* 317 (1998): 1181-1184.

92 No author, "Assessment tools used in the care and treatment of patients with schizophrenia and other major psychiatric disorders," accessed on 05 MAR 2003 at: http://www.psychiatry-in-practice.com/html/resources/assessment_tools.asp

93 No author, "Brief Psychiatric Rating Scale (BPRS)," accessed 05 MAR 2003 on-line at: http://www.psychiatry-in-practice.com/html/resources/BPRS.asp

94 No author, "Positive and Negative Syndrome Scale (PANSS)," accessed 05 MAR 2003 on-line at: http://www.psychiatry-in-practice.com/html/resources/PANSS.asp

95 No author, "Scale for the Assessment of Negative Symptoms (SANS)," accessed 05 MAR 2003 on-line at: http://www.psychiatry-in-practice.com/html/resources/SANS.asp

96 No author, "Clinical Global Impression (CGI)," accessed 05 MAR 2003 on-line at: http://www.psychiatry-in-practice.com/html/resources/CGI.asp

97 Jonathan O. Cole, Gerald L. Klerman, Solomon C. Goldberg, Dean J. Clyde, Edwin M. Davidson, et. al., "Phenothiazine Treatment in Acute Schizophrenia," *Archives of General Psychiatry* 10 (1964): 246-260.

98 *Ibid.*

99 *Ibid.*

100 John Kane, Gilbert Honigfeld, Jack Singer, Herbert Meltzer, and the Clozaril Collaborative Study Group, *Archives of General Psychiatry* 45 (1988): 789-796.

101 Healy, *The Creation of Psychopharmacology.*

102 Johannes Kornhuber, Andreas Schultz, Jens Wiltfang, Ingolf Meineke, Christoph H. Gleiter, Robert Zochling, Karl-Werner Boissl, Friedrich Leblhuber, and Peter Riederer, "Persistence of Haloperidol in Human Brain Tissue," *American Journal of Psychiatry* 156 (1999): 885-890.

103 Colin Ross and John Read, "Antipsychotic Medications: myths and facts."

104 NDA 20-592 [Eli Lilly's New Drug Application for Zyprexa], Review and Evaluation of Clinical Data, September 30, 1996, Department of Health and Human Services, Food and Drug Administration, Rockville, Maryland.

105 *Ibid.*, pp. 120, 137.

106 NDA 20-592, Statistical Review and Evaluation, February 14, 1996, pp. 1-4.

107 NDA 20-592, Review and Evaluation of Clinical Data, September 30, 1996, pp. 120, 137.

108 Emmanuel Stip, "Happy Birthday neuroleptics! 50 year [sic] later: *la folie du doute*," European Psychiatry 17 (2002): 1-5.

109 S. Leucht, G. Pitschel-Walz, D. Abraham, and W. Kissling, "Efficacy and extrapyramidal side-effects of the new antipsychotics olanzapine, quetiapine, risperidone, and sertindole compared to conventional antipsychotics and placebo [Abstract]," *Schizophrenia Research* 35 (1999): 51-68.

110 Miranda Chakos, Jeffrey Lieberman, Elaine Hoffman, Daniel Bradford, and Brian Sheitman, "Effectiveness of Second-Generation Antipsychotics in Patients With Treatment-Resistant Schizophrenia: A Review and Meta-Analysis of Randomized Trials," *American Journal of Psychiatry* 158 (2001): 518-526.

111 *Ibid.*, p. 518.

112 John Geddes, Nick Freemantle, Paul Harrison, and Paul Bebbington, "Atypical antipsychotics in the treatment of schizophrenia: systematic overview and meta-regression analysis," *British Medical Journal* 321 (2000): 1371-1376.

113 Robert Rosenheck, Deborah Perlick, Stephen Bingham, Wen Liu-Mares, Joseph Collins, et. al., "Effectiveness and Cost of Olanzapine and Haloperidol in the Treatment of Schizophrenia," *JAMA* 290 (2003): 2693-2702.

114 *Ibid.*, p. 2693.

115 Jeffrey A. Lieberman, Gary Tollefson, Mauricio Tohen, Alan I. Green, Raquel E. Gur, et. al., "Comparative Efficacy and Safety of Atypical and Conventional Antipsychotic Drugs in First-Episode Psychosis: A Randomized, Double-Blind Trial of Olanzapine Versus Haloperidol," *American Journal of Psychiatry* 160 (2003): 1396-1404.

116 A.C. Viguera, R.J. Baldessarini, J.D. Hegarty, D.P. Van Kammen, and M. Tohen, "Clinical risk following abrupt and gradual withdrawal of maintenance neuroleptic treatment [Abstract]," *Archives of General Psychiatry* 54 (1997): 49-55.

117 Richard Tranter and David Healy, "Neuroleptic Discontinuation Syndromes," *Journal of Psychopharmacology* 12 (1998): 401-406.

118 *Ibid.*, pp. 404-405.

119 Philip G. Janicak, John M. Davis, Sheldon H. Preskorn, and Frank J. Ayd, Jr., *Principles and Practice of Psychopharmacology*, p. 149.

120 *Ibid.*, pp. 140-141.

121 J.M. Davis, C.B. Schaffer, G.A. Killian, C. Kinard, and C. Chan, "Important issues in the drug treatment of schizophrenia [Abstract]," *Schizophrenia Bulletin* 6 (1980): 70-87.

122 Patricia L. Gilbert, M. Jackuelyn Harris, Lou Ann McAdams, and Dilip V. Jeste, "Neuroleptic Withdrawal in Schizophrenia Patients," *Archives of General Psychiatry* 52 (1995): 173-188.

123 Ross J. Baldessarini and Adele C. Viguera, "Neuroleptic Withdrawal in Schizophrenic Patients," *Archives of General Psychiatry* 52 (1995): 189-192.

124 Robert Whitaker, "The case against antipsychotic drugs: a 50-year record of doing more harm than good," p.6.

125 Ross J. Baldessarini and Adele C. Viguera, "Neuroleptic Withdrawal in Schizophrenic Patients," pp. 190-191.

126 *Ibid.*, p. 191.

127 Peter J. Weiden and Mark Olfson, "Cost of relapse in schizophrenia," Schizophrenia Bulletin 21 (1995): 419-429.

128 *Ibid.*

129 *Ibid.*

130 Mauricio Tohen, John Hennen, Carlos M. Zarate, Ross J. Baldessarini, Stephen M. Strakowski, Andrew L. Stoll, Gianni L. Faedda, Trisha Suppes, Priscilla Gebre-Medhin, and Bruce M. Cohen, "Two-Year Syndromal and Functional Recovery in 219 Cases of First-Episode Major Affective Disorder With Psychotic Features," *American Journal of Psychiatry* 157 (2000): 220-228.

131 Alan S. Bellack, Nina R. Schooler, Stephen R. Marder, John M. Kane, Clayton H. Brown, and Ye Yang, "Do Clozapine and Risperidone Affect Social Competence and Problem Solving?" *American Journal of Psychiatry* 161 (2004): 364-367.

132 *Ibid.*, p. 366.

133 James D. Hegarty, Ross J. Baldessarni, Mauricio Tohen, Christine Waternaux, and Godehard Oepen, "One Hundred Years of Schizophrenia: A Meta-Analysis of the Outcome Literature," *American Journal of Psychiatry* 151 (1994): 1409-1416.

134 *Ibid.*, p. 1414.

135 Cohen, "A Critique of the Use of Neuroleptic Drugs," p. 203.

136 S. Kasper and E. Resinger, "Cognitive effects and antipsychotic treatment [Abstract]," *Psychoneuroendocrinology* 28 Suppl (2003): 27-38.

137 Cohen, "A Critique of the Use of Neuroleptic Drugs," pp. 182-183.

138 *Ibid.*, p. 183.

139 Elkhonon Goldberg, "Akinesia, Tardive Dysmentia, and Frontal Lobe Disorder in Schizophrenia," *Schizophrenia Bulletin* 11 (1985): 255-263.

140 Michael S. Myslobodsky, "Anosognosia in Tardive Dyskinesia: 'Tardive Dysmentia' or 'Tardive Dementia?'" *Schizophrenia Bulletin* 12 (1986): 1-6.

141 Ian C. Wilson, James C. Garbutt, Clayton F. Lanier, Joseph Moylan, William Nelson, and Arthur J. Prange, Jr., "Is There a Tardive Dysmentia?" *Schizophrenia Bulletin* 9 (1983): 187-192.

142 K.L. Davis and G.S. Rosenberg, "Is there a limbic system equivalent of tardive dyskinesia?" *Biological Psychiatry* 14 (1979): 699-703.

143 T. Lewander, "Neuroleptics and the neuroleptic-induced deficit syndrome," *Acta Psychiatrica Scandinavica* 89 suppl 380 (1994): 8-13.

144 Malcolm H. Lader, "Neurolepic-Induced Deficit Syndrome (NIDS)," *Journal of Clinical Psychiatry* 54 (1993): 493-500.

145 N.R. Schooler, "Deficit symptoms in schizophrenia: negative symptoms versus neuroleptic-induced deficits," *Acta Psychiatrica Scandinavica* 89 suppl 380 (1994): 21-26.

146 Richard S.E. Keefe, Susan G. Silva, Diana O. Perkins, and Jeffrey A. Lieberman, "The Effects of Atypical Antipsychotic Drugs on Neurocognitive Impairment in Schizophrenia: A Review and Meta-Analysis," *Schizophrenia Bulletin* 25 (1999): 201-222.

147 *Ibid.*, pp. 212-213.

148 Michael J. Minzenberg, John H. Poole, Cynthia Benton, and Sophia Vinogradov, "Association of Anticholinergic Load With Impairment of Complex Attention and Memory in Schizophrenia," *American Journal of Psychiatry* 161 (2004): 116-124.

149 *Ibid.*, pp. 122-123.

150 B. Vitiello, A. Martin, J. Hill, C. Mack, S. Molchan, R. Martinez, D.L. Murphy, and T. Sunderland, "Cognitive and behavioral effects of cholinergic, dopaminergic, and serotonergic blockade in humans [Abstract]," *Neuropsychopharmacology* 16 (1997): 15-24.

151 C.S. Peretti, J.M. Danion, F. Kauffmann-Muller, D. Grange, A. Patat, and P. Rosenzweig, "Effects of haloperidol and amisulpride on motor and cognitive skill learning in healthy volunteers [Abstract]," *Psychopharmacology* 131 (1997): 329-338.

152 C. Papageorgiou, P. Oulis, C. Vasios, G.K. Matsopoulos, N. Uzunoglu, A. Rabavilas, and G.N. Christodoulou, "Do atypical antipsychotics fail to exert cognitive sparing effects [Abstract]?" *Neuroreport* 14 (2003): 505-509.

153 J.A. Sweeney, J.G. Keilp, G.L. Haas, J. Hill, and P.J. Weiden, "Relationships between medication treatments and neuropsychological test performance in schizophrenia [Abstract]," *Psychiatry Research* 37 (1991): 297-308.

154 B. Vitiello, A. Martin, J. Hill, C. Mack, S. Molchan, R. Martinez, D.L. Murphy, and T. Sunderland, "Cognitive and behavioral effects of cholinergic, dopaminergic, and serotonergic blockade in humans."

155 M.W. Gilbertson and D.P. van Kammen, "Recent and remote memory dissociation: medication effects and hippocampal function in schizophrenia [Abstract]," *Biological Psychiatry* 42 (1997): 585-595.

156 M.A. Mehta, F.F. Manes, G Magnolfi, B.J. Sahakian, and T.W. Robbins, "Impaired set-shifting and dissociable effects on tests of spatial working memory following the dopamine D2 receptor antagonist sulpiride in human volunteers [Abstract]," *Psychopharmacology* 176 (2004): 331-342.

157 G. Cassens, A.K. Inglis, P.S. Appelbaum, and T.G. Gutheil, "Neuroleptics: Effects on neuropsychological function in chronic schizophrenic patients [Abstract]," *Schizophrenia Bulletin* 16 (1990): 477-500.

158 D.J. King, "Psychomotor impairment and cognitive disturbances induced by neuroleptics," *Acta Psychiatrica Scandinavica* 89 suppl 380 (1994): 53-58.

159 F. Ridout and I. Hindmarch, "The effects of acute doses of fexofenadine, promethazine, and placebo on cognitive and psychomotor function in healthy Japanese volunteers [Abstract]," *Annals of Allergy, Asthma, and Immunology* 90 (2003): 404-410.

160 G. Brebion, X. Amador, M.J. Smith, and J.M. Gorman, "Memory impairment and schizophrenia: the role of processing speed [Abstract]," *Schizophrenia Research* 27 (1998): 31-39.

161 J.M. Cleghorn, R.D. Kaplan, B. Szechtman, H. Szechtman, and G.M. Brown, "Neuroleptic drug effects on cognitive function in schizophrenia [Abstract]," *Schizophrenia Research* 3 (1990): 211-219.

162 T.H. Rammsayer, "Are there dissociable roles of the mesostriatal and mesolimbocortical dopamine systems on temporal information processing in humans [Abstract]?" *Neuropsychobiology* 35 (1997): 36-45.

163 T.H. Rammsayer, "On dopaminergic modulation of temporal information processing [Abstract]," *Biological Psychiatry* 36 (1993): 209-222.

164 D. McCartan, R. Bell, J.F. Green, C. Campbell, K. Trimble, A. Pickering, and D.J. King, "The differential effects of chlorpromazine and haloperidol on latent inhibition in healthy volunteers [Abstract]," *Journal of Psychopharmacology* 15 (2001): 96-104.

165 T.H. Rammsayer, S. Rodewald, and D. Groh, "Dopamine-antagonistic, anticholinergic, and GABAergic effects on declarative and procedural memory functions [Abstract]," *Brain Research: Cognitive Brain Research* 9 (2000): 61-71.

166 H. Scherer, M.A. Bedard, E. Stip, F. Paquet, F. Richer, M. Beriault, J.P. Rodriguez, and J.P. Motard, "Procedural learning in schizophrenia can reflect the pharmacologic properties of the antipsychotic treatments [Abstract]," *Cognitive and Behavioral Neurology* 17 (2004): 32-40.

167 F. Paquet, J.P. Soucy, E. Stip, M. Levesque, A. Elie, and M.A. Bedard, "Comparison between olanazpine and haloperidol on procedural learning and the relationship with striatal D2 receptor occupancy in schizophrenia [Abstract]," *Journal of Neuropsychiatry and Clinical Neuroscience,"* 16 (2004): 47-56.

168 S. Kagerer, C. Winter, H.J. Moller, and M. Soyka, "Effects of haloperidol and atypical neuroleptics on psychomotor performance and driving ability in schizophrenic patients. Results from an experimental study [Abstract] ," *Neuropsychobiology* 47 (2003): 212-218.

169 Kevan R. Wylie, David J. Thompson, and Hiram J. Wildgust, "Effects of depot neuroleptics on driving performance in chronic schizophrenic patients," *Journal of Neurology, Neurosurgery, and Psychiatry* 56 (1993): 910-913.

170 Richard S.E. Keefe, Susan G. Silva, Diana O. Perkins, and Jeffrey A. Lieberman, "The Effects of Atypical Antipsychotic Drugs on Neurocognitive Impairment in Schizophrenia: A Review and Meta-Analysis," pp. 214-215.

171 John A. Harvey, "Role of the Serotonin 5HT2A Receptor in Learning," *Learning and Memory* 10 (2003): 355-362.

172 G.V. Williams, S.G. Rao, and P.S. Goldman-Rakic, "The physiological role of 5HT2A receptors in working memory [Abstract]," *Journal of Neuroscience* 22 (2002): 2843-2854.

173 P.J. Tyson, K.H. Roberts, and A.M. Mortimer, "Are the cognitive effects of atypical antipsychotics influenced by their affinity to 5HT2A receptors [Abstract]?" *International Journal of Neuroscience* 114 (2004): 593-611.

174 B.M. Li and Z.T. Mei, "Delayed response deficit induced by local injection of the alpha-2 antagonist yohimbine into the dorsolateral prefrontal cortex in young adult monkeys [Abstract]," *Behavioral and Neural Biology* 62 (1994): 134-139.

175 A.F.T. Arnsten and T.A. Contant, "alpha2 Adrenergic agonists decrease distractability in aged monkeys performing the delayed response task [Abstract]," *Psychopharmacology* 108 (1992): 159-169.

176 R.B. Fields, D.P. Van Kammen, J.L. Peters, J. Rosen, W.B. Van Kammen, A. Nugent, M. Stipetic, and M. Linnoila, "Clonidine improves memory function in schizophrenia independently from change in psychosis [Abstract]," *Schizophrenia Research* 1 (1988): 417-423.

177 D.B. Sternberg, D. Korol, G.D. Novack, and J.L. McGaugh, "Epinephrine-induced memory facilitation: attenuation by adrenoreceptor antagonists [Abstract]," *European Journal of Pharmacology* 129 (1986): 189-193.

178 A.F. Arnsten, J.C. Steere, and R.D. Hunt, "The contribution of alpha 2 noradrenergic mechanisms of prefrontal cortical cognitive function. Potential significance for attention-deficit hyperactivity disorder [Abstract]," *Archives of General Psychiatry* 53 (1996): 448-455.

179 John W. Olney, Nuri B. Farber, David F. Wozniak, Vesna Jevtovic-Todorovic, and Chrysanthy Ikonomidou, "Environmental Agents That Have the Potential to Trigger Massive Apoptotic Neurodegeneration in the Developing Brain," *Environmental Health Perspectives* 108 Suppl S3 (2000): 383-388.

180 K.E. Jardemark, X. Liang, V. Arvanov, and R.Y. Wang, "Subchronic treatment with either clozapine, olanzapine, or haloperidol produces a hyposensitive response of the rat cortical cells to N-methyl-D-aspartate [Abstract]," *Neuroscience* 100 (2000): 1-9.

181 J.B. Levine, G. Martin, A. Wilson, and S.N. Treistman, "Clozapine inhibits isolated N-methyl-D-aspartate receptors expressed in xenopus oocytes in a subunit specific manner [Abstract]," *Neuroscience Letter* 346 (2003): 125-128.

182 T. Hanaoka, H. Toyoda, T. Mizuno, H. Kikuyama, K. Morimoto, R. Takahata, H. Matsumura, and H. Yoneda, "Alterations in NMDA receptor subunit levels in the brain regions of rats chronically administered typical or atypical antipsychotic drugs [Abstract]," *Neurochemistry Research* 28 (2003): 919-924.

183 F.I. Tarazi, R.J. Baldessarini, N.S. Kula, and K. Zhang, "Long-term effects of olanzapine, risperidone, and quetiapine on ionotropic glutamate receptor types: implications for antipsychotic drug treatment [Abstract]," *Journal of Pharmacology and Experimental Therapeutics* 306 (2003): 1145-1151.

184 A.J. Mishizen-Eberz, R.A. Rissman, T.L. Carter, M.D. Ikonomovic, B.B. Wolfe, and D.M. Armstrong, "Biochemical and molecular studies of NMDA receptor subunits NR1/2A/2B in hippocampal subregions throughout progression of Alzheimer's disease pathology [Abstract]," *Neurobiology of Disease* 15 (2004): 80-92.

185 A. Gemperle and H.R. Olpe, "Effects of subchronic clozapine treatment on long-term potentiation in rat prefrontal cortex [Abstract]," *European Neuropsychopharmacology* 14 (2004): 340-346.

186 Michael S. Gazzaniga, Richard B. Ivry, and George R. Mangun, *Cognitive Neuroscience: The Biology of the Mind* (New York: W.W. Norton & Company, 1998), pp. 283-287.

187 A.L. Hoff, W.O. Faustman, M. Wieneke, S. Espinoza, M. Costa, O. Wolkowitz, and J.G. Csernansky, "The effects of clozapine on symptom reduction, neurocognitive function, and clinical management in treatment-refractory state hospital schizophrenic patients [Abstract]," *Neuropsychopharmacology* 15 (1996): 361-369.

188 G. Ellison, "The N-methyl-D-aspartate antagonists phencyclidine, ketamine and dizocilpine as both behavioral and anatomical models of the dementias [Abstract]," *Brain Research: Brain Research Reviews* 20 (1995): 250-267.

189 G. Eillson, "Competetive and non-competitive NMDA antagonists induce similar limbic degeneration [Abstract]," *Neuroreport* 5 (1994): 2688-2692.

190 L.M. Rowland, R.S. Astur, R.E. Jung, J.R. Bustillo, J. Lauriello, and R.A. Yeo, "Selective Cognitive Impairments Associated with NMDA Receptor Blockade in Humans [Abstract]," *Neuropsychopharmacology* 30 (2005): 633-639.

191 T.H. Rammsayer, "Effects of pharmacologically induced changes in NMDA-receptor activity on long-term memory in humans," *Learning and Memory* 8 (2001): 20-25.

192 B. Fagerlund, T. Mackeprang, A. Gade, and B.Y. Glenthoj, "Effects of low-dose risperidone and low-dose zuclopenthixol on cognitive functions in first-episode drug-naïve schizophrenic patients [Abstract]," *CNS Spectrum* 9 (2004): 364-374.

193 C.A. Galletly, C.R. Clark, A.C. McFarlane, and D.L. Weber, "The effect of clozapine on the speed and accuracy of information processing [Abstract]," *Progress in Neuropsychopharmacology and Biological Psychiatry* 24 (2000): 1329-1338.

194 T.E. Goldberg and D.R. Weinberger, "The effects of clozapine on neurocognition: an overview," Journal of Clinical Psychiatry 55 suppl B (1994): 88-90.

195 T.E. Goldberg, R.D. Greenberg, S.J. Griffin, J.M. Gold, J.E. Kleinman, D. Pickar, S.C. Schulz, and D.R. Weinberger, "The effect of clozapine on cognition and psychiatric symptoms in patients with schizophrenia [Abstract]," *British Journal of Psychiatry* 162 (1993): 43-48.

196 J.M. Kane, S.R. Marder, N.R. Schooler, W.C.Wirshing, D. Umbricht, R.W. Baker, D.A. Wirshing, A. Safferman, R. Ganguli, M. McMeniman, and M. Borenstein, "Clozapine and haloperidol in moderately refractory schizophrenia: a six-month randomized and double-blind comparison [Abstract]," *Archives of General Psychiatry* 58 (2001): 965-972.

197 M.K. Laker, R.S. Duffett, and J.C. Cookson, "Long-term outcome with clozapine: comparison of patients continuing and discontinuing treatment [Abstract]," *International Clinical Psychopharmacology* 13 (1998): 75-78.

198 E. Elomaa, "The secret of clozapine: to sleep while awake?" *Medical Hypotheses* 43 (1994): 245-246.

199 O. Freudenreich, R.D. Weiner, and J.P. McEvoy, "Clozapine-induced electroencephalogram changes as a function of clozapine serum levels [Abstract]," *Biological Psychiatry* 42 (1997): 132-137.

200 I.A. Treves and M.Y. Neufeld, "EEG abnormalities in clozapine-treated schizophrenic patients [Abstract]," *European Neuropsychopharmacology* 6 (1996): 93-94.

201 G. Adler, S. Griesharber, V. Faude, B. Thebaldi, and H. Dressing, "Clozapine in patients with chronic schizophrenia: serum level, EEG and memory performance [Abstract]," *Pharmacopsychiatry* 35 (2002): 190-194.

202 Lakshmi P. Voruganti and A. George Awad, "Is Neuroleptic Dysphoria a Variant of Drug-Induced Extrapyramidal Side Effects?" *Canadian Journal of Psychiatry* 49 (2004): 285-289.

203 *Ibid.*

204 M. Laruelle, C.D. D'Souza, R.M. Baldwin, and A. Abi-Dargham, "Imaging D2 receptor occupancy by endogenous dopamine in humans [Abstract]," *Neuropsychopharmacology* 17 (1997): 162-174.

205 L. Voruganti, P. Slomka, P. Zabel, G. Costa, A. So, A. Mattar, and A.G. Awad, "Subjective effects of AMPT-induced dopamine depletion in schizophrenia: the correlation between D2 binding ratio and dysphoric response [Abstract]," *Neuropsychopharmacology* 25 (2001): 642-650.

206 M. Fujita, N.P. Verhoeff, A. Varrone, S. Zoghbi, R.M. Baldwin, P.A. Jatlow, G.M. Anderson, J.P. Siebyl, and R.B. Innis, "Imaging extrastriatal dopamine D(2) receptor occupancy by endogenous dopamine in healthy humans [Abstract]," *European Journal of Pharmacology* 387 (2000): 179-188.

207 J. Hietala, E. Syvalahsi, H. Vilkman, K. Vuorio, V. Rakkolainen, J. Bergman, et. al., "Depressive symptoms and presynaptic dopamine function in neuroleptic-naïve schizophrenia [Abstract]," *Schizophrenia Research* 35 (1999): 41-50.

208 Lieuwe de Haan, Jules Lavalaye, Don Linszen, Peter M.A.J. Dingemans, and Jan Booij, "Subjective Experience and Striatal Dopamine D2 Receptor Occupancy in Patients With Schizophrenia Stabilized by Olanzapine or Risperidone," *American Journal of Psychiatry* 157 (2000): 1019-1020.

209 T.I. Lidsky, "Reevaluation of the mesolimbic hypothesis of antipsychotic drug action [Abstract]," *Schizophrenia Bulletin* 21 (1995): 67-74.

210 P. Andres, "Frontal cortex as the central executive of working memory: time to revise our view [Abstract]," *Cortex* 39 (2003): 871-895.

211 Shitij Kapur, "Psychosis as a State of Aberrant Salience: A Framework Linking Biology, Phenomenology, and Pharmacology in Schizophrenia," *American Journal of Psychiatry* 160 (2003): 13-23.

212 *Ibid.*, pp. 14-15.

213 *Ibid.*, p. 16.

214 *Ibid.*, pp. 17-18.

215 K.J. Feasey-Truger, C. Alzheimer, and G. ten Bruggencate, "Chronic clozapine versus chronic haloperidol treatment: differential effects on electrically evoked dopamine efflux in the rat caudate putamen, but not in the nucleus accumbens [Abstract]," *Naunyn Schmiedebergs Archives of Pharmacology* 354 (1996): 725-730.

216 J. Ma, N. Ye, N. Lange, and B.M. Cohen, "Dynorphinergic GABA neurons are a target of both typical and atypical antipsychotic drugs in the nucleus accumbens shell, central amygdaloid nucleus and the thalamic central medical nucleus [Abstract]," *Neuroscience* 121 (2003): 991-998.

217 P. Phillips and S. Johnson, "How does [sic] drug and alcohol misuse develop among people with psychotic illness? A literature review[Abstract]," *Social Psychiatry and Psychiatric Epidemiology* 36 (2001): 269-276.

218 L.N. Voruganti, R.J. Heslegrave, and A.G. Awad, "Neuroleptic dysphoria may be the missing link between schizophrenia and substance abuse [Abstract]," *Journal of Nervous and Mental Disease* 185 (1997): 463-465.

219 Guy Chouinard, Barry D. Jones, and Lawrence Annable, "Neuroleptic-Induced Supersensitivity Psychosis," *American Journal of Psychiatry* 135 (1978): 1409-1410.

220 G. Chouinard, I. Creese, D. Boisvert, L. Annable, J. Bradwejn, and B. Jones, "High Neuroleptic Plasma Levels in Patients Manifesting Supersensitivity Psychosis," *Biological Psychiatry* 17 (1982): 849-852.

221 T.J. Taiminen, R.K. Salokangas, S. Saarijarvi, H. Niemi, V. Ahola, and E. Syvalahti, "Smoking and cognitive deficits in schizophrenia: a pilot study [Abstract]," *Addiction and Behavior* 23 (1998): 263-266.

222 R.K. Salokangas, H. Vilkman, T. Ilonen, T. Taiminen, J. Bergman, M. Haaparanta, O. Solin, A. Alanen, E. Syvalahti, and J. Hietala, "High levels of dopamine activity in the basal ganglia of cigarette smokers [Abstract]," *American Journal of Psychiatry* 157 (2000): 632-634.

223 S. Silvestri, J.C. Negrete, M.V. Seeman, C.M. Shammi, and P. Seeman, "Does nicotine affect D2 receptor upregulation [Abstract]?" *Acta Psychiatrica Scandinavica* 109 (2004): 313-317.

224 R.K. Salokangas, S. Saarijarvi, T. Taiminen, H. Lehto, H. Niemi, V. Ahola, and E. Syvalahti, "Effect of smoking on neuroleptics in schizophrenia [Abstract]," *Schizophrenia Research* 23 (1997): 55-60.

225 K. Castagnoli, S.J. Steyn, G. Magnin, C.J. Van Der Schyf, I. Fourie, A. Khalil, and N. Castagnoli, Jr., "Studies on the interaction of tobacco leaf and tobacco smoke constituents and monoamine oxidase [Abstract]," *Neurotoxicology Research* 4 (2002): 151-160.

226 K. Castagnoli and T. Murugesan, "Tobacco leaf, smoke and smoking, MAO inhibitors, Parkinson's disease and neuroprotection: are there links [Abstract]?" *Neurotoxicology* 25 (2004): 279-291.

227 Kenneth L. Davis and Gordon S. Rosenberg, "Is There a Limbic System Equivalent of Tardive Dyskinesia?" *Biological Psychiatry* 14 (1979): 699-703.

228 David P. Moore, "Tardive Psychosis [Abstract]," *Journal of the Kentucky Medical Association* 84 (1986): 351-353.

229 S. Silvestri, M.V. Seeman, J.C. Negrete, S. Houle, C.M. Shammi, G.J. Remington, S. Kapur, R.B. Zipursky, A.A. Wilson, B.K. Christensen, and P. Seeman, "Increased dopamine D2 receptor binding after long-term treatment with antipsychotics in humans: a clinical PET study [Abstract]," *Psychopharmacology* 152 (2000): 174-180.

230 Thomas A. Kent and Robert D. Wilber, "Reserpine Withdrawal Psychosis: The Possible Role of Denervation Supersensitivity of Receptors," *Journal of Nervous and Mental Disease* 170 (1982): 502-504.

231 Mong-Liang Lu, Jan-Jhy Pan, Hiu-Wen Teng, Kuan-Pin Su, and Winston W. Shen, "Metoclopramide-Induced Supersensitivity Psychosis," *Annals of Pharmacotherapy* 36 (2002): 1387-1390.

232 Ian C. Wilson, James C. Garbutt, Clayton F. Lanier, Joseph Moylan, William Nelson, and Arthur J. Prange, Jr., "Is There a Tardive Dysmentia?" pp.187-192.

233 Elkhonon Goldberg, "Akinesia, Tardive Dysmentia, and Frontal Lobe Disorder in Schizophrenia ," pp. 255-263.

234 Michael S. Myslobodsky, "Anosognosia in Tardive Dyskinesia: 'Tardive Dysmentia' or 'Tardive Dementia'?" pp. 1-6.

235 Perminder Sachdev, "The development of the concept of akathisia: a historical overview," *Schizophrenia Research* 16 (1995): 33-45.

236 *Ibid.*, p. 37.

237 *Ibid.*

238 C. Leung, D.W. Chung, I.W. Kam, and K.H. Wat, "Multiple rib fractures secondary to severe tardive dystonia and respiratory dyskinesia [Abstract]," *Journal of Clinical Psychiatry* 61 (2000): 215-216.

239 T. Hayashi, T. Nishikawa, I. Koga, Y. Uchida, and S. Yamawaki, "Prevalence of and risk factors for respiratory dyskinesia [Abstract]," *Clinical Neuropharmacology* 19 (1996): 390-398.

240 Jane Kruk, Perminder Sachdev, and Subba Singh, "Neuroleptic-Induced Respiratory Dyskinesia," *Journal of Neuropsychiatry* 7 (1995): 223-229.

241 Guochuan Tsai, Donald C. Goff, Robert W. Chang, James Flood, Lee Baer, and Joseph T. Coyle, "Markers of Glutamatergic Neurotransmission and Oxidative Stress Associated With Tardive Dyskinesia," *American Journal of Psychiatry* 155 (1998): 1207-1213.

242 Robert Miller and Guy Chouinard, "Loss of Striatal Cholinergic Neurons as a Basis for Tardive and L-Dopa-Induced Dyskinesias, Neuroleptic-Induced Supersensivity Psychosis and Refractory Schizophrenia," *Biological Psychiatry* 34 (1993): 713-738.

243 D. Tarsy and R.J. Baldessarini, "The pathophysiologic basis of tardive dyskinesia [Abstract]," *Biological Psychiatry* 12 (1977): 431-450.

244 William C. Wirshing, "Movement Disorders Associated With Neuroleptic Treatment," *Journal of Clinical Psychiatry* 62 suppl 21 (2001): 15-18.

245 Daniel Casey, "Tardive Dyskinesia: Pathophysiology and Animal Models," *Journal of Clinical Psychiatry* 61 suppl 4 (2000): 5-9.

246 Colin Ross and John Read, "Antipsychotic Medications: myths and facts," p. 108.

247 Cohen, "A Critique of the Use of Neuroleptic Drugs," p. 211.

248 William M. Glazer, "Extrapyramidal Side Effects, Tardive Dyskinesia, and the Concept of Atypicality," *Journal of Clinical Psychiatry* 61 suppl 3 (2000): 16-21.

249 Dilip V. Jeste, Jonathan P. Lacro, Barton Palmer, Enid Rockwell, M. Jackuelyn Harris, and Michael P. Caliguri, "Incidence of Tardive Dyskinesia in Early Stages of Low-Dose Treatment with Typical Neuroleptics in Older Patients," *American Journal of Psychiatry* 156 (1999): 309-311.

250 Piet P. Oosthuizen, Robin A. Emsley, J. Stephanus Maritz, Jadri A. Turner, and N. Keyter, "Incidence of Tardive Dyskinesia in First-Episode Psychosis Patients Treated With Low-Dose Haloperidol," *Journal of Clinical Psychiatry* 64 (2003): 1075-1080.

251 Wayne S. Fenton, "Prevalence of Spontaneous Dyskinesia in Schizophrenia," *Journal of Clinical Psychiatry* 61 suppl 4 (2000): 10-14.

252 L. Ganzini, D.E. Casey, W.F. Hoffman, and A.L. McCall, "The prevalence of metoclopramide-induced tardive dyskinsia and acute extrapyramidal movement disorders [Abstract]," *Archives of Internal Medicine* 153 (1993): 1469-1475.

253 S.R. Cheyette, J.L. Cummings, "Encephalitis lethargica: lessons for contemporary neuropsychiatry [Abstract]," *Journal of Neuropsychiatry and Clinical Neuroscience* 7 (1995): 125-134.

254 J.C. Krusz, W.C. Koller, and D.K. Ziegler, "Historical review: abnormal movements associated with epidemic encephalitis lethargica [Abstract]," *Movement Disorders* 2 (1987): 137-141.

255 S.B. Blunt, R.J. Lane, N. Turjanki, and G.D. Perkin, "Clinical features and management of two cases of encephalitis lethargica [Abstract]," *Movement Disorders* 12 (1997): 154-159.

256 C. Pacchetti, S. Cristina, and G. Nappi, "Reversible chorea and focal dystonia in vitamin B12 deficiency [Abstract]," *NEJM* 347 (2002): 295.

257 S.C. Hung, S.H. Hung, D.C. Tarng, W.C. Yang, and T.P. Huang, "Chorea induced by thiamine deficiency in hemodialsysis patients [Abstract]," *American Journal of Kidney Disease* 37 (2001): 427-430.

258 S.A. Chong, S. Mythily, and G. Remington, "Tardive dyskinesia and iron status [Abstract]," *Journal of Clinical Psychopharmacology* 24 (2004): 235-236.

259 S.B. Blunt, M. Silva, C. Kennard, and R. Wise, "Vitamin B12 deficiency presenting with severe pseudoathetosis of upper limbs [Abstract]," *Lancet* 343 (1994): 550.

260 J. Joubert and P.H. Jourbert, "Chorea and psychiatric changes in organophosphate poisoning.   A report of two further cases [Abstract]," *South African Medical Journal* 74 (1988): 32-34.

261 Wayne S. Fenton, "Prevalence of Spontaneous Dyskinesia in Schizophrenia."

262 L.C. Kopala, K.P. Good, and W.G. Honer, "Extrapyramidal signs and clinical symptoms in first-episode schizophrenia: response to low-dose risperidone [Abstract]," *Journal of Clinical Psychopharmacology* 17 (1997): 308-313.

263 W.W. Fleischhacker, P. Lemmens, and B. van Baelen, "A qualitative assessment of the neurological safety of antipsychotic drugs: an analysis of a risperidone database [Abstract]," *Pharmacopsychiatry* 34 (2001): 104-110.

264 D.Tarsy, R.J. Baldessarini, and F.I. Tarazi, "Effects of newer antipsychotics on extrapyramidal function [Abstract]," *CNS Drugs* 16 (2002): 23-45.

265 Philip Seeman and Shitij Kapur, "Clozapine Occupies High Levels of Dopamine D2 Receptors," *Life Sciences* 60 (1997): PL207-PL216.

266 Philip Seeman, "Dopamine Receptors: Clinical Correlates," accessed 27 MAR 2005 on-line at http://64.233.161.104/search?q=cache:9WqFhedbQbMJ:www.acnp.org/g4/GN401000027/CH027.html

267 P. Seeman and T. Tallerico, "Antipsychotic drugs which elicit little or no parkinsonism bind more loosely than dopamine to brain D2 receptors, yet occupy high levels of these receptors [Abstract]," *Molecular Psychiatry* 3 (1998): 123-134.

268 Philip Seeman, "Dopamine Receptors: Clinical Correlates."

269 *Ibid.*

270 Philip Seeman and Shitij Kapur, "Clozapine Occupies High Levels of Dopamine D2 Receptors," p. PL-215.

271 S. Kapur and P. Seeman, "Antipsychotic agents differ in how fast they come off the dopamine D2 receptors. Implications for atypical antipsychotic action [Abstract]," *Journal of Psychiatry and Neuroscience* 25 (2000): 161-166.

272 Seong S. Shim, "Action of Atypical Antipsychotics," *American Journal of Psychiatry* 159 (2002): 154-155.

273 D.E. Casey and G.A. Keepers, "Neuroleptic side effects: acute extrapyramidal syndromes and tardive dyskinesia," in D.E. Casey and A.V. Christensen, Eds., *Psychopharmacology: Current Trends* (Berlin: Springer Verlag, 1988), pp. 74-93.

274 A. Malla, R. Norman, D. Scholten, L. Townsend, R. Manchanda, J. Takhar, and R. Haricharan, "A comparison of two novel antipsychotics in first episode non-affective psychosis: one-year outcome on symptoms, motor side effects, and cognition," *Psychiatry Research* 129 (2004): 159-169.

275 J. Peuskens and C.G. Link, "A comparison of quetiapine and chlorpromazine in the treatment of schizophrenia [Abstract]," *Acta Psychiatrica Scandinavica* 96 (1997): 265-273.

276 L.C. Kopala, K.P. Good, and W.G. Honer, "Extrapyramidal signs and clinical symptoms in first-episode schizophrenia: response to low-dose risperidone."

277 B.M. Cohen, P.E. Keck, A. Satlin, and J.O. Cole, "Prevalence and severity of akathisia in patients on clozapine [Abstract]," *Biological Psychiatry* 29 (1991): 1215-1219.

278 L. Peacock, T. Solgaard, H. Lublin, and J. Gerlach, "Clozapine versus typical antipsychotics. A retro- and prospective study of extrapyramidal side effects [Abstract]," *Psychopharmacology* 124 (1996): 188-196.

279 William M. Glazer, "Extrapyramidal Side Effects, Tardive Dyskinesia, and the Concept of Atypicality."

280 D.V. Jeste, A. Okamoto, J. Napolitano, J.M. Kane, and R.A. Martinez, "Low incidence of persistent tardive dyskinesia in elderly patients with dementia treated with risperidone," *American Journal of Psychiatry* 157 (2000): 1150-1155.

281 A. Claus, J. Bollen, H. DeCuyper, M. Eneman, M. Malfroid, J. Peuskens, and S. Heylen, "Risperidione versus haloperidol in the treatment of chronic schizophrenic inpatients: a multicentre double-blind comparative study [Abstract]," *Acta Psychiatrica Scandinavica* 85 (1992): 295-305.

282 J. Ananth, K.S. Burgoyne, D. Niz, and M. Smith, "Tardive dyskinesia in 2 patients treated with ziprasidone," *Journal of Psychiatry and Neuroscience* 29 (2004): 467-469.

283 Martin E. Keck, Marianne B. Muller, Elisabeth B. Binder, Annette Sonntag, and Florian Holsboer, "Ziprasidone-Related Tardive Dyskinesia," *American Journal of Psychiatry* 161 (2004): 175-176.

284 Klara J. Rosenquist, Susan S. Walker, and S. Nassir Ghaemi, "Tardive Dyskinesia and Ziprasidone," *American Journal of Psychiatry* 159 (2002): 1436.

285 Maria Alexiadis, David Whitehorn, Hazel Woodley, and Lili Kopala, "Prolactin Elevation With Quetiapine," *American Journal of Psychiatry* 59 (2002): 1608-1609.

286 M. Wudarsky, R. Nicolson, S.D. Hamburger, L. Spechler, P. Gochman, J. Bedwell, MC. Lenane, and J.L. Rapoport, "Elevated prolactin in pediatric patients on typical and atypical antipsychotics [Abstract]," *Journal of Child and Adolescent Psychopharmacology* 9 (1999): 239-245.

287 P. Turrone, S. Kapur, M.V. Seeman, and A.J. Flint, "Elevation of prolactin levels by atypical antipsychotics," *American Journal of Psychiatry* 159 (2002): 133-135.

288 M.G. Subramanian, C.L. Kowalczyk, R.E. Leach, D.M. Lawson, C.M. Blacker, K.A. Ginsburg, J.F. Randolph, Jr., M.P. Diamond, and K.S. Moghissi, "Midcycle increase of prolactin seen in normal women is absent in subjects with unexplained infertility [Abstract]," *Fertility and Sterility* 67 (1997): 644-647.

289 K. Asukai, T. Uemara, and H. Minaguchi, "Occult hyperprolactinemia in infertile women [Abstract]," *Fertility and Sterility* 60 (1993): 423-427.

290 S. Andersen, N.H. Bruun, K.M. Pedersen, and P. Laurberg, "Biologic variation is important for interpretation of thyroid function tests [Abstract]," *Thyroid* 13 (2003): 1069-1078.

291 M.D. Sauro and N.E. Zorn, "Prolactin induces proliferation of vascular smooth muscle cells through a protein kinase C-dependent mechanism [Abstract]," *Journal of Cellular Physiology* 148 (1991): 133-138.

292 A.M. Meaney and V. O'Keane, "Prolactin and schizophrenia: clinical consequences of hyperprolactinemia [Abstract]," *Life Sciences* 71 (2002): 979-992.

293 G.A. Arneson, "Phenothiazine derivatives and glucose metabolism [Abstract]," *Journal of Neuropsychiatry* 5 (1964): 181-185.

294 B.W. Hiles, "Hyperglycemia and glycosuria following chlorpromazine therapy,"*JAMA* 162 (1956): 1651 as cited in D. Kohen, "Diabetes mellitus and schizophrenia: historical perspective," *British Journal of Psychiatry* (suppl) 47 (2004): S64-66.

295 E. Thonnard-Neumann, "Phenothiazines and diabetes in hospitalized women [Abstract],"*American Journal of Psychiatry* 124 (1968): 978-982.

296 S. Hagg, L. Joelsson, T. Mjorndal, O. Spigset, G. Oja, and R. Dahlqvist, "Prevalence of diabetes and impaired glucose tolerance in patients treated with clozapine compared with patients treated with conventional depot neuroleptic medications [Abstract]," *Journal of Clinical Psychiatry* 59 (1998): 294-299.

297 Dan W. Haupt and John W. Newcomer, "Hyperglycemia and Antipsychotic Medication," *Journal of Clinical Psychiatry* 62 suppl 27 (2001): 18.

298 D.C. Henderson, E. Cagliero, C. Gray, R.A. Nasrallah, D.L. Hayden, D.A. Schoenfeld, and D.C. Goff, "Clozapine, diabetes mellitus, weight gain, and lipid abnormalities: A five-year naturalistic study," *American Journal of Psychiatry* 157 (2000): 975-981.

299 Dan W. Haupt and John W. Newcomer, "Hyperglycemia and Antipsychotic Medication."

300 *Ibid.*

301 Jambur Ananth, Ravi Venkatesh, Karl Burgoyne, and Sarath Gunatilake, "Atypical Antipsychoic Drug Use and Diabetes," *Psychotherapy and Psychosomatics* 71 (2002): 244-254.

302 *Ibid.*

303 J. Bobes, M.P. Garcia-Portilla, J. Rejas, G. Hernandez, M. Garcia-Garcia, F. Rico-Villademoros, and A. Porras, "Frequency of Sexual Dysfunction and Other Reproductive Side-effects in Patients with Schizophrenia Treated with Risperidone, Olanzapine, Quetiapine, or Haloperidol: The Results of the EIRE Study," *Journal of Sex & Marital Therapy* 29 (2003): 125-147.

304 K.R. Fontaine, M. Heo, E.P. Harrigan, C.L. Shear, M. Lakshminarayanan, D.E. Casey, and D.B. Allison, "Estimating the consequences of anti-psychotic induced weight gain on health and mortality rate [Abstract]," *Psychiatry Research* 101 (2001): 277-288.

305 Anthony L. Pelonero, James L. Levenson, and Anand K. Pandurangi, "Neuroleptic Malignant Syndrome: A Review," *Psychiatric Services* 49 (1998): 1163-1172.

306 Urban Osby, Nestor Correia, Anders Ekbom, and Par Sparen, "Time trends in schizophrenia mortality in Stockholm County, Sweden: cohort study," *British Medical Journal* 321 (2000): 483-484.

307 David Healy, "Service utilization in 1896 and 1996: morbidity and mortality data from North Wales [Abstract]," *History of Psychiatry* 16 (2005): 27-41.

308 M.C. Bralet, V. Yon, G. Loas, and C. Noisette, "Cause of mortality in schizophrenic patients: prospective study of years of a cohort of 150 chronic schizophrenic patients [Abstract]," *Encephale* 26 (2000): 32-41.

309 John L. Waddington, Hanafy A. Youssef, and Anthony Kinsella, "Mortality in schizophrenia: Antipsychotic polypharmacy and absence of adjunctive anticholinergics over the course of a 10-year prospective study," *British Journal of Psychiatry* 173 (1998): 325-329.

310 Sabine M.J.M. Straus, Gysele S. Bleumink, Jeanne P. Dieleman, Johan van der Lei, Geert W. 't Jong, J. Herre Kingma, Miriam C.J.M. Sturkenboom, and Bruno H.C. Stricker, "Antipsychotics and the Risk of Sudden Cardiac Death," *Archives of Internal Medicine* 164 (2004): 1293-1297.

311 M.L. Barnard, K.M. Ridge, F. Saldias, E. Friedman, M. Gare, C. Guerrero, E. Leucona, A.M. Bertorello, A.I. Katz, and J.I. Sznajder, "Stimulation of the dopamine 1 receptor increases lung edema clearance [Abstract]," *American Journal of Critical Care Medicine* 160 (1999): 982-986.

312 M.L. Barnard, W.G. Olivera, D.M. Rutschman, A.M. Bertorello, A.I. Katz, and J.I. Sznajder, "Dopamine stimulates sodium transport and liquid clearance in rat lung [Abstract]," *American Journal of Respiratory Critical Care Medicine* 156 (1997): 709-714.

313 David Ruschena, Paul E. Mullen, Simon Palmer, Philip Burgess, Stephen M. Cordner, Olaf H. Drummer, Cameron Wallace, and Justin Barry-Walsh, "Choking deaths: the role of antipsychotic medication," *British Journal of Psychiatry* 183 (2003); 446-450.

314 Alex Handiside, "Our Physical Health...Who Cares?" Occasional Paper No. 5, (April 2004), New Zealand Mental Health Commission, accessed 12 JUL 2004 on-line at: http://www.mhc.govt.nz/pages/publications

315 *Ibid.*

316 Bertram P. Karon, *The Tragedy of Schizophrenia*, (Tustin, CA: Kevco Publishing, 1999).

317 *Ibid.*, p. 8.

318 *Ibid.*, p. 4.

319 Edward Shorter, *A History of Psychiatry: From the Era of the Asylum to the Age of Prozac*, (New York: John Wiley & Sons, Inc., 1997).

320 J. Sanbourne Bockoven and Harry C. Solomon, "Comparison of Two Five-Year Follow-Up Studies: 1947 to 1952 and 1967 to 1972," *American Journal of Psychiatry* 132 (1975): 796-801.

321 *Ibid.*, pp. 800-801.

322 Courtenay M. Harding, George W. Brooks, Takamaru Ashikaga, John S. Strauss, and Alan Breier, "The Vermont Longitudinal Study of Persons With Severe Mental Illness, I: Methodology, Study Sample, and Overall Status 32 Years Later," *American Journal of Psychiatry* 144 (1987): 718-726.

323 Courtenay M. Harding, George W. Brooks, Takamaru Ashikaga, John S. Strauss, and Alan Breier, "The Vermont Longitudinal Study of Persons With Severe Mental Illness, II: Long-Term Outcome of Subjects Who Retrospectively Met *DSM-III* Criteria for Schizophrenia.

324 *Ibid.*, p. 730.

325 Bertram P. Karon, *The Tragedy of Schizophrenia*, p. 3.

326 *Ibid.*, pp. 10-11.

327 Arthur Deikman and Leighton Whitaker, "Humanizing a Psychiatric Ward," *Psychotherapy Theory, Research and Practice* 16 (1979), accessed 03 APR 2005 on-line at: http://www.deikman. com/humanizing.html

328 *Ibid.*

329 John R. Bola and Loren R. Mosher, "Treatment of Acute Psychosis Without Neuroleptics: Two-Year Outcomes From the Soteria Project," *Journal of Nervous and Mental Disease* 191 (2003): 219-229.

330 Loren R. Mosher and Voyce Hendrix, *Soteria: Through Madness to Deliverance,* (USA: XLibris, 2004).

331 John R. Bola and Loren R. Mosher, "Treatment of Acute Psychosis Without Neuroleptics: Two-Year Outcomes From the Soteria Project."

332 Maurice Rappaport, H. Kenneth Hopkins, Karyl Hall, Teodoro Belleza and Julian Silverman, "Are There Schizophrenics for Whom Drugs May be Unnecessary or Contraindicated?" *International Pharmacopsychiatry* 13 (1978): 100-111.

333 *Ibid.,* p. 107.

334 *Ibid.*

335 V. Lehtinen, J. Aaltonen, T. Koffert, V. Rakkolainen, and E. Syvalahti, "Two-year outcome in first-episode psychosis treated according to an integrated model. Is immediate neuroleptisation always needed?"

336 *Ibid.,* pp. 318-319.

337 David S. Cohen, "A Critique of the Use of Neuroleptic Drugs," pp. 190-191.

338 Garry Prouty, "Pre-Therapy: A Newer Development of Schizophrenia," *Journal of the American Academy of Psychoanalysis and Dynamic Psychiatry* 31 (2003): 59-73.

339 Garry Prouty, *Theoretical Evolutions in Person-Centered / Experiential Therapy: Applications to Schizophrenic and Retarded Psychoses,* (Westport, Connecticut: Praeger, 1994).

340 Garry Prouty, Dion Van Werde, and Marlis Portner, *Pre-Therapy: Reaching contact-impaired clients,* (Ross-on-Wye: PCCS Books, 2002).

Chapter Nine

Stimulant Medications and ADHD

1 David Healy, *The Creation of Psychopharmacology*, (Cambridge, Massachusetts: Harvard University Press, 2002), pp. 56-69.

2 Solomon H. Snyder, *Drugs and the Brain*, (New York: Scientific American Library, 1999), pp. 121-133.

3 Daniel M. Perrine, *The Chemistry of Mind-Altering Drugs*, (Washington, DC: American Chemical Society, 1996), pp. 193-205.

4 No author, "Amphetamine," Answers.com, accessed 17 JUN 2005 on-line at: http://www.answers.com/topic/amphetamine

5 Solomon H. Snyder, *Drugs and the Brain*, p. 131.

6 *Ibid.*, p. 132.

7 No author, "Amphetamine," *Answers.com*.

8 Mortimer D. Gross, "Origin of Stimulant Use for Treatment of Attention Deficit Disorder," *American Journal of Psychiatry* 152 (1995): 298-299.

9 Peter Schrag and Diane Divoky, *The Myth of the Hyperactive Child*, (New York: Pantheon Books, 1975), pp. 76-81.

10 Healy, *The Creation of Psychopharmacology*.

11 CHADD, "About Us," accessed 22 OCT 2004 on-line at: http://www.chadd.org/webpage.cfm?cat_id=2

12 No author, "United Nations' Warnings on Ritalin: Two Press Releases," (28 February 1996, 04 March 1997), accessed 14 OCT 2004 on-line at: http://216.239.41.104/search?q=cache:6RroSjUcTPsJ:www.pbs.org/wgbh/pages/frontline/shows/medicating/backlash/un.html+ritalin+abuse+in+canada&hl=en

13 NAMI, "Mission and History," accessed 22 OCT 2004 on-line at: http://madman-bbs.dyndns.org/mirrors/nami/web.nami.org/history.htm

14 Scott Lurie and Aglaia O'Quinn, "Neuroendocrine Responses to Methylphenidate and d-Amphetamine: Applications to Attention-Deficit Disorder," *Journal of Neuropsychiatry* 3 (1991): 41-50.

15 Daniel M. Perrine, *The Chemistry of Mind-Altering Drugs*, p. 195.

16 Ronald Kuczenski and David S. Segal, "Effects of Methylphenidate on Extracellular Dopamine, Serotonin, and Norepinephrine: Comparison with Amphetamine [Abstract]," *Journal of Neurochemistry* 68 (1997): 2032-2037.

17 Lurie and O'Quinn, "Neuroendocrine Responses to Methylphenidate and d-Amphetamine: Applications to Attention-Deficit Disorder."

18 Brian Vastag, "Pay Attention: Ritalin Acts Much Like Cocaine," *JAMA* 286 (2001): 905-906.

19 Oscar Larrosa, Yolanda de la Llave, Soledad Barrio, Juan Jose Granzio, and Diego Garcia-Borreguero, "Stimulant and Anticataplectic Effects of Reboxetine in Patients with Narcolepsy: A Pilot Study," *Sleep* 24 (2001): 282-285.

20 Hege Salvesen Blix, WHO Collaborating Centre for Drug Statistics Methodology, personal communication, (October 13, 2004).

21 No author, WHO Collaborating Centre for Drug Statistics and Methodology, accessed 20 OCT 2004 on-line at: http://www.whocc. no/atcddd/indexdatabase/index.php?query=N06BA09

22 "Sympathomimetic." *Stedman's Pocket Medical Dictionary* (Baltimore: Williams & Wilkins, 1987).

23 No author, WHO Collaborating Centre for Drug Statistics and Methodology, accessed 19 OCT 2004 on-line at: http://whocc.no/ atcddd/atcsystem.html

24 Eric J. Nestler, Steven E. Hyman, and Robert C. Malenka, *Molecular Neuropharmacology: A Foundation for Clinical Neuroscience*, (New York: The McGraw-Hill Companies, Inc., 2001), p. 177.

25 P. Seeman and B. Madras, "Methylphenidate elevates resting dopamine which lowers the impulse-triggered release of dopamine: a hypothesis [Abstract]," Behavioural Brain Research 130 (2002): 79-83.

26 A.A. Grace, "The tonic/phasic model of dopamine system regulation and its implications for understanding alcohol and psychostimulant craving [Abstract]," *Addiction* 95 (2000): 119-128.

27 Nora D. Volkow, Gene-Jack Wang, Joanna S. Fowler, Jean Logan, Madina Gerasimov, Laurence Maynard, Yu-Shin Ding, Samuel J. Gatley, Andrew Gifford, and Dinko Franceschi, "Therapeutic Doses of Oral Methylphenidate Significantly Increase Extracellular Dopamine in the Human Brain," Journal of Neuroscience 21 (2001): 1-5.

28 Teena D. Chase, Richard E. Brown, Normand Carrey, and Michael Wilkinson, "Daily methylphenidate administration attenuates c-fos expression in the striatum of prepubertal rats," *Neuroreport* 14 (2003): 769-772.

29 Terry E. Robinson and Bryan Kolb, "Persistent Structural Modifications in Nucleus Accumbens and Prefrontal Cortex Neurons Produced by Previous Experience with Amphetamine," *The Journal of Neuroscience* 17 (1997): 8491-8497.

30 Gunther H. Moll, Sharmila Hause, Eckart Ruther, Aribert Rothenberger, and Gerald Huether, "Early Methylphenidate Administration to Young Rats Causes a Persistent Reduction in the Density of Striatal Dopamine Transporters," *Journal of Child and Adolescent Psychopharmacology* 11 (2001): 15-24.

31 Nathalie Ginovart, Lars Farde, Christer Halldin, and Carl-Gunnar Swahn, "Changes in Striatal D2-Receptor Density Following Chronic Treatment With Amphetamine as Assessed With PET in Nonhuman Primates," *Synapse* 31 (1999): 154-162.

32 Terry E. Robinson and Bryan Kolb, "Structural plasticity associated with exposure to drugs of abuse," *Neuropharmacology* 47 (2004): 33-46.

33 J.S.H. Vles, F.J.M. Feron, J.G.M. Hendriksen, J. Jolles, M.J.P.G. van Kroonenburgh, and W.E.J. Weber, "Methylphenidate Down-Regulates the Dopamine Receptor and Transporter System in Children with Attention Deficit Hyperkinetic Disorder (ADHD)," *Neuropediatrics* 34 (2003): 77-80.

34 Nora D. Volkow and James M. Swanson, "Variables That Affect the Clinical Use and Abuse of Methylphenidate in the Treatment of ADHD," *American Journal of Psychiatry* 160 (2003): 1909-1918.

35 C.K. Varley, J. Vincent, P. Varley, and R. Chalderon, "Emergence of tics in children with attention deficit hyperactivity disorder treated with stimulant medications [Abstract]," *Comprehensive Psychiatry* 42 (2001): 228-233.

36 Theodore A. Henderson, "Effects of Methylphenidate (Ritalin) On Mammalian Myocardial Ultrastructure," *The American Journal of Cardiovascular Pathology* 5 (1994): 68-78.

37 Daniel J. Safer, Julie M. Zito, and Eric M. Fine, "Increased Methylphenidate Usage for Attention Deficit Disorder in the 1990s," *Pediatrics* 98 (1996): 1084-1088.

38 George Bush, Presidential Proclamation 6158, (July 17, 1990) accessed 23 OCT 2004 on-line at: http://www.loc.gov/loc/brain/proclaim.html

39 Mark Olfson, Marc J. Gameroff, Steven C. Marcus, and Peter S. Jensen, "National Trends in the Treatment of Attention Deficit Hyperactivity Disorder," *American Journal of Psychiatry* 160 (2003): 1071-1077.

40 Daniel J. Safer, Julie M. Zito, and Eric M. Fine, "Increased Methylphenidate Usage for Attention Deficit Disorder in the 1990s."

41 Eliot Marshall, "Duke Study Faults Overuse of Stimulants for Children," *Science* 289 (2000): 721.

42 Gretchen B. LeFever, Keila V. Dawson, and Ardythe L. Morrow, "The Extent of Drug Therapy for Attention Deficit-Hyperactivity Disorder Among Children in Public Schools," *American Journal of Public Health* 89 (1999): 1359-1364.

43 Marsha D. Rappley, Joseph C. Gardiner, James R. Jetton, and Richard T. Houang, "The Use of Methylphenidate in Michigan," *Archives of Pediatric and Adolescent Medicine* 149 (1995): 675-679.

44 Julie Magno Zito, Daniel J. Safer, Susan dosReis, Laurence S. Magder, and Mark A. Riddle, "Methylphenidate Patterns Among Medicaid Youths," *Psychopharmacology Bulletin* 33 (1997): 143-147.

45 Ralph Olsen, "Pediatric Practice: Whose Mood Are We Altering?" *Pediatrics* 47 (1971): 961.

46 Karen M. Stockl, Tom E. Hughes, Manal A. Jarrar, Kristina Secnik, and Amy R. Perwien, "Physician Perceptions of the Use of Medications for Attention Deficit Hyperactivity Disorder," *Journal of Managed Care Pharmacy* 9 (2003): 416-423.

47 Howard M. Schachter, Ba Pham, Jim King, Stephanie Langford, and David Moher, "How efficacious and safe is short-acting methylphenidate for the treatment of attention-deficit disorder in children and adolescents? A meta-analysis," *CMAJ* 165 (2001): 1475-1488.

48 *Ibid.*

49 The MTA Cooperative Group, "A 14-Month Randomized Clinical Trial of Treatment Strategies for Attention-Deficit/Hyperactivity Disorder," *Archives of General Psychiatry* 56 (1999): 1073-1086.

50 The MTA Cooperative Group, "Moderators and Mediators of Treatment Response for Children With Attention-Deficit/Hyperactivity Disorder," *Archives of General Psychiatry* 56 (1999): 1088-1096.

51 Ross W. Greene and J. Stuart Ablon, "What Does the MTA Study Tell us About Effective Psychosocial Treatment for ADHD?" *Journal of Clinical Child Psychology* 30 (2001): 114-121.

52 MTA Cooperative Group, "National Institute of Mental Health Multimodal Treatment Study of ADHD Follow-up: Changes in Effectiveness and Growth After the End of Treatment," *Pediatrics* 113 (2004): 762-769.

53 Salvatore Mannuzza, Rachel G.Klein, Noreen Bonagura, Patricia Malloy, Tina L. Giampino, and Kathy A. Addalli, "Hyperactive Boys Almost Grown Up," *Archives of General Psychiatry* 48 (1991): 77-83.

54 Salvatore Mannuzza, Rachel G. Klein, Abrah Bessler, Patricia Malloy, and Maria LaPadula, "Adult Psychiatric Status of Hyperactive Boys Grown Up," *American Journal of Psychiatry* 155 (1998): 493-498.

55 Salvatore Mannuzza, Rachel G.Klein, Noreen Bonagura, Patricia Malloy, Tina L. Giampino, and Kathy A. Addalli, "Hyperactive Boys Almost Grown Up," p. 83.

56 Salvatore Mannuzza, Rachel G. Klein, Abrah Bessler, Patricia Malloy, and Maria LaPadula, "Adult Psychiatric Status of Hyperactive Boys Grown Up."

57 Betsy Hoza, William E Pelham, Daniel A. Waschbusch, Heidi Kipp, and Julie Sarno Owens, "Academic Task Persistence of Normally Achieving ADHD and Control Boys: Performance, Self-Evaluations, and Attributions," *Journal of Consulting and Clinical Psychology* 69 (2001): 271-283.

58 Betsy Hoza, Daniel A. Waschbusch, William E. Pelham, Brook S.G. Molina, and Richard Milich, "Attention-Deficit/Hyperactivity Disordered and Control Boys' Responses to Social Success and Failure," *Child Development* 71 (2000): 432-446.

59 Carol K. Whalen, Barbara Henker, Barry E. Collins, Sharon McAuliffe, and Alan Vaux, "Peer Interaction in a Structured Communication Task: Comparisons of Normal and Hyperactive Boys and of Methylphenidate (Ritalin) and Placebo Effects," *Child Development* 50 (1979): 388-401.

60 Carol K. Whalen, Barbara Henker, Stephen P. Hinshaw, Tracy Heller, and Alice Huber-Dressler, "Messages of Medication: Effects of Actual Versus Informed Medication Status on Hyperactive Boys' Expectancies and Self-Evaluations," *Journal of Consulting and Clinical Psychology* 59 (1991): 602-606.

61 *Ibid.*

62 John C. Hill and Eugene P. Schoener, "Age-Dependent Decline of Attention Deficit Hyperactivity Disorder," *American Journal of Psychiatry* 153 (1996): 1143-1146.

63 Brad J. Bushman and Roy F. Baumeister, "Threatened Egoism, Narcissism, Self-Esteem, and Direct and Displaced Aggression: Does Self-Love or Self-Hate Lead to Violence?" *Journal of Personality and Social Psychology* 75 (1998): 219-229.

64 Peter A. Ahmann, Stuart J. Waltonen, Kurt A. Olson, Fred W. Theye, Alayne J. Van Erem, and Robert J. LaPlant, "Placebo-Controlled Evaluation of Ritalin Side Effects," *Pediatrics* 91 (1993): 1101-1106.

65 Daryl Efron, Frederick Jarman, and Melinda Barker, "Side Effects of Methylphenidate and Dexamphetamine in Children With Attention Deficit Hyperactivity Disorder: A Double-blind, Crossover Trial," *Pediatrics* 100 (1997): 662-666.

66 A. Poulton and C.T. Cowell, "Slowing of growth in height and weight on stimulants: A characteristic pattern," *Journal of Paediatrics and Child Health* 39 (2003): 180-185.

67 William J. Pizzi, Emil C. Rode, and June E. Barnhart, "Differential Effects of Methylphenidate on the Growth of Neonatal and Adolescent Rats," *Neurotoxicology and Teratology* 9 (1987): 107-111.

68 Megan C. Lisska and Scott A. Rivkees, "Daily Methylphenidate Use Slows the Growth of Children: A Community Based Study," *Journal of Pediatric Endocrinology & Metabolism* 16 (2003): 711-718.

69 MTA Cooperative Group, "National Institute of Mental Health Multimodal Treatment Study of ADHD Follow-up: Changes in Effectiveness and Growth After the End of Treatment."

70 Scott Lurie and Aglaia O'Quinn, "Neuroendocrine Responses to Methylphenidate and d-Amphetamine: Applications to Attention-Deficit Disorder."

71 D. Aarskog, F.O. Fevang, H. Klove, K.F. Stoa, and T. Thorsen, "The effect of the stimulant drugs, dextroamphetamine and methylphenidate, on secretion of growth hormone in hyperactive children," *The Journal of Pediatrics* 90 (1977): 136-139.

72 B.S. Kilgore, L.C. Dickinson, C.R. Burnett, J. Lee, H.K. Schedewie, and M.J. Elders, "Alterations in cartilage metabolism by neurostimulant drugs [Abstract]," *Journal of Pediatrics* 94 (1979): 542-545.

73 Kristian Holtkamp, Birgitta Peters-Wallraf, Stefan Wuller, Roland Pfaafle, and Beate Herpertz-Dahlmann, "Methylphenidate-Related Growth Impairment," *Journal of Child and Adolescent Psychopharmacology* 12 (2002): 55-61.

74 Thomas J. Speech, Stephen M. Rao, David C. Osmon, and Len T. Sperry, "A double-blind controlled study of methylphenidate treatment in closed head injury," *Brain Injury* 7 (1993): 333-338.

75 Sharon E. Williams, M. Douglas Ris, Rita Ayyangar, Bruce K. Schefft, and Daniel Berch, "Recovery in Pediatric Brain Injury: Is Psychostimulant Medication Beneficial?" *Journal of Head Trauma Rehabilitation* 13 (1998): 73-81.

76 Henry A. Nasrallah, Jan Loney, Stephen C. Olson, Mona McCalley-Whitters, John Kramer, and Charles G. Jacoby, "Cortical Atrophy in Young Adults With a History of Hyperactivity in Childhood," *Psychiatry Research* 17 (1986): 241-246.

77 Gene-Jack Wang, Nora D. Volkow, Joanna S. Fowler, Richard Ferrieri, David J. Schlyer, David Alexoff, Naomi Pappas, Jeffrey Lieberman, Payton King, Donald Warner, Christopher Wong, Robert J. Hitzemann, and Alfred P. Wolf, "Methylphenidate Decreases Regional Cerebral Blood Flow in Normal Human Subjects," *Life Sciences* 54 (1994): PL143-146.

78 *Ibid.*, p. PL-144.

79 Gene-Jack Wang, personal communication, (October 12, 2004).

80 Victoria T. Shea, "State-Dependent Learning in Children Receiving Methylphenidate," *Psychopharmacology* 78 (1982): 266-270.

81 James M. Swanson and Marcel Kinsbourne, "Stimulant-Related State-Dependent Learning in Hyperactive Children," *Science* 192 (1976): 1354-1357.

82 R.L. Sprague and E.K. Sleator, "Methylphenidate in hyperkinetic children: Differences in dose effects on learning and social behavior [Abstract]," *Science* 198 (1977): 1274-1276.

83 V.I. Douglas, R.G. Barr, K. Amin, M.E. O'Neill, and B.G. Britton, "Dosage effects and individual responsivity to methylphenidate in attention deficit disorder [Abstract]," *Journal of Child Psychology and Psychiatry* 29 (1988): 452-475.

84 Lorraine Campbell, Molly A. Malone, John R. Kershner, Wendy Roberts, Thomas Humphries, and William J. Logan, "Methylphenidate Slows Right Hemisphere Processing in Children with Attention-Deficit/Hyperactivity Disorder," *Journal of Child and Adolescent Psychopharmacology* 6 (1996): 229-239.

85 Jane Shields, "Semantic-pragmatic disorder: a right hemisphere syndrome?" *British Journal of Disorders of Communication* 26 (1991): 383-392, accessed 20 MAY 2004 on-line at: http://www.mugsy.org/shields1.htm

86 Jon Bonne, "'Go Pills: A war on drugs?'" MSNBC (January 9, 2003), accessed 15 MAY 2004 on-line at: http://msnbc.msn.com/id/3071789/

87 Brad Knickerbocker, "Military looks to drugs for battle readiness," The Christian Science Monitor (August 9, 2002), accessed 15 MAY 2004 on-line at: http://www.csmonitor.com/2002/0809/p01s04-usmi.html

88 *Ibid.*

89 Bill Berkowitz, "Bombs and Speed Kill in Afghanistan," AlterNet.org (August 7, 2002), accessed 15 MAY 2004 on-line at: http://www.alternet.org/story.html?StoryID=13791

90 Russell A. Barkley, Kevin R. Murphy, and Denise Kwasnik, "Motor Vehicle Driving Competencies and risks in Teens and Young Adults with Attention Deficit Hyperactivity Disorder," *Pediatrics* 6 (1996): 1089-1095.

91 Esther Cherland and Renee Fitzpatrick, "Psychotic Side Effects of Psychostimulants: A 5-Year Review," *Canadian Journal of Psychiatry* 44 (1999): 811-813.

92 Christopher S. Sarampote, Lisa A. Efron, Adelaide S. Robb, Phillip L. Pearl, and Mark A. Stein, "Can Stimulant Rebound Mimic Pediatric Bipolar Disorder?" *Journal of Child and Adolescent Psychopharmacology* 12 (2002): 63-67.

93 F.X. Vollenweider, R.P. Maguire, K.L. Leenders, K. Mathys, and J. Angst, "Effects of high amphetamine dose on mood and cerebral glucose metabolism in normal volunteers using positron emission tomography (PET)," *Psychiatry Research* 83 (1998): 149-162.

94 M.P. Delbello, C.A. Soutullo, W. Hendricks, R.T. Niemeier, S.L. McElroy, and S.M. Strakowski, "Prior stimulant treatment in adolescents with bipolar disorder: association with age at onset [Abstract]," *Bipolar Disorders* 3 (2001): 53-57.

95 C.A. Soutullo, M.P. DelBello, J.E. Ochsner, S.L. McElroy, S.A. Taylor, S.M. Strakowski, and P.E. Keck, Jr., "Severity of bipolarity in hospitalized manic adolescents with history of stimulant or antidepressant treatment [Abstract]," *Journal of Affective Disorders* 70 (2002): 323-327.

96 No author, "United Nations' Warnings on Ritalin: Two Press Releases," (28 February 1996, 04 March 1997).

97 Joseph Biederman, "Pharmacotherapy for attention-deficit/ hyperactivity disorder (ADHD) decreases the risk for substance abuse: findings from a longitudinal follow-up of youths with and without ADHD [Abstract]," *Journal of Clinical Psychiatry* 64 Suppl 11 (2003): 3-8.

98 Timothy Wilens, Stephen V. Faraone, Joseph Biederman, and Samantha Gunawardene, "Does stimulant therapy of ADHD beget later substance abuse? Meta-analytic Review of the Literature," *Pediatrics* 111 (2003): 179-185.

99 Nora D. Volkow and James M. Swanson, "Variables That Affect the Clinical Use and Abuse of Methylphenidate in the Treatment of ADHD."

100 Susan Schenk and Sari Izenwasser, "Pretreatment with methylphenidate sensitizes rats to the reinforcing effects of cocaine," *Pharmacology, Biochemistry and Behavior* 72 (2002): 651-657.

101 Cindy L. Brandon, Michela Marinelli, Lorinda K. Baker, and Francis J. White, "Enhanced Reactivity and Vulnerability to Cocaine Following Methylphenidate Treatment in Adolescent Rats," *Neuropsychopharmacology* 25 (2001): 651-661.

102 Nadine M. Lambert and Carolyn S. Hartsough, "Prospective Study of Tobacco Smoking and Substance Dependencies among Samples of ADHD and Non-ADHD Participants," *Journal of Learning Disabilities* 31 (1998): 533-544.

103 Russell A. Barkley, Mariellen Fischer, Lori Smallish, and Kenneth Fletcher, "Does the Treatment of Attention-Deficit/Hyperactivity Disorder With Stimulants Contribute to Drug Use/Abuse? A 13-Year Prospective Study," *Pediatrics* 111 (2003): 97-109.

104 H. Schubiner, A. Tzelepis, S. Milberger, N. Lockhart, M. Kruger, B.J. Kelley, E.P. Schoener, "Prevalence of attention-deficit/hyperactivity disorder and conduct disorder among substance abusers [Abstract]," *Journal of Clinical Psychiatry* 61 (2000): 244-251.

105 K.M. Carroll and B.J. Rounsaville, "History and significance of childhood attention deficit disorder in treatment-seeking cocaine abusers [Abstract]," *Comprehensive Psychiatry* 34 (1993): 75-82.

106 B.R. Horner and K.E. Scheibe, "Prevalence and implications of attention-deficit hyperactivity disorder among adolescents in treatment for substance abuse [Abstract]," *Journal of the American Academy of Child and Adolescent Psychiatry* 36 (1997): 30-36.

107 J. Grabowski, J.D. Roache, J.M. Schmitz, H. Rhoades, D. Creson, and A. Korszun, "Replacement medication for cocaine dependence: methylphenidate [Abstract]," *Journal of Clinical Psychopharmacology* 17 (1997): 485-488.

108 F. Gawin, C. Riordan, and H. Kleber, "Methylphenidate treatment of cocaine abusers without attention deficit disorder: a negative report [Abstract]," *American Journal of Drug and Alcohol Abuse* 11 (1985): 193-197.

109 H. Schubiner, K.K. Saules, C.L. Arfken, C.E. Johanson, C.R. Schuster, N. Lockhart, A. Edwards, J. Donlin, and E. Pihlgren, "Double-blind placebo-controlled trial of methylphenidate in the treatment of adult ADHD patients with comorbid cocaine dependence [Abstract]," *Experimental and Clinical Psychopharmacology* 10 (2002): 286-294.

110 Scott H. Kollins, Emily K. MacDonald, and Craig R. Rush, "Assessing the abuse potential of methylphenidate in nonhuman and human subjects," *Pharmacology, Biochemistry and Behavior* 68 (2001): 611-627.

111 William E. Pelham, Jr., Elizabeth M. Gnagy, Andrew R. Greiner, Betsy Hoza, Stephen P. Hinshaw, James M. Swanson, Steve Simpson, Cheri Shapiro, Oscar Bukstein, Carrie Baron-Myak, and Keith McBurnett, "Behavioral versus Behavioral and Pharmacological Treatment in ADHD Children Attending a Summer Treatment Program," *Journal of Abnormal Child Psychology* 28 (2000): 507-525.

112 *Ibid.*, p. 520.

113 Tiffany M. Field, Olga Quintino, Maria Hernandez-Reif, and Gabrielle Koslovsky, "Adolescents With Attention Deficit Hyperactivity Disorder Benefit From Massage Therapy," *Adolescence* 33 (1998): 104-108.

114 Nancy A. Jackson, "A Survey of Music Therapy Methods and Their Role in the Treatment of Early Elementary School Children with ADHD," *Journal of Music Therapy* 4 (2003): 302-323.

115 Steven P. Hinshaw, Barbara Henker, C.K. Whalen, "Self-control in hyperactive boys in anger-inducing situations: effects of cognitive-behavioral training and of methylphenidate [Abstract]," *Journal of Abnormal Child Psychology* 12 (1984): 55-77.

116 Katherine B. Suzman, Robin D. Morris, Mary K. Morris, and Michael A. Milan, "Cognitive-Behavioral Remediation of Problem Solving Deficits in Children With Acquired Brain Injury," *Journal of Behavioral Therapy & Experimental Psychiatry* 28 (1997): 203-212.

117 Wendy B. Marlowe, "An Intervention for Children With Disorders of Executive Functions," *Developmental Neuropsychology* 18 (2000): 445-454.

118 T. Fuchs, N. Birbaumer, W. Lutzenberger, J.H. Gruzelier, and J. Kaiser, "Neurofeedback treatment for attention-deficit/hyperactivity disorder in childen: a comparison with methylphenidate [Abstract]," *Applied Psychophysiology and Biofeedback* 28 (2003): 1-12.

119 N.L. VandenBerg, "The use of a weighted vest to increase on-task behavior in children with attentional difficulties [Abstract]," *American Journal of Occupational Therapy* 55 (2001): 621-628.

120 Shauna L. Shapiro and Roger Walsh, "An Analysis of Recent Meditation Research and Suggestions for Future Directions," *The Humanistic Psychologist* 31 (2003): 86-113.

121 Jeffrey M. Schwartz and Sharon Begley, *The Mind and the Brain: Neuroplasticity and the Power of Mental Force,* (New York, NY: Harper Collins, 2002).

Epilogue

The Need for An Adequately Informed Consent to Care

1 Seymour Kety, "Hearings of the National Commission on Health Sciences and Society," 90th 'Congress, 2nd Session, 1968, as quoted in David Healy, *The Creation of Psychopharmacology*, (Cambridge, Massachusetts: Harvard University Press, 2002), p. 334.

2 Simon N. Whitney, Amy L. McGuire, and Laurence B. McCullough, "A Typology of Shared Decision Making, Informed Consent, and Simple Consent," *Annals of Internal Medicine* 140 (2003): 54-59.

3 C.W. Van Staden and C. Kruger, "Incapacity to give informed consent owing to mental disorder," *Journal of Medical Ethics Online* 29 (2003): 41-43, accessed 10 APR 2005 on-line at: http://jme.bmjjournals.com/cgi/content/full/29/1/41

5 David Healy, *The Creation of Psychopharmacology*, (Cambridge, Massachusetts: Harvard University Press, 2002), pp. 363-371.

6 Chris Horrocks and Zoran Jevtic, *Introducing Baudrillard*, (Lanham, MD: Totem Books, 1997).

7 Jean Baudrillard, *Simulacra and Simulation*, as translated by Sheila Faria Glaser, (Ann Arbor: The University of Michigan Press, 1994).

8 Kathryn Schulz, "Did Antidepressants Depress Japan?" originally published in *The New York Times* (August 22, 2004), accessed 02 SEP 2004 on-line at: http://www.journalismfellowships.org/stories/japan/japan_depressed.htm

9 Nortin M. Hadler, The Last Well Person: How to Stay Well Despite the Health-Care System, (Ithaca: McGill-Queen's University Press, 2004).

10 David Healy, *The Creation of Psychopharmacology*, pp. 371-381.

11 *Ibid.*, p. 311.

12 Jeffrey M. Drazen and Gregory D. Curfman, "Financial Associations of Authors," *New England Journal of Medicine* 346 (2002): 1901-1902.

13 Phil B. Fontanarosa, Drummond Rennie, and Catherine D. DeAngelis, "Postmarketing Surveillance – Lack of Vigilance, Lack of Trust," *JAMA* 292 (2004): 2647-2650.

14 *Ibid.*, p. 2647.

15 Vera Sharav, "Pfizer Zoloft Warnings to Canadian Doctors Contrast to US – FDA Caves In to Pharma Lobbying," (February 10, 2005), accessed 11 APR 2005 on-line at: http://www.ahrp.org/infomail/05/02/10.php

16 Russell Katz, "FDA Labeling Change Request Letter for Antidepressant Medications," (October 28, 2004), Department of Health and Human Services, U.S. Food and Drug Administration, CDER website, accessed 11 APR 2005 on-line at: http://www.fda.cder/drug/antidepressants/SSRIlabelChange.htm

17 No author, "Class Suicidality Labeling Language for Antidepressants," (January 26, 2005), Department of Health and Human Services, U.S. Food and Drug Administration, CDER website, accessed 11 APR 2005 on-line at: http://www.fda.gov/cder/drug/antidepressants/PI_template.pdf

18 Christine Kilgore, "Antidepressant Use Dropped 10% in Youth," *Family Practice News* (March 15, 2005), p. 47.

19 Robert Stieinbrook, "Financial Conflicts of Interest and the NIH," *New England Journal of Medicine* 350 (2004): 327-330.

20 Ted Agres, "NIH bans all consulting," *The Scientist* (February 2, 2005), accessed 11 APR 2005 on-line at: http://www.biomedcentral.com/news/20050202/02

21 Rick Weiss, "NIH Workers Angered by New Ethics Rules," Washington Post (February 3, 2005), accessed 10 APR 2005 on-line at: http://www.washingtonpost.com/wp-dyn/articles/A58845-2005Feb2.html

22 Marc Kaufman, "Many FDA Scientists Had Drug Concerns, 2002 Survey Shows," *Washington Post* (December 16, 2004), accessed 14 FEB 2005 on-line at: http://washingtonpost.com/ac2/wp-dyn/A3135-2004Dec15?language=printer

23 John Solomon, "Climate of alarm described at NIH," *The New York Times* (April 10, 2005), accessed 12 APR 2005 on-line at: http://www.ahrp.org/infomail/05/04/11.php

24 *Ibid.*

25 Christopher Lee, "HHS Backs Protection For Special Consultant," *Washington Post* (February 2, 2005), p. A21.

26 No author, "Frequently Asked Questions," HonestDoctor.org (official website of Dr. Jonathan M. Fishbein), accessed 12 APR 2005 on-line at: http://www.honestdoctor.org/faqs.html#1

Index

neuroleptic discontinuation syndrome 34, 205, 211

neuroleptic induced deficit syndrome (NIDS) 67

Neuroleptic Malignant Syndrome (NMS) 141, 377

neuron 45–47, 77, 78, 125, 126, 164, 167–171, 184, 192, 263

neurosyphilis 163

neurotransmitters 45, 47–52, 59, 62, 64, 71, 72, 76, 77, 80, 81, 84, 85, 87, 124, 125, 155, 156, 163–169, 175, 217, 222, 233, 237, 238, 263, 264, 266

Neurotransmitter Depletion Studies 87

nicotine 177, 228, 260, 298, 370

nigrostriatal 164, 171, 178, 226, 232, 237, 268

NMDA (N-methyl-d-aspartate) 221, 222, 365, 366

Non-equivalent dosing 28

norepinephrine 45, 52, 71, 76, 84, 86–89, 93, 135, 137, 164, 165, 221, 229, 233, 263, 264

Novartis 160, 261

O

obesity 66, 240, 242, 244, 260, 262

Observed Cases 150

obsessive compulsive disorder 126, 340

Olanzapine (Zyprexa) 352, 358, 368, 377

oligodendrocytes 45

opiates 69

osteoporosis 56, 92

oxidative stress 184, 185, 354

P

panic attacks 72, 127

Parkinson, James 163

Parkinson's disease 126, 158, 164, 184, 232, 268, 370

parkinsonism 178, 204, 225, 226, 232, 234, 239, 352, 374

patent extensions 115, 302

Patient Years of Exposure (PYEs) 120

Paxil 72, 74, 83, 90, 91, 105, 116, 117, 121, 146

PDAC (Psychopharmacologic Drug Advisory Committee) 113

PDUFA (Prescription Drug User Fee Act) 308

pemoline (Cylert) 264, 272, 288, 305

Perkinism 17

PE (pulmonary embolism) 246

Pharmacodynamic mechanisms 61

Pharmacokinetic mechanisms 61

pharmacological stress factors 204, 211

phenothiazines 69, 153, 154, 157, 185, 194, 195, 199, 200, 227, 240, 252

phobia 283

pituitary 52, 62, 66, 89, 91, 140, 178, 239, 288, 331, 332

placebos 9, 15, 19, 21, 98, 106, 336

placebo washout 30–32, 99, 196, 197, 198

positive illusory bias 280, 281, 283

pre-Therapy 380

prolactin 56, 89, 91, 92, 93, 138, 158, 159, 178, 239, 240, 243, 331–333, 375, 376

proof in principle 10, 190

Prouty, Garry 259, 380

Prozac 26, 27, 30, 33, 35, 55, 72, 74, 75, 81, 86, 90, 93, 95–106, 112–116, 114, 118, 120, 121, 126, 139, 140, 145, 146, 318, 319, 320, 325, 326, 329, 335–338, 379

psychic indifference 154, 176, 215, 227

psychoanalysis 5, 380

psychodynamic 149, 248

psychosis 26, 28, 35, 67, 100, 112, 136, 138, 153, 155–157, 159, 160, 164, 165, 176, 186, 187, 192, 194, 197, 201, 205, 211, 212, 216, 221–223, 226, 228, 229, 230, 235, 236, 240, 244, 247, 253, 254, 256–259, 259, 293, 355, 364, 374, 380
psychotherapy 253
Publication bias 39
pyridinium 55, 184, 323, 352, 353

Q

Quarti, Cornelia 154
quetiapine (Seroquel) 33, 159, 197, 221, 237, 239, 358, 365, 374

R

racemic mixtures 74
randomization 15, 20, 22, 27, 102, 190, 216
Randomized Controlled Trial (RCT) xi, 12, 14, 15, 17, 19, 20, 273, 315, 319
Rationalists 12
Rauwolfia serpentina (reserpine) 69, 153
reactive oxygen species (ROS) 184, 185, 186, 353
Reality Based Medicine 13
rebound xii, 63, 103, 287, 294
Rechtshaffen, Allan 136
recovery 109, 149, 150, 211, 360, 388
recurrence 63, 107, 108, 110, 152, 337
redundant publication 37, 38, 321
relapse 88, 107, 151, 204, 249
relaxation 40, 303
remission 88, 89, 107, 146, 150, 186, 195, 239
REM sleep 55, 56, 133–137, 152, 342
REM sleep behavior disorder 135, 341, 342

reserpine 69–71, 112, 113, 153, 155, 163, 164, 229
respiratory dyskinesia 246, 371
retrograde ejaculation 244
Richet, Charles 18
risperidone (Risperdal) 34, 56, 159, 161, 186, 200, 212, 213, 217, 221, 223, 225, 236, 239, 358, 365, 366, 373, 373–375
Ritalin (methylphenidate) 56, 59, 261, 264, 267, 269–273, 285–288, 290, 291, 292, 294–298, 300, 305, 381, 382, 384, 386, 387, 390
Rivers, W.H.R. 19
rollback phenomenon 123, 124

S

Sacks, Oliver 155
Schildkraut, Joseph 71, 325
schizoaffective disorder 201
schizophrenia 4, 5, 34, 158, 159, 160, 161, 163, 164, 177, 180, 181, 183, 185–187, 190–192, 195–197, 200, 201–203, 207, 208, 209, 213, 215, 216–218, 221, 224, 230, 234, 236, 240, 241, 245, 246, 247, 248, 251, 253–256, 257, 319, 351, 353–356, 358, 359, 361–364, 367–370, 373, 374, 376–378
Seeman, Phil 237, 370, 373
selection bias 27
self-fulfilling prophecy 283
semantic-pragmatic disorder 292, 389
sensitization xii, 55, 56, 58, 59, 60, 267, 275, 299, 300, 324
serotonin 55, 70, 71, 72, 76–83
serotonin reuptake inhibitors (SSRIs) 35, 38, 55, 71, 81, 85, 126, 305, 326, 331
serotonin reuptake transporter 84
serotonin reuptake transporter (SERT) 72, 79, 81, 83, 85
serotonin syndrome 141

Z

About the Author

Dr. Grace Jackson is a board certified psychiatrist who graduated summa cum laude from California Lutheran University with a Bachelor of Arts in Political Science and a Bachelor of Science in Biology, as well as a Masters Degree in Public Administration. She earned her Medical Degree from the University of Colorado Health Sciences Center in 1996 and completed her internship and residency while in the U.S. Navy. Following her service as a staff psychiatrist at Bethesda Naval Hospital, she worked in the North Carolina prison system.

Dr. Jackson has lectured widely in the United States and Europe, and has testified as an expert witness in forced medication trials. Her interests include philosophy, history, politics, and law.